I've recently started jogging. To be more specific, I'm training for the 10K run that I signed my entire staff up for. Now that I have a goal, I'm "racing" to get there. What have I gotten myself into this time? But I've never really minded running, so I'm enjoying it. Being active not only refreshes my spirit, it also gives me a real sense of accomplishment. Now to keep it up!! (My current weight is 70 kg!! The fight's only just begun!!)

—Mitsutoshi Shimabukuro, 2012

Mitsutoshi Shimabukuro made his debut in **Weekly Shonen Jump** in 1996. He is best known for **Seikimatsu Leader Den Takeshi!** for which he won the 46th Shogakukan Manga Award for children's manga in 2001. His current series, **Toriko**, began serialization in Japan in 2008.

TORIKO VOL. 19
SHONEN JUMP Manga Edition

STORY AND ART BY MITSUTOSHI SHIMABUKURO

Translation/Christine Dashiell
Touch-Up Art & Lettering/Elena Diaz
Design/Matt Hinrichs
Editor/Hope Donovan

TORIKO © 2008 by Mitsutoshi Shimabukuro
All rights reserved. First published in Japan in 2008 by SHUEISHA Inc., Tokyo.
English translation rights arranged by SHUEISHA Inc.

Printed in Canada

Published by VIZ Media, LLC
P.O. Box 77010
San Francisco, CA 94107

10 9 8 7 6 5 4 3 2 1
First printing, December 2013

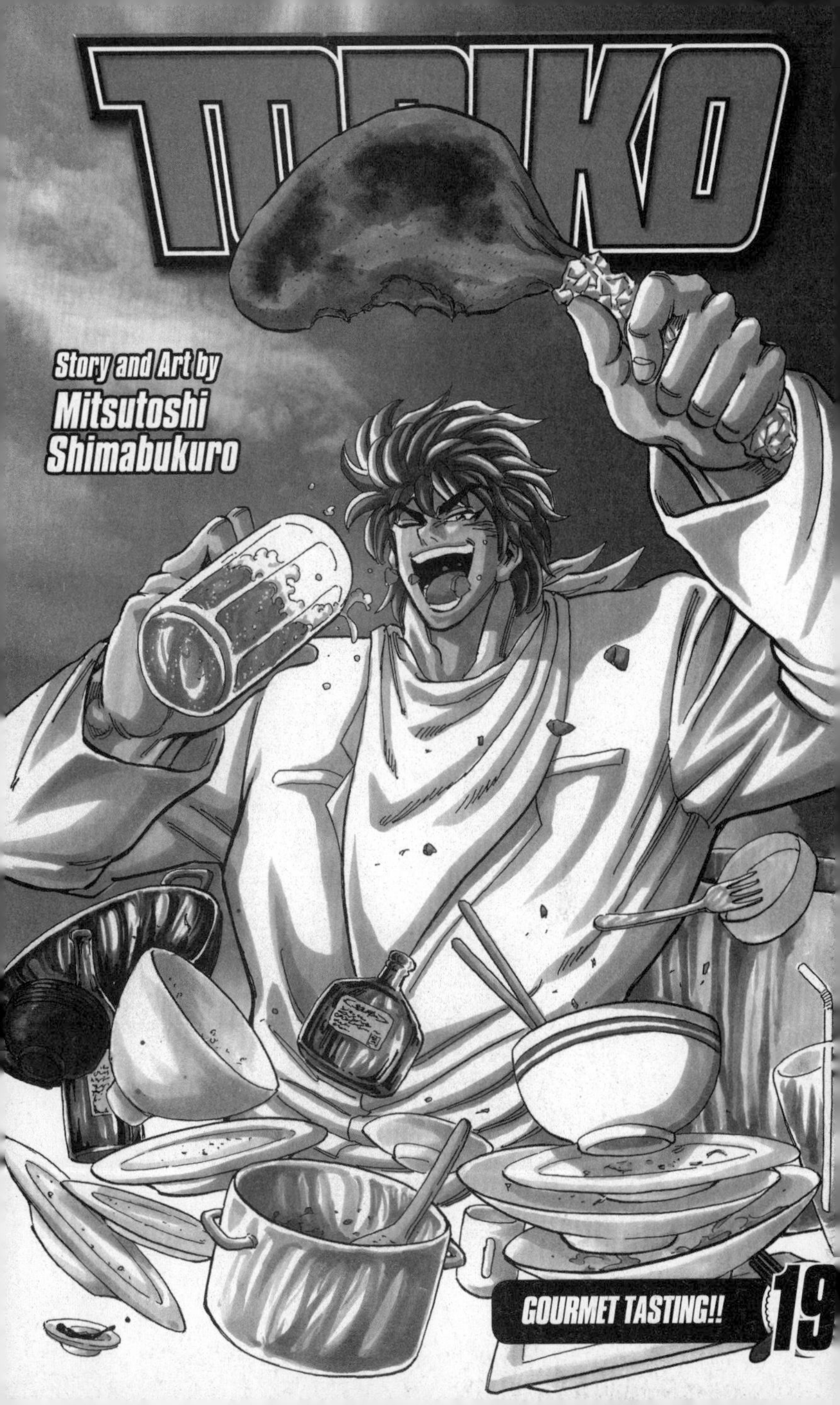

TORIKO
Story and Art by
Mitsutoshi Shimabukuro
GOURMET TASTING!!
19

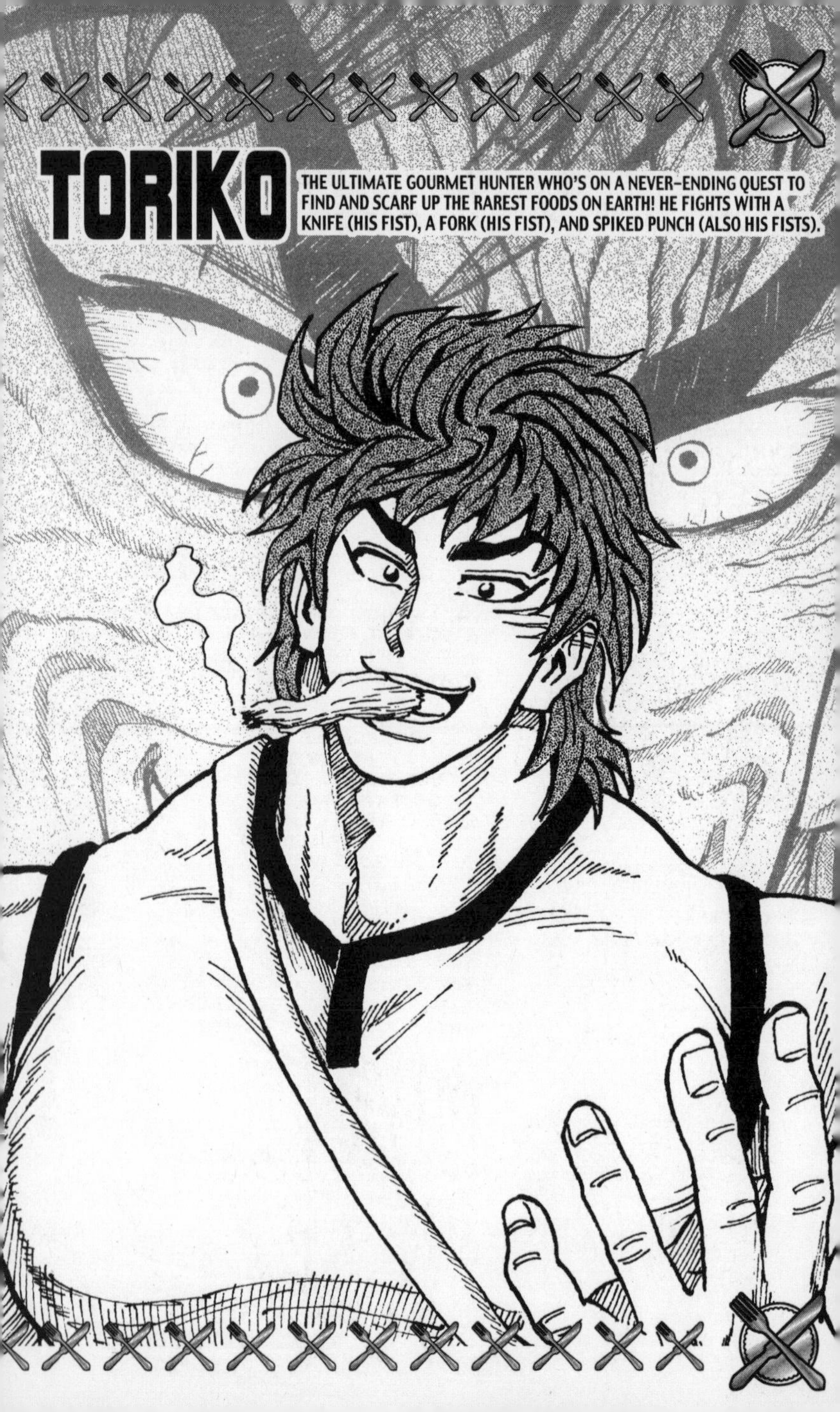
TORIKO
THE ULTIMATE GOURMET HUNTER WHO'S ON A NEVER-ENDING QUEST TO FIND AND SCARF UP THE RAREST FOODS ON EARTH! HE FIGHTS WITH A KNIFE (HIS FIST), A FORK (HIS FIST), AND SPIKED PUNCH (ALSO HIS FISTS).

WHAT'S FOR DINNER

IT'S THE AGE OF GOURMET! KOMATSU, THE HEAD CHEF AT THE HOTEL OWNED BY THE IGO (INTERNATIONAL GOURMET ORGANIZATION), BECAME FAST FRIENDS WITH THE LEGENDARY GOURMET HUNTER TORIKO WHILE GATOR HUNTING. NOW KOMATSU ACCOMPANIES TORIKO ON HIS LIFELONG QUEST TO CREATE THE PERFECT FULL-COURSE MEAL.

ALTHOUGH THEY OFTEN FIND THEMSELVES PITTED AGAINST GOURMET CORP.'S NEFARIOUS AGENTS, THERE'S NOTHING THAT CAN STOP THEIR ADVENTURES! TORIKO AND KOMATSU COME AWAY FROM THEIR QUEST FOR CENTURY SOUP EMPTY-HANDED, BUT KOMATSU RE-CREATES THE SOUP TO WORLDWIDE ACCLAIM. THEN, AT THE URGING OF THE IGO PRESIDENT, TORIKO AND KOMATSU FORMED THE ULTIMATE HUNTER-CHEF PARTNERSHIP! TO PREPARE FOR ENTRY INTO THE GOURMET WORLD, THEY SET ABOUT GATHERING FOODS FROM A TRAINING LIST PROVIDED BY THE PRESIDENT.

ONE DAY, THE DUO ACCOMPANIES COCO TO THE SHADY JIDDAL KINGDOM TO WIN GOURMET CASINO'S METEOR GARLIC. WHILE THERE, THEY'RE REUNITED WITH THE GOURMET MAFIA DON, MATCH, AND AFTER THE FOUR MEN MASTER THE FLOOR GAMES, THEY'RE ESCORTED INTO THE VIP AREA. THEY QUICKLY LEARN THE UNDERGROUND COOKING WORLD WAGERS PEOPLE'S LIVES. THEN, THE OWNER INVITES THEM *BEYOND* THE VIP AREA!

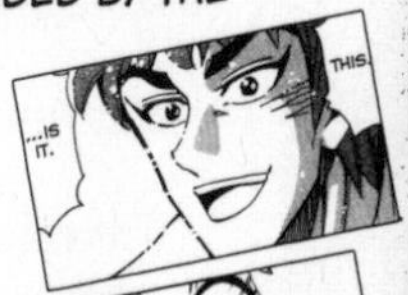
THIS.
...IS IT.

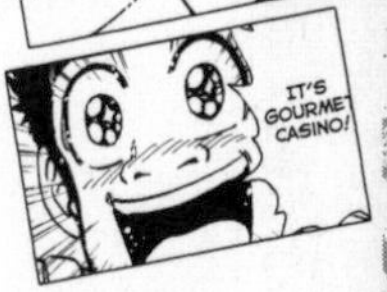
IT'S GOURMET CASINO!

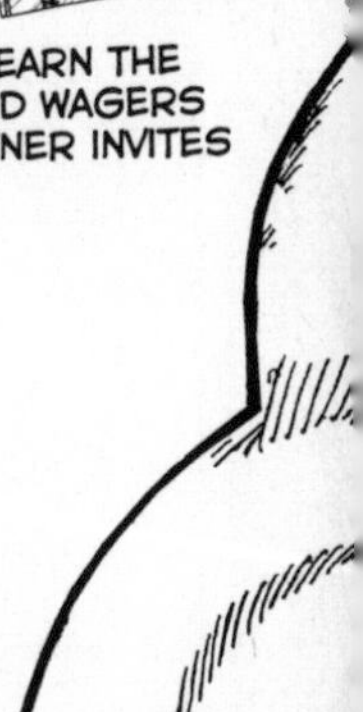

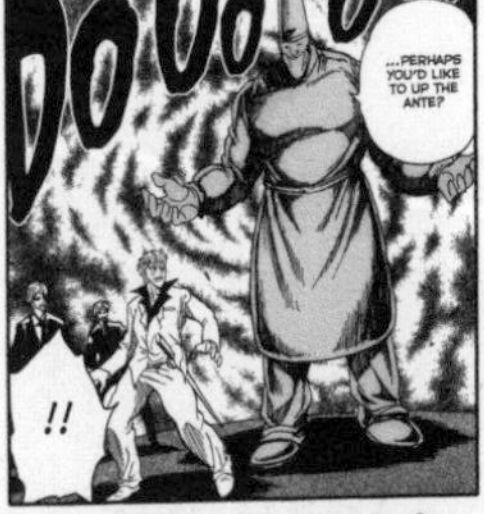
...PERHAPS YOU'D LIKE TO UP THE ANTE?
!!

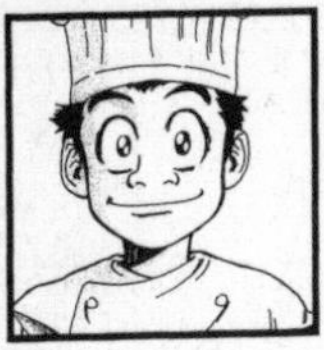

● KOMATSU
TALENTED IGO HOTEL CHEF AND TORIKO'S #1 FAN

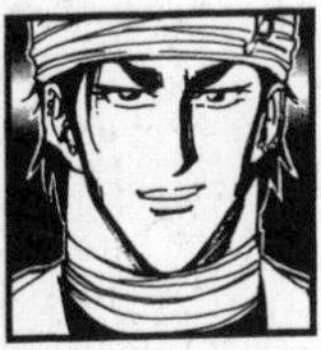

● COCO
ONE OF THE FOUR KINGS, THOUGH HE IS ALSO A FORTUNETELLER. SPECIAL ABILITY: POISON FLOWS IN HIS VEINS.

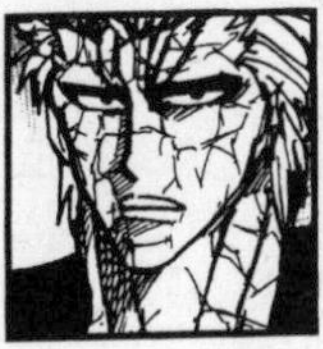

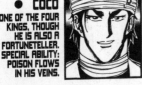

● MATCH
MAFIA DON FROM NERG CITY. A GOURMET HUNTER. HIS SPECIALTY IS HIS TRIPLE SLICE ATTACK.

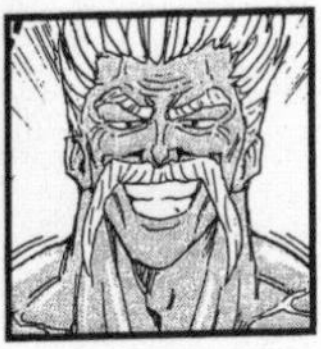

● ICHIRYU
HARDY IGO PRESIDENT AND DISCIPLE OF THE LATE GOURMET GOD ACACIA.

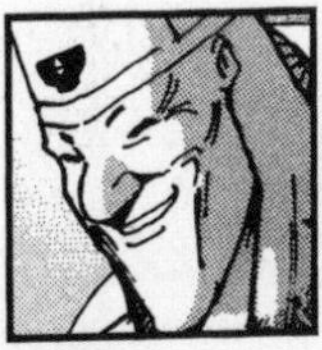

● LIVEBEARER
BOSS OF THE UNDERGROUND COOKING WORLD AND OWNER OF GOURMET CASINO.

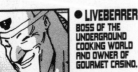

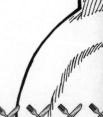

Contents

TORIKO

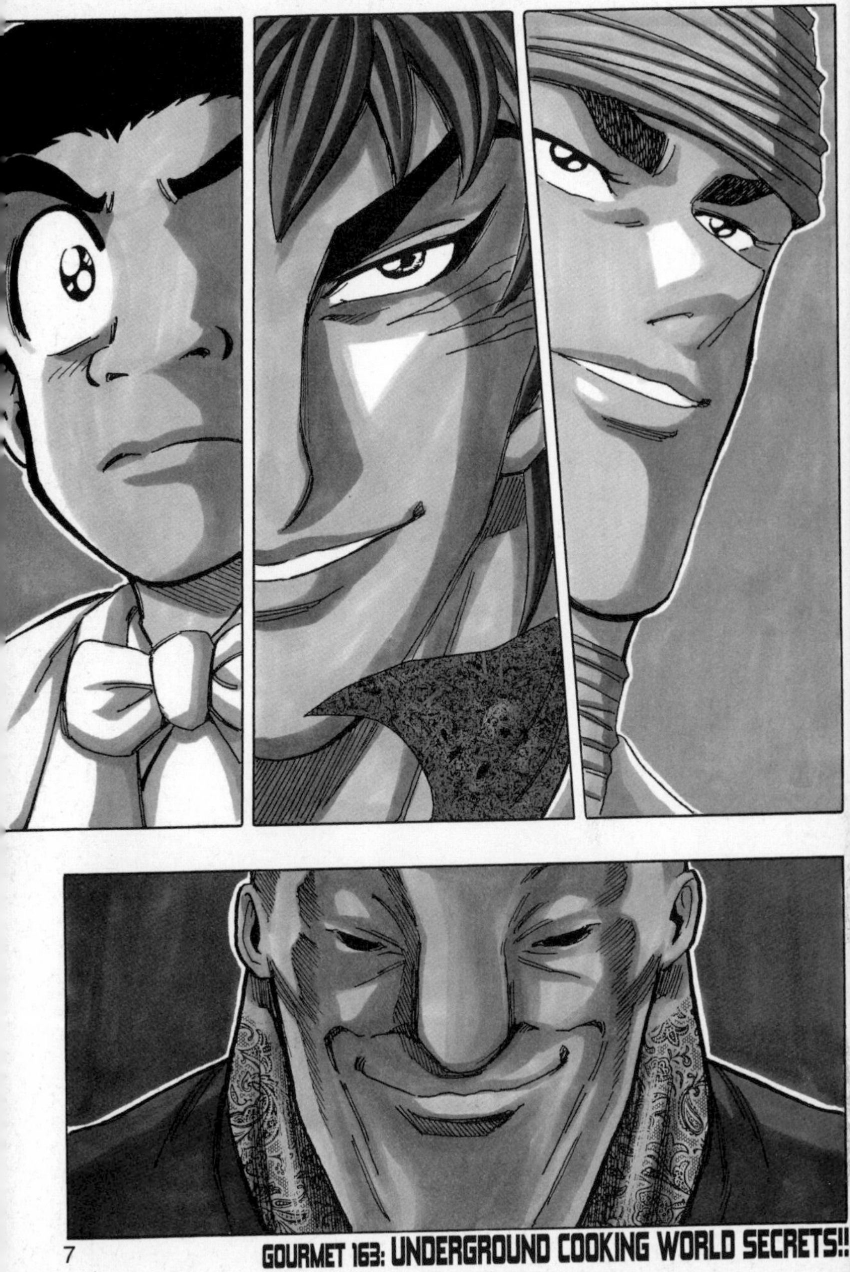

GOURMET 163: UNDERGROUND COOKING WORLD SECRETS!!

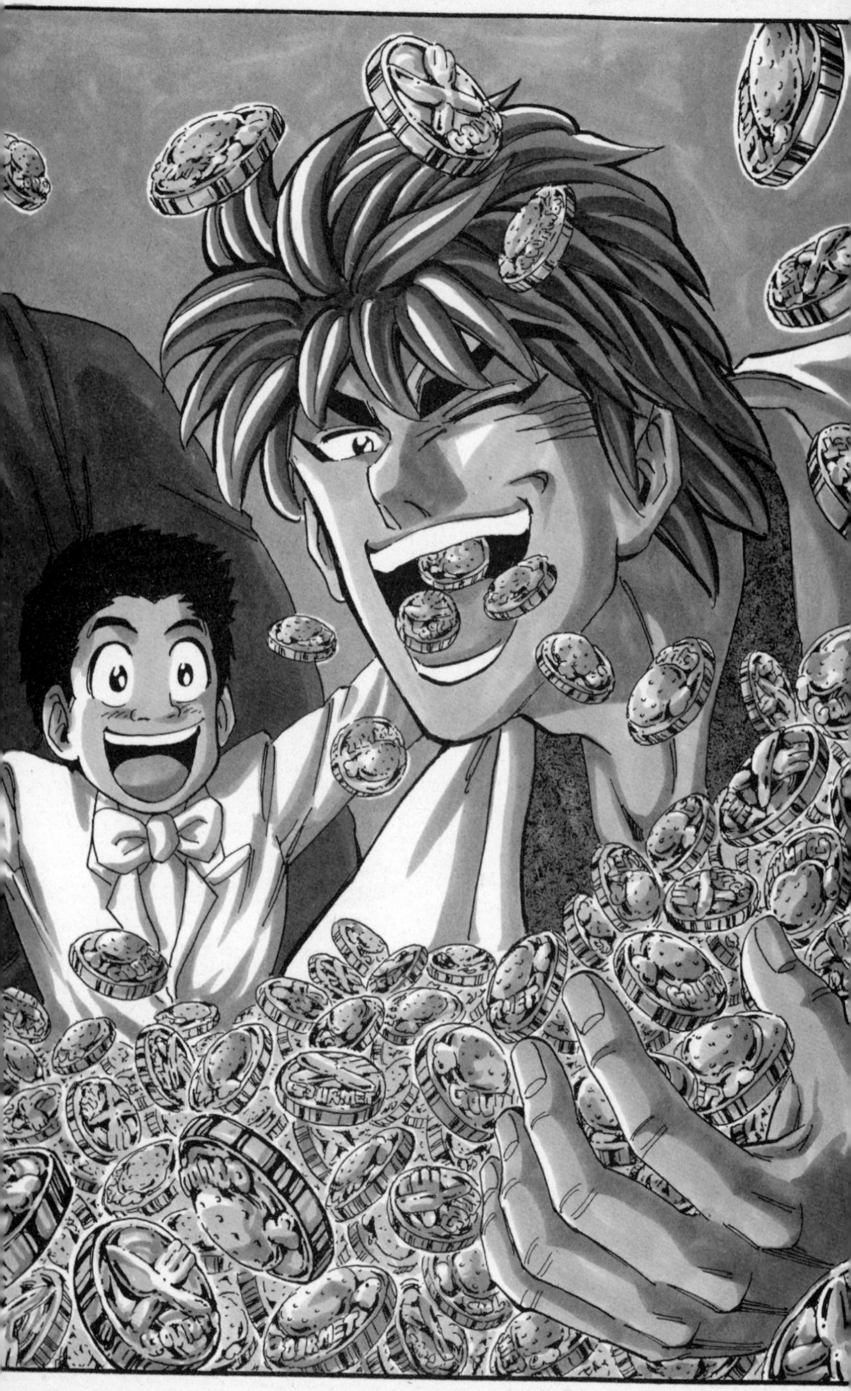
GOURMET

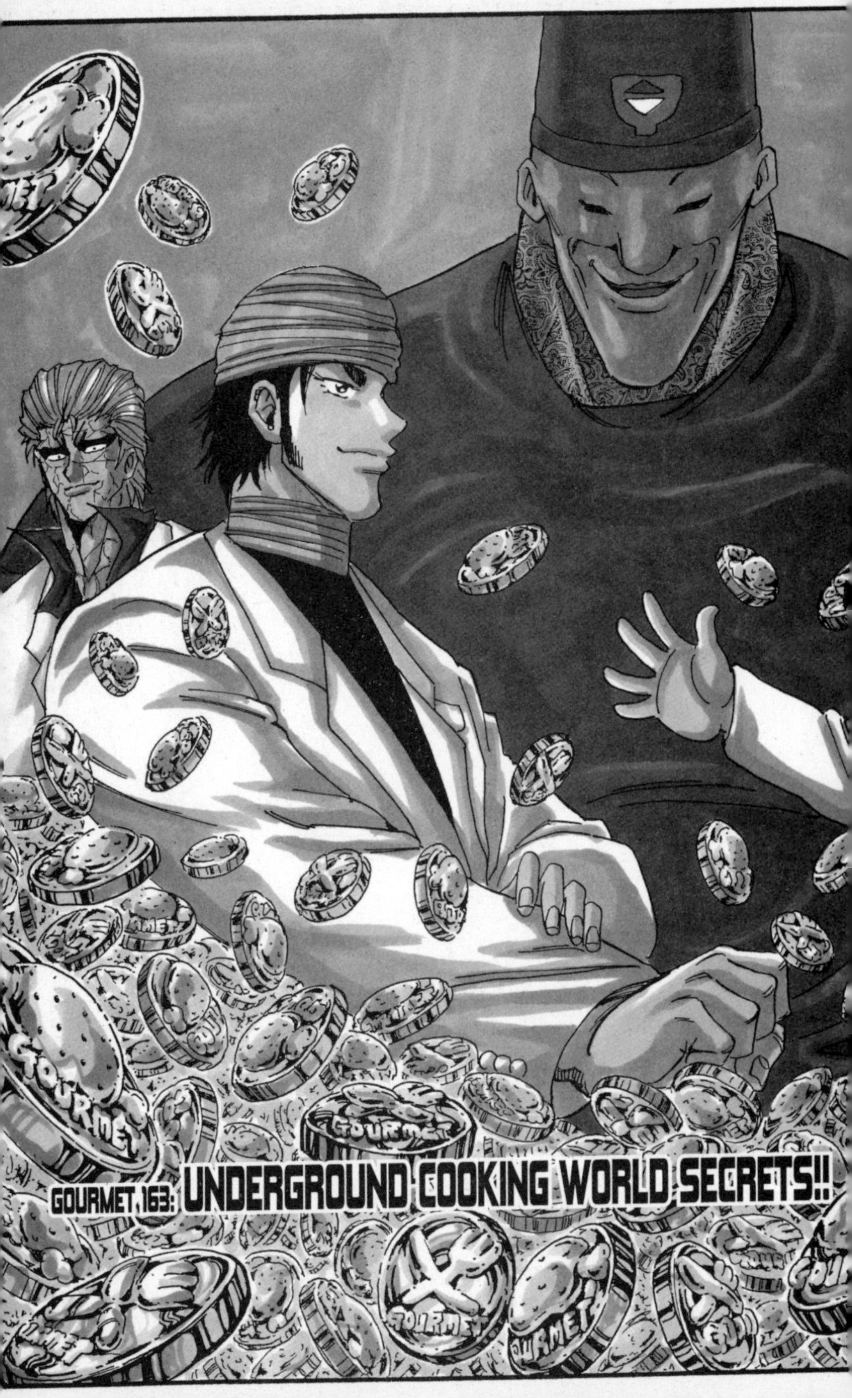
GOURMET 163: UNDERGROUND COOKING WORLD SECRETS!!

TORIKO

GOURMET CHECKLIST

Vol. 193

GORGONCLOPS
(MAMMAL)

CAPTURE LEVEL: 42
HABITAT: GOURMET PYRAMID
LENGTH: ---
HEIGHT: 22 METERS
WEIGHT: 18 TONS
PRICE: 100 G / 300 YEN

SCALE

A BIPEDAL MAMMAL THAT LIVES IN THE UPPER LEVELS OF THE GOURMET PYRAMID.
THIS CYCLOPS HAS SNAKE-LIKE HAIR AND A FEROCIOUS DISPOSITION TO MATCH ITS
ABOMINABLE APPEARANCE. IT WILL ATTACK ANY CREATURE IT ENCOUNTERS WITHOUT
A SECOND THOUGHT. THE GORGONCLOPS IS SO FORMIDABLE THAT MOST WHO ENTER
GOURMET PYRAMID IN HOPES OF REACHING MELLOW COLA IN THE SUBTERRANEAN
LEVELS END UP ITS PREY. HOWEVER, UNLESS YOU'RE STRONG ENOUGH TO DEFEAT THE
GORGONCLOPS AND FEAST ON ITS FLESH, YOU'RE MOST LIKELY NO MATCH FOR THE
REST OF GOURMET PYRAMID.

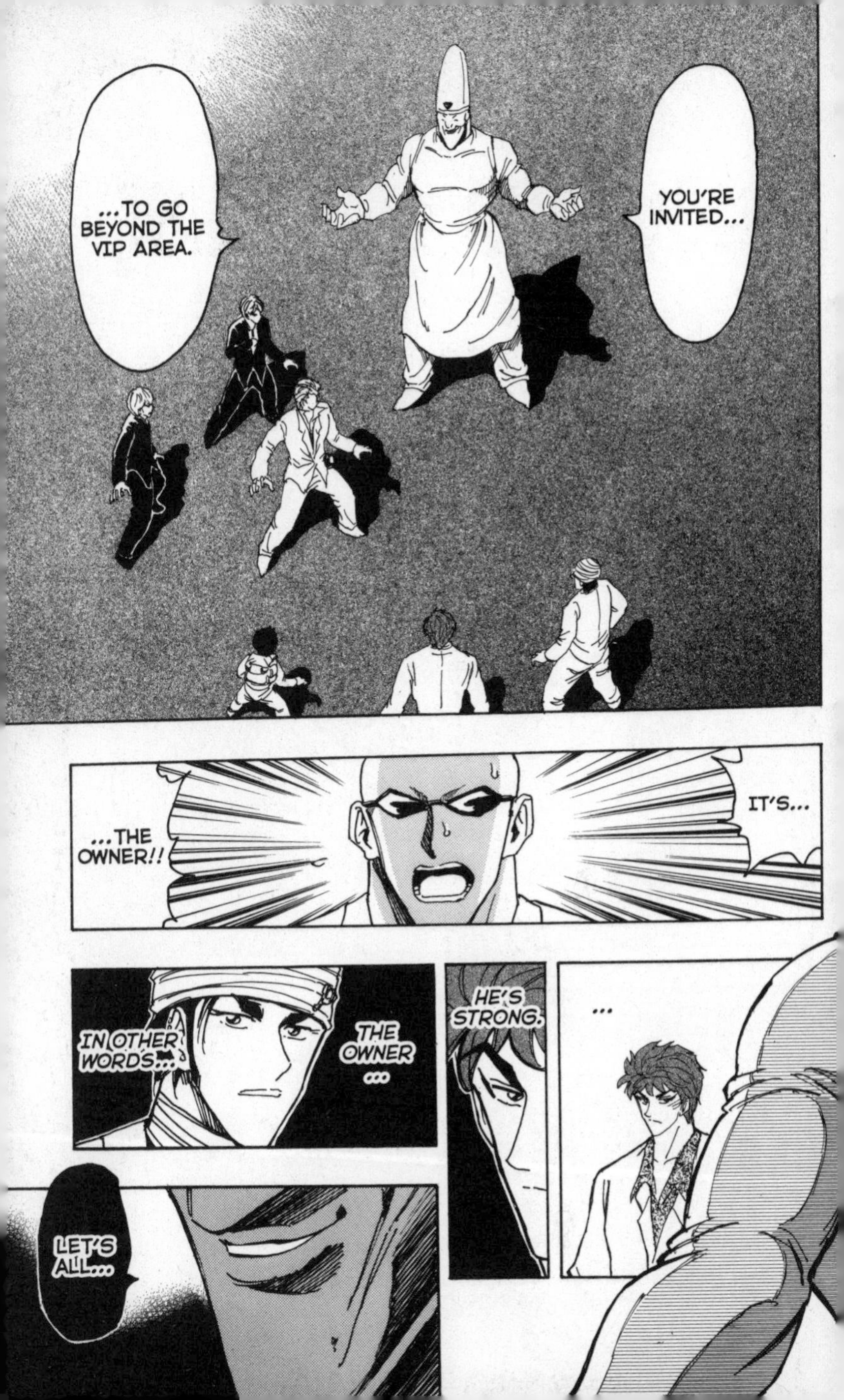
YOU'RE INVITED...
...TO GO BEYOND THE VIP AREA.
IT'S...
...THE OWNER!!
...
HE'S STRONG.
THE OWNER...
IN OTHER WORDS...
LET'S ALL...

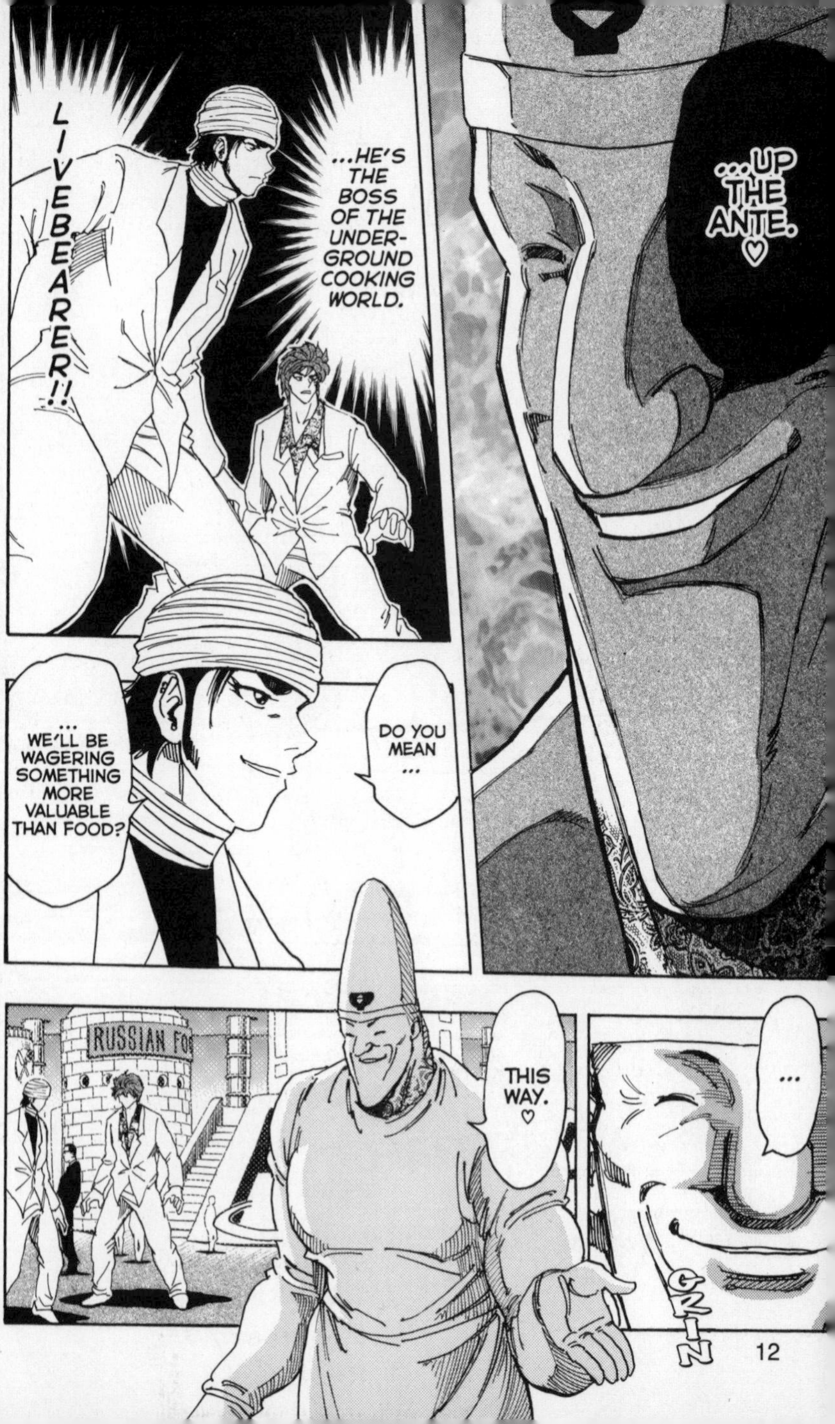
...UP THE ANTE. ♡
...HE'S THE BOSS OF THE UNDER-GROUND COOKING WORLD.
LIVEBEARER!!
DO YOU MEAN ...
... WE'LL BE WAGERING SOMETHING MORE VALUABLE THAN FOOD?
...
GRIN
THIS WAY. ♡
RUSSIAN FO

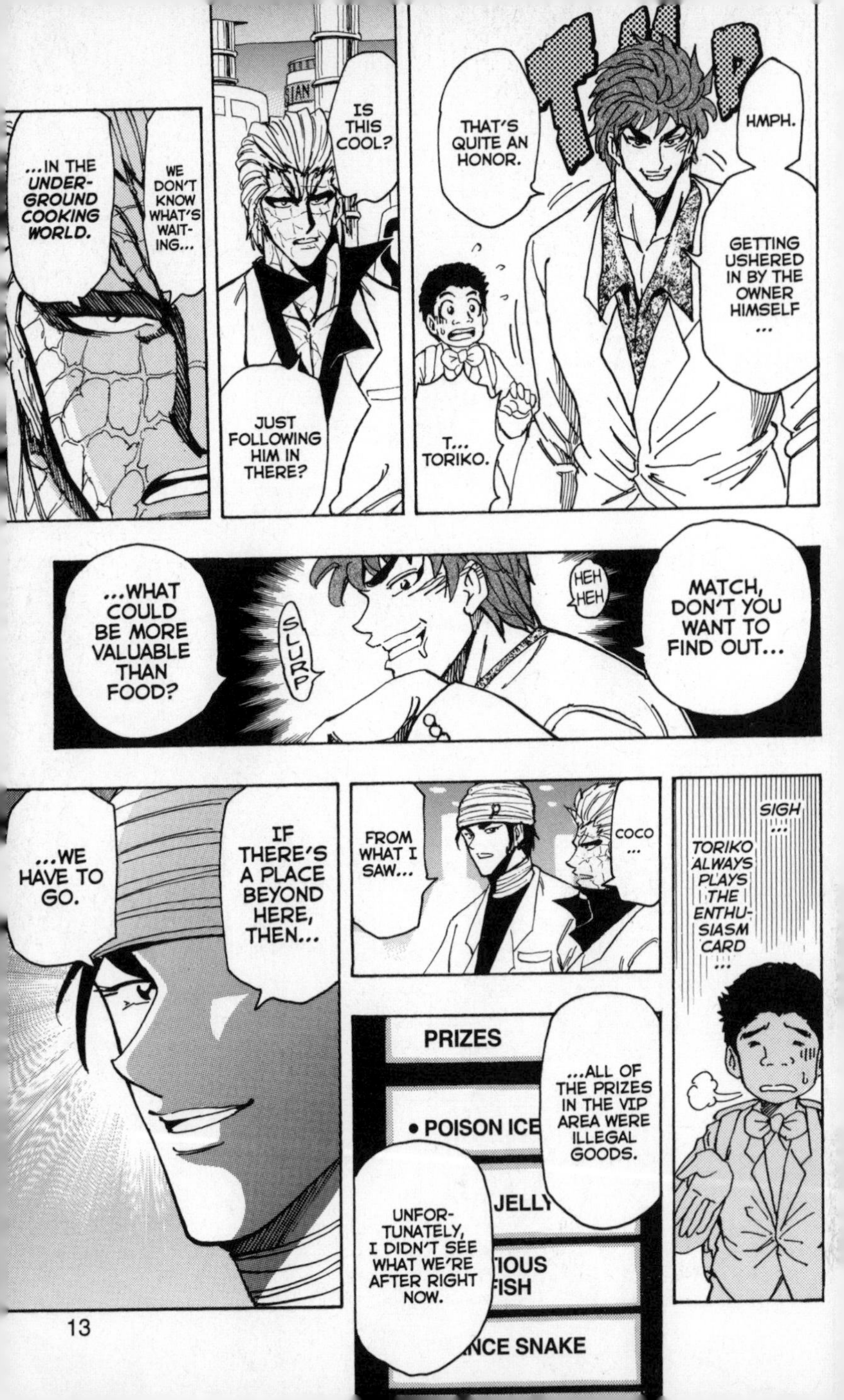
HMPH.
GETTING USHERED IN BY THE OWNER HIMSELF...
THAT'S QUITE AN HONOR.
T... TORIKO.
IS THIS COOL?
JUST FOLLOWING HIM IN THERE?
WE DON'T KNOW WHAT'S WAITING...
...IN THE UNDERGROUND COOKING WORLD.
HEH HEH
MATCH, DON'T YOU WANT TO FIND OUT...
SLURP
...WHAT COULD BE MORE VALUABLE THAN FOOD?
SIGH...
TORIKO ALWAYS PLAYS THE ENTHUSIASM CARD...
COCO...
FROM WHAT I SAW...
PRIZES
• POISON ICE
...ALL OF THE PRIZES IN THE VIP AREA WERE ILLEGAL GOODS.
UNFORTUNATELY, I DIDN'T SEE WHAT WE'RE AFTER RIGHT NOW.
IF THERE'S A PLACE BEYOND HERE, THEN...
...WE HAVE TO GO.

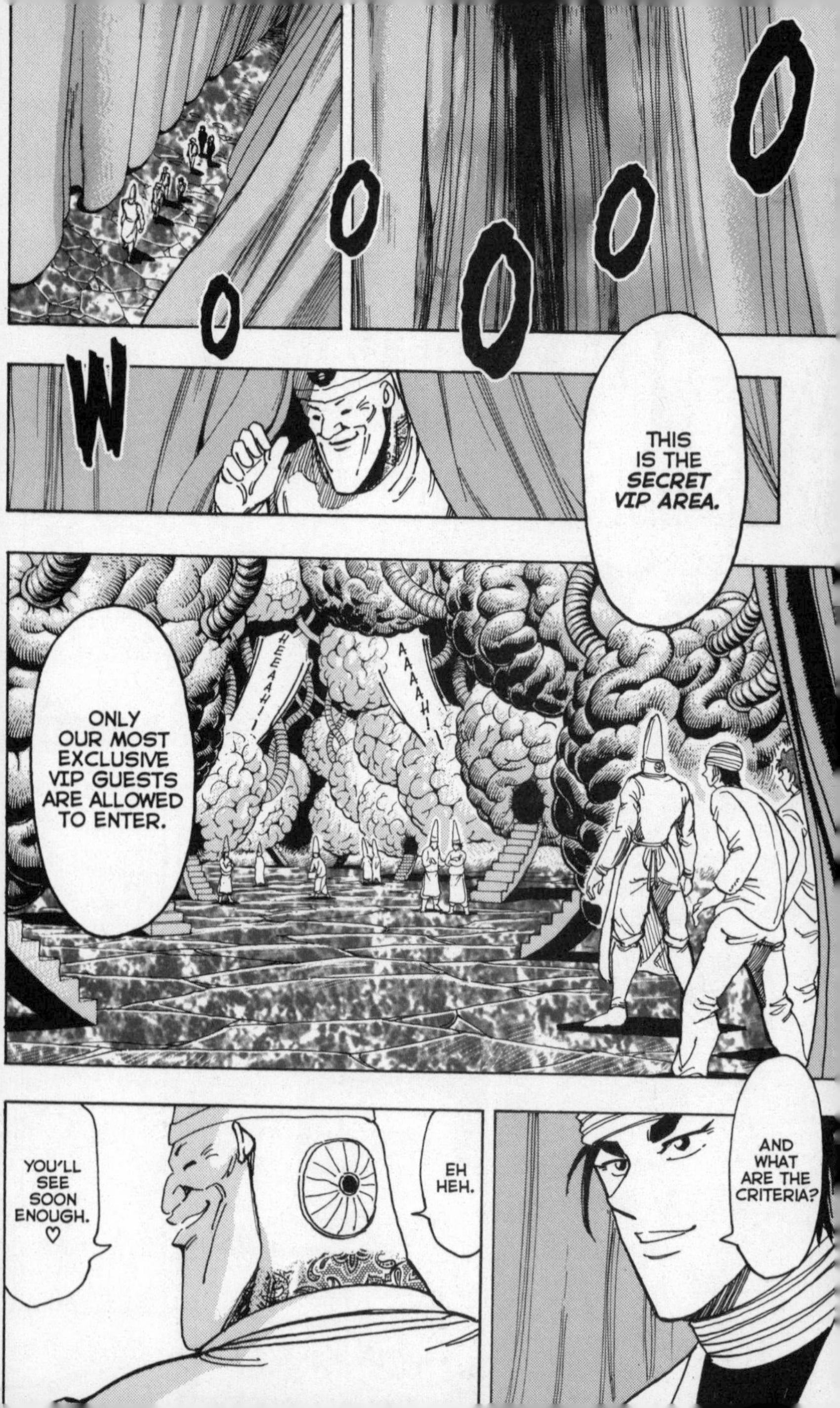
WOOOOO
THIS IS THE SECRET VIP AREA.
AAAAH!!
HEEAAAH!!
ONLY OUR MOST EXCLUSIVE VIP GUESTS ARE ALLOWED TO ENTER.
AND WHAT ARE THE CRITERIA?
EH HEH.
YOU'LL SEE SOON ENOUGH. ♡

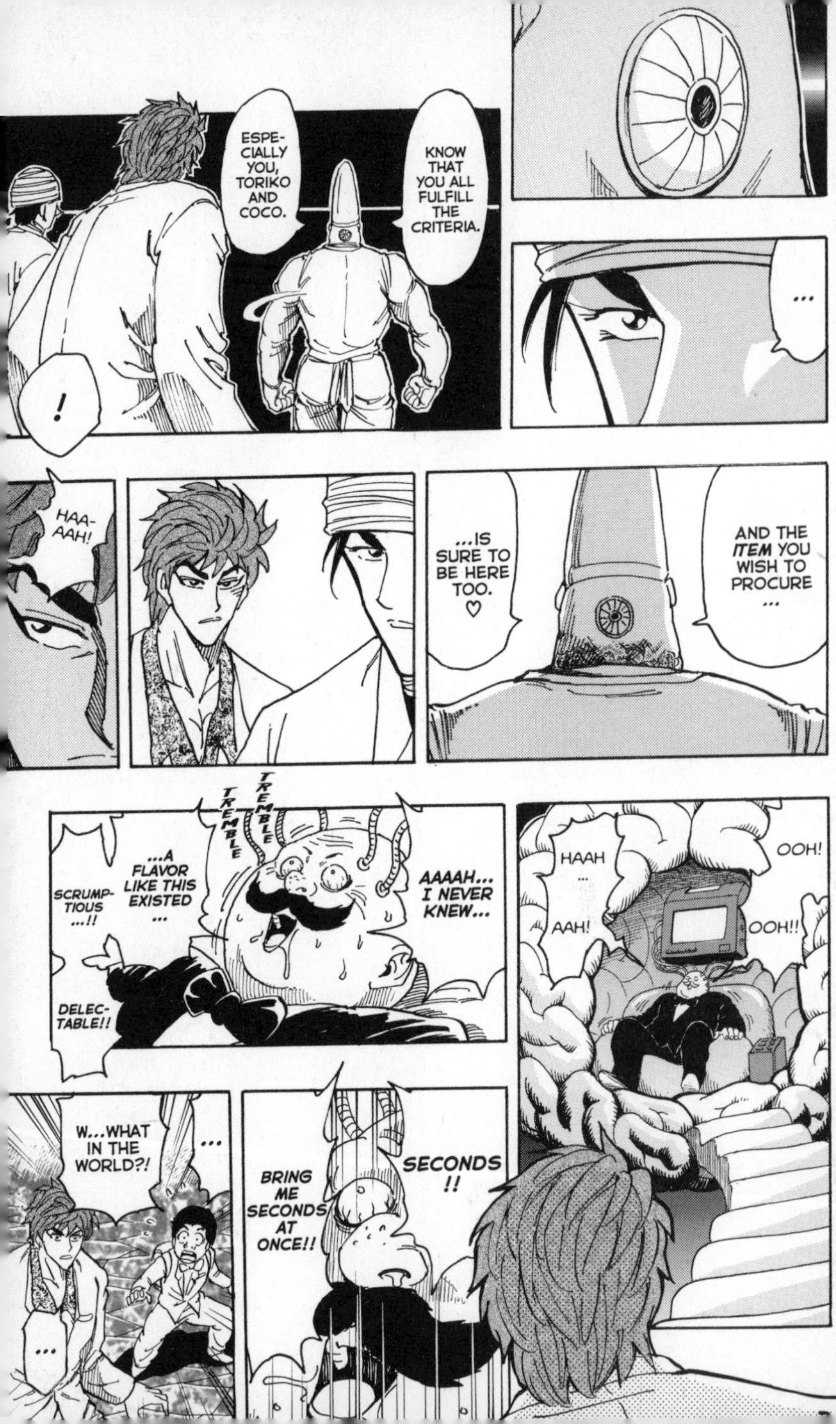
...
KNOW THAT YOU ALL FULFILL THE CRITERIA.
ESPECIALLY YOU, TORIKO AND COCO.
!
AND THE *ITEM* YOU WISH TO PROCURE ...
...IS SURE TO BE HERE TOO. ♡
HAA-AAH!
OOH!
HAAH ...
OOH!!
AAH!
AAAAH... I NEVER KNEW...
TREMBLE
TREMBLE
...A FLAVOR LIKE THIS EXISTED ...
SCRUMPTIOUS ...!!
DELECTABLE!!
SECONDS !!
BRING ME SECONDS AT ONCE!!
...
W...WHAT IN THE WORLD?!
...

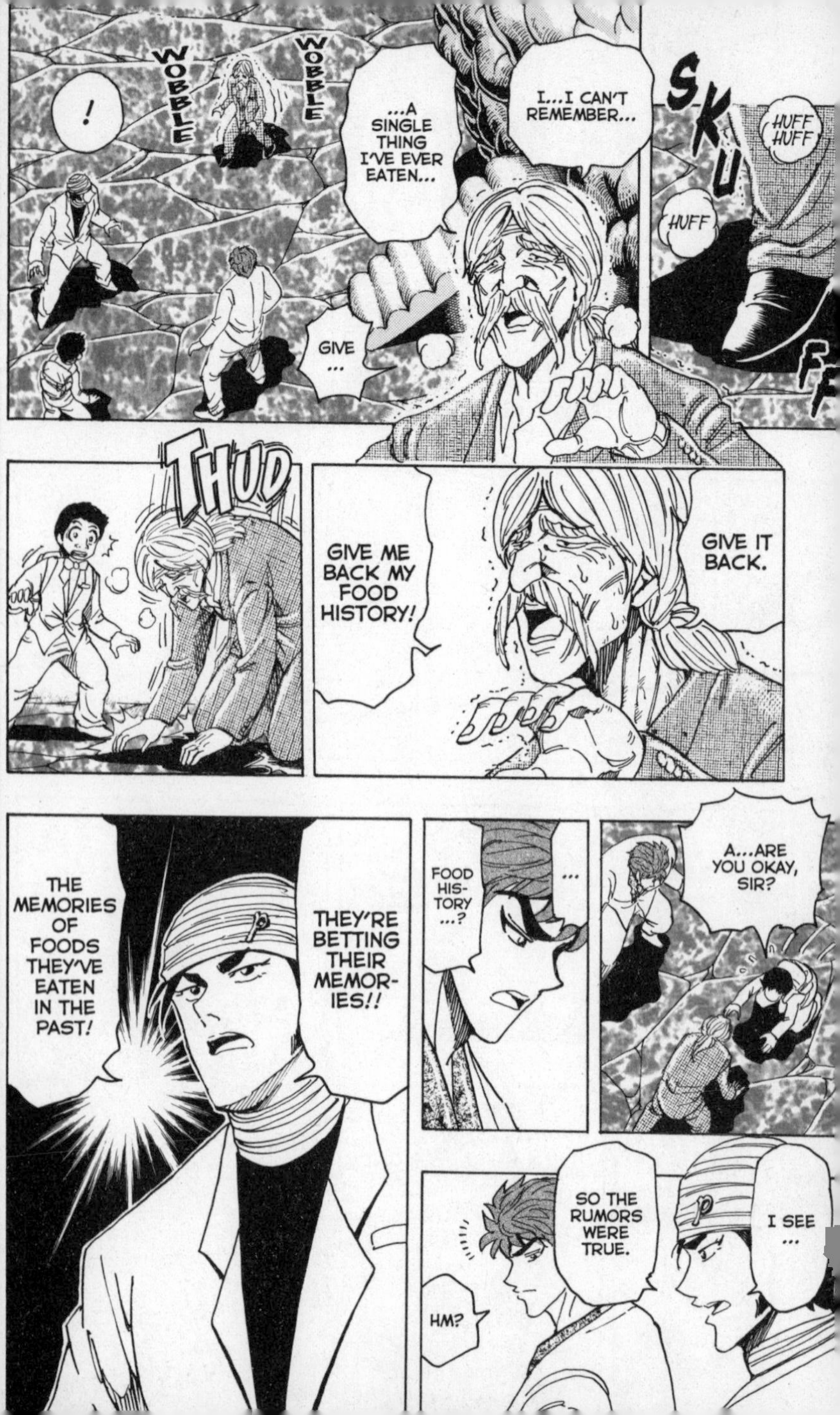
SKUFF
HUFF HUFF
HUFF
I...I CAN'T REMEMBER...
...A SINGLE THING I'VE EVER EATEN...
GIVE ...
WOBBLE
WOBBLE
!
GIVE IT BACK.
GIVE ME BACK MY FOOD HISTORY!
THUD
A...ARE YOU OKAY, SIR?
...
FOOD HISTORY ...?
I SEE ...
SO THE RUMORS WERE TRUE.
HM?
THEY'RE BETTING THEIR MEMORIES!!
THE MEMORIES OF FOODS THEY'VE EATEN IN THE PAST!

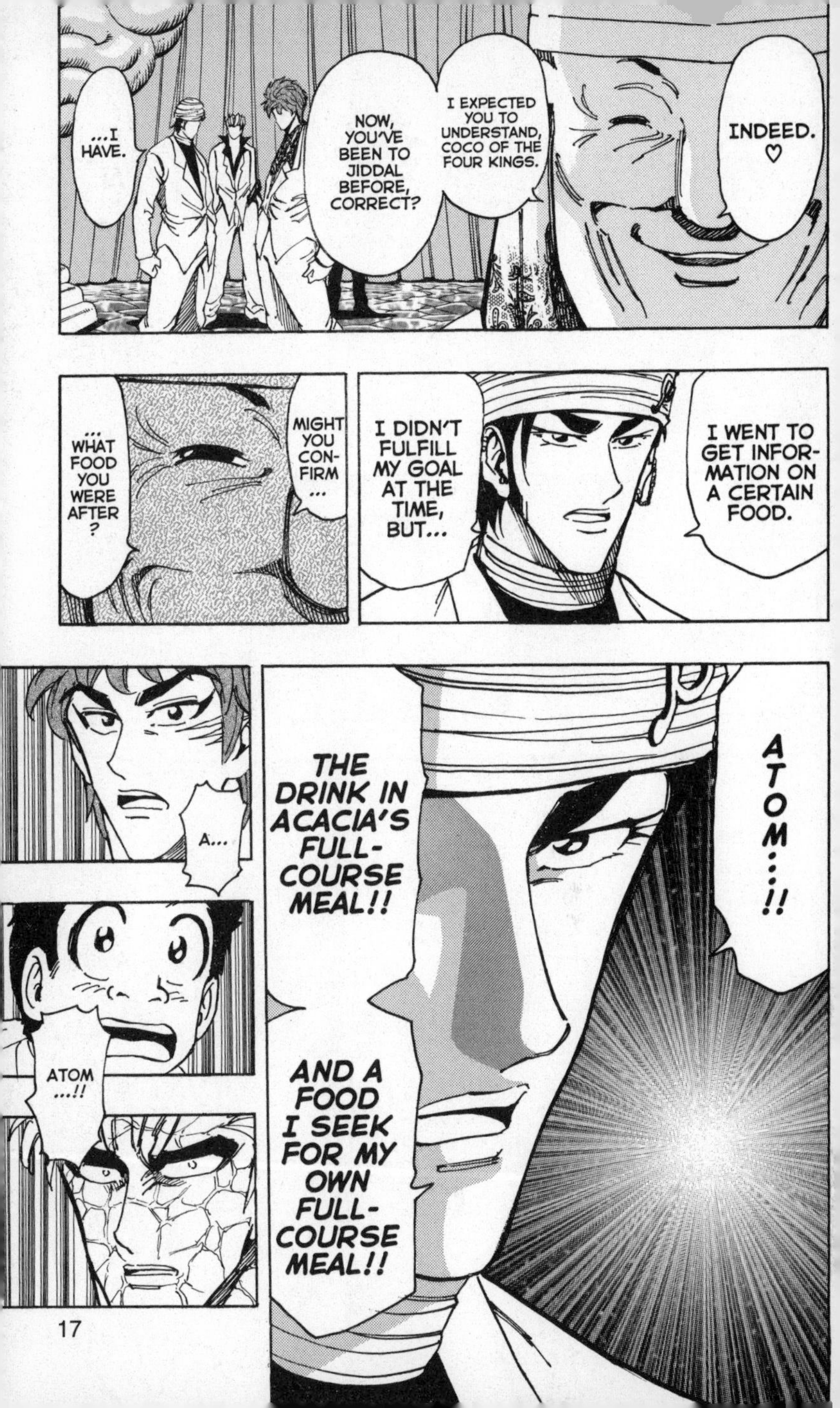
INDEED. ♡
I EXPECTED YOU TO UNDERSTAND, COCO OF THE FOUR KINGS.
NOW, YOU'VE BEEN TO JIDDAL BEFORE, CORRECT?
...I HAVE.
I WENT TO GET INFORMATION ON A CERTAIN FOOD.
I DIDN'T FULFILL MY GOAL AT THE TIME, BUT...
MIGHT YOU CONFIRM...
...WHAT FOOD YOU WERE AFTER?
ATOM...!!
THE DRINK IN ACACIA'S FULL-COURSE MEAL!!
AND A FOOD I SEEK FOR MY OWN FULL-COURSE MEAL!!
A...
ATOM...!!

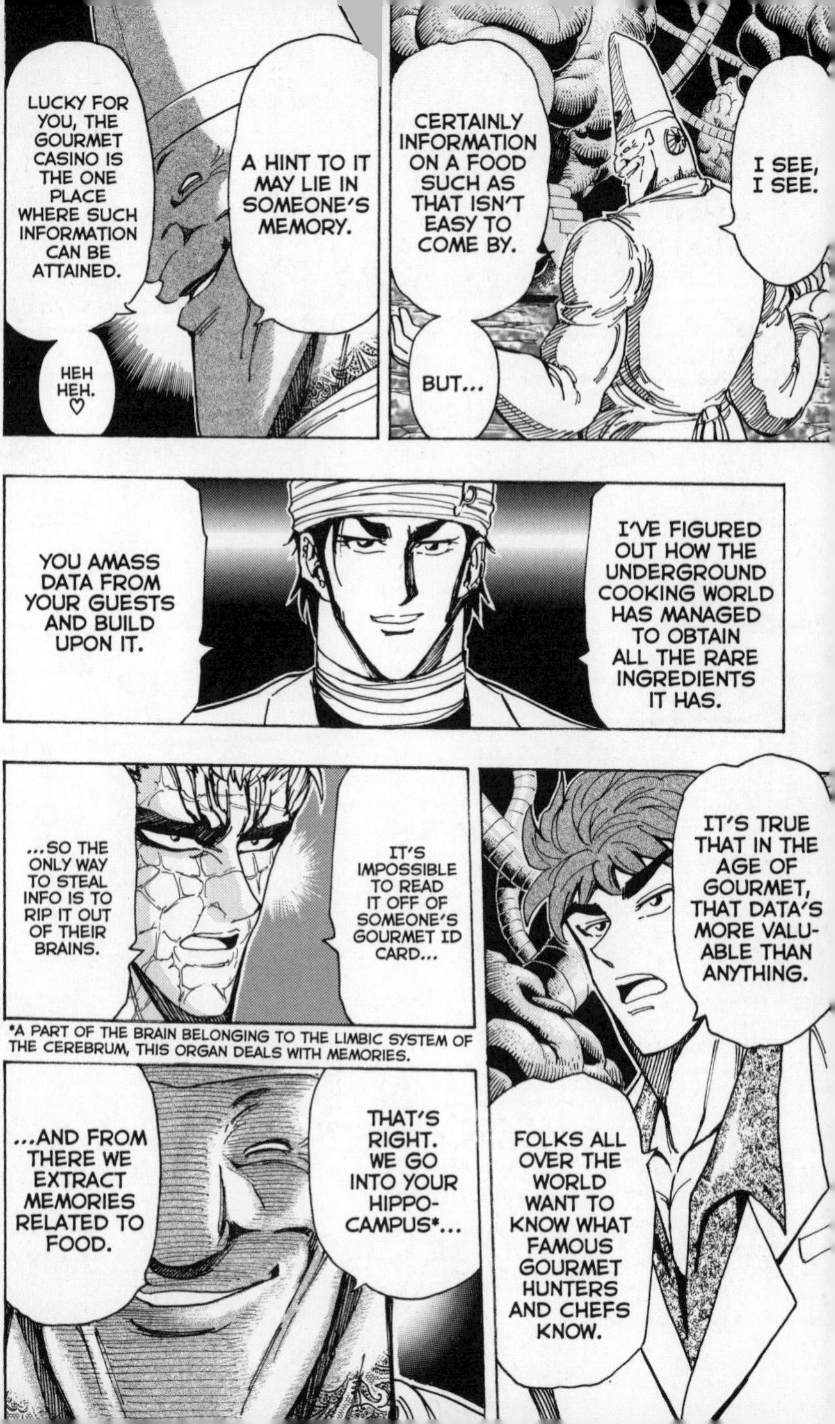
I SEE, I SEE.
CERTAINLY INFORMATION ON A FOOD SUCH AS THAT ISN'T EASY TO COME BY.
BUT...
A HINT TO IT MAY LIE IN SOMEONE'S MEMORY.
LUCKY FOR YOU, THE GOURMET CASINO IS THE ONE PLACE WHERE SUCH INFORMATION CAN BE ATTAINED.
HEH HEH. ♡
I'VE FIGURED OUT HOW THE UNDERGROUND COOKING WORLD HAS MANAGED TO OBTAIN ALL THE RARE INGREDIENTS IT HAS.
YOU AMASS DATA FROM YOUR GUESTS AND BUILD UPON IT.
IT'S TRUE THAT IN THE AGE OF GOURMET, THAT DATA'S MORE VALU-ABLE THAN ANYTHING.
FOLKS ALL OVER THE WORLD WANT TO KNOW WHAT FAMOUS GOURMET HUNTERS AND CHEFS KNOW.
IT'S IMPOSSIBLE TO READ IT OFF OF SOMEONE'S GOURMET ID CARD...
...SO THE ONLY WAY TO STEAL INFO IS TO RIP IT OUT OF THEIR BRAINS.
*A PART OF THE BRAIN BELONGING TO THE LIMBIC SYSTEM OF THE CEREBRUM, THIS ORGAN DEALS WITH MEMORIES.
THAT'S RIGHT. WE GO INTO YOUR HIPPO-CAMPUS*...
...AND FROM THERE WE EXTRACT MEMORIES RELATED TO FOOD.

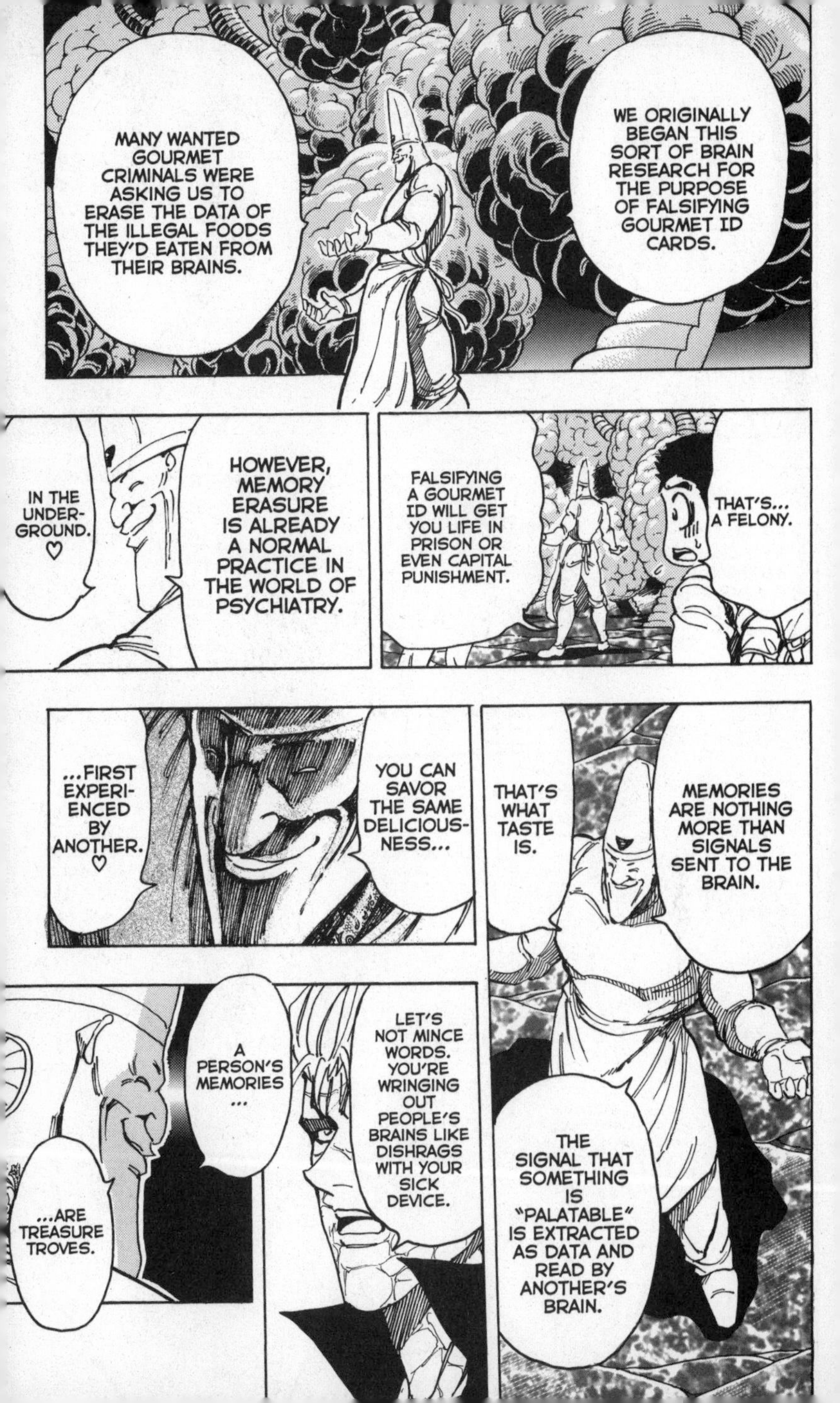
WE ORIGINALLY BEGAN THIS SORT OF BRAIN RESEARCH FOR THE PURPOSE OF FALSIFYING GOURMET ID CARDS.
MANY WANTED GOURMET CRIMINALS WERE ASKING US TO ERASE THE DATA OF THE ILLEGAL FOODS THEY'D EATEN FROM THEIR BRAINS.
THAT'S... A FELONY.
FALSIFYING A GOURMET ID WILL GET YOU LIFE IN PRISON OR EVEN CAPITAL PUNISHMENT.
HOWEVER, MEMORY ERASURE IS ALREADY A NORMAL PRACTICE IN THE WORLD OF PSYCHIATRY.
IN THE UNDER-GROUND. ♡
MEMORIES ARE NOTHING MORE THAN SIGNALS SENT TO THE BRAIN.
THAT'S WHAT TASTE IS.
THE SIGNAL THAT SOMETHING IS "PALATABLE" IS EXTRACTED AS DATA AND READ BY ANOTHER'S BRAIN.
YOU CAN SAVOR THE SAME DELICIOUS-NESS...
...FIRST EXPERI-ENCED BY ANOTHER. ♡
LET'S NOT MINCE WORDS. YOU'RE WRINGING OUT PEOPLE'S BRAINS LIKE DISHRAGS WITH YOUR SICK DEVICE.
A PERSON'S MEMORIES ...
...ARE TREASURE TROVES.

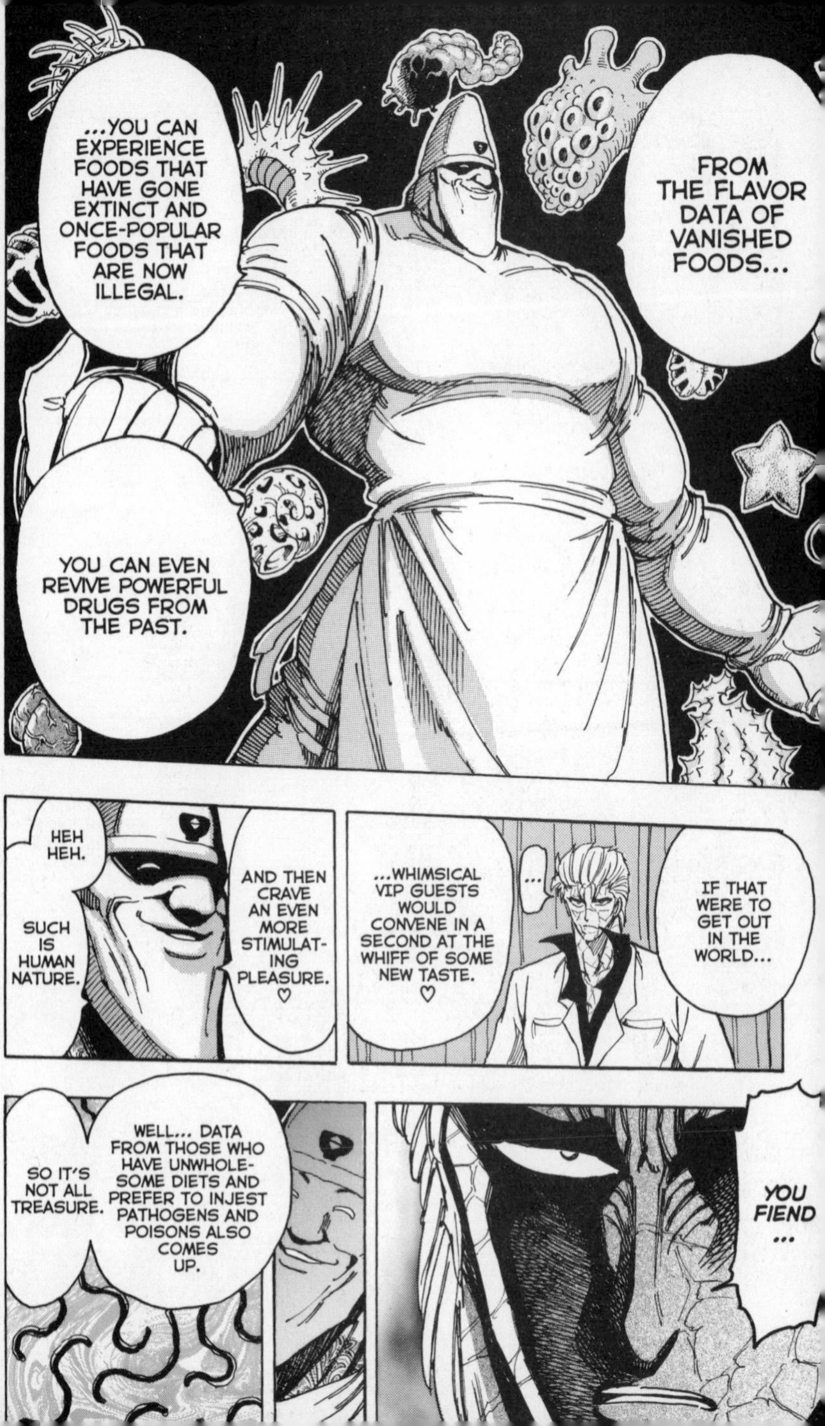
FROM THE FLAVOR DATA OF VANISHED FOODS...
...YOU CAN EXPERIENCE FOODS THAT HAVE GONE EXTINCT AND ONCE-POPULAR FOODS THAT ARE NOW ILLEGAL.
YOU CAN EVEN REVIVE POWERFUL DRUGS FROM THE PAST.
IF THAT WERE TO GET OUT IN THE WORLD...
...
...WHIMSICAL VIP GUESTS WOULD CONVENE IN A SECOND AT THE WHIFF OF SOME NEW TASTE. ♡
AND THEN CRAVE AN EVEN MORE STIMULAT-ING PLEASURE. ♡
HEH HEH.
SUCH IS HUMAN NATURE.
YOU FIEND ...
WELL... DATA FROM THOSE WHO HAVE UNWHOLE-SOME DIETS AND PREFER TO INJEST PATHOGENS AND POISONS ALSO COMES UP.
SO IT'S NOT ALL TREASURE.

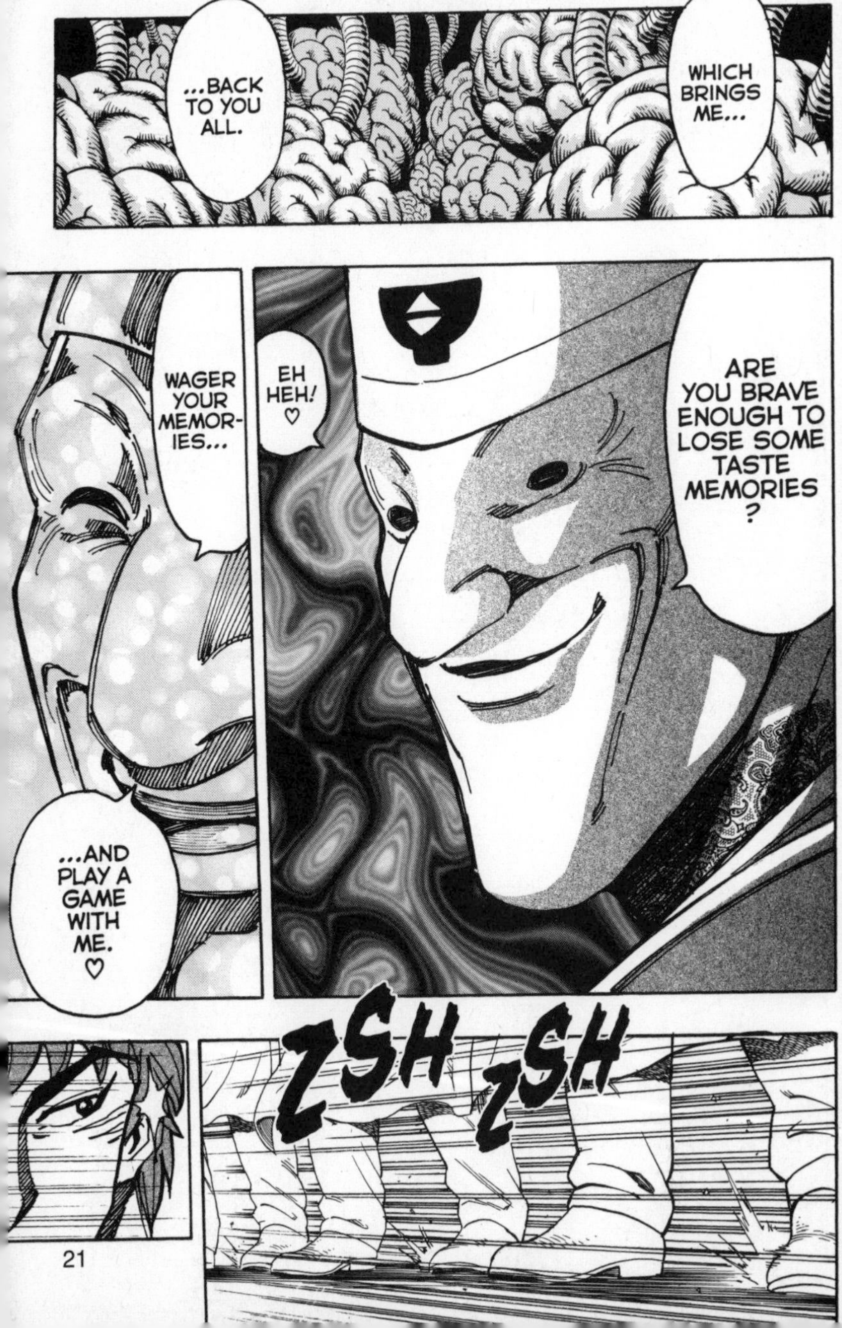
WHICH BRINGS ME...
...BACK TO YOU ALL.
ARE YOU BRAVE ENOUGH TO LOSE SOME TASTE MEMORIES?
EH HEH! ♡
WAGER YOUR MEMOR-IES...
...AND PLAY A GAME WITH ME. ♡
ZSH ZSH

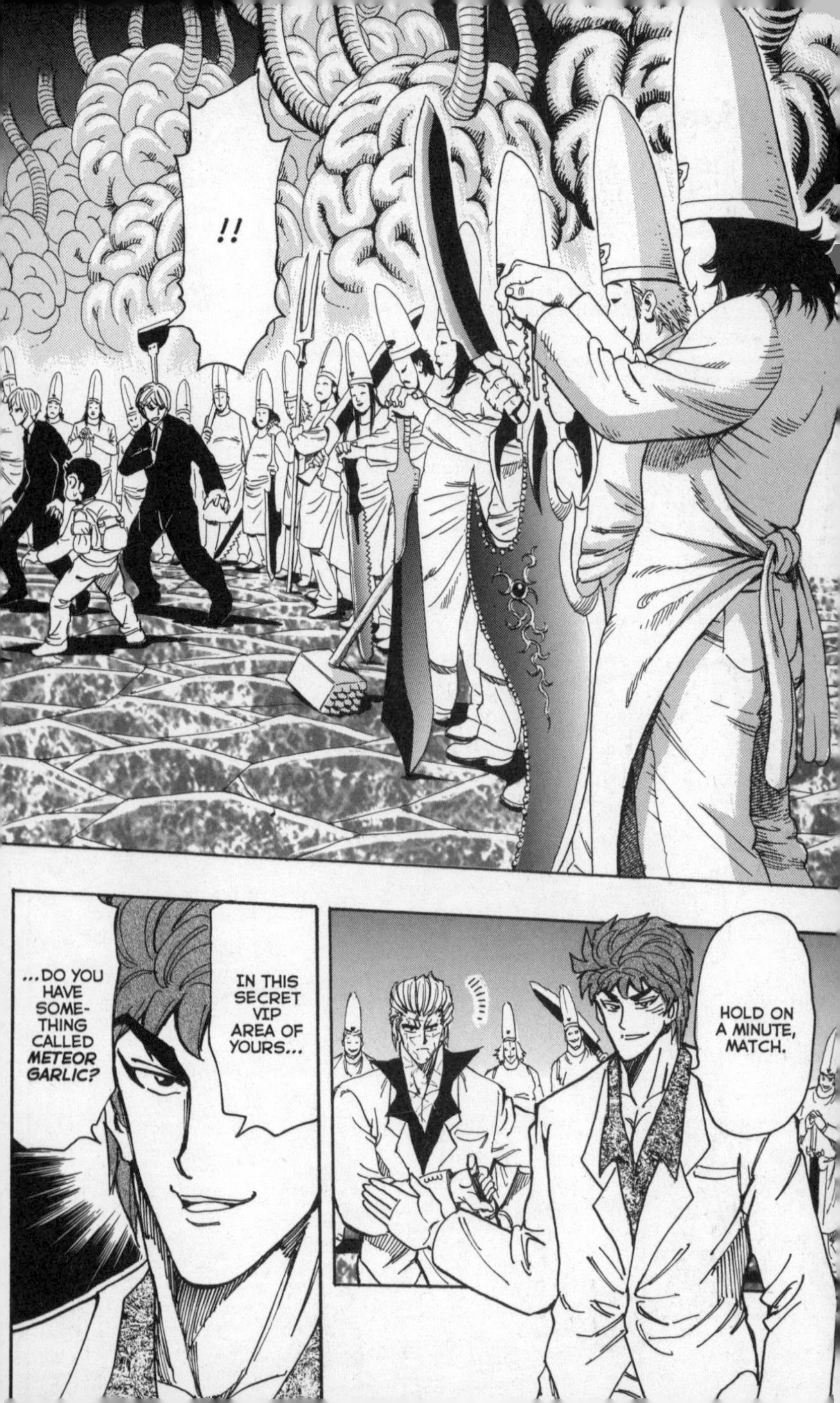
!!
HOLD ON A MINUTE, MATCH.
IN THIS SECRET VIP AREA OF YOURS...
...DO YOU HAVE SOME-THING CALLED *METEOR GARLIC?*

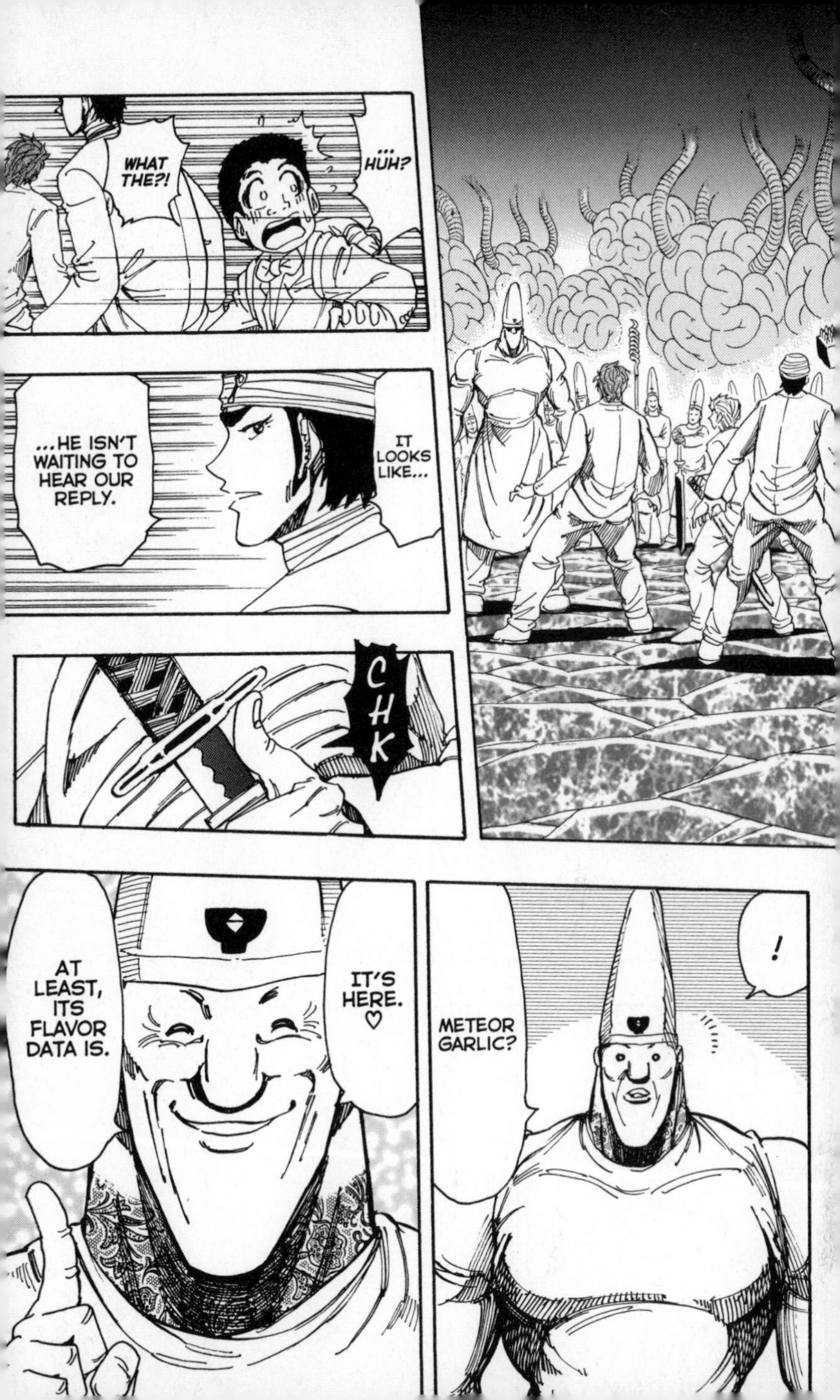
...HUH?
WHAT THE?!
IT LOOKS LIKE...
...HE ISN'T WAITING TO HEAR OUR REPLY.
CHK
!
METEOR GARLIC?
IT'S HERE. ♡
AT LEAST, ITS FLAVOR DATA IS.

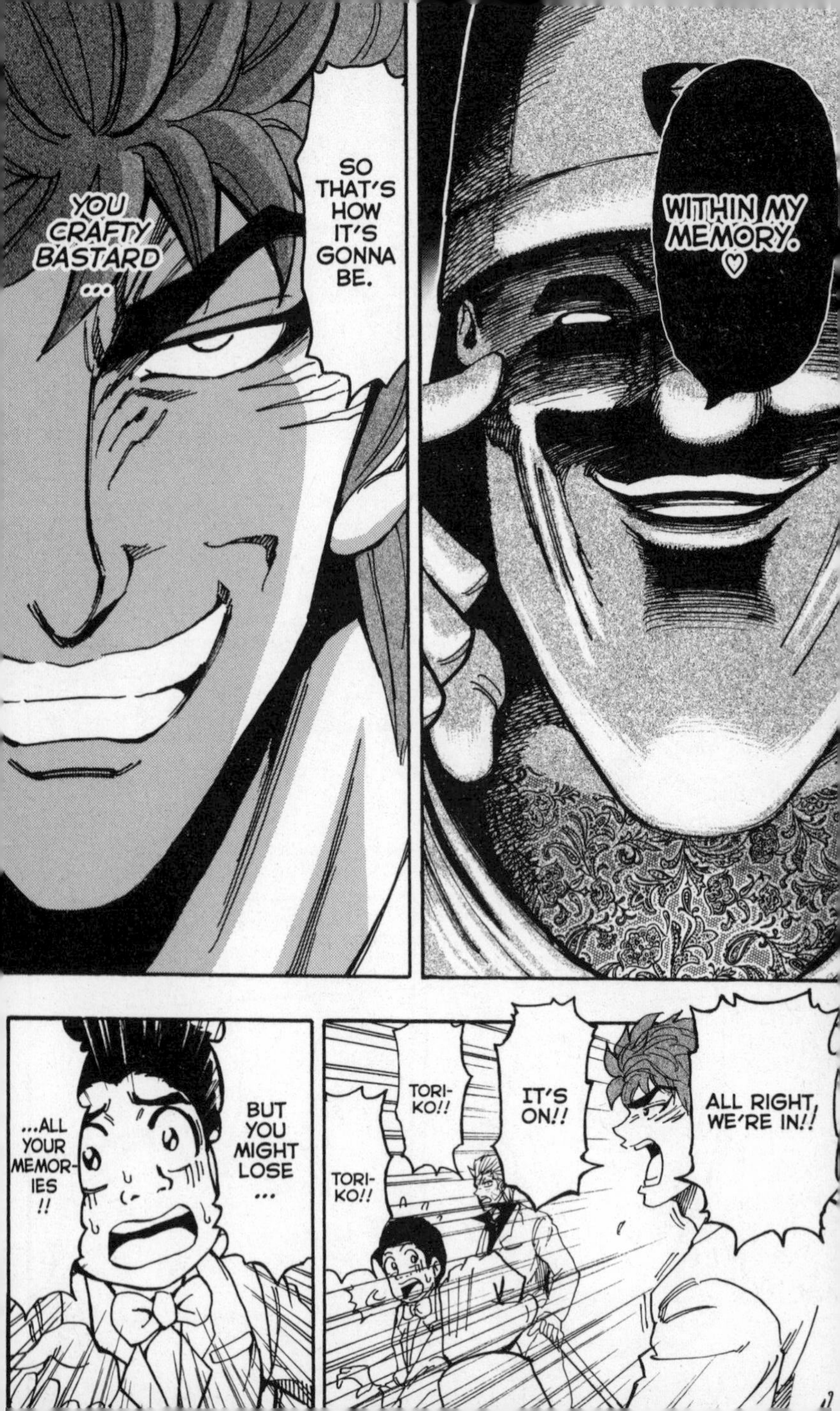

WITHIN MY MEMORY. ♡
SO THAT'S HOW IT'S GONNA BE.
YOU CRAFTY BASTARD...
ALL RIGHT, WE'RE IN!!
IT'S ON!!
TORI-KO!!
TORI-KO!!
BUT YOU MIGHT LOSE...
...ALL YOUR MEMOR-IES!!

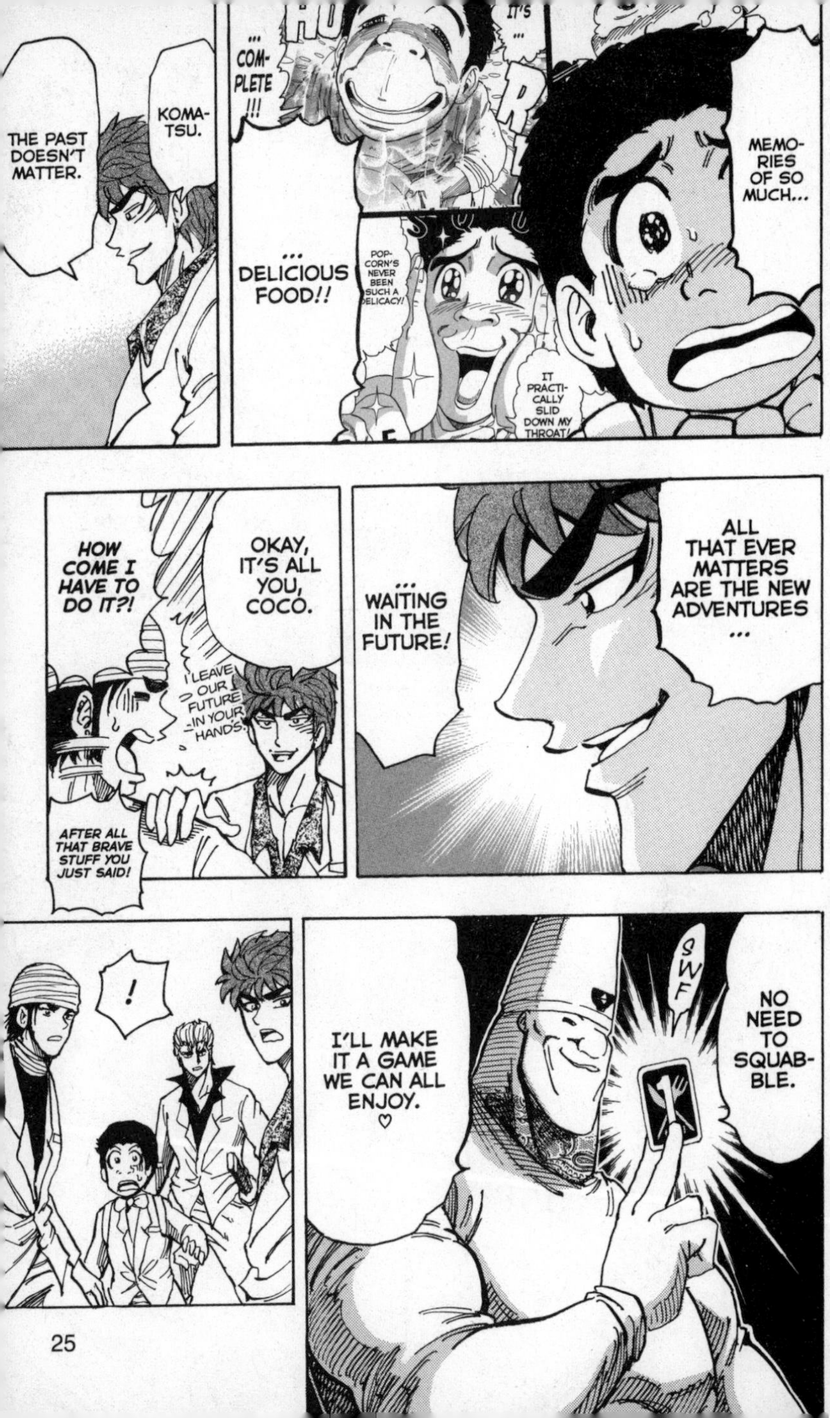
MEMORIES OF SO MUCH...
IT'S ...
... COMPLETE!!!
... DELICIOUS FOOD!!
POPCORN'S NEVER BEEN SUCH A DELICACY!
IT PRACTICALLY SLID DOWN MY THROAT!
KOMATSU.
THE PAST DOESN'T MATTER.
ALL THAT EVER MATTERS ARE THE NEW ADVENTURES ...
... WAITING IN THE FUTURE!
OKAY, IT'S ALL YOU, COCO.
I LEAVE OUR FUTURE IN YOUR HANDS.
HOW COME I HAVE TO DO IT?!
AFTER ALL THAT BRAVE STUFF YOU JUST SAID!
NO NEED TO SQUABBLE.
SWF
I'LL MAKE IT A GAME WE CAN ALL ENJOY. ♡
!

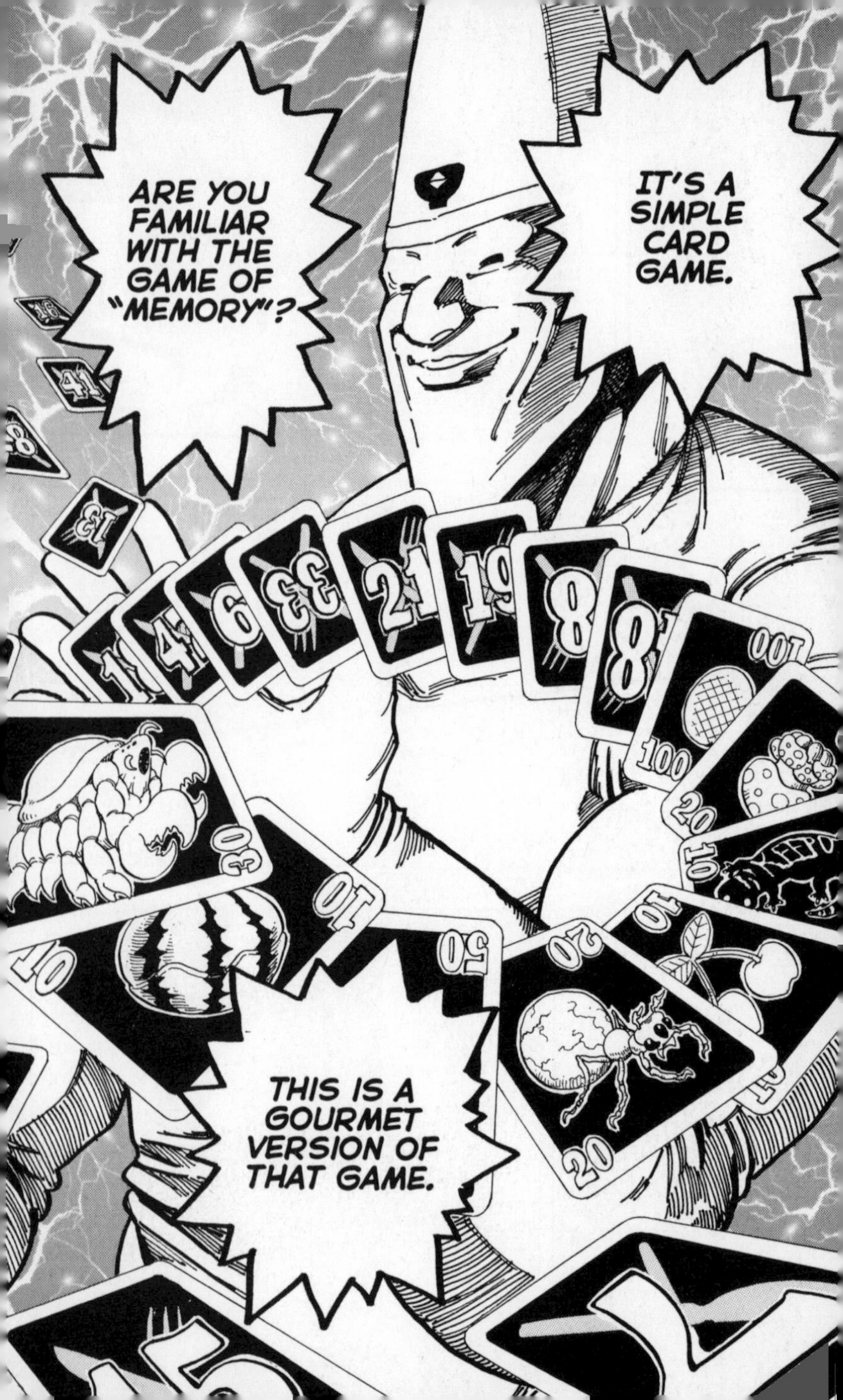
IT'S A SIMPLE CARD GAME.
ARE YOU FAMILIAR WITH THE GAME OF "MEMORY"?
THIS IS A GOURMET VERSION OF THAT GAME.

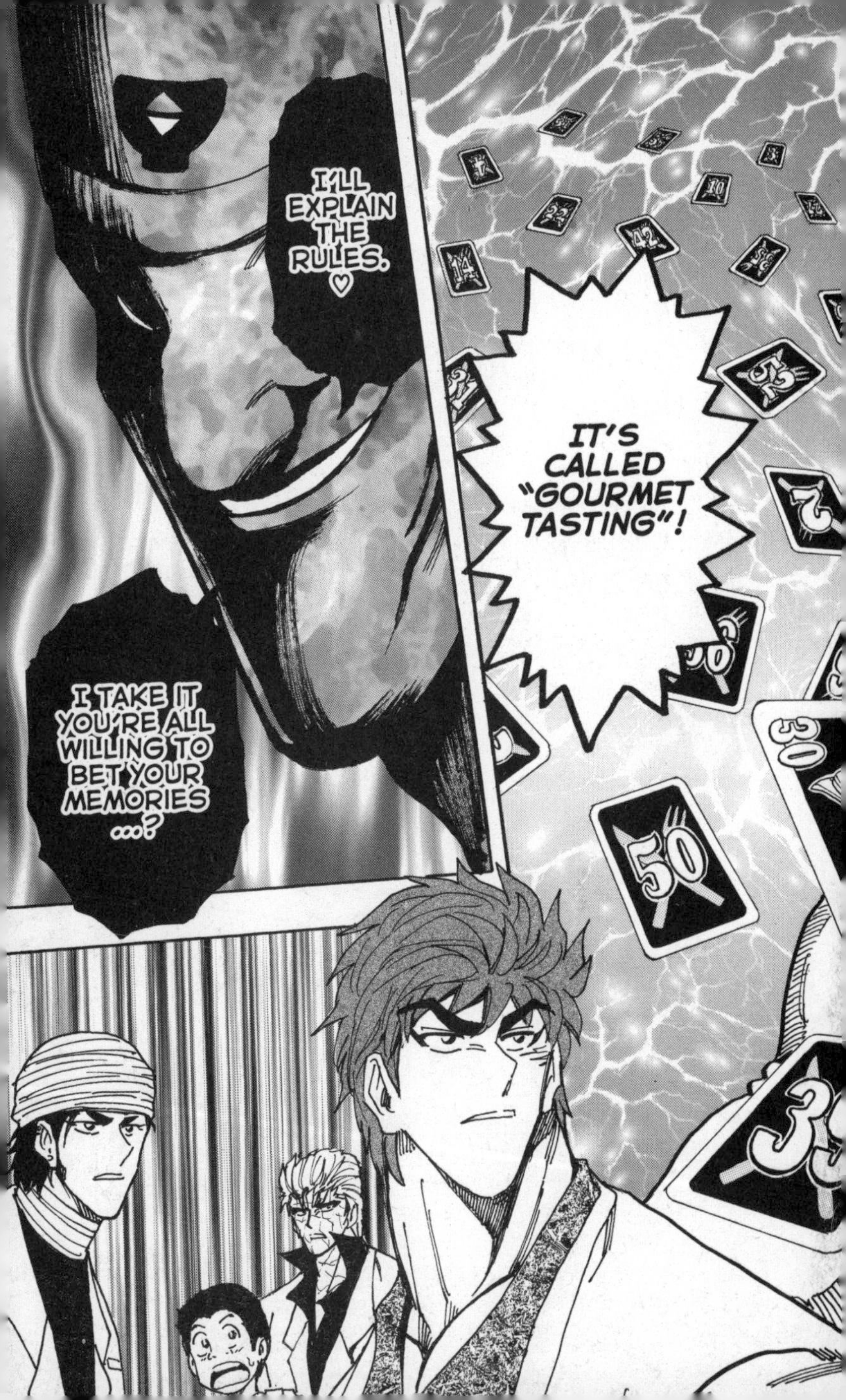
IT'S CALLED "GOURMET TASTING"!
I'LL EXPLAIN THE RULES. ♡
I TAKE IT YOU'RE ALL WILLING TO BET YOUR MEMORIES ...?

TORIKO

GOURMET CHECKLIST

Vol. 194

UNICORN CERBERUS

(MAMMAL)

CAPTURE LEVEL: 63

HABITAT: GOURMET PYRAMID

LENGTH: 20 METERS

HEIGHT: 15 METERS

WEIGHT: 35 TONS

PRICE: 100 G / 150 YEN;
STUFFED SPECIMEN /
2 BILLION

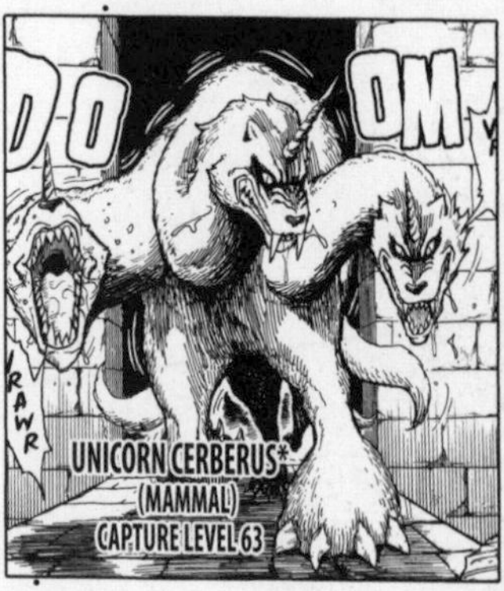
D-O
OM
RAWR
UNICORN CERBERUS*
(MAMMAL)
CAPTURE LEVEL 63

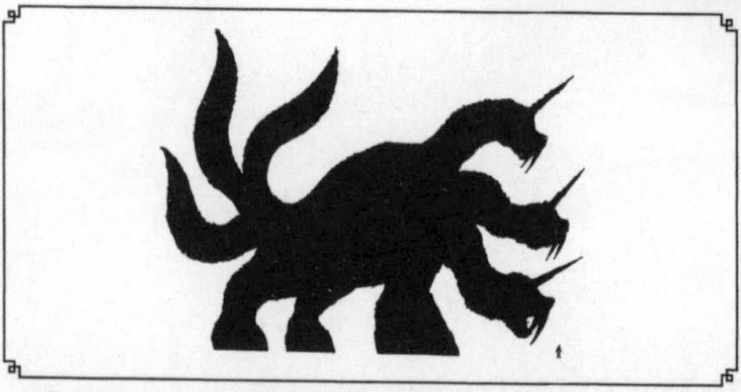

SCALE

A THREE-HEADED UNICORN THAT HAS LIVED IN GOURMET PYRAMID SINCE ANCIENT TIMES. ITS FLESH IS TOO TOUGH TO EAT AND NOT VERY RICH IN NUTRIENTS. HOWEVER, IT OFFERS 100 KILOCALORIES OF ENERGY FOR EVERY 100 GRAMS OF ITS MEAT, MUCH LIKE THE BREAST MEAT OF A CHICKEN, SO IN THE UTTERLY FOOD-DEVOID GOURMET PYRAMID, IT IS A PRECIOUS ENERGY SOURCE. ITS HORNS AND FANGS FETCH A HIGH PRICE AS MATERIALS FOR ORNAMENTATION AND A FULLY INTACT STUFFED UNICORN CERBERUS AS AN ART OBJECT IS SO RARE THAN WHEN ONE ACTUALLY MAKES IT ONTO THE MARKET, IT SELLS FOR TEN TO ONE HUNDRED TIMES THE PRICE OF ITS HORN OR FANGS ALONE.

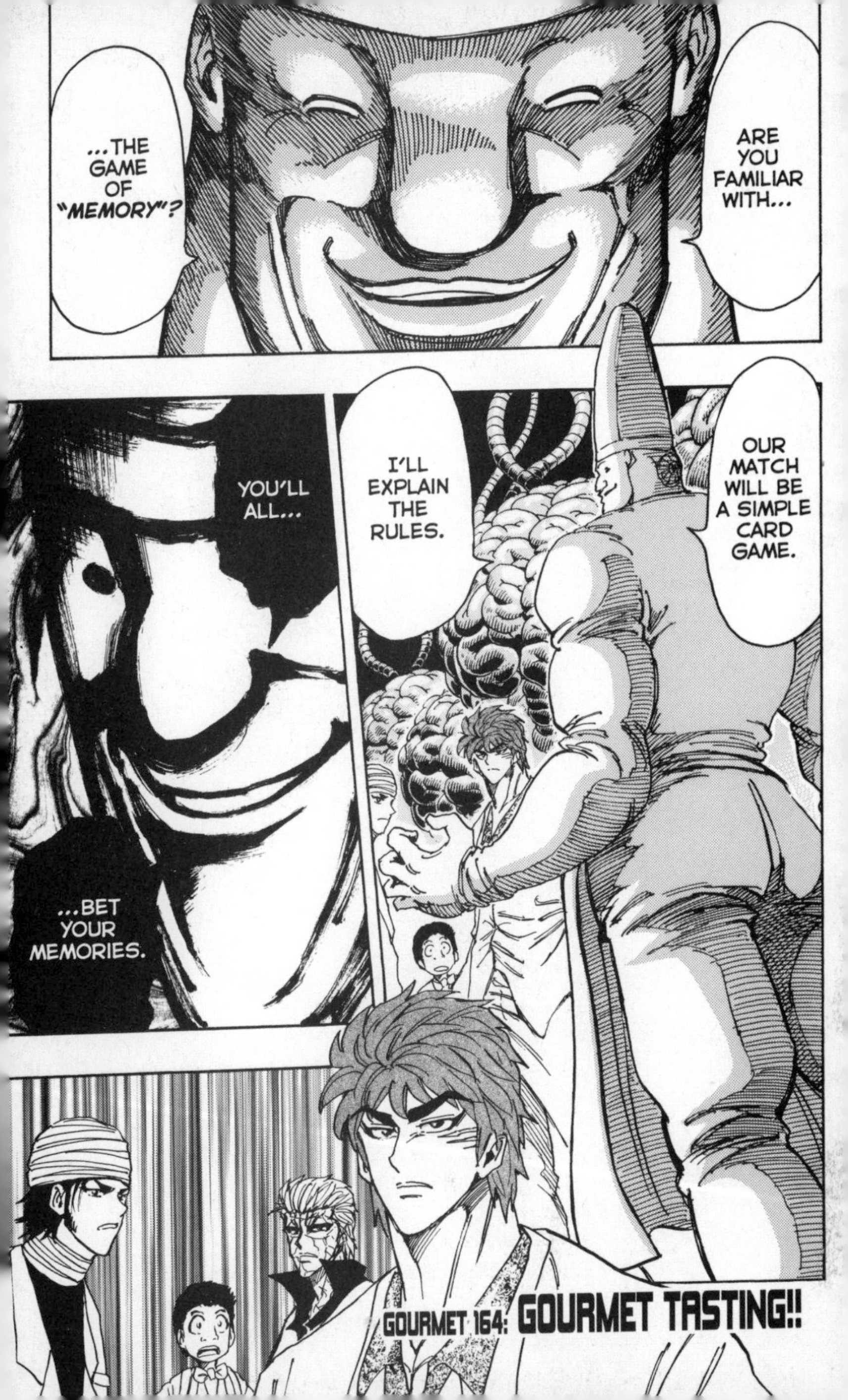
ARE YOU FAMILIAR WITH...
...THE GAME OF "MEMORY"?
OUR MATCH WILL BE A SIMPLE CARD GAME.
I'LL EXPLAIN THE RULES.
YOU'LL ALL...
...BET YOUR MEMORIES.
GOURMET 164: GOURMET TASTING!!

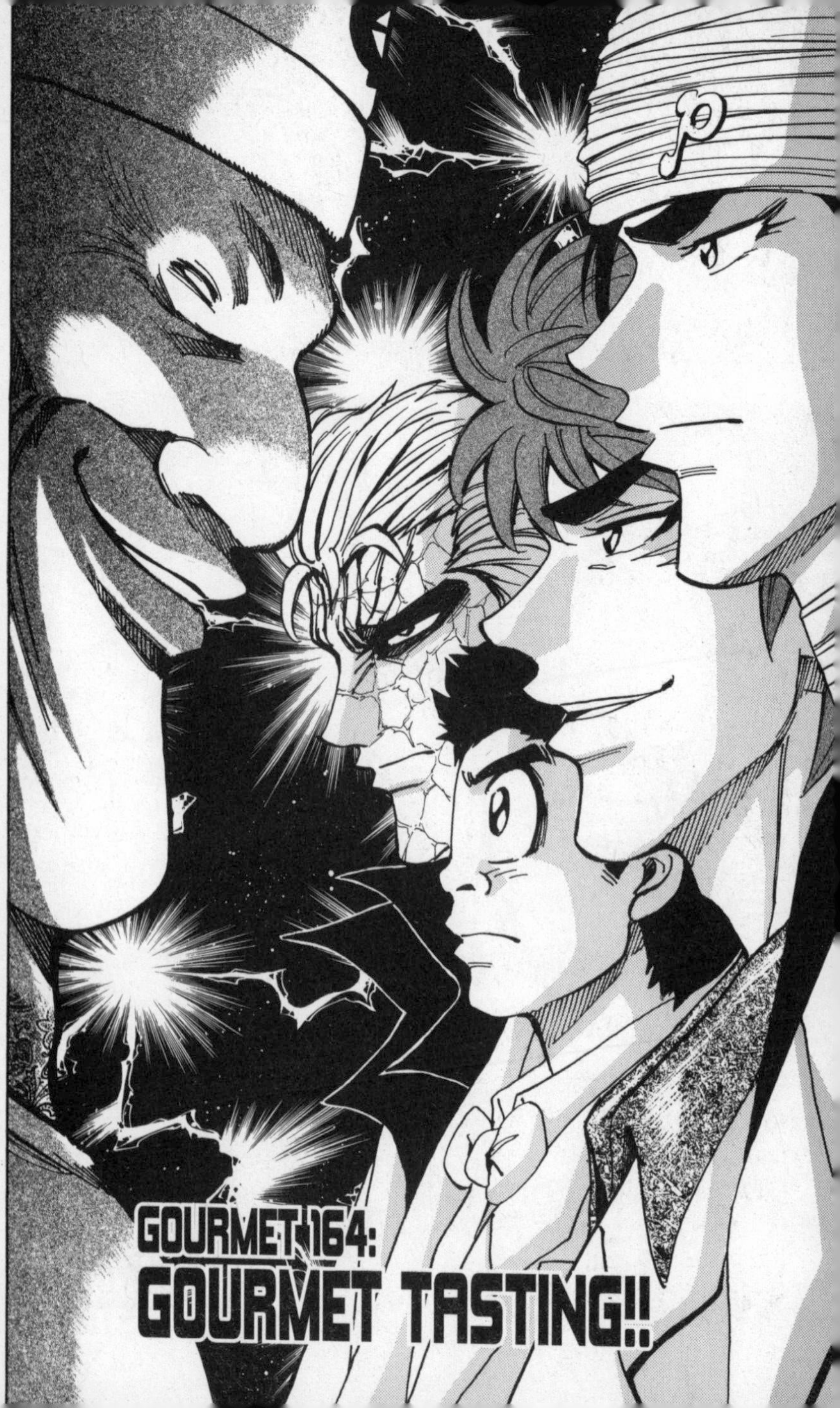
GOURMET 164:
GOURMET TASTING!!

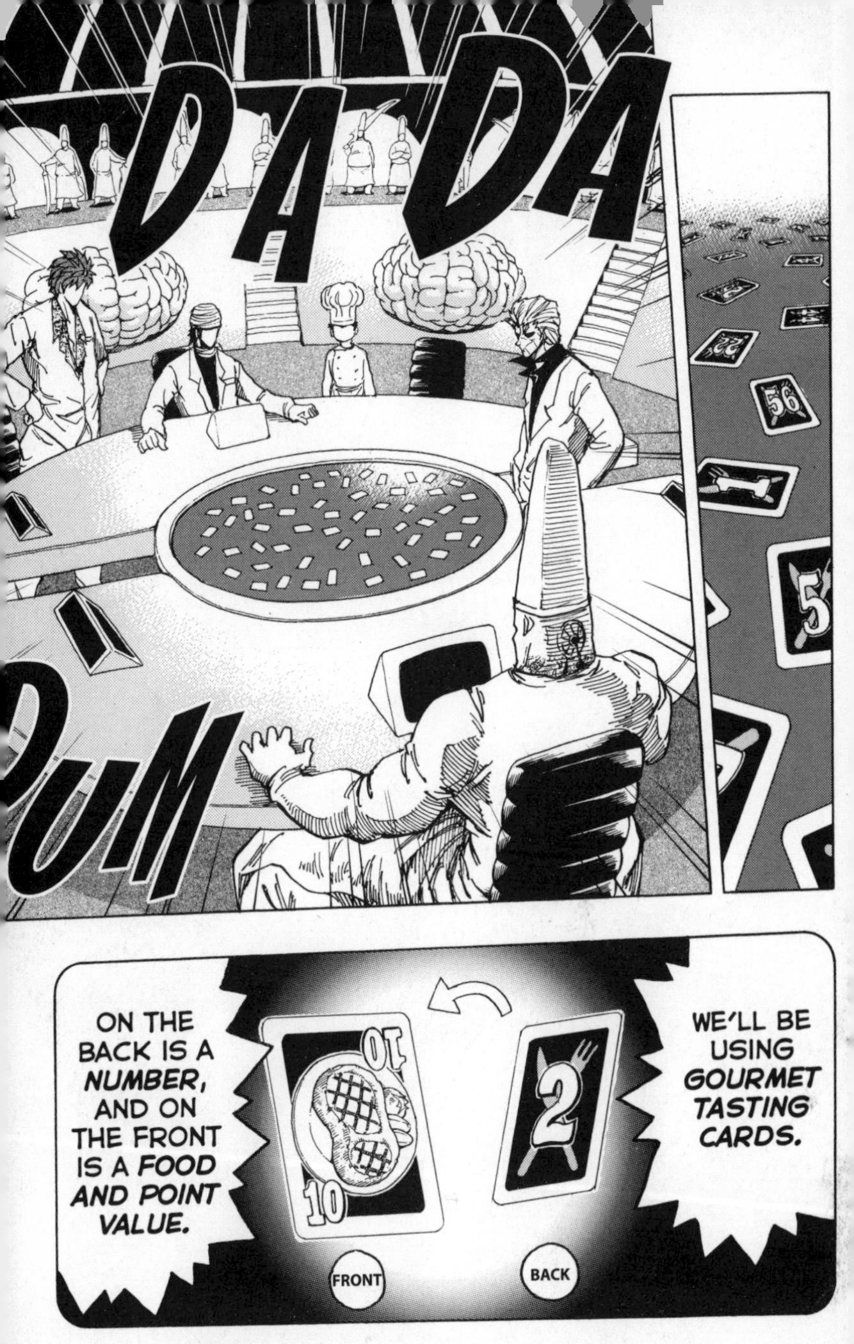
DA DA
DUM
WE'LL BE USING *GOURMET TASTING CARDS.*
ON THE BACK IS A *NUMBER,* AND ON THE FRONT IS A *FOOD AND POINT VALUE.*
FRONT
BACK

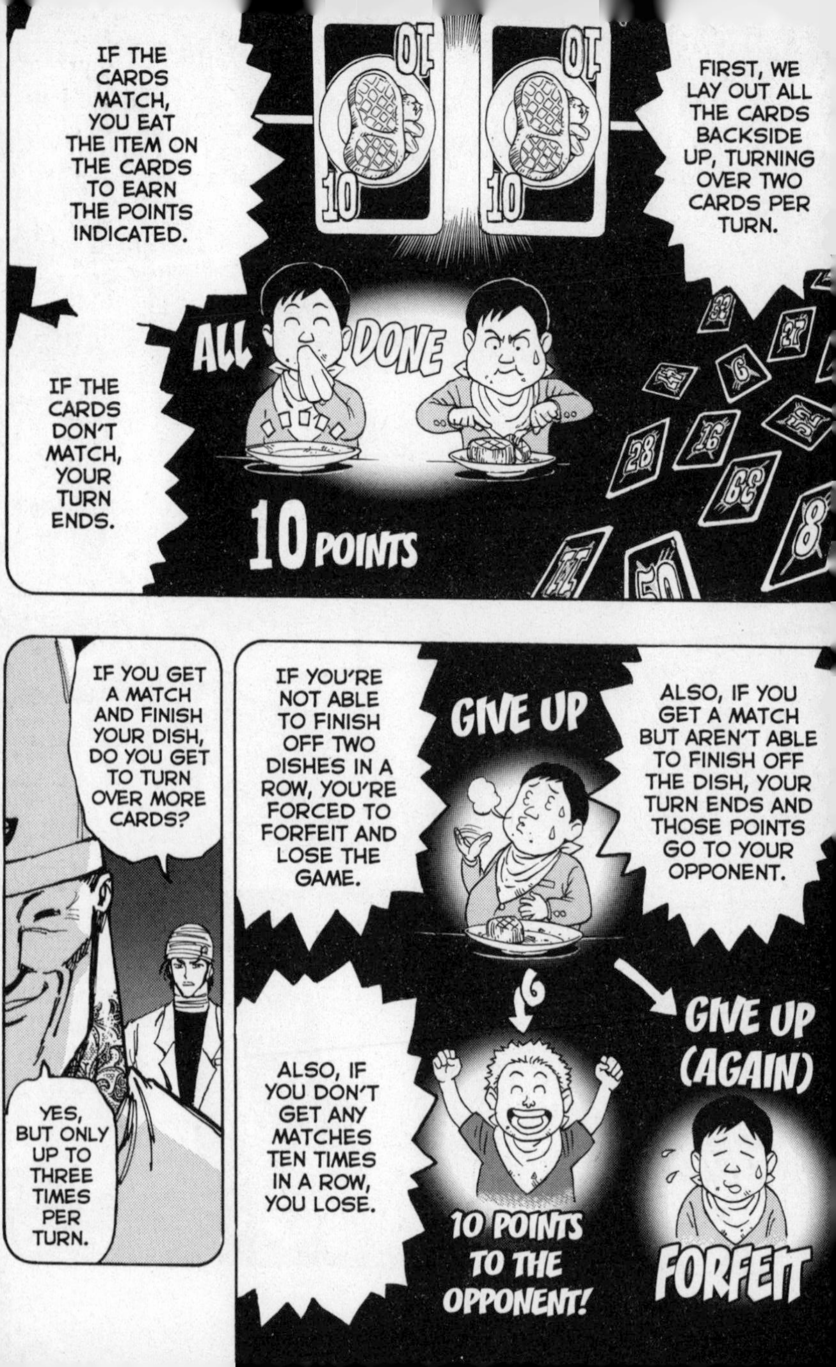
FIRST, WE LAY OUT ALL THE CARDS BACKSIDE UP, TURNING OVER TWO CARDS PER TURN.
IF THE CARDS MATCH, YOU EAT THE ITEM ON THE CARDS TO EARN THE POINTS INDICATED.
ALL DONE
10 POINTS
IF THE CARDS DON'T MATCH, YOUR TURN ENDS.
ALSO, IF YOU GET A MATCH BUT AREN'T ABLE TO FINISH OFF THE DISH, YOUR TURN ENDS AND THOSE POINTS GO TO YOUR OPPONENT.
GIVE UP
IF YOU'RE NOT ABLE TO FINISH OFF TWO DISHES IN A ROW, YOU'RE FORCED TO FORFEIT AND LOSE THE GAME.
GIVE UP (AGAIN)
FORFEIT
10 POINTS TO THE OPPONENT!
ALSO, IF YOU DON'T GET ANY MATCHES TEN TIMES IN A ROW, YOU LOSE.
IF YOU GET A MATCH AND FINISH YOUR DISH, DO YOU GET TO TURN OVER MORE CARDS?
YES, BUT ONLY UP TO THREE TIMES PER TURN.

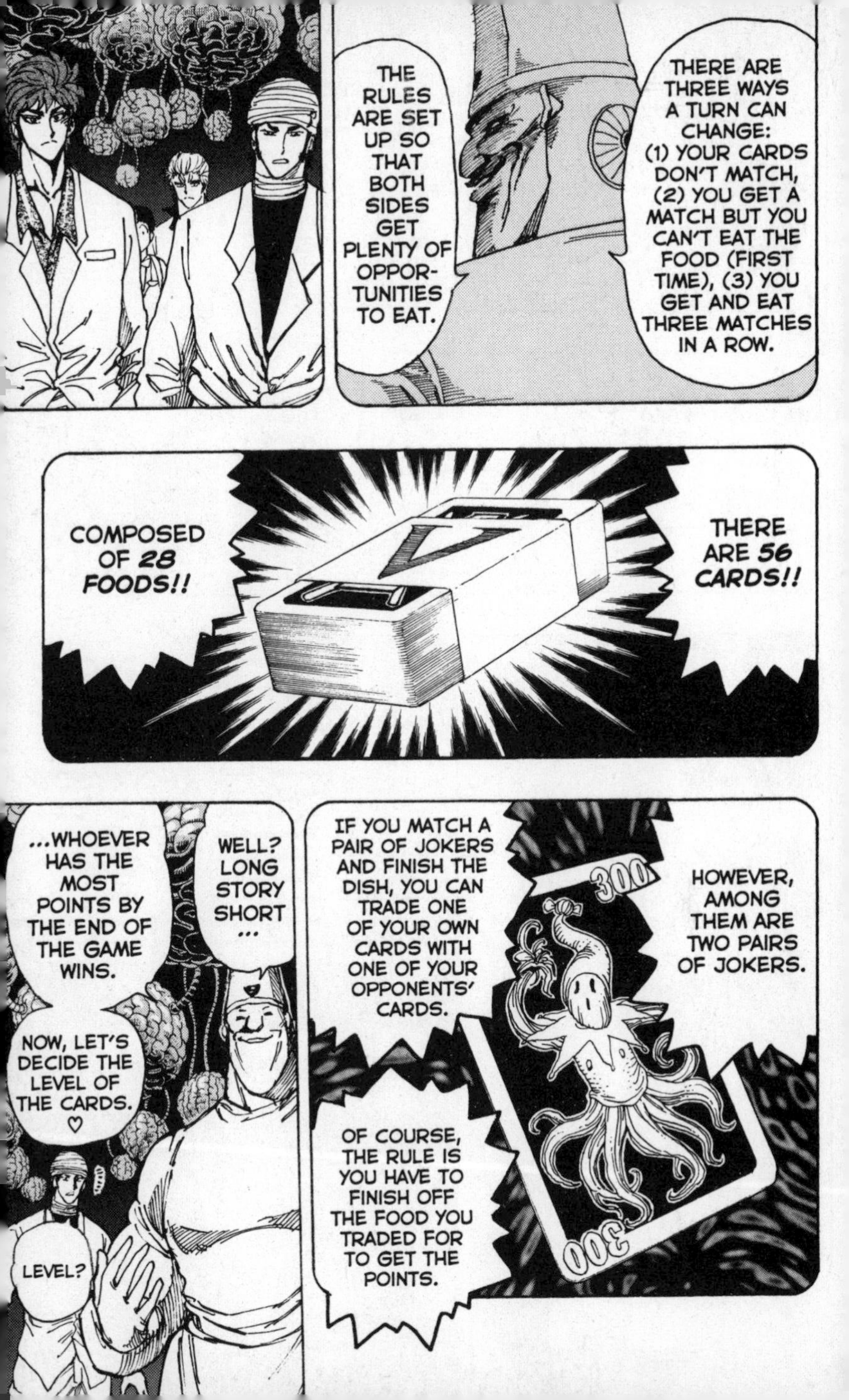
THERE ARE THREE WAYS A TURN CAN CHANGE: (1) YOUR CARDS DON'T MATCH, (2) YOU GET A MATCH BUT YOU CAN'T EAT THE FOOD (FIRST TIME), (3) YOU GET AND EAT THREE MATCHES IN A ROW.
THE RULES ARE SET UP SO THAT BOTH SIDES GET PLENTY OF OPPOR-TUNITIES TO EAT.
THERE ARE 56 CARDS!!
COMPOSED OF 28 FOODS!!
HOWEVER, AMONG THEM ARE TWO PAIRS OF JOKERS.
300
300
IF YOU MATCH A PAIR OF JOKERS AND FINISH THE DISH, YOU CAN TRADE ONE OF YOUR OWN CARDS WITH ONE OF YOUR OPPONENTS' CARDS.
OF COURSE, THE RULE IS YOU HAVE TO FINISH OFF THE FOOD YOU TRADED FOR TO GET THE POINTS.
WELL? LONG STORY SHORT ...
...WHOEVER HAS THE MOST POINTS BY THE END OF THE GAME WINS.
NOW, LET'S DECIDE THE LEVEL OF THE CARDS. ♡
LEVEL?

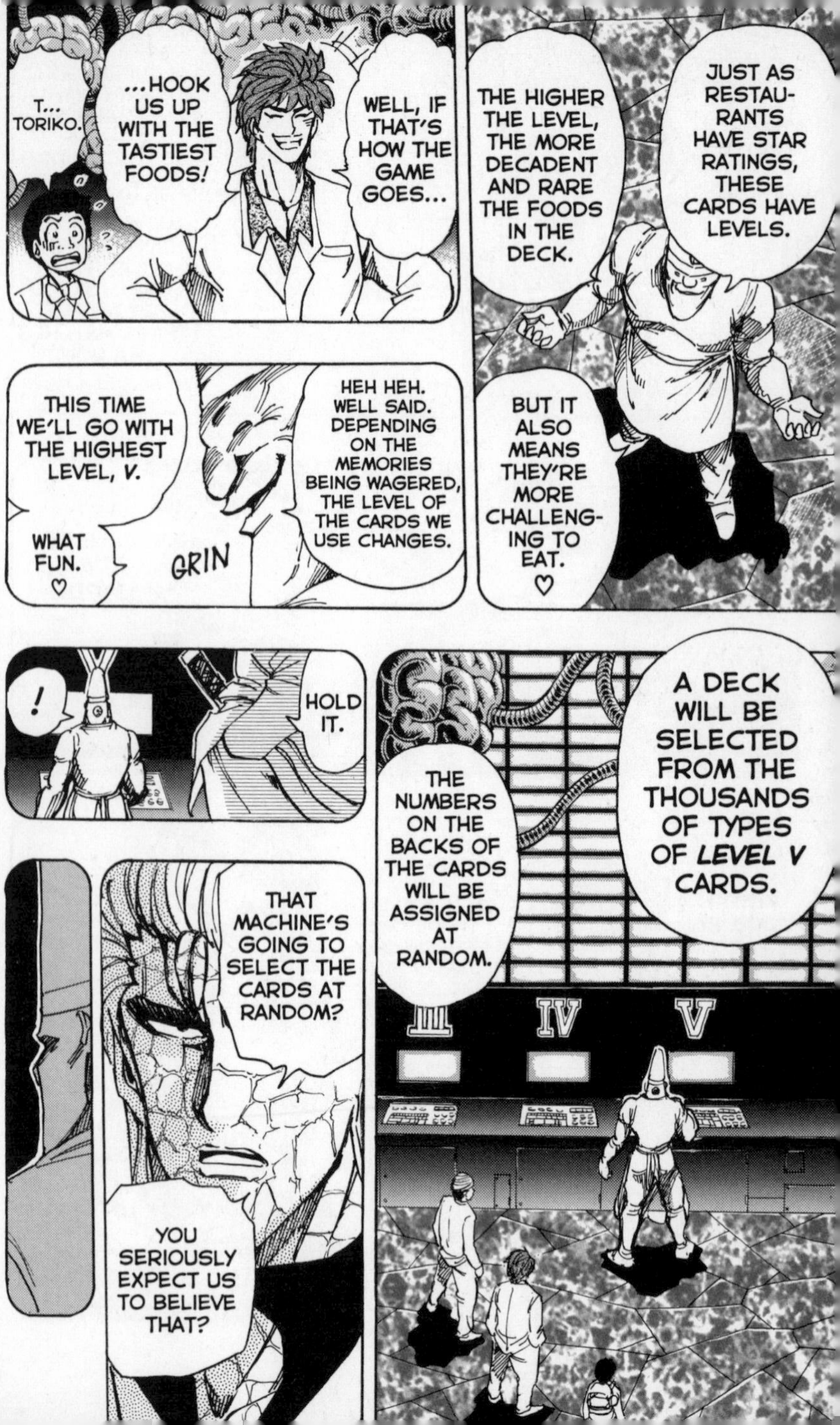
JUST AS RESTAURANTS HAVE STAR RATINGS, THESE CARDS HAVE LEVELS.
THE HIGHER THE LEVEL, THE MORE DECADENT AND RARE THE FOODS IN THE DECK.
BUT IT ALSO MEANS THEY'RE MORE CHALLENGING TO EAT. ♡
WELL, IF THAT'S HOW THE GAME GOES...
...HOOK US UP WITH THE TASTIEST FOODS!
T... TORIKO.
HEH HEH. WELL SAID. DEPENDING ON THE MEMORIES BEING WAGERED, THE LEVEL OF THE CARDS WE USE CHANGES.
GRIN
THIS TIME WE'LL GO WITH THE HIGHEST LEVEL, *V*.
WHAT FUN. ♡
A DECK WILL BE SELECTED FROM THE THOUSANDS OF TYPES OF ***LEVEL V*** CARDS.
THE NUMBERS ON THE BACKS OF THE CARDS WILL BE ASSIGNED AT RANDOM.
III
IV
V
HOLD IT.
!
THAT MACHINE'S GOING TO SELECT THE CARDS AT RANDOM?
YOU SERIOUSLY EXPECT US TO BELIEVE THAT?

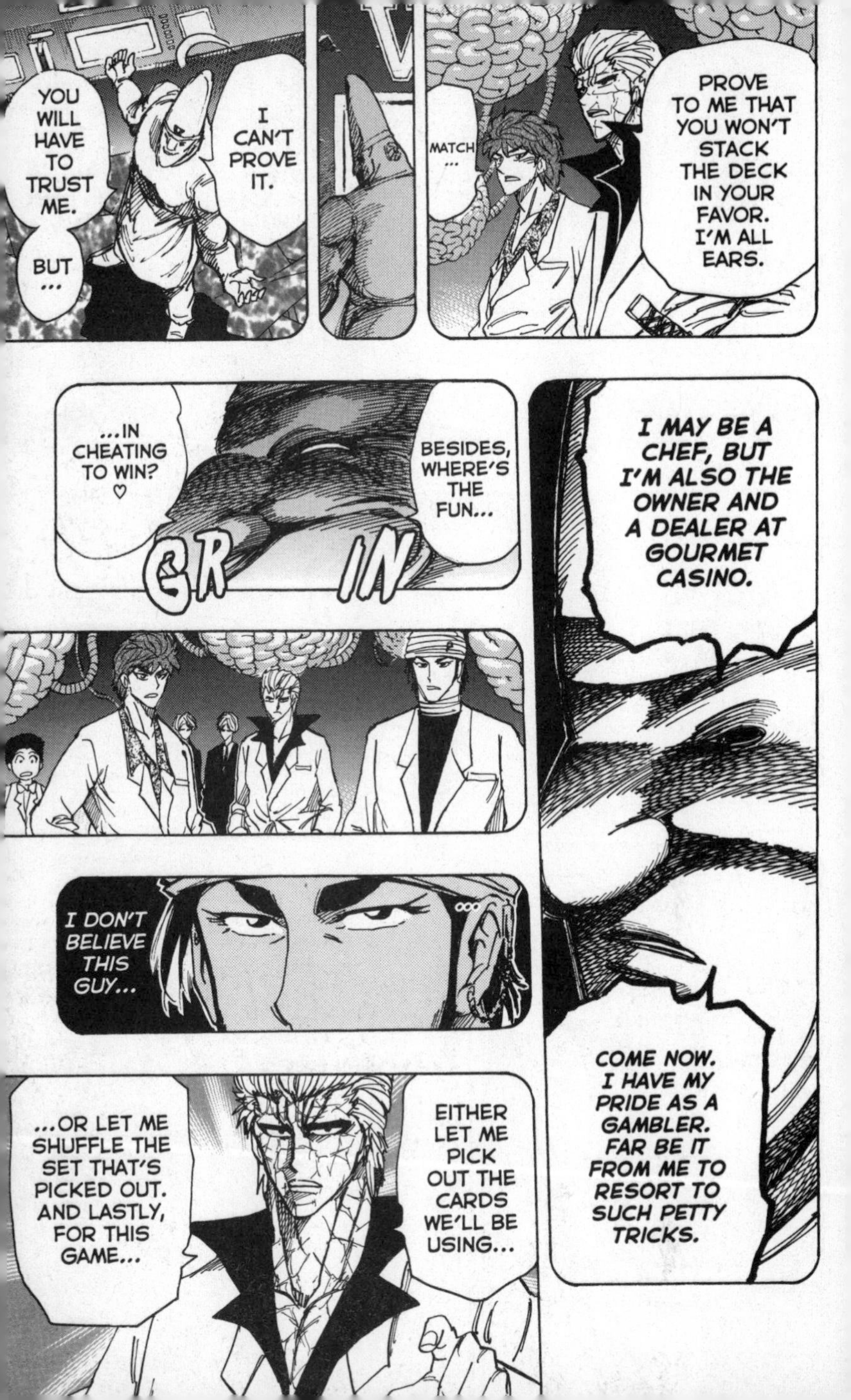
PROVE TO ME THAT YOU WON'T STACK THE DECK IN YOUR FAVOR. I'M ALL EARS.
MATCH...
I CAN'T PROVE IT.
YOU WILL HAVE TO TRUST ME.
BUT...
I MAY BE A CHEF, BUT I'M ALSO THE OWNER AND A DEALER AT GOURMET CASINO.
COME NOW. I HAVE MY PRIDE AS A GAMBLER. FAR BE IT FROM ME TO RESORT TO SUCH PETTY TRICKS.
BESIDES, WHERE'S THE FUN...
...IN CHEATING TO WIN? ♡
GR IN
I DON'T BELIEVE THIS GUY...
EITHER LET ME PICK OUT THE CARDS WE'LL BE USING...
...OR LET ME SHUFFLE THE SET THAT'S PICKED OUT. AND LASTLY, FOR THIS GAME...

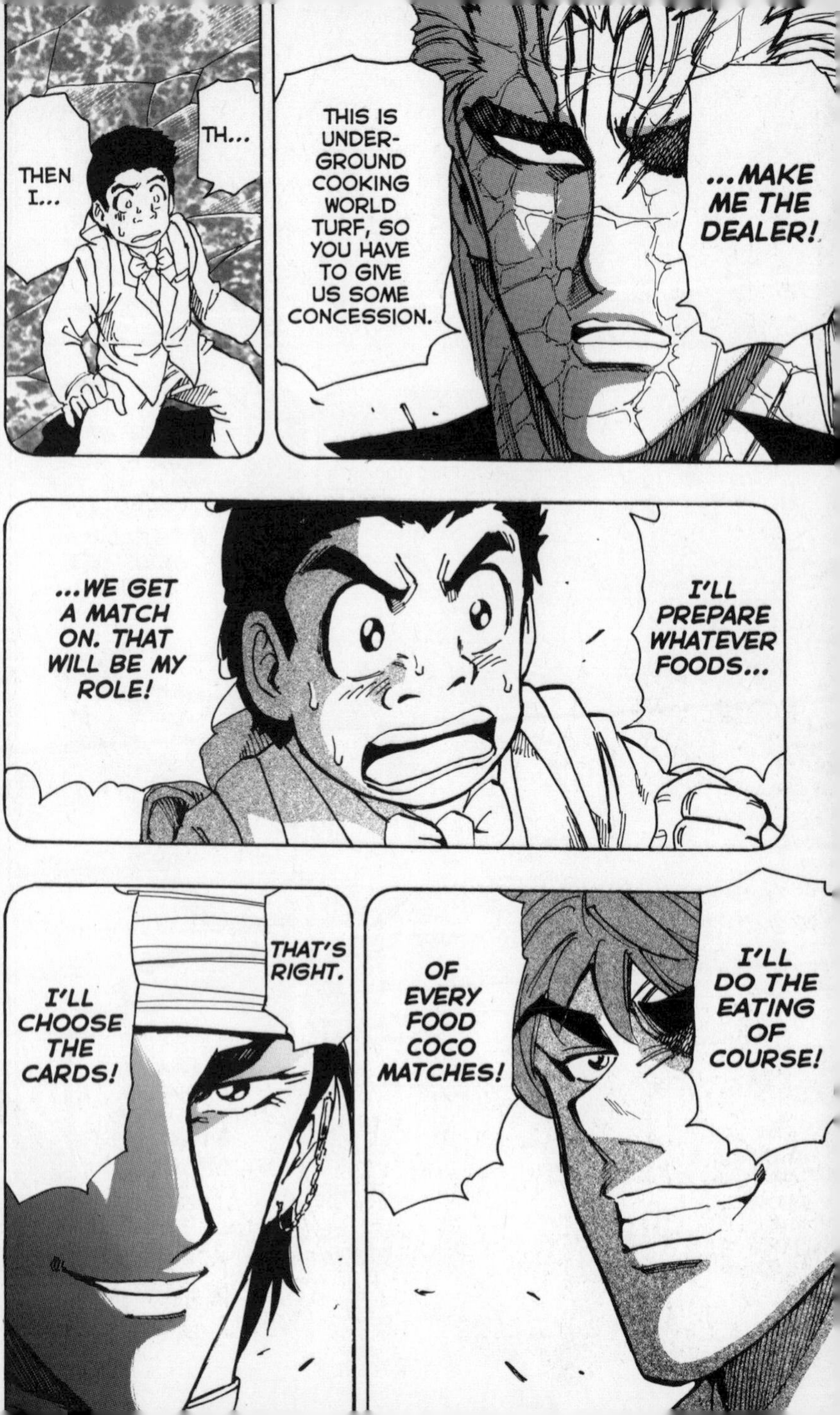
THIS IS UNDER-GROUND COOKING WORLD TURF, SO YOU HAVE TO GIVE US SOME CONCESSION.
...MAKE ME THE DEALER!
TH...
THEN I...
I'LL PREPARE WHATEVER FOODS...
...WE GET A MATCH ON. THAT WILL BE MY ROLE!
I'LL DO THE EATING OF COURSE!
OF EVERY FOOD COCO MATCHES!
THAT'S RIGHT.
I'LL CHOOSE THE CARDS!

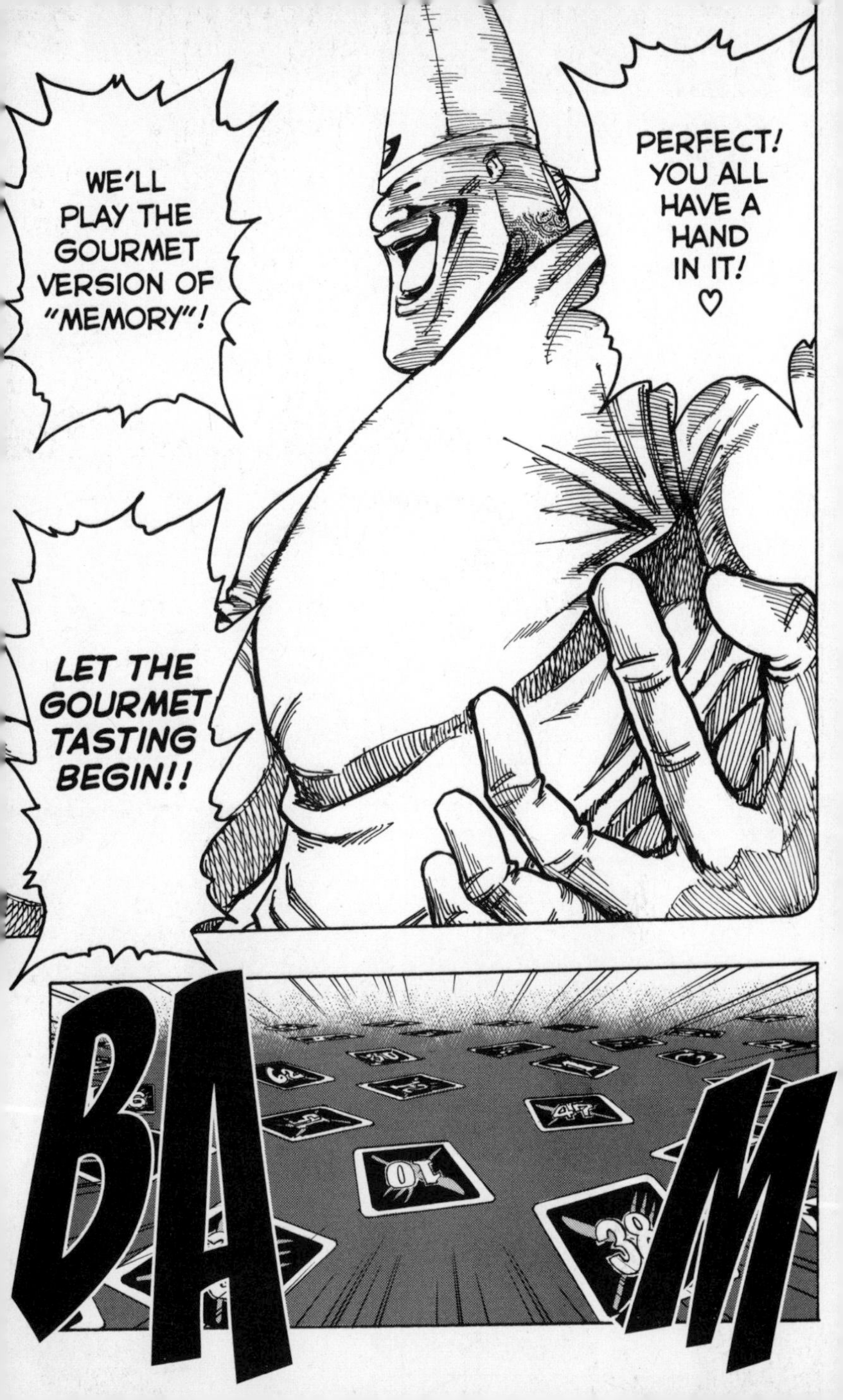
PERFECT! YOU ALL HAVE A HAND IN IT! ♡
WE'LL PLAY THE GOURMET VERSION OF "MEMORY"!
LET THE GOURMET TASTING BEGIN!!
BAM

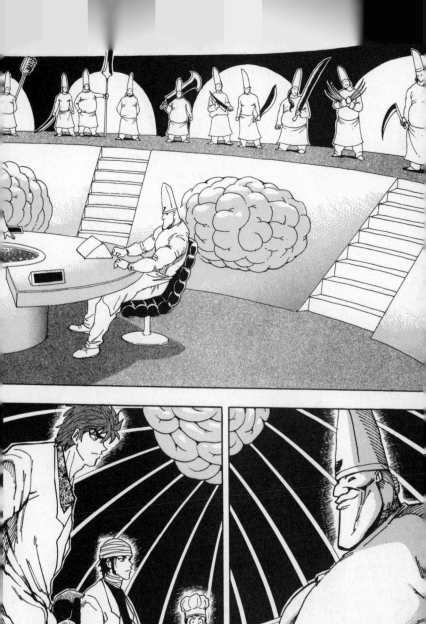

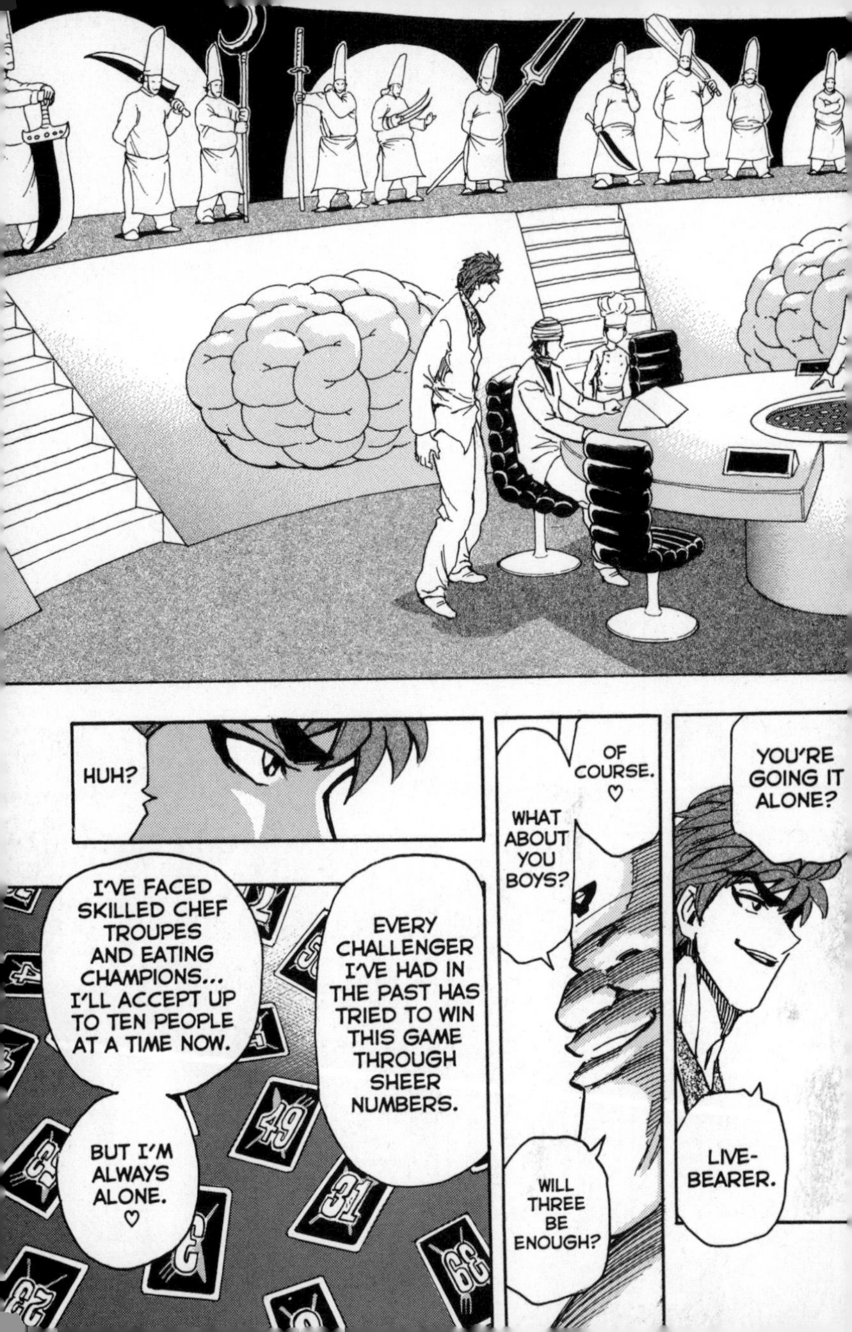
YOU'RE GOING IT ALONE?
LIVE-BEARER.
OF COURSE. ♡
WHAT ABOUT YOU BOYS?
WILL THREE BE ENOUGH?
HUH?
EVERY CHALLENGER I'VE HAD IN THE PAST HAS TRIED TO WIN THIS GAME THROUGH SHEER NUMBERS.
I'VE FACED SKILLED CHEF TROUPES AND EATING CHAMPIONS... I'LL ACCEPT UP TO TEN PEOPLE AT A TIME NOW.
BUT I'M ALWAYS ALONE. ♡

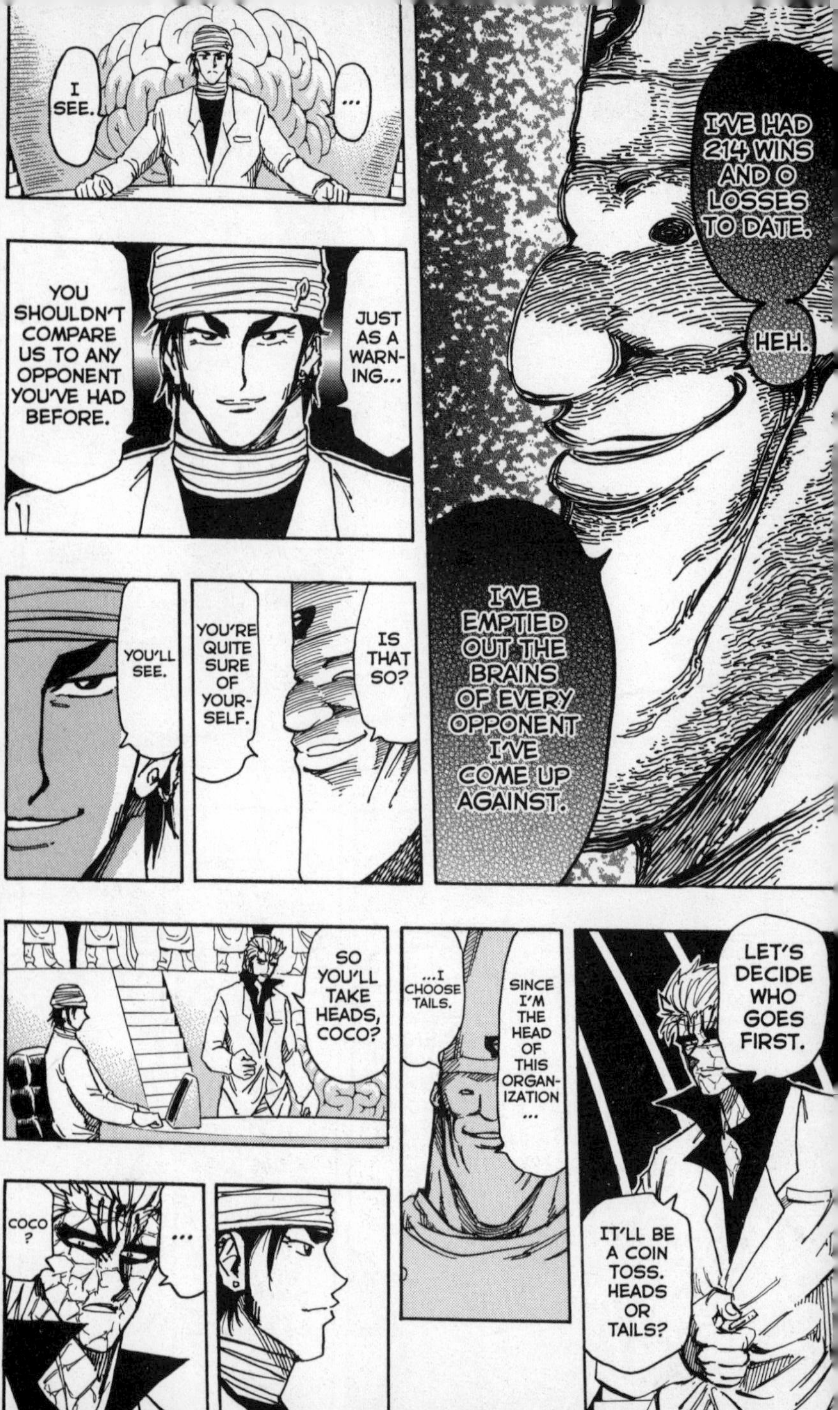
I'VE HAD 214 WINS AND 0 LOSSES TO DATE.
HEH.
I'VE EMPTIED OUT THE BRAINS OF EVERY OPPONENT I'VE COME UP AGAINST.
...
I SEE.
JUST AS A WARNING...
YOU SHOULDN'T COMPARE US TO ANY OPPONENT YOU'VE HAD BEFORE.
IS THAT SO?
YOU'RE QUITE SURE OF YOURSELF.
YOU'LL SEE.
LET'S DECIDE WHO GOES FIRST.
IT'LL BE A COIN TOSS. HEADS OR TAILS?
SINCE I'M THE HEAD OF THIS ORGANIZATION...
...I CHOOSE TAILS.
SO YOU'LL TAKE HEADS, COCO?
...
COCO?

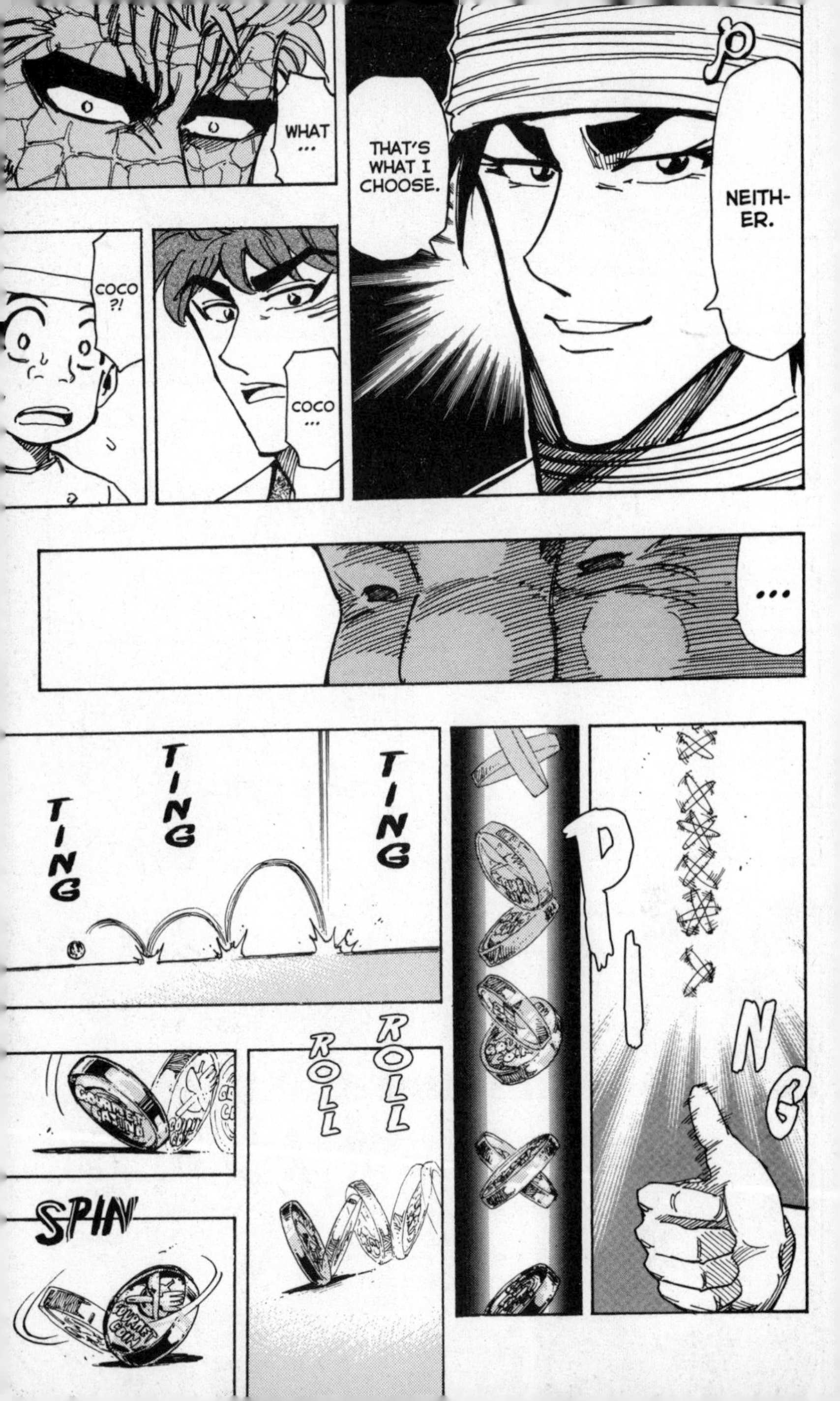
NEITHER.
THAT'S WHAT I CHOOSE.
WHAT...
COCO...
COCO?!
...
PING
TING
TING
TING
ROLL
ROLL
SPIN

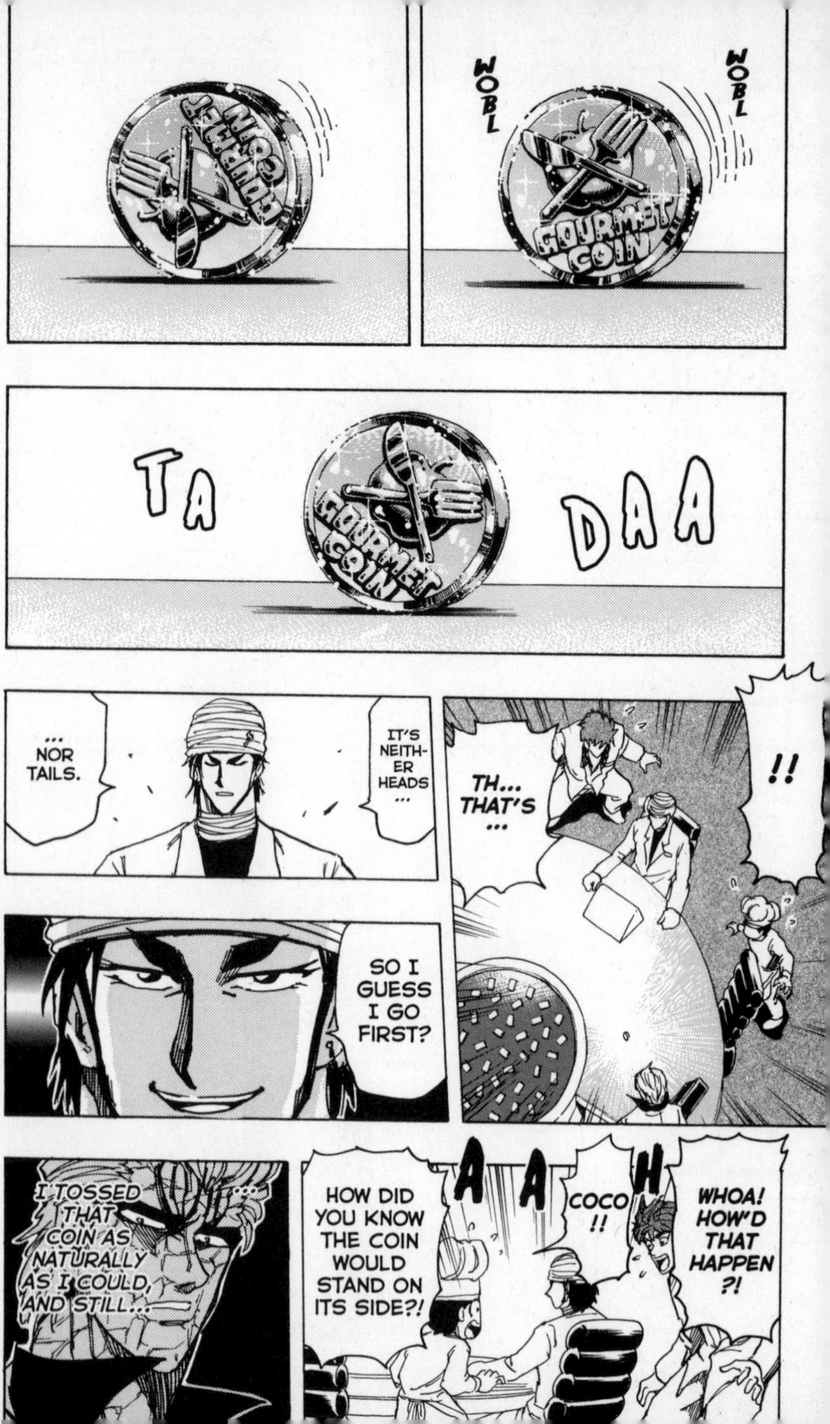
WOBL
WOBL
GOURMET COIN
TA
DAA
GOURMET COIN
!!
TH... THAT'S ...
IT'S NEITH-ER HEADS ...
... NOR TAILS.
SO I GUESS I GO FIRST?
WHOA! HOW'D THAT HAPPEN ?!
AAH
COCO !!
HOW DID YOU KNOW THE COIN WOULD STAND ON ITS SIDE?!
I TOSSED THAT COIN AS NATURALLY AS I COULD, AND STILL...

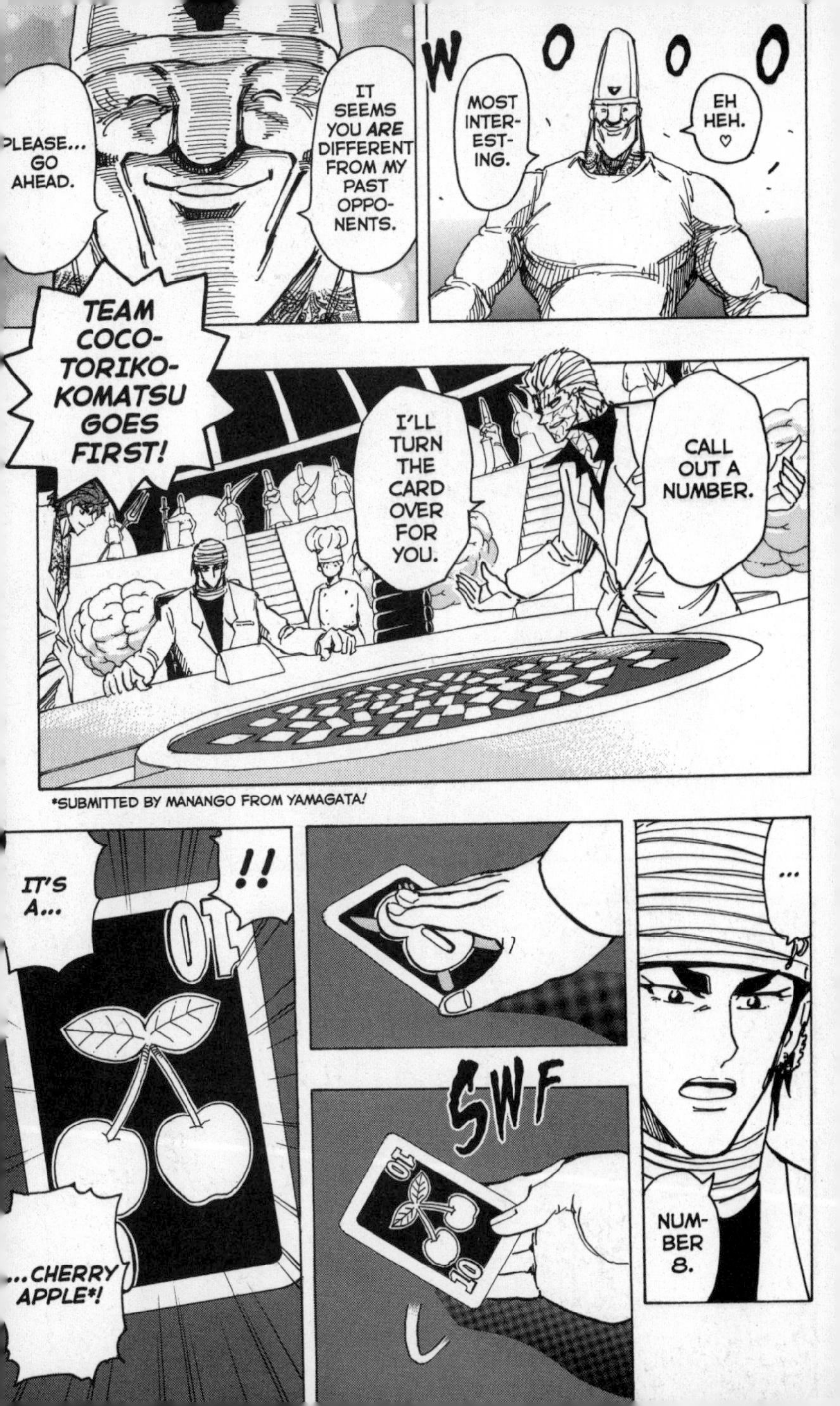
WOOOO
EH HEH. ♡
MOST INTER-EST-ING.
IT SEEMS YOU ARE DIFFERENT FROM MY PAST OPPONENTS.
PLEASE... GO AHEAD.
TEAM COCO-TORIKO-KOMATSU GOES FIRST!
CALL OUT A NUMBER.
I'LL TURN THE CARD OVER FOR YOU.
...
NUMBER 8.
SWF
!!
IT'S A...
...CHERRY APPLE*!

*SUBMITTED BY MANANGO FROM YAMAGATA!

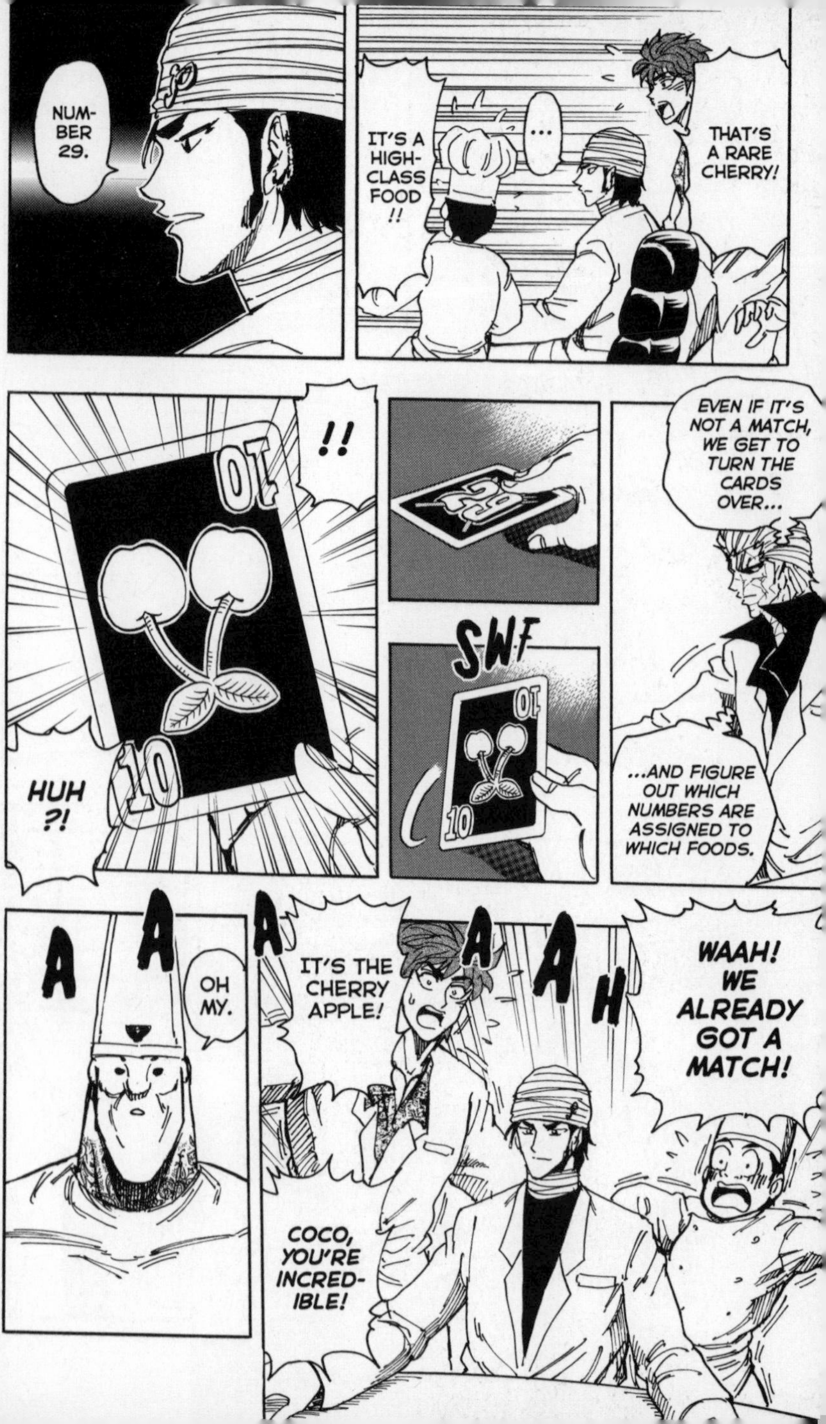
THAT'S A RARE CHERRY!
...
IT'S A HIGH-CLASS FOOD !!
NUMBER 29.
EVEN IF IT'S NOT A MATCH, WE GET TO TURN THE CARDS OVER...
...AND FIGURE OUT WHICH NUMBERS ARE ASSIGNED TO WHICH FOODS.
SWF
10
!!
10
HUH ?!
WAAH! WE ALREADY GOT A MATCH!
AAAAAH
IT'S THE CHERRY APPLE!
COCO, YOU'RE INCREDIBLE!
OH MY.

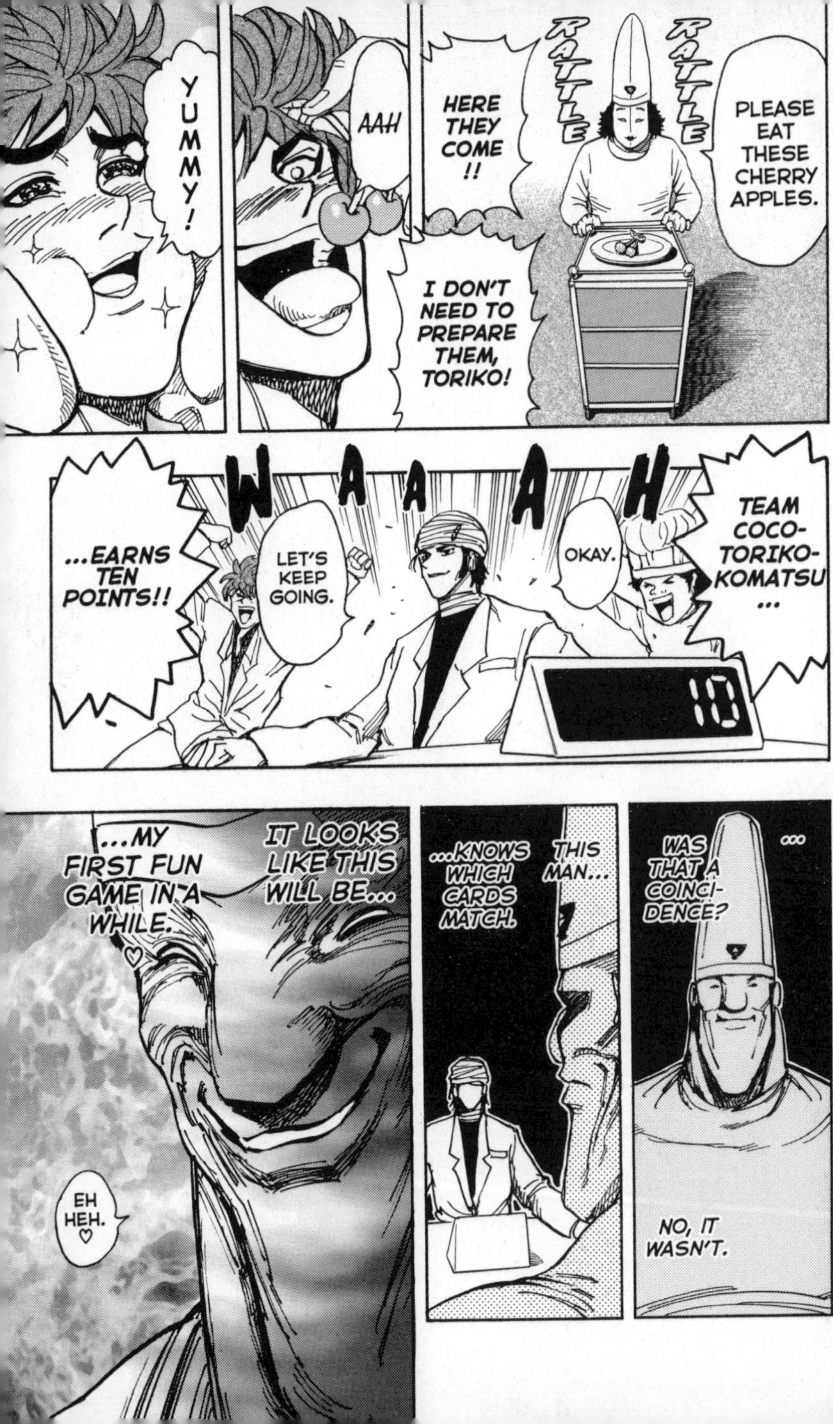
RATTLE RATTLE
PLEASE EAT THESE CHERRY APPLES.
HERE THEY COME!!
I DON'T NEED TO PREPARE THEM, TORIKO!
AAH
YUMMY!
TEAM COCO-TORIKO-KOMATSU...
WAAAAH
OKAY.
LET'S KEEP GOING.
...EARNS TEN POINTS!!
10
...
WAS THAT A COINCIDENCE?
NO, IT WASN'T.
THIS MAN...
...KNOWS WHICH CARDS MATCH.
IT LOOKS LIKE THIS WILL BE...
...MY FIRST FUN GAME IN A WHILE. ♡
EH HEH. ♡

TORIKO

GOURMET CHECKLIST
Vol. 195

JOWLCARGOT
(MOLLUSK)

CAPTURE LEVEL: 38
HABITAT: GOURMET PYRAMID
LENGTH: 6 METERS
HEIGHT: 5 METERS
WEIGHT: 3.5 TONS
PRICE: 100 G / 30,000 YEN

JOWLCARGOT
(MOLLUSK)
CAPTURE LEVEL 38

SCALE

A MONSTROUS MOLLUSK THAT FORMS A SYMBIOTIC RELATIONSHIP WITH A CREATURE IT LIVES OFF OF. ITS SHELL BOASTS A POWERFUL JAW. PREDATORS APPROACH WITH HOPES OF SNACKING ON ITS SOFT SNAIL PARTS, BUT WILL BE ATTACKED BY THE BULLET-FAST JAWS. THEY'RE EXPANDABLE AND POISONOUS TOO. ITS MEAT IS A WELL-KNOWN DELICACY TOUTED OVER ALL OTHER ESCARGOT.

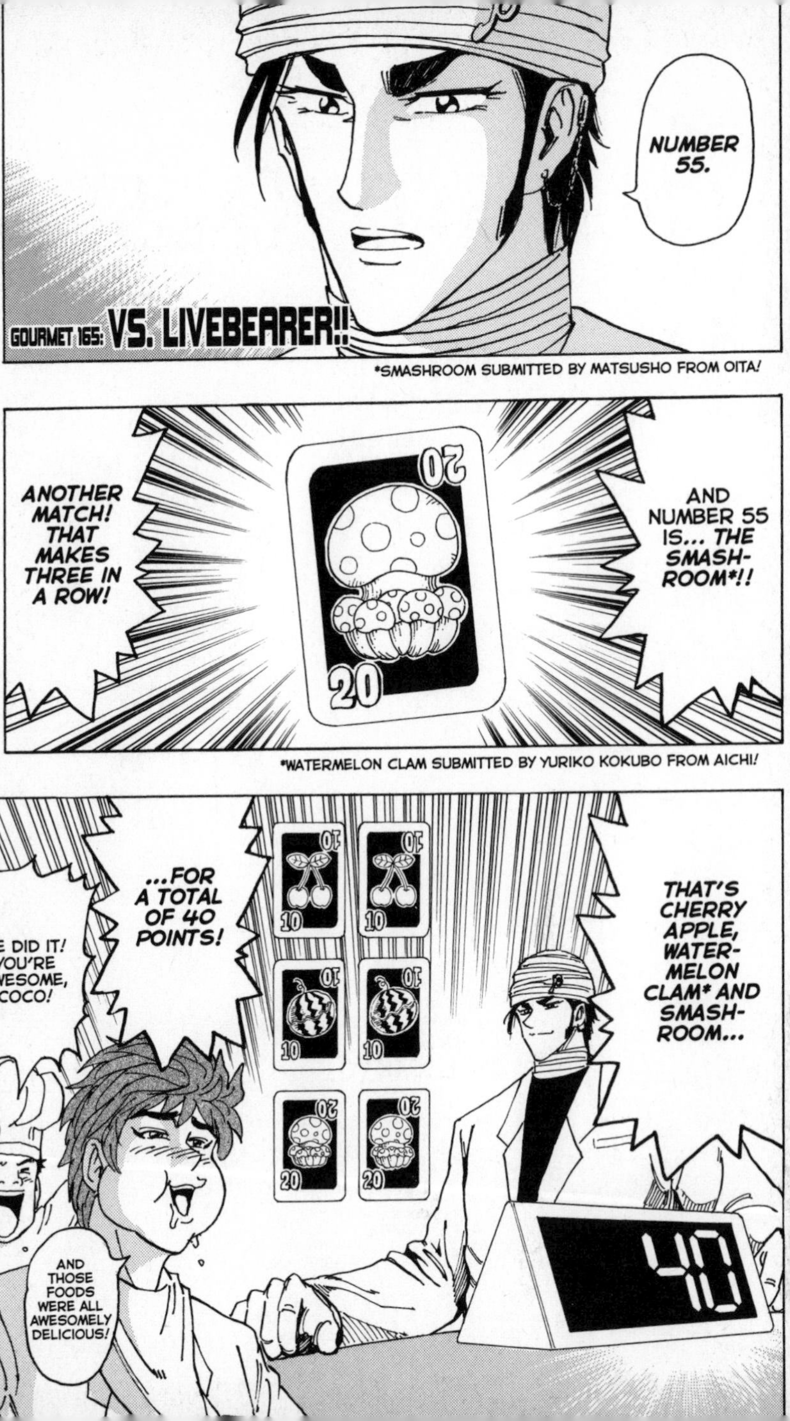
GOURMET 165: VS. LIVEBEARER!!
NUMBER 55.
*SMASHROOM SUBMITTED BY MATSUSHO FROM OITA!
AND NUMBER 55 IS... THE SMASH-ROOM*!!
ANOTHER MATCH! THAT MAKES THREE IN A ROW!
*WATERMELON CLAM SUBMITTED BY YURIKO KOKUBO FROM AICHI!
THAT'S CHERRY APPLE, WATER-MELON CLAM* AND SMASH-ROOM...
...FOR A TOTAL OF 40 POINTS!
WE DID IT! YOU'RE AWESOME, COCO!
AND THOSE FOODS WERE ALL AWESOMELY DELICIOUS!

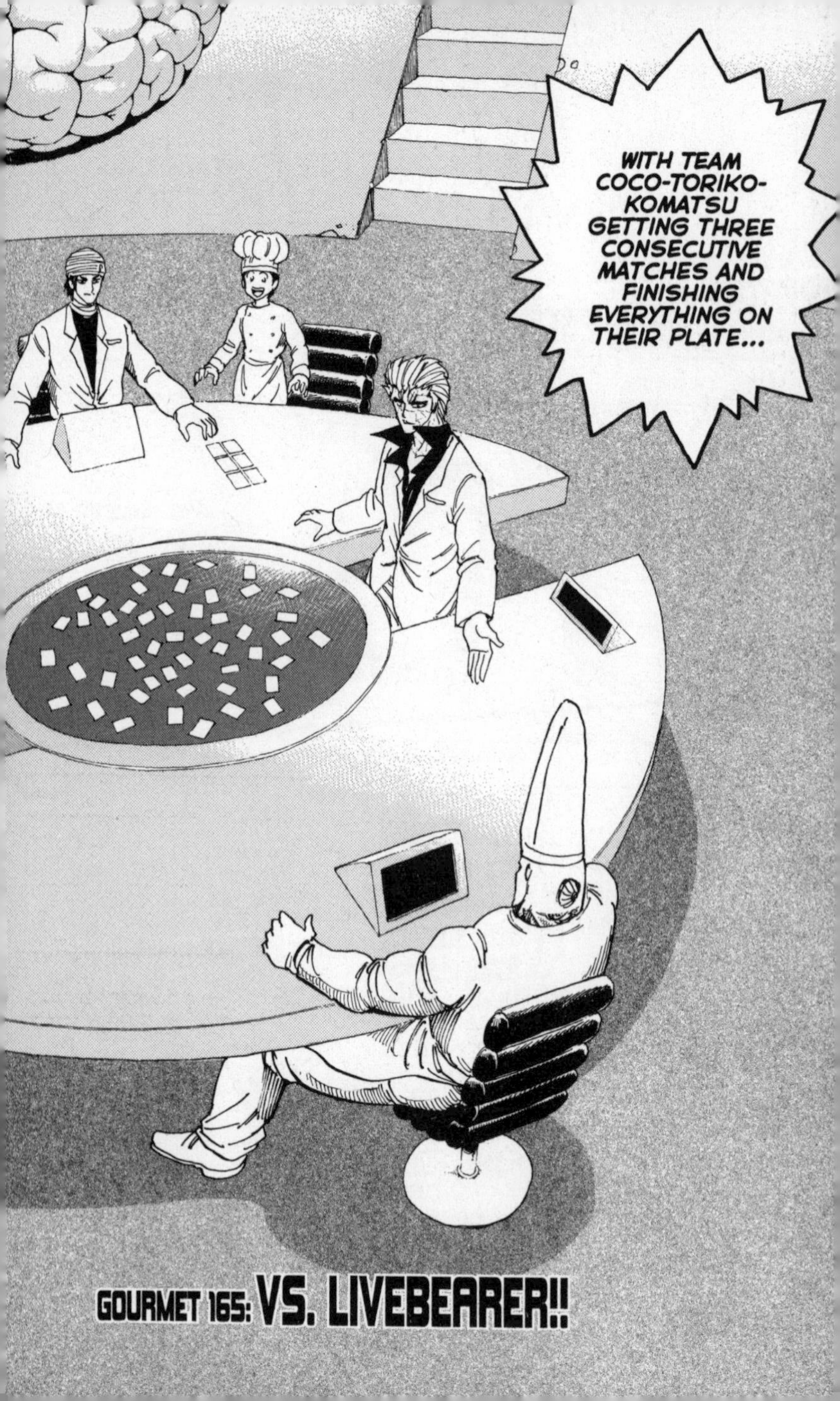
WITH TEAM COCO-TORIKO-KOMATSU GETTING THREE CONSECUTIVE MATCHES AND FINISHING EVERYTHING ON THEIR PLATE...
GOURMET 165: VS. LIVEBEARER!!

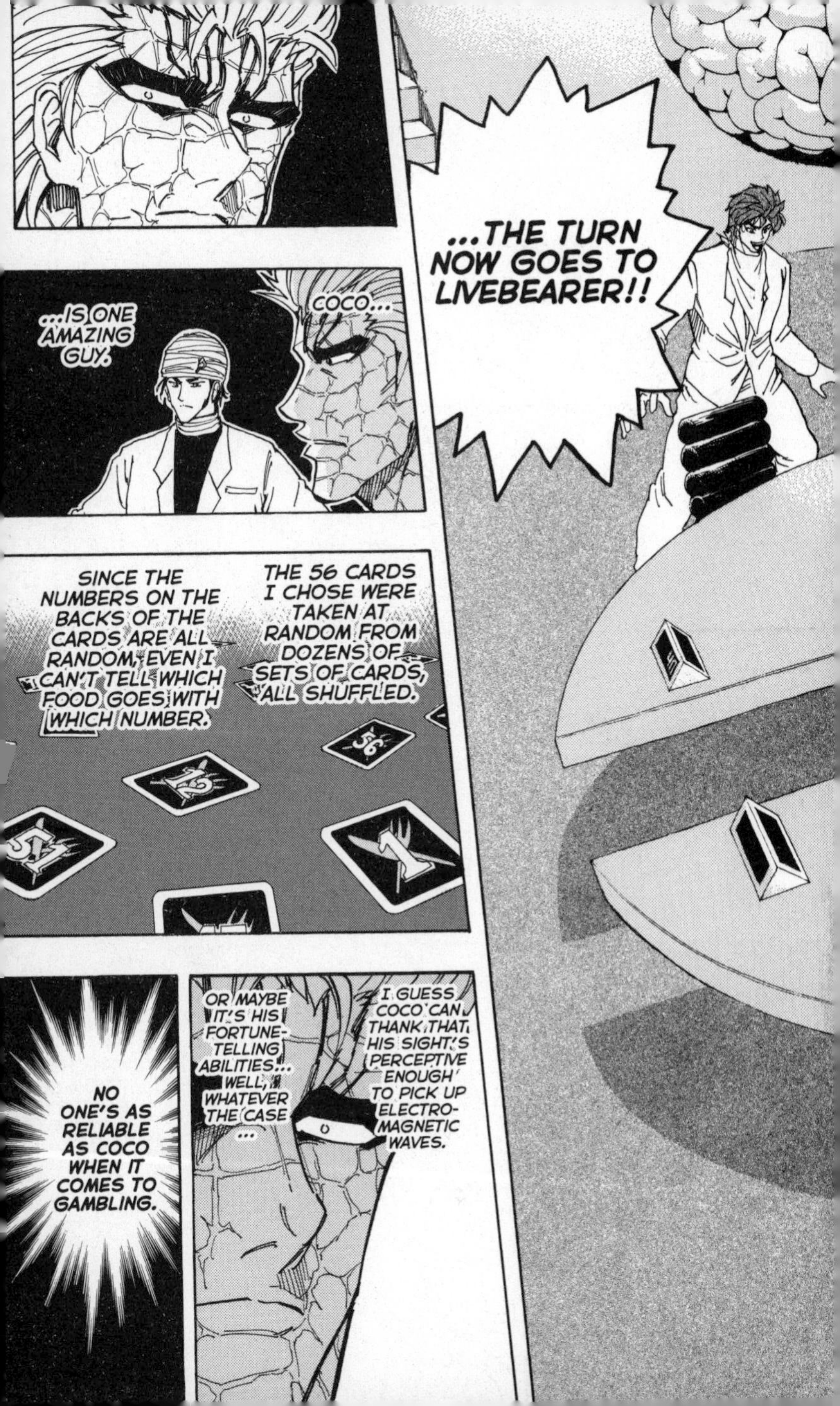
...THE TURN NOW GOES TO LIVEBEARER!!
COCO...
...IS ONE AMAZING GUY.
THE 56 CARDS I CHOSE WERE TAKEN AT RANDOM FROM DOZENS OF SETS OF CARDS, ALL SHUFFLED.
SINCE THE NUMBERS ON THE BACKS OF THE CARDS ARE ALL RANDOM, EVEN I CAN'T TELL WHICH FOOD GOES WITH WHICH NUMBER.
56
12
1
I GUESS COCO CAN THANK THAT HIS SIGHT'S PERCEPTIVE ENOUGH TO PICK UP ELECTRO-MAGNETIC WAVES.
OR MAYBE IT'S HIS FORTUNE-TELLING ABILITIES... WELL, WHATEVER THE CASE ...
NO ONE'S AS RELIABLE AS COCO WHEN IT COMES TO GAMBLING.

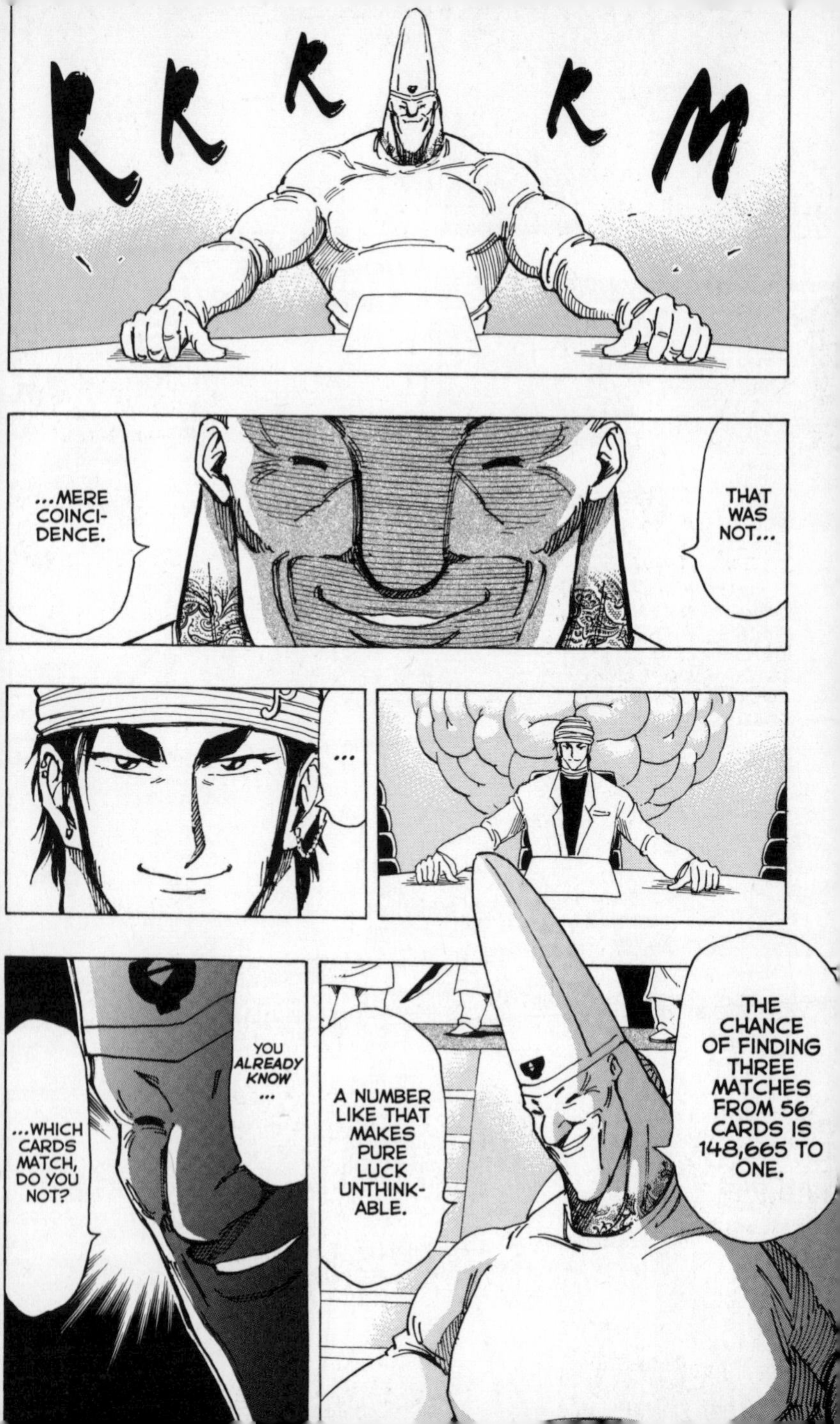
RRRRM
THAT WAS NOT...
...MERE COINCIDENCE.
...
THE CHANCE OF FINDING THREE MATCHES FROM 56 CARDS IS 148,665 TO ONE.
A NUMBER LIKE THAT MAKES PURE LUCK UNTHINKABLE.
YOU ALREADY KNOW ...
...WHICH CARDS MATCH, DO YOU NOT?

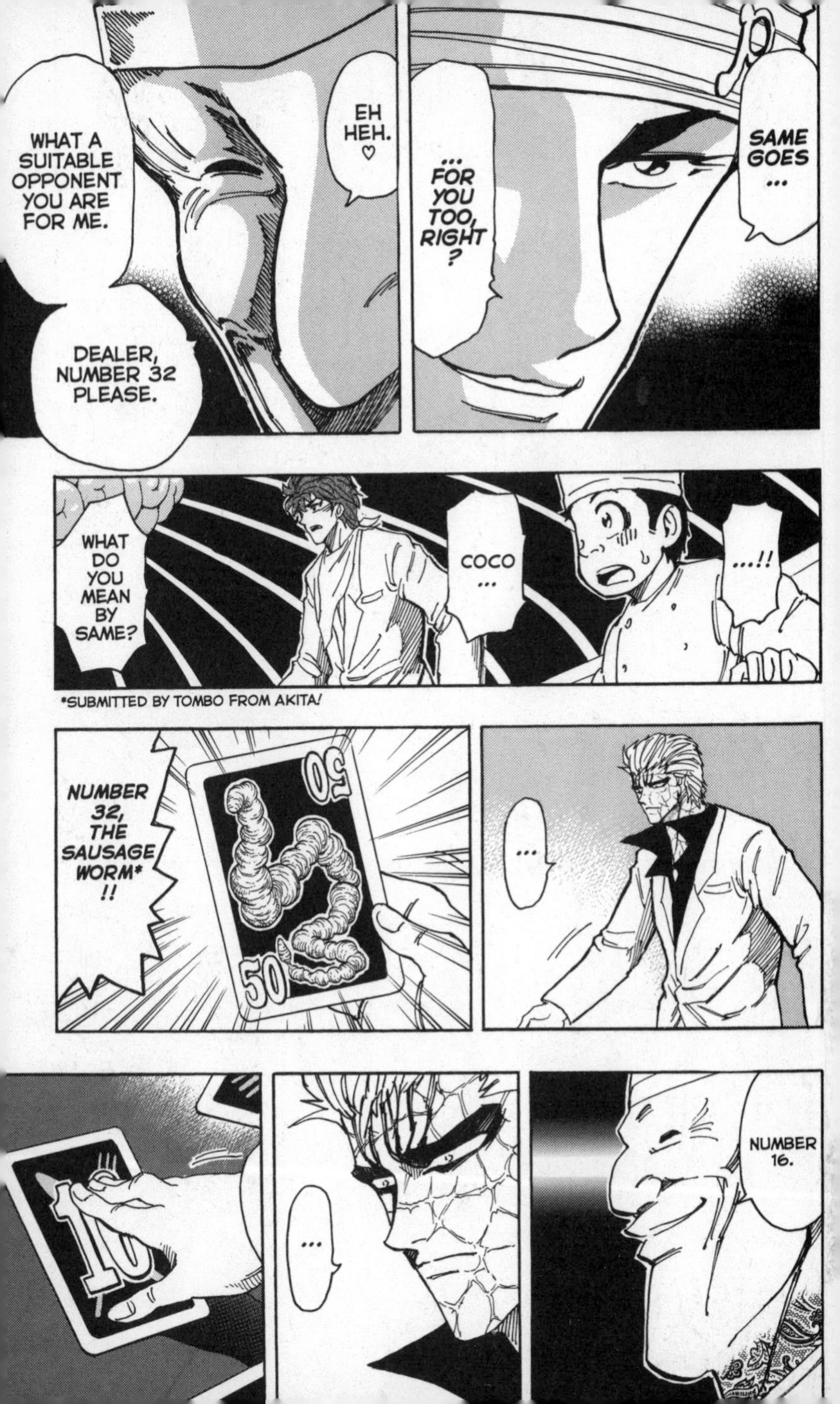
SAME GOES ...
... FOR YOU TOO, RIGHT?
EH HEH. ♡
WHAT A SUITABLE OPPONENT YOU ARE FOR ME.
DEALER, NUMBER 32 PLEASE.
...!!
COCO ...
WHAT DO YOU MEAN BY SAME?
*SUBMITTED BY TOMBO FROM AKITA!
...
NUMBER 32, THE SAUSAGE WORM* !!
50
NUMBER 16.
...

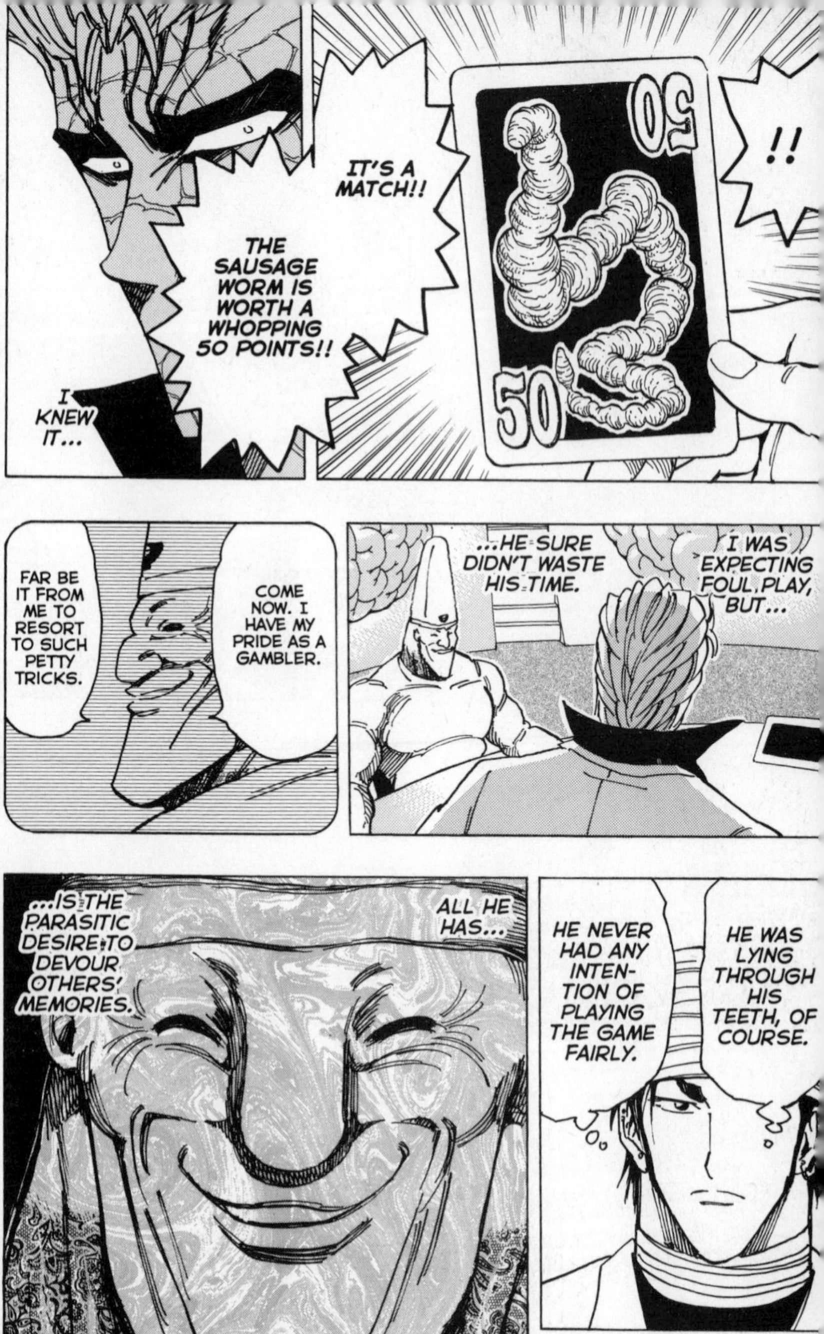

!!
50
50
IT'S A MATCH!!
THE SAUSAGE WORM IS WORTH A WHOPPING 50 POINTS!!
I KNEW IT...
I WAS EXPECTING FOUL PLAY, BUT...
...HE SURE DIDN'T WASTE HIS TIME.
COME NOW. I HAVE MY PRIDE AS A GAMBLER.
FAR BE IT FROM ME TO RESORT TO SUCH PETTY TRICKS.
HE WAS LYING THROUGH HIS TEETH, OF COURSE.
HE NEVER HAD ANY INTEN-TION OF PLAYING THE GAME FAIRLY.
ALL HE HAS...
...IS THE PARASITIC DESIRE TO DEVOUR OTHERS' MEMORIES.

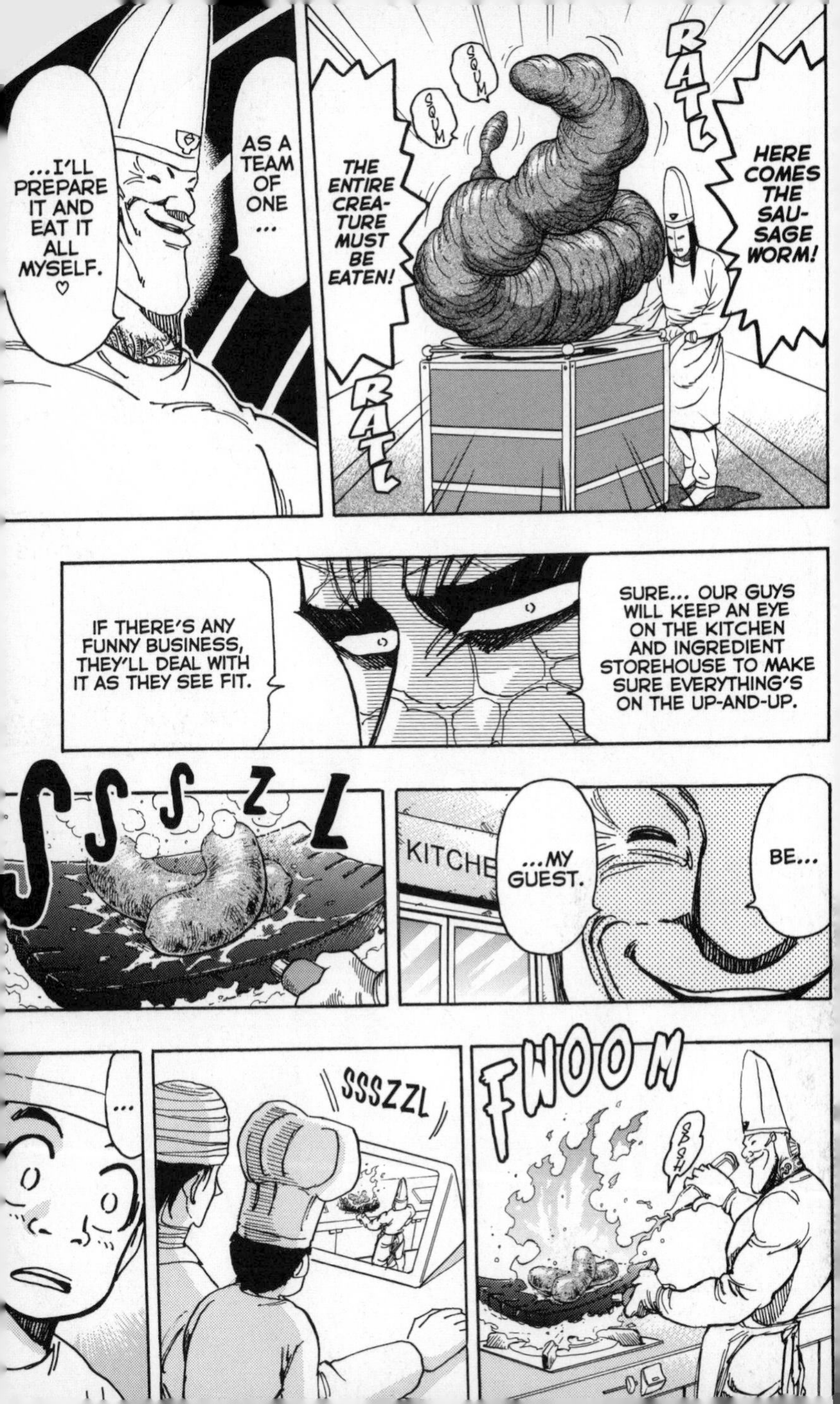

HERE COMES THE SAUSAGE WORM!
RATTL
THE ENTIRE CREATURE MUST BE EATEN!
SQUM
SQUM
RATTL
AS A TEAM OF ONE...
...I'LL PREPARE IT AND EAT IT ALL MYSELF. ♡
SURE... OUR GUYS WILL KEEP AN EYE ON THE KITCHEN AND INGREDIENT STOREHOUSE TO MAKE SURE EVERYTHING'S ON THE UP-AND-UP.
IF THERE'S ANY FUNNY BUSINESS, THEY'LL DEAL WITH IT AS THEY SEE FIT.
BE...
...MY GUEST.
KITCHE
SSSZZL
FWOOM
SPSH
SSSZZL
...

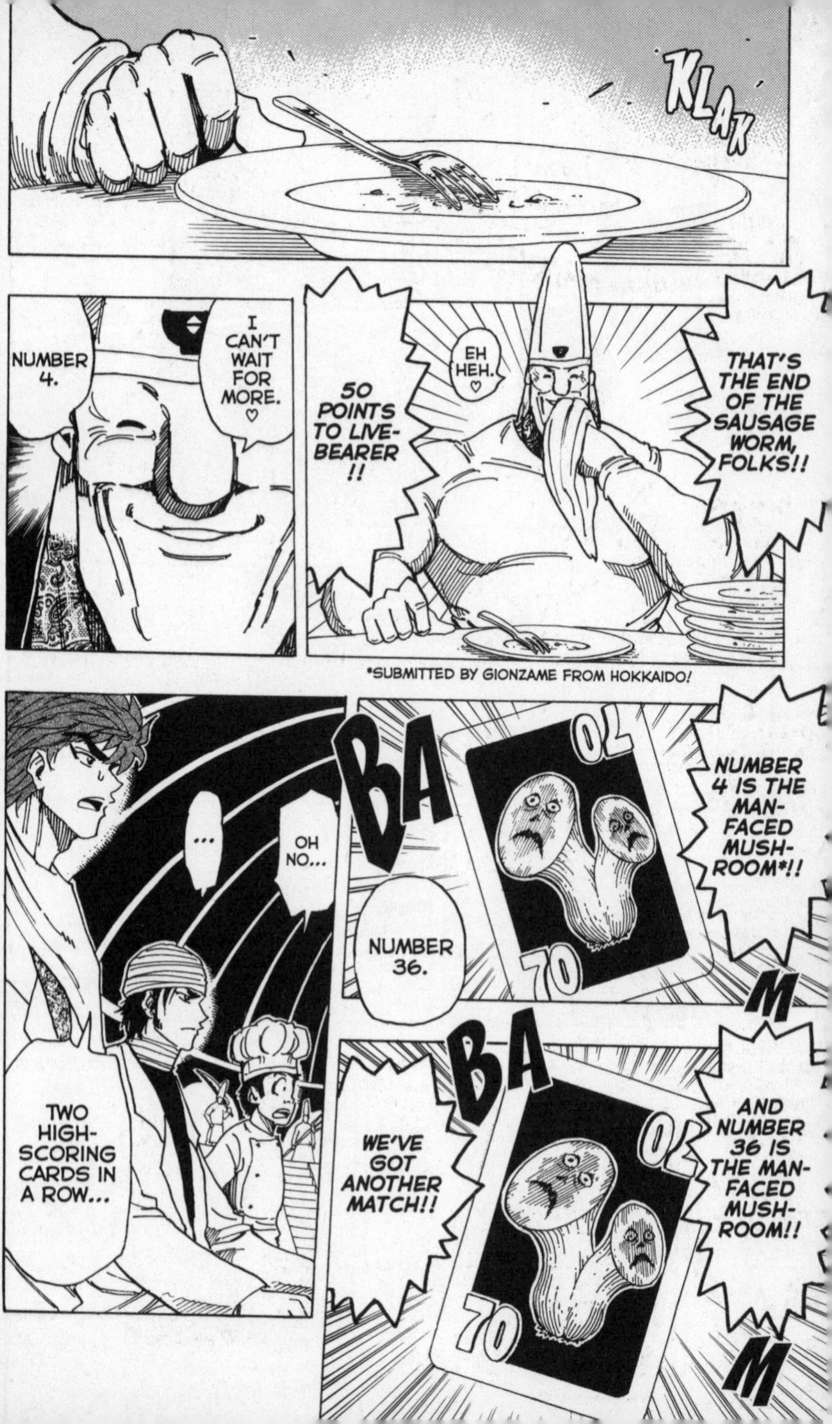
KLAK
THAT'S THE END OF THE SAUSAGE WORM, FOLKS!!
EH HEH. ♡
50 POINTS TO LIVE-BEARER !!
I CAN'T WAIT FOR MORE. ♡
NUMBER 4.
NUMBER 4 IS THE MAN-FACED MUSH-ROOM*!!
BA
M
70
NUMBER 36.
OH NO...
...
AND NUMBER 36 IS THE MAN-FACED MUSH-ROOM!!
BA
M
70
WE'VE GOT ANOTHER MATCH!!
TWO HIGH-SCORING CARDS IN A ROW...

*SUBMITTED BY GIONZAME FROM HOKKAIDO!

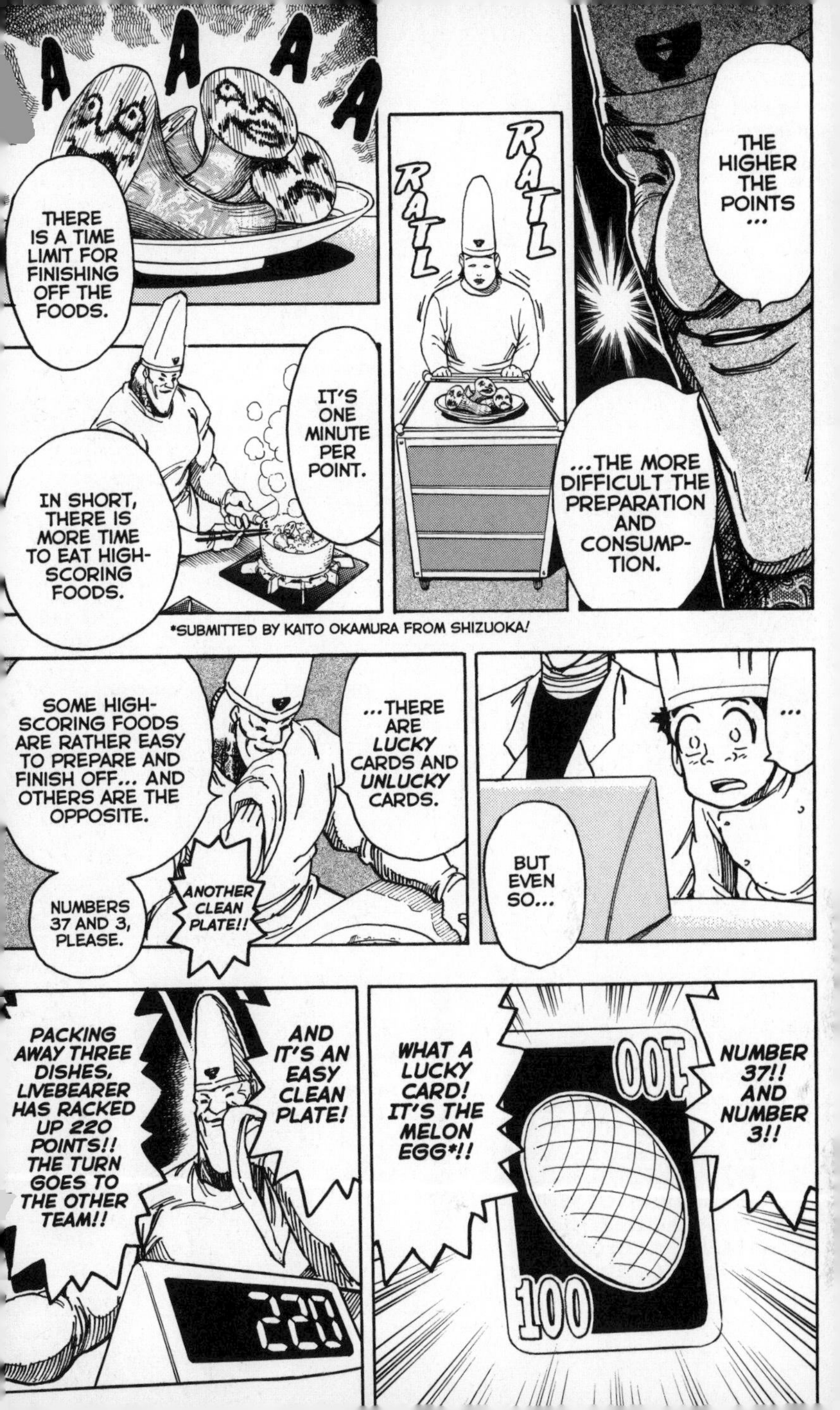
THE HIGHER THE POINTS ...
...THE MORE DIFFICULT THE PREPARATION AND CONSUMPTION.
RATTL
RATTL
A
A
A
A
THERE IS A TIME LIMIT FOR FINISHING OFF THE FOODS.
IT'S ONE MINUTE PER POINT.
IN SHORT, THERE IS MORE TIME TO EAT HIGH-SCORING FOODS.
...
BUT EVEN SO...
...THERE ARE LUCKY CARDS AND UNLUCKY CARDS.
SOME HIGH-SCORING FOODS ARE RATHER EASY TO PREPARE AND FINISH OFF... AND OTHERS ARE THE OPPOSITE.
ANOTHER CLEAN PLATE!!
NUMBERS 37 AND 3, PLEASE.
NUMBER 37!! AND NUMBER 3!!
100
WHAT A LUCKY CARD! IT'S THE MELON EGG*!!
100
AND IT'S AN EASY CLEAN PLATE!
PACKING AWAY THREE DISHES, LIVEBEARER HAS RACKED UP 220 POINTS!! THE TURN GOES TO THE OTHER TEAM!!
220

*SUBMITTED BY KAITO OKAMURA FROM SHIZUOKA!

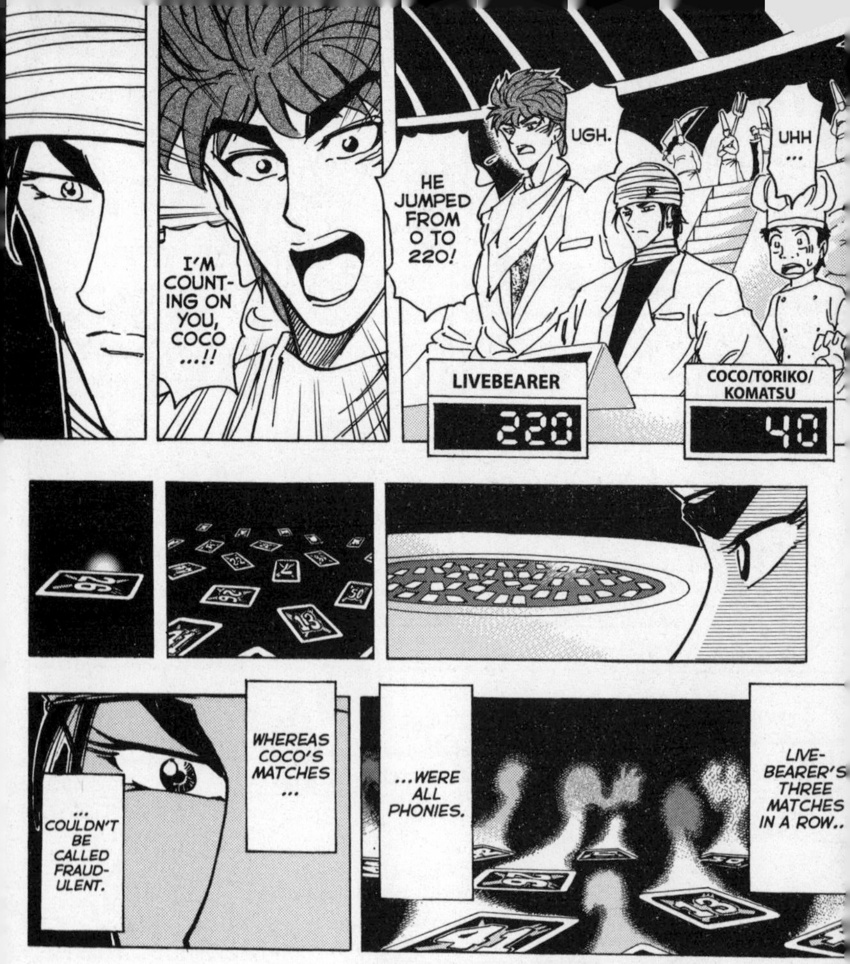
UHH ...
UGH.
HE JUMPED FROM 0 TO 220!
LIVEBEARER
220
COCO/TORIKO/KOMATSU
40
I'M COUNTING ON YOU, COCO ...!!
LIVE-BEARER'S THREE MATCHES IN A ROW..
...WERE ALL PHONIES.
WHEREAS COCO'S MATCHES ...
... COULDN'T BE CALLED FRAUD-ULENT.

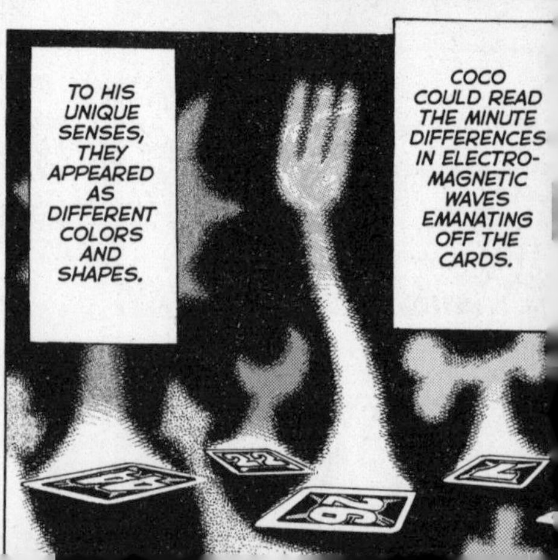
COCO COULD READ THE MINUTE DIFFERENCES IN ELECTRO-MAGNETIC WAVES EMANATING OFF THE CARDS.
TO HIS UNIQUE SENSES, THEY APPEARED AS DIFFERENT COLORS AND SHAPES.

■ SYNESTHESIA

A SENSORY PHENOMENON IN WHICH A STIMULUS IS INTERPRETED NOT ONLY BY THE APPROPRIATE SENSORY PATHWAY FOR IT, BUT BY ANOTHER KIND OF SENSORY PATHWAY ALTOGETHER, SUCH AS SEEING A COLOR WHEN A CERTAIN SOUND IS HEARD.

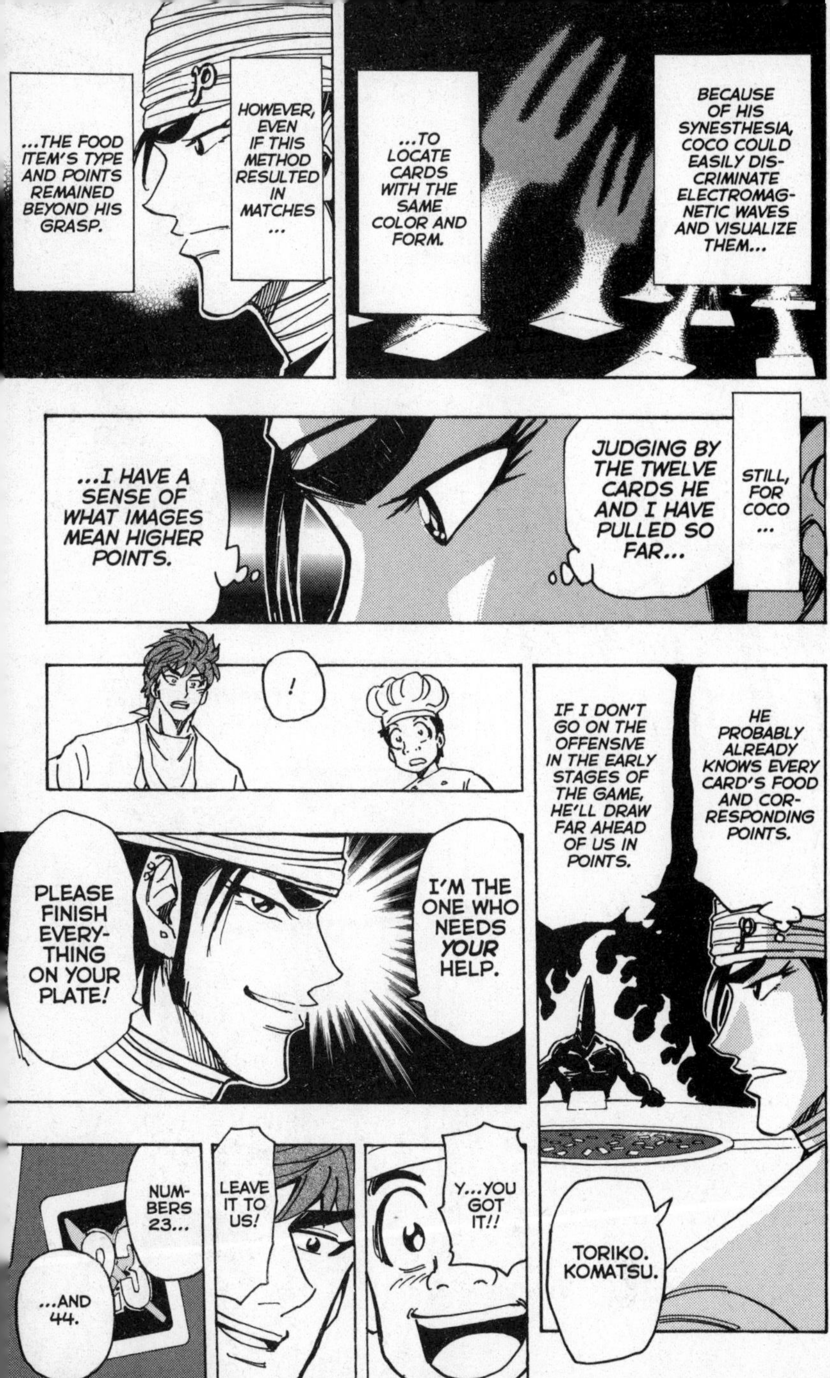
BECAUSE OF HIS SYNESTHESIA, COCO COULD EASILY DISCRIMINATE ELECTROMAGNETIC WAVES AND VISUALIZE THEM...
...TO LOCATE CARDS WITH THE SAME COLOR AND FORM.
HOWEVER, EVEN IF THIS METHOD RESULTED IN MATCHES...
...THE FOOD ITEM'S TYPE AND POINTS REMAINED BEYOND HIS GRASP.
STILL, FOR COCO...
JUDGING BY THE TWELVE CARDS HE AND I HAVE PULLED SO FAR...
...I HAVE A SENSE OF WHAT IMAGES MEAN HIGHER POINTS.
HE PROBABLY ALREADY KNOWS EVERY CARD'S FOOD AND CORRESPONDING POINTS.
IF I DON'T GO ON THE OFFENSIVE IN THE EARLY STAGES OF THE GAME, HE'LL DRAW FAR AHEAD OF US IN POINTS.
TORIKO. KOMATSU.
!
I'M THE ONE WHO NEEDS *YOUR* HELP.
PLEASE FINISH EVERYTHING ON YOUR PLATE!
Y...YOU GOT IT!!
LEAVE IT TO US!
NUMBERS 23...
...AND 44.

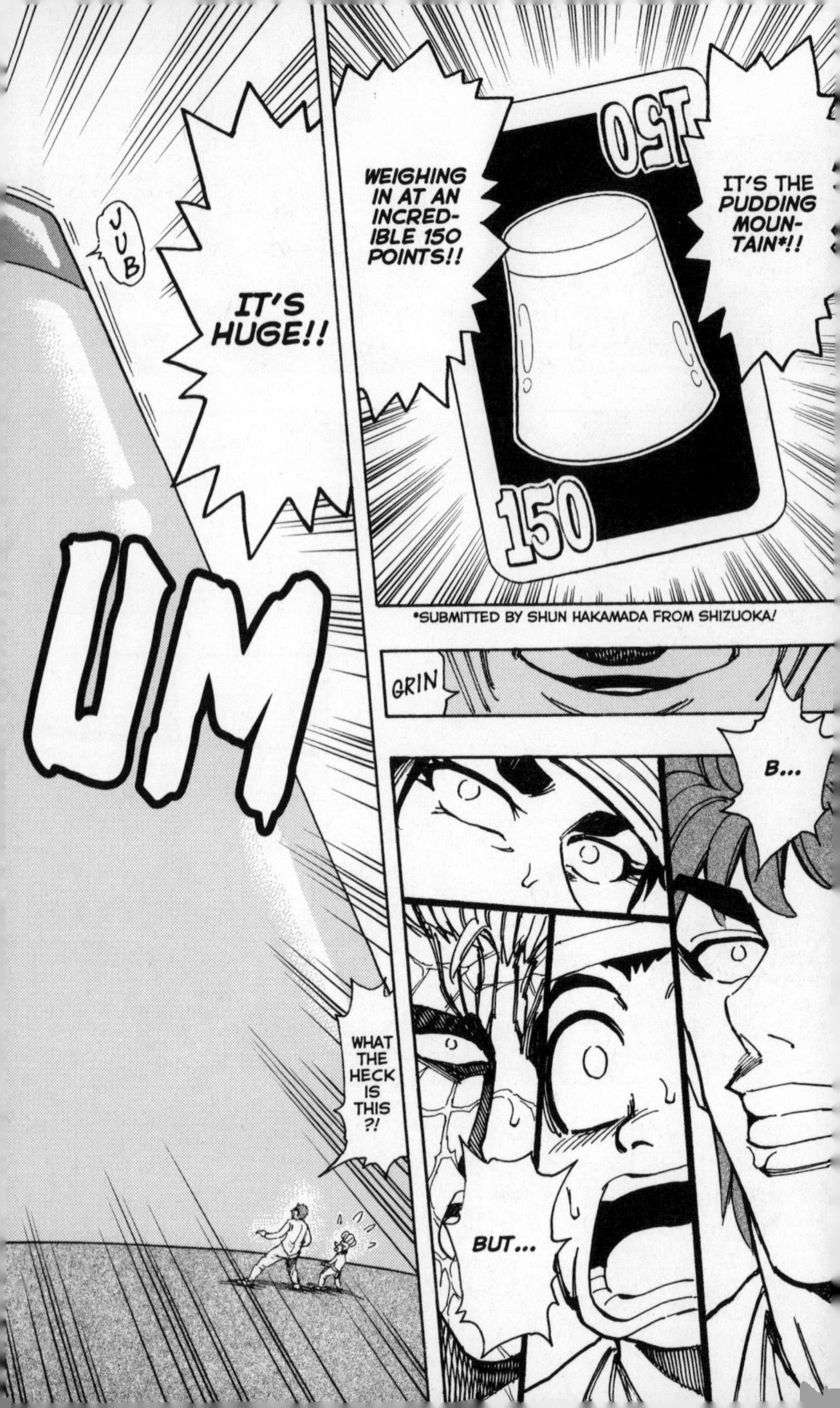
IT'S THE PUDDING MOUNTAIN*!!
WEIGHING IN AT AN INCREDIBLE 150 POINTS!!
150
*SUBMITTED BY SHUN HAKAMADA FROM SHIZUOKA!
GRIN
B...
BUT...
WHAT THE HECK IS THIS?!
JUB
IT'S HUGE!!
UM

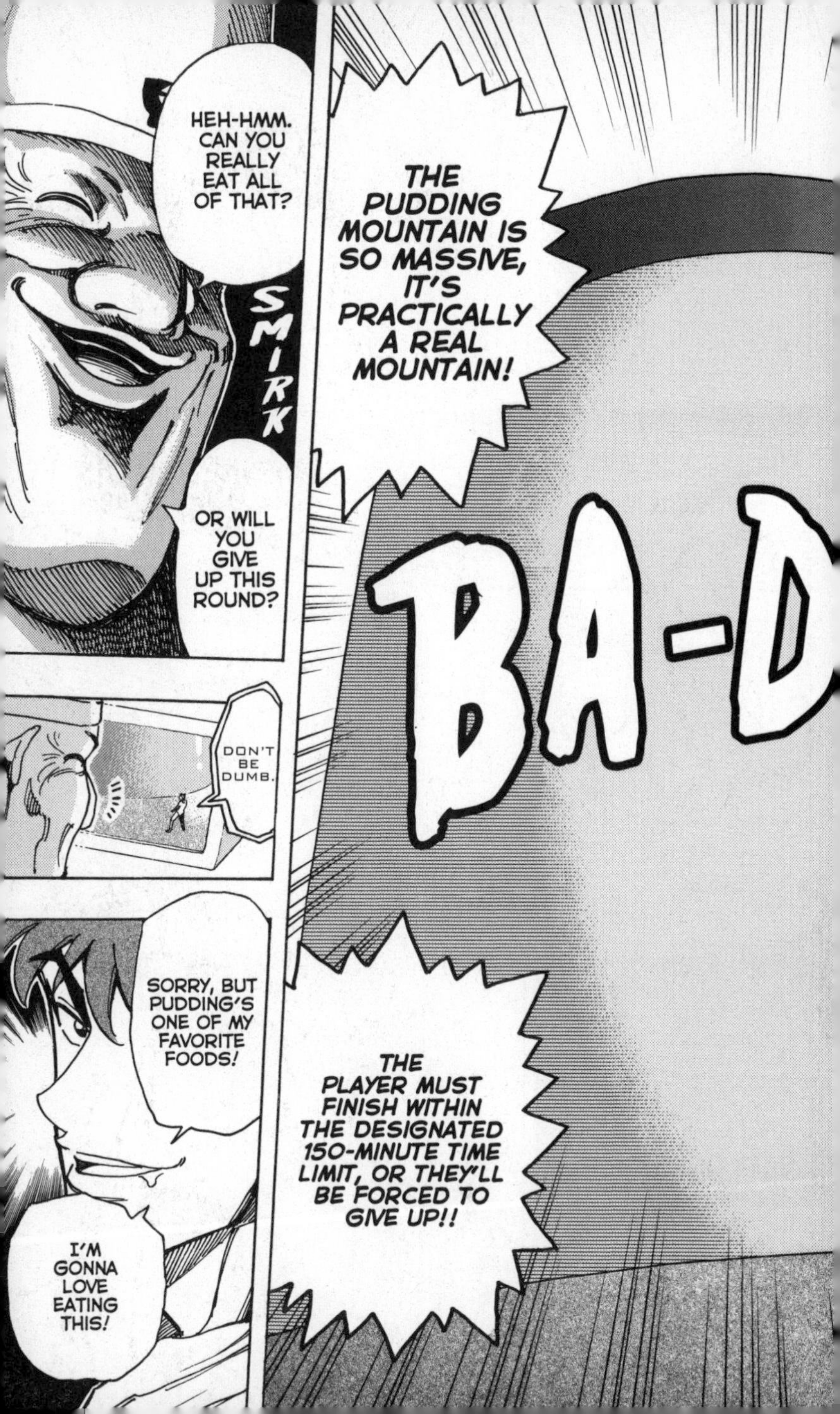
THE PUDDING MOUNTAIN IS SO MASSIVE, IT'S PRACTICALLY A REAL MOUNTAIN!
BA-D
THE PLAYER MUST FINISH WITHIN THE DESIGNATED 150-MINUTE TIME LIMIT, OR THEY'LL BE FORCED TO GIVE UP!!
HEH-HMM. CAN YOU REALLY EAT ALL OF THAT?
SMIRK
OR WILL YOU GIVE UP THIS ROUND?
DON'T BE DUMB.
SORRY, BUT PUDDING'S ONE OF MY FAVORITE FOODS!
I'M GONNA LOVE EATING THIS!

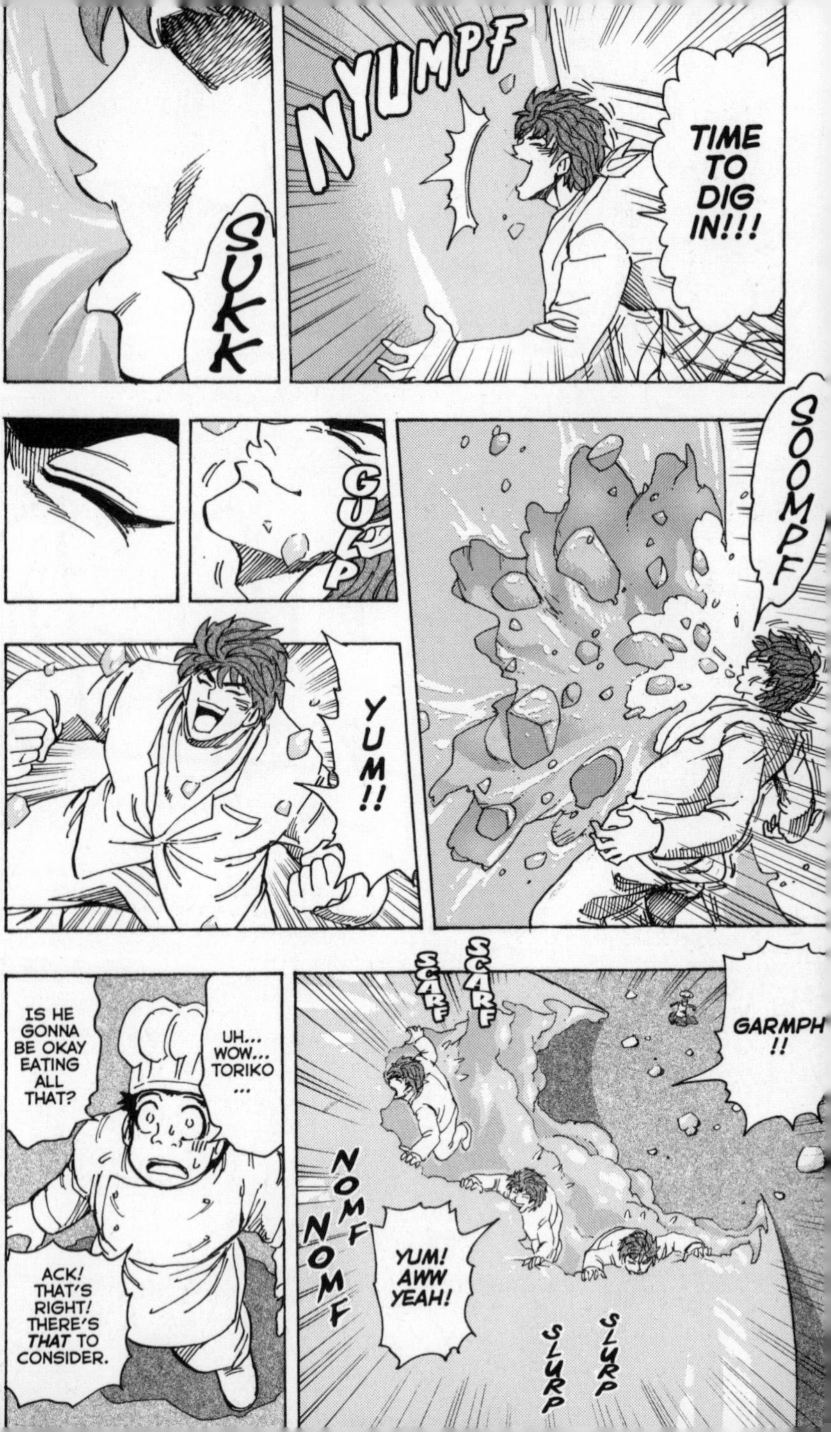
TIME TO DIG IN!!!
NYUMPF
SUKK
SOOOMPF
GULP
YUM!!
GARMPH!!
SCARF SCARF
NOMF NOMF
YUM! AWW YEAH!
SLURP SLURP
UH... WOW... TORIKO...
IS HE GONNA BE OKAY EATING ALL THAT?
ACK! THAT'S RIGHT! THERE'S *THAT* TO CONSIDER.

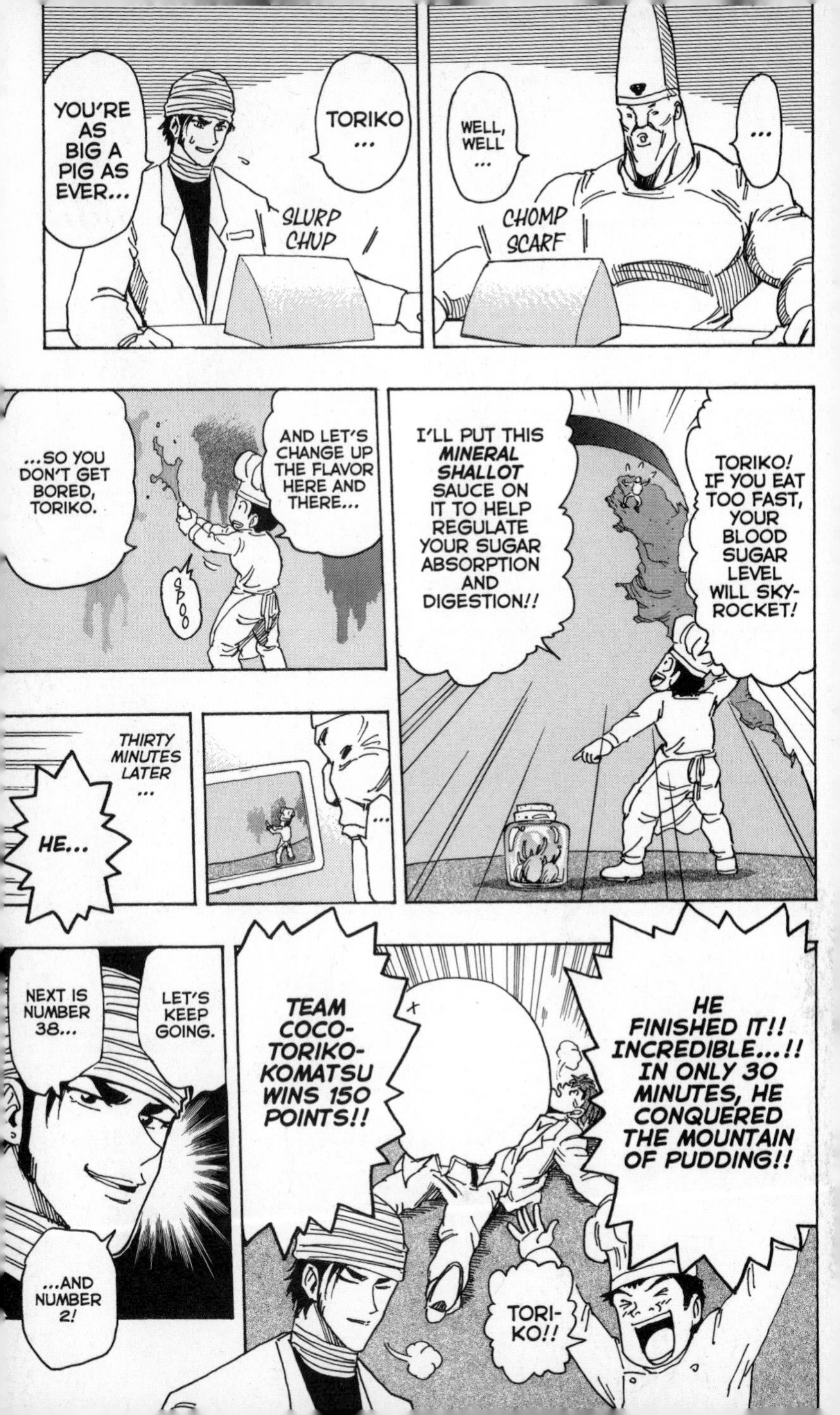
...
WELL, WELL...
CHOMP SCARF
TORIKO...
YOU'RE AS BIG A PIG AS EVER...
SLURP CHUP
TORIKO! IF YOU EAT TOO FAST, YOUR BLOOD SUGAR LEVEL WILL SKY-ROCKET!
I'LL PUT THIS ***MINERAL SHALLOT*** SAUCE ON IT TO HELP REGULATE YOUR SUGAR ABSORPTION AND DIGESTION!!
AND LET'S CHANGE UP THE FLAVOR HERE AND THERE...
...SO YOU DON'T GET BORED, TORIKO.
SPOO
...
THIRTY MINUTES LATER...
HE...
HE FINISHED IT!! INCREDIBLE...!! IN ONLY 30 MINUTES, HE CONQUERED THE MOUNTAIN OF PUDDING!!
TEAM COCO-TORIKO-KOMATSU WINS 150 POINTS!!
TORI-KO!!
LET'S KEEP GOING.
NEXT IS NUMBER 38...
...AND NUMBER 2!

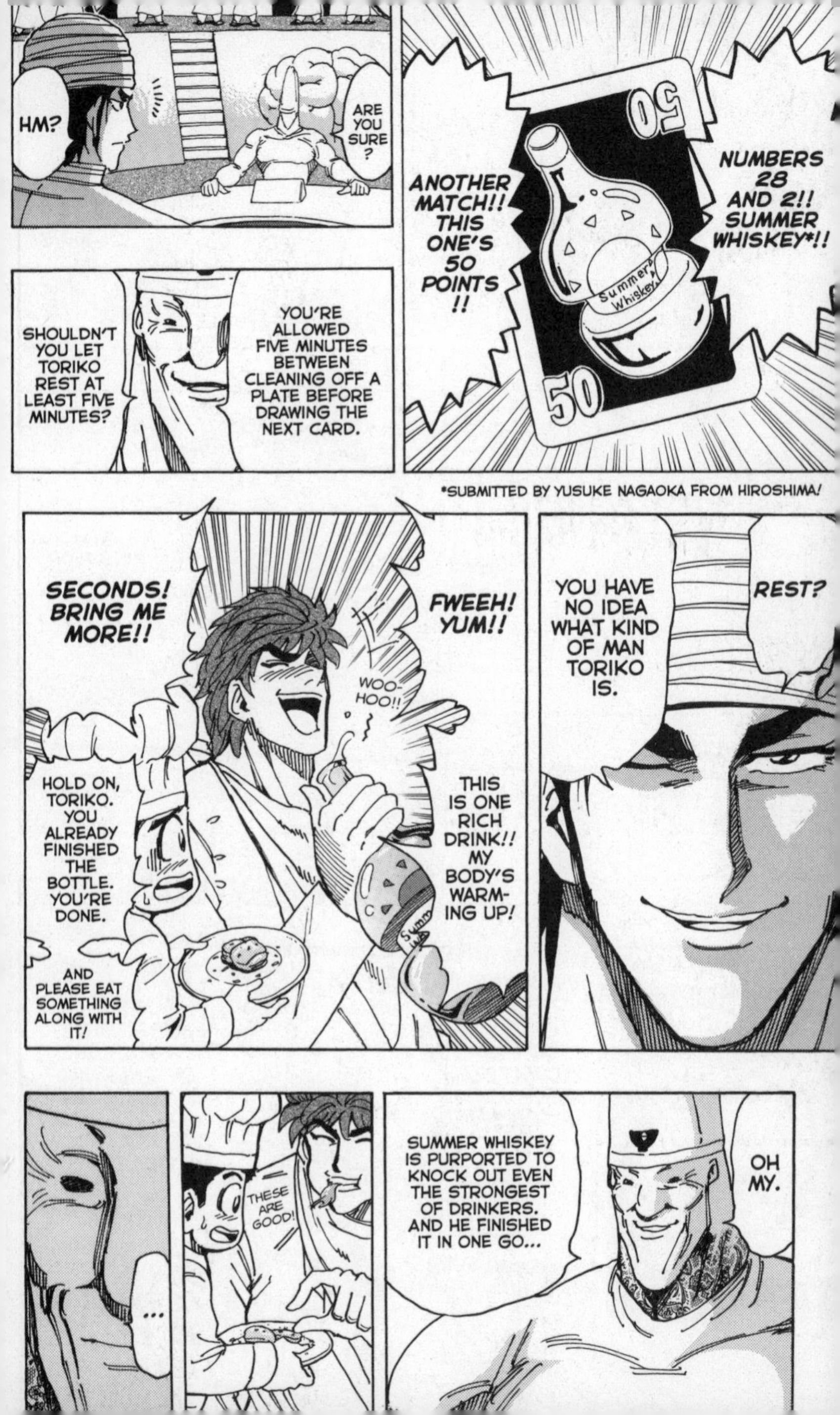
NUMBERS 28 AND 2!! SUMMER WHISKEY*!!
ANOTHER MATCH!! THIS ONE'S 50 POINTS!!
50
Summer Whiskey
50
ARE YOU SURE?
HM?
YOU'RE ALLOWED FIVE MINUTES BETWEEN CLEANING OFF A PLATE BEFORE DRAWING THE NEXT CARD.
SHOULDN'T YOU LET TORIKO REST AT LEAST FIVE MINUTES?
*SUBMITTED BY YUSUKE NAGAOKA FROM HIROSHIMA!
REST?
YOU HAVE NO IDEA WHAT KIND OF MAN TORIKO IS.
FWEEH! YUM!!
SECONDS! BRING ME MORE!!
WOO-HOO!!
THIS IS ONE RICH DRINK!! MY BODY'S WARMING UP!
HOLD ON, TORIKO. YOU ALREADY FINISHED THE BOTTLE. YOU'RE DONE.
AND PLEASE EAT SOMETHING ALONG WITH IT!
OH MY.
SUMMER WHISKEY IS PURPORTED TO KNOCK OUT EVEN THE STRONGEST OF DRINKERS. AND HE FINISHED IT IN ONE GO...
THESE ARE GOOD!
...

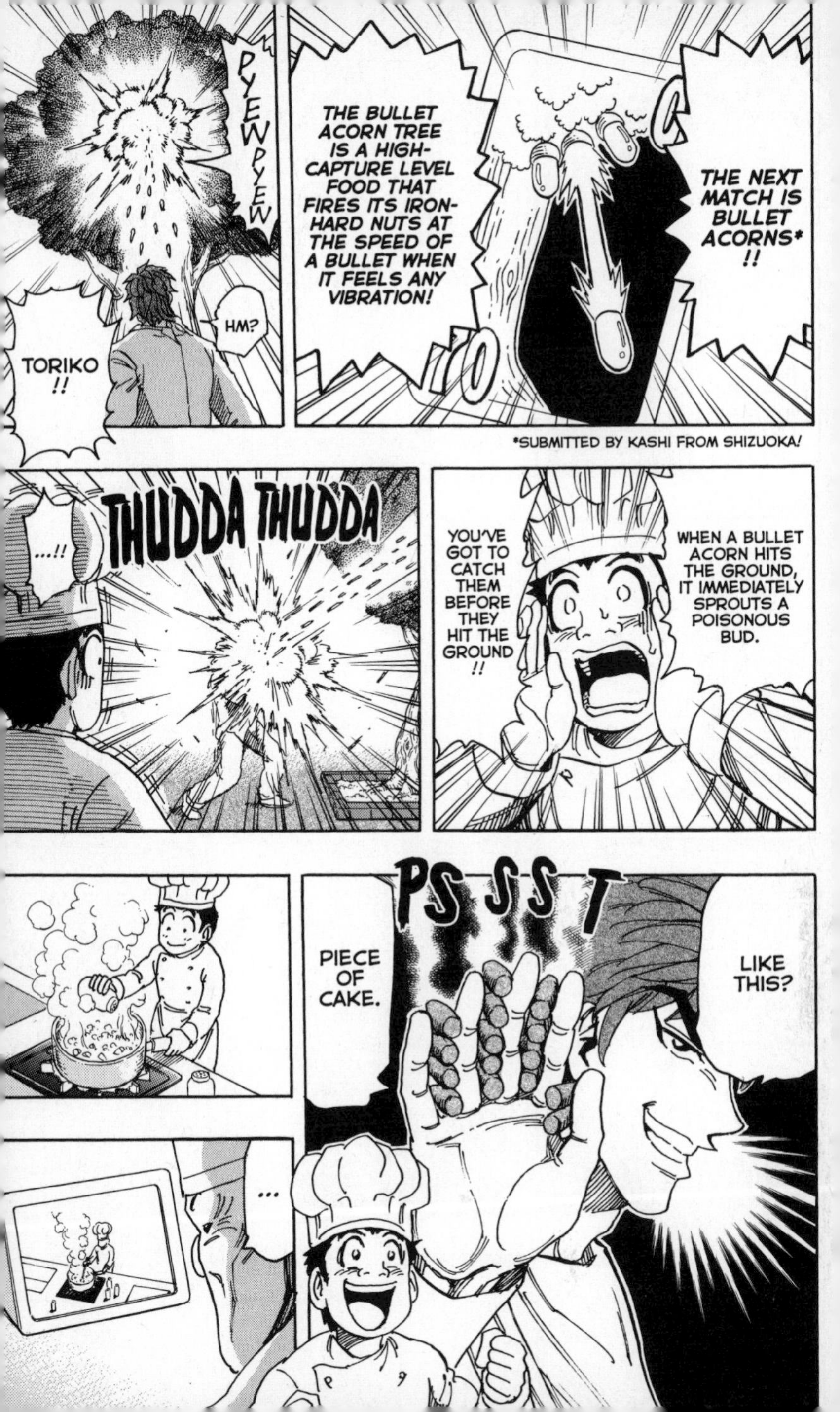
THE NEXT MATCH IS BULLET ACORNS* !!
THE BULLET ACORN TREE IS A HIGH-CAPTURE LEVEL FOOD THAT FIRES ITS IRON-HARD NUTS AT THE SPEED OF A BULLET WHEN IT FEELS ANY VIBRATION!
PYEW PYEW
HM?
TORIKO !!
*SUBMITTED BY KASHI FROM SHIZUOKA!
WHEN A BULLET ACORN HITS THE GROUND, IT IMMEDIATELY SPROUTS A POISONOUS BUD.
YOU'VE GOT TO CATCH THEM BEFORE THEY HIT THE GROUND !!
THUDDA THUDDA
...!!
PSSST
LIKE THIS?
PIECE OF CAKE.
...

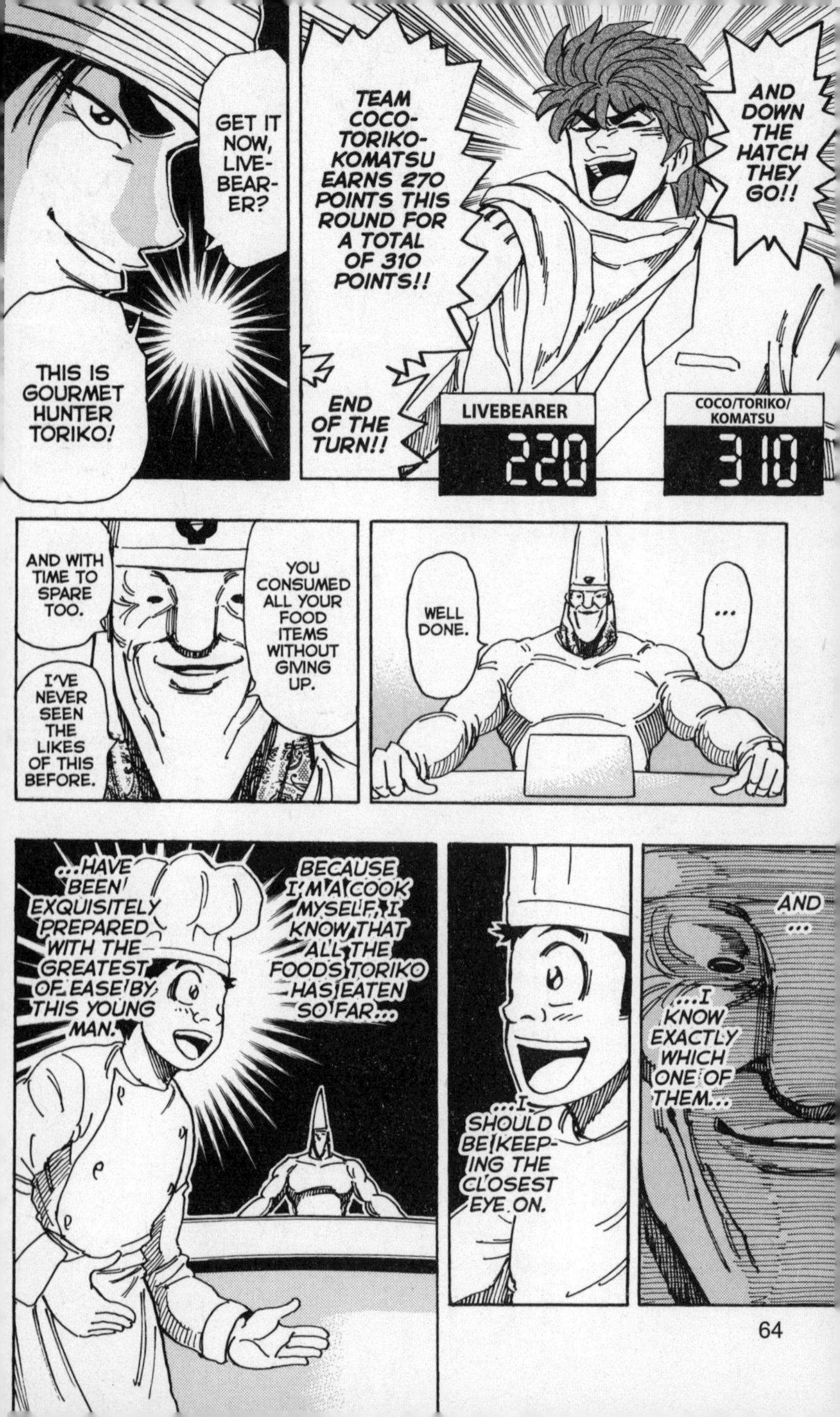
AND DOWN THE HATCH THEY GO!!
TEAM COCO-TORIKO-KOMATSU EARNS 270 POINTS THIS ROUND FOR A TOTAL OF 310 POINTS!!
COCO/TORIKO/KOMATSU 310
LIVEBEARER 220
END OF THE TURN!!
GET IT NOW, LIVE-BEARER?
THIS IS GOURMET HUNTER TORIKO!
...
WELL DONE.
YOU CONSUMED ALL YOUR FOOD ITEMS WITHOUT GIVING UP.
AND WITH TIME TO SPARE TOO.
I'VE NEVER SEEN THE LIKES OF THIS BEFORE.
AND...
...I KNOW EXACTLY WHICH ONE OF THEM...
...I SHOULD BE KEEPING THE CLOSEST EYE ON.
BECAUSE I'M A COOK MYSELF, I KNOW THAT ALL THE FOODS TORIKO HAS EATEN SO FAR...
...HAVE BEEN EXQUISITELY PREPARED WITH THE GREATEST OF EASE BY THIS YOUNG MAN.

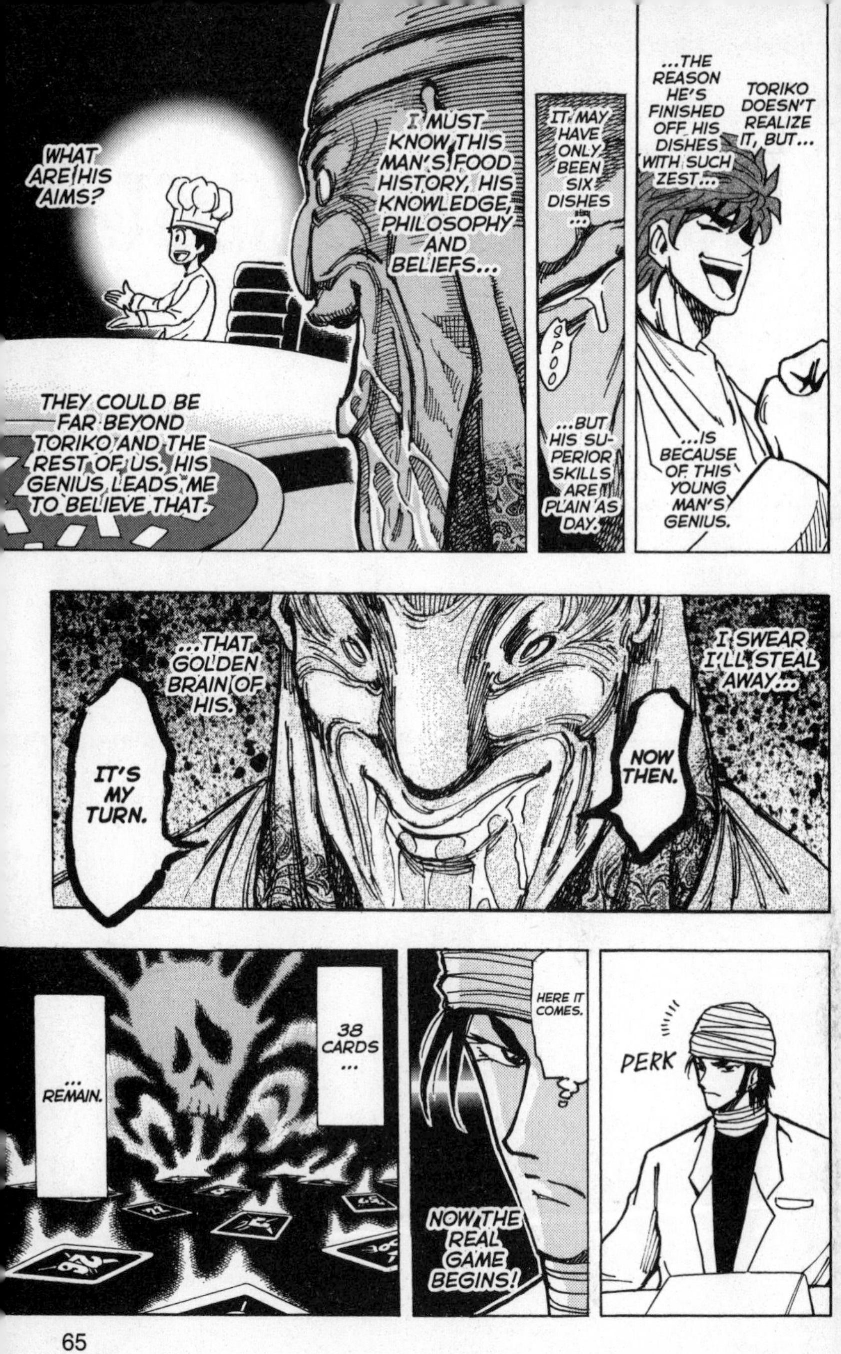
TORIKO DOESN'T REALIZE IT, BUT...
...THE REASON HE'S FINISHED OFF HIS DISHES WITH SUCH ZEST...
...IS BECAUSE OF THIS YOUNG MAN'S GENIUS.
IT MAY HAVE ONLY BEEN SIX DISHES...
SPOO
...BUT HIS SUPERIOR SKILLS ARE PLAIN AS DAY.
I MUST KNOW THIS MAN'S FOOD HISTORY, HIS KNOWLEDGE, PHILOSOPHY AND BELIEFS...
WHAT ARE HIS AIMS?
THEY COULD BE FAR BEYOND TORIKO AND THE REST OF US. HIS GENIUS LEADS ME TO BELIEVE THAT.
I SWEAR I'LL STEAL AWAY...
...THAT GOLDEN BRAIN OF HIS.
NOW THEN.
IT'S MY TURN.
PERK
HERE IT COMES.
NOW THE REAL GAME BEGINS!
38 CARDS...
...REMAIN.

TORIKO

GOURMET CHECKLIST

Vol. 196

DANGOL
(CRUSTACEAN)

CAPTURE LEVEL: 40
HABITAT: GOURMET PYRAMID
LENGTH: 70 CM
HEIGHT: ---
WEIGHT: 50 KG
PRICE: TYPICALLY NOT FIT FOR CONSUMPTION BUT CAPTURED CORRECTLY IT CAN BE 100G / 10,000 YEN

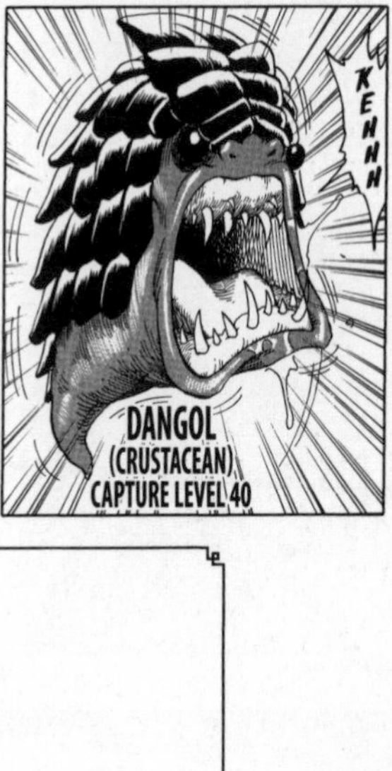
KENHH
DANGOL
(CRUSTACEAN)
CAPTURE LEVEL 40

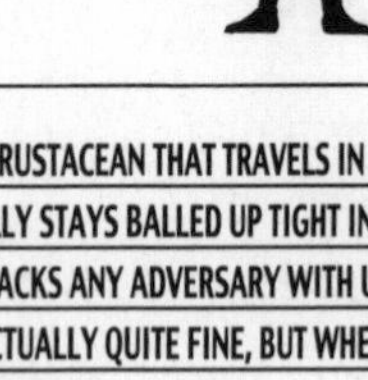

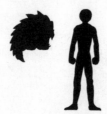

SCALE

A COWARDLY CRUSTACEAN THAT TRAVELS IN PACKS. TERRIFIED OF OUTSIDE THREATS, A DANGOL USUALLY STAYS BALLED UP TIGHT IN ITS ARMOR-HARD SHELL. HOWEVER, WHEN PUSHED, IT ATTACKS ANY ADVERSARY WITH UNBRIDLED FEROCITY. THE MEAT OF ITS SOFT BITS IS ACTUALLY QUITE FINE, BUT WHEN IT BUNCHES UP, NO ORDINARY PERSON CAN WRENCH IT OPEN.

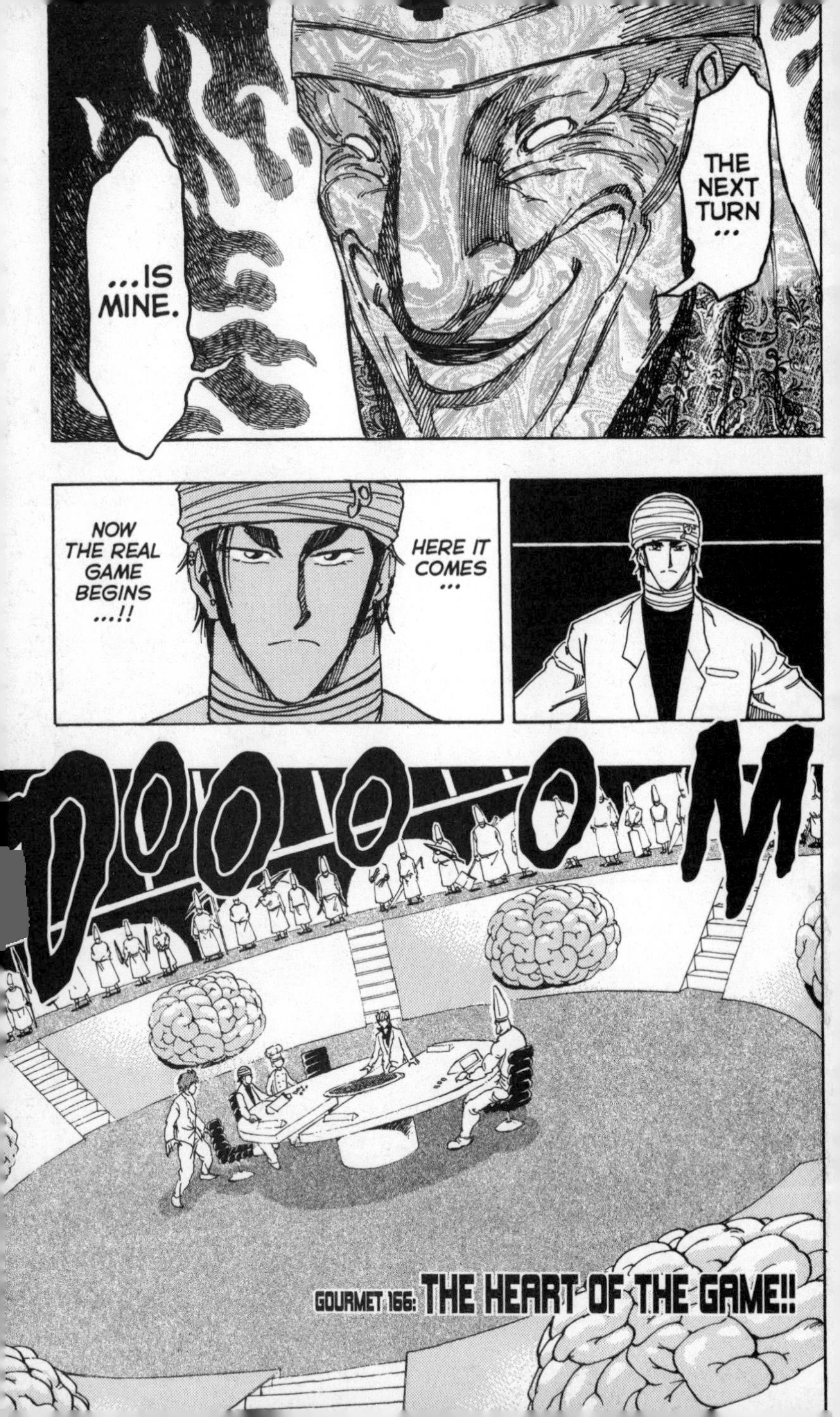
THE NEXT TURN ...
...IS MINE.
HERE IT COMES ...
NOW THE REAL GAME BEGINS ...!!
DOOOO-O-OM
GOURMET 166: THE HEART OF THE GAME!!

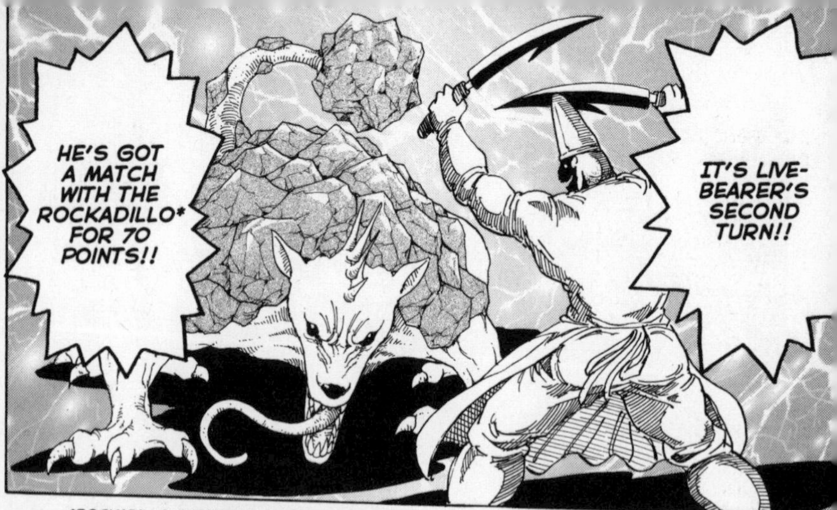
IT'S LIVE-BEARER'S SECOND TURN!!
HE'S GOT A MATCH WITH THE ROCKADILLO* FOR 70 POINTS!!

*ROCKADILLO SUBMITTED BY SNAKE FROG FROM TOKYO!

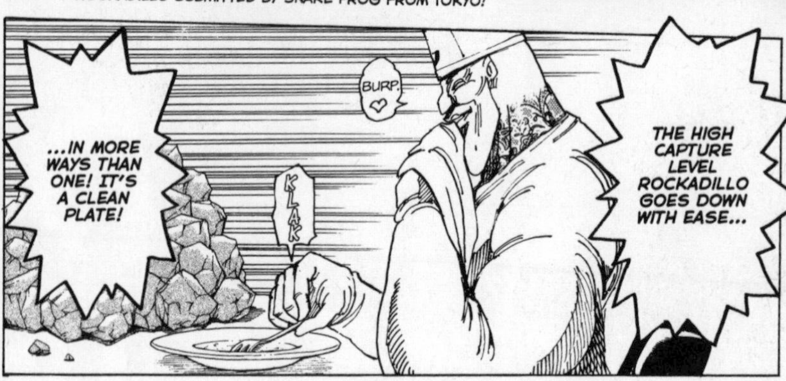
THE HIGH CAPTURE LEVEL ROCKADILLO GOES DOWN WITH EASE...
BURP ♡
KLAK
...IN MORE WAYS THAN ONE! IT'S A CLEAN PLATE!

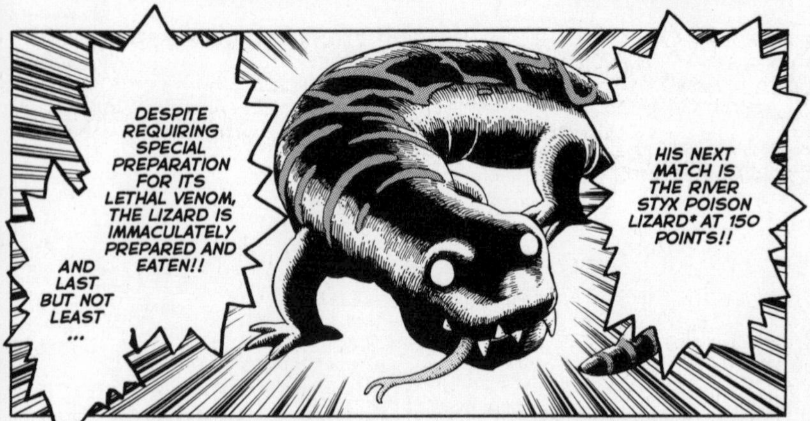
HIS NEXT MATCH IS THE RIVER STYX POISON LIZARD* AT 150 POINTS!!
DESPITE REQUIRING SPECIAL PREPARATION FOR ITS LETHAL VENOM, THE LIZARD IS IMMACULATELY PREPARED AND EATEN!!
AND LAST BUT NOT LEAST ...

*RIVER STYX POISON LIZARD SUBMITTED BY TAKUYA KURIHARA FROM IBARAKI!

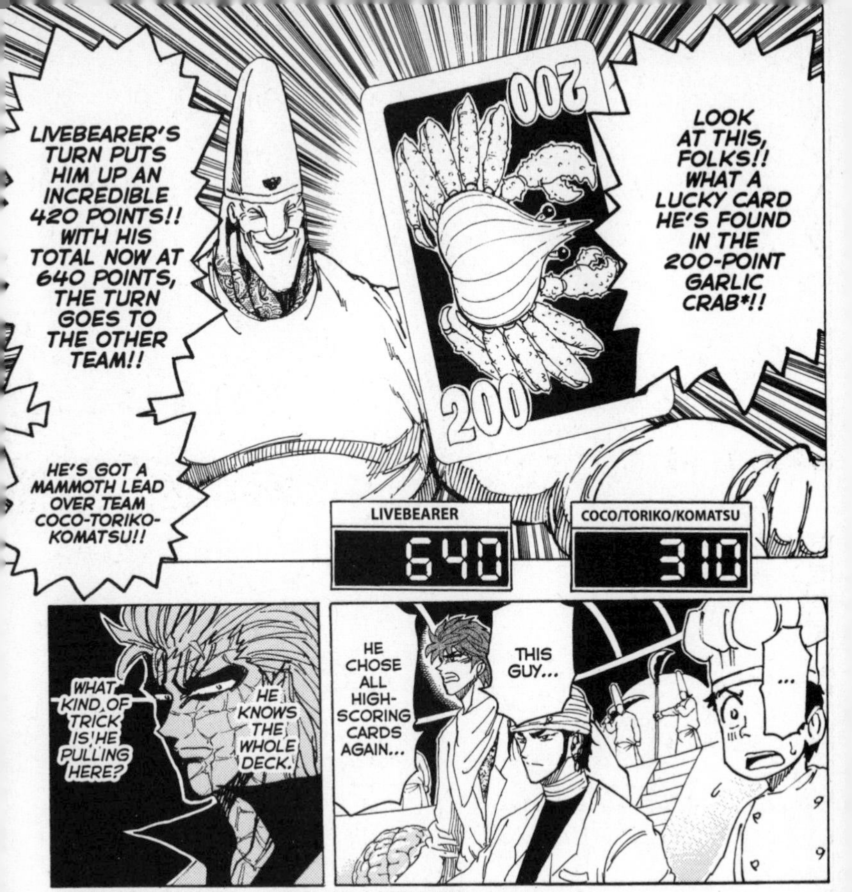
200
200
LOOK AT THIS, FOLKS!! WHAT A LUCKY CARD HE'S FOUND IN THE 200-POINT GARLIC CRAB*!!
LIVEBEARER'S TURN PUTS HIM UP AN INCREDIBLE 420 POINTS!! WITH HIS TOTAL NOW AT 640 POINTS, THE TURN GOES TO THE OTHER TEAM!!
HE'S GOT A MAMMOTH LEAD OVER TEAM COCO-TORIKO-KOMATSU!!
LIVEBEARER
640
COCO/TORIKO/KOMATSU
310
...
THIS GUY...
HE CHOSE ALL HIGH-SCORING CARDS AGAIN...
HE KNOWS THE WHOLE DECK.
WHAT KIND OF TRICK IS HE PULLING HERE?

*GARLIC CRAB SUBMITTED BY RYUTA UMEDA FROM OITA!

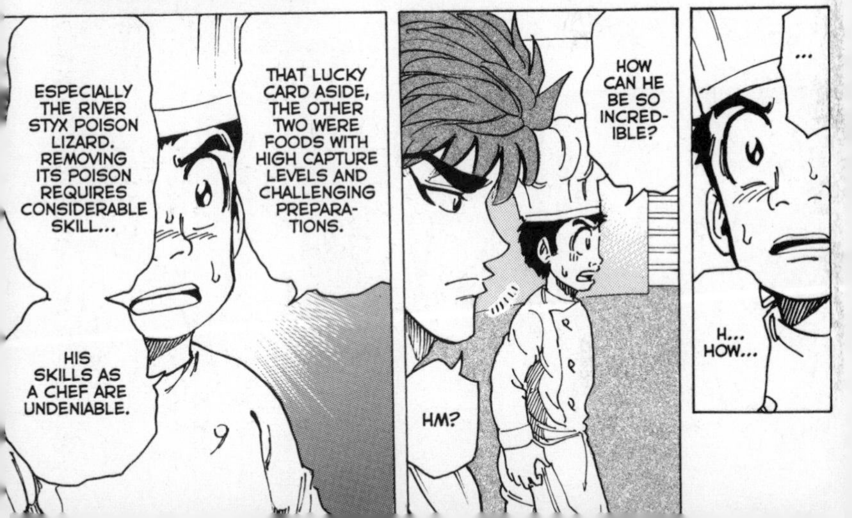
...
H... HOW...
HOW CAN HE BE SO INCREDIBLE?
HM?
THAT LUCKY CARD ASIDE, THE OTHER TWO WERE FOODS WITH HIGH CAPTURE LEVELS AND CHALLENGING PREPARATIONS.
ESPECIALLY THE RIVER STYX POISON LIZARD. REMOVING ITS POISON REQUIRES CONSIDERABLE SKILL...
HIS SKILLS AS A CHEF ARE UNDENIABLE.

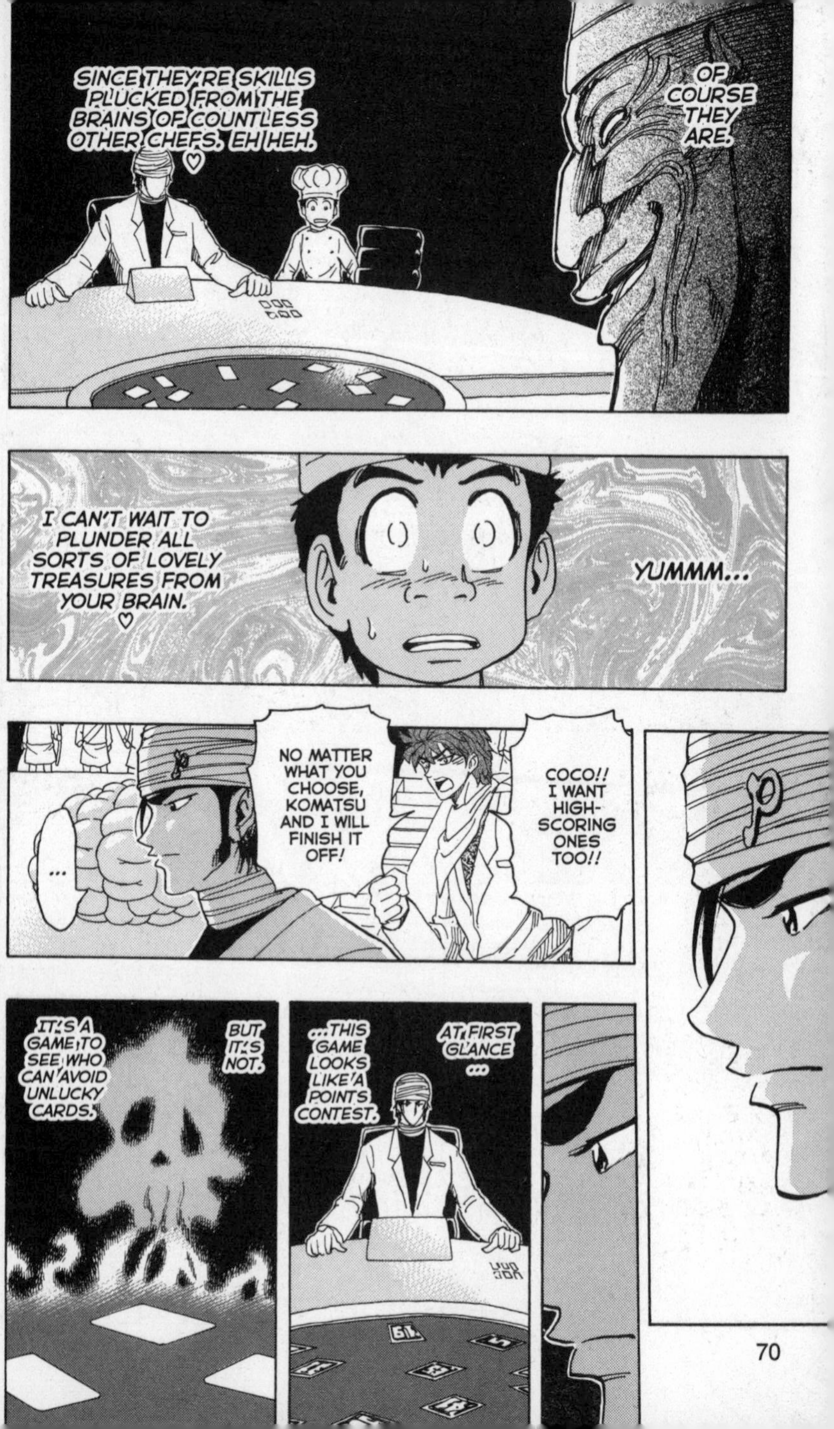

OF COURSE THEY ARE.
SINCE THEY'RE SKILLS PLUCKED FROM THE BRAINS OF COUNTLESS OTHER CHEFS. EH HEH. ♡
YUMMM...
I CAN'T WAIT TO PLUNDER ALL SORTS OF LOVELY TREASURES FROM YOUR BRAIN. ♡
COCO!! I WANT HIGH-SCORING ONES TOO!!
NO MATTER WHAT YOU CHOOSE, KOMATSU AND I WILL FINISH IT OFF!
...
AT FIRST GLANCE...
...THIS GAME LOOKS LIKE A POINTS CONTEST.
BUT IT'S NOT.
IT'S A GAME TO SEE WHO CAN AVOID UNLUCKY CARDS.

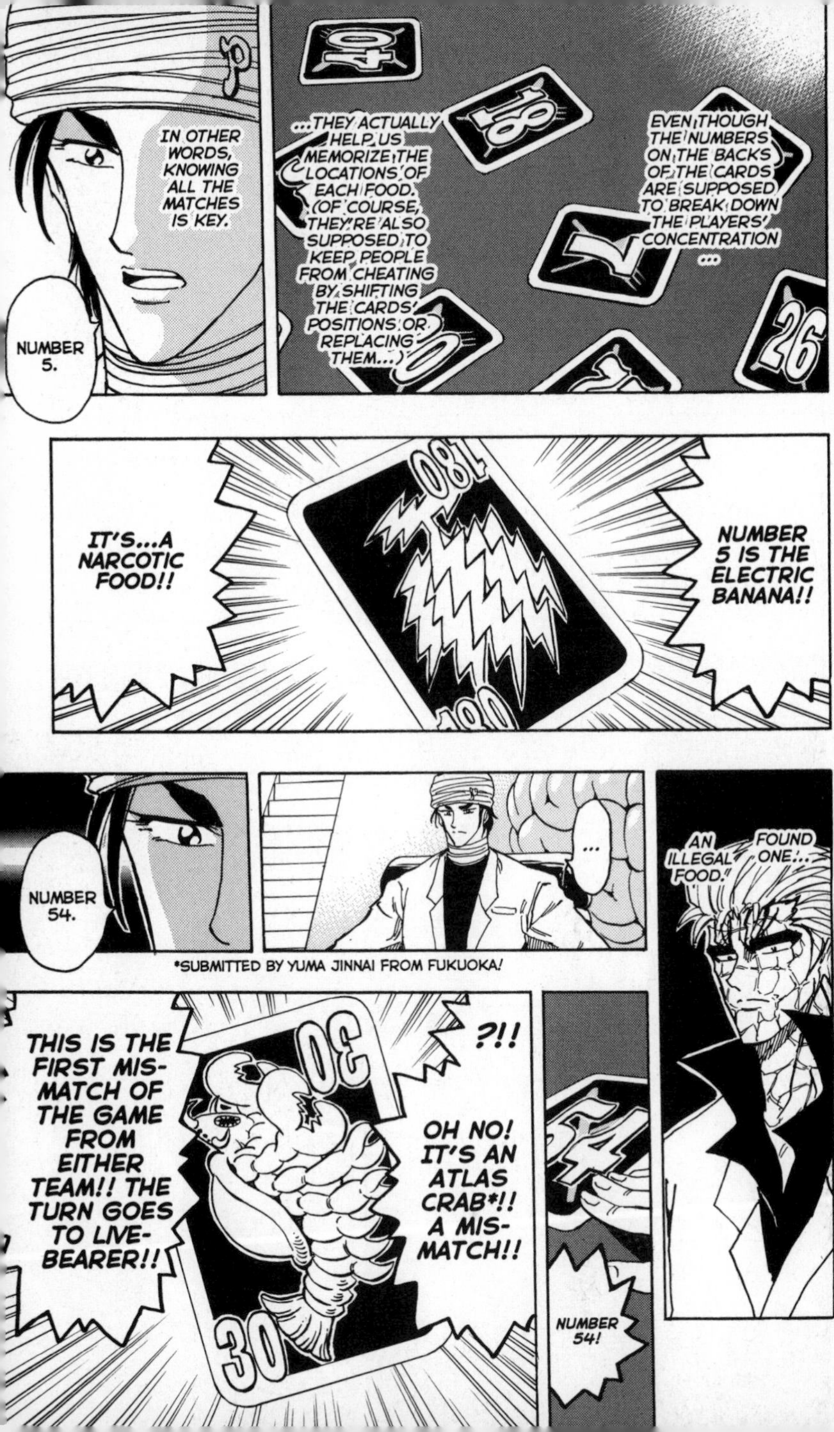
EVEN THOUGH THE NUMBERS ON THE BACKS OF THE CARDS ARE SUPPOSED TO BREAK DOWN THE PLAYERS' CONCENTRATION...
...THEY ACTUALLY HELP US MEMORIZE THE LOCATIONS OF EACH FOOD. (OF COURSE, THEY'RE ALSO SUPPOSED TO KEEP PEOPLE FROM CHEATING BY SHIFTING THE CARDS' POSITIONS OR REPLACING THEM...)
IN OTHER WORDS, KNOWING ALL THE MATCHES IS KEY.
NUMBER 5.
NUMBER 5 IS THE ELECTRIC BANANA!!
IT'S...A NARCOTIC FOOD!!
FOUND ONE...
AN ILLEGAL FOOD.
...
NUMBER 54.
NUMBER 54!
?!!
OH NO! IT'S AN ATLAS CRAB*!! A MIS-MATCH!!
THIS IS THE FIRST MIS-MATCH OF THE GAME FROM EITHER TEAM!! THE TURN GOES TO LIVE-BEARER!!

*SUBMITTED BY YUMA JINNAI FROM FUKUOKA!

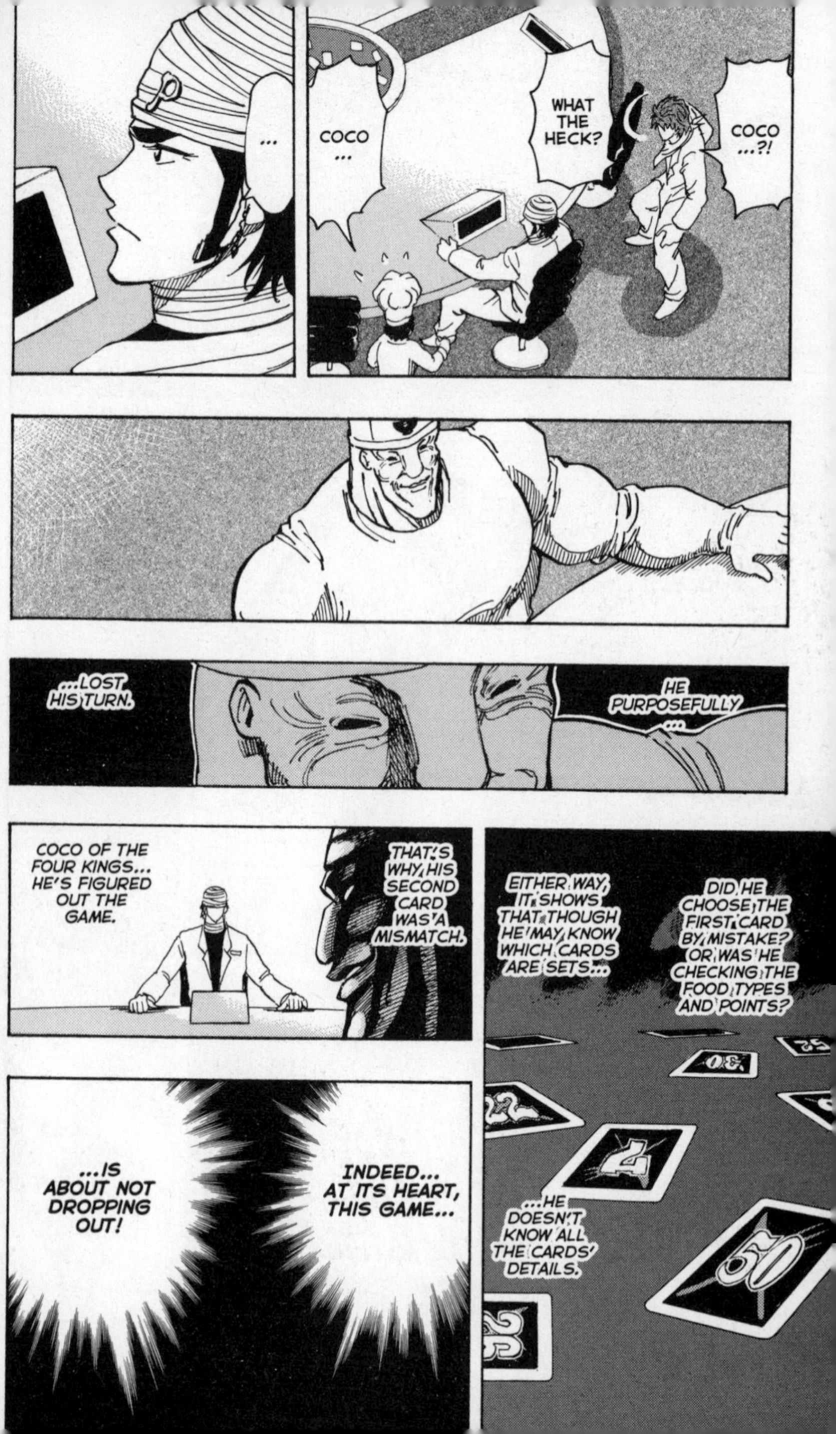
COCO ...?!
WHAT THE HECK?
COCO ...
...
HE PURPOSEFULLY ...
...LOST HIS TURN.
DID HE CHOOSE THE FIRST CARD BY MISTAKE? OR WAS HE CHECKING THE FOOD TYPES AND POINTS?
EITHER WAY, IT SHOWS THAT THOUGH HE MAY KNOW WHICH CARDS ARE SETS...
...HE DOESN'T KNOW ALL THE CARDS' DETAILS.
THAT'S WHY HIS SECOND CARD WAS A MISMATCH.
COCO OF THE FOUR KINGS... HE'S FIGURED OUT THE GAME.
INDEED... AT ITS HEART, THIS GAME...
...IS ABOUT NOT DROPPING OUT!

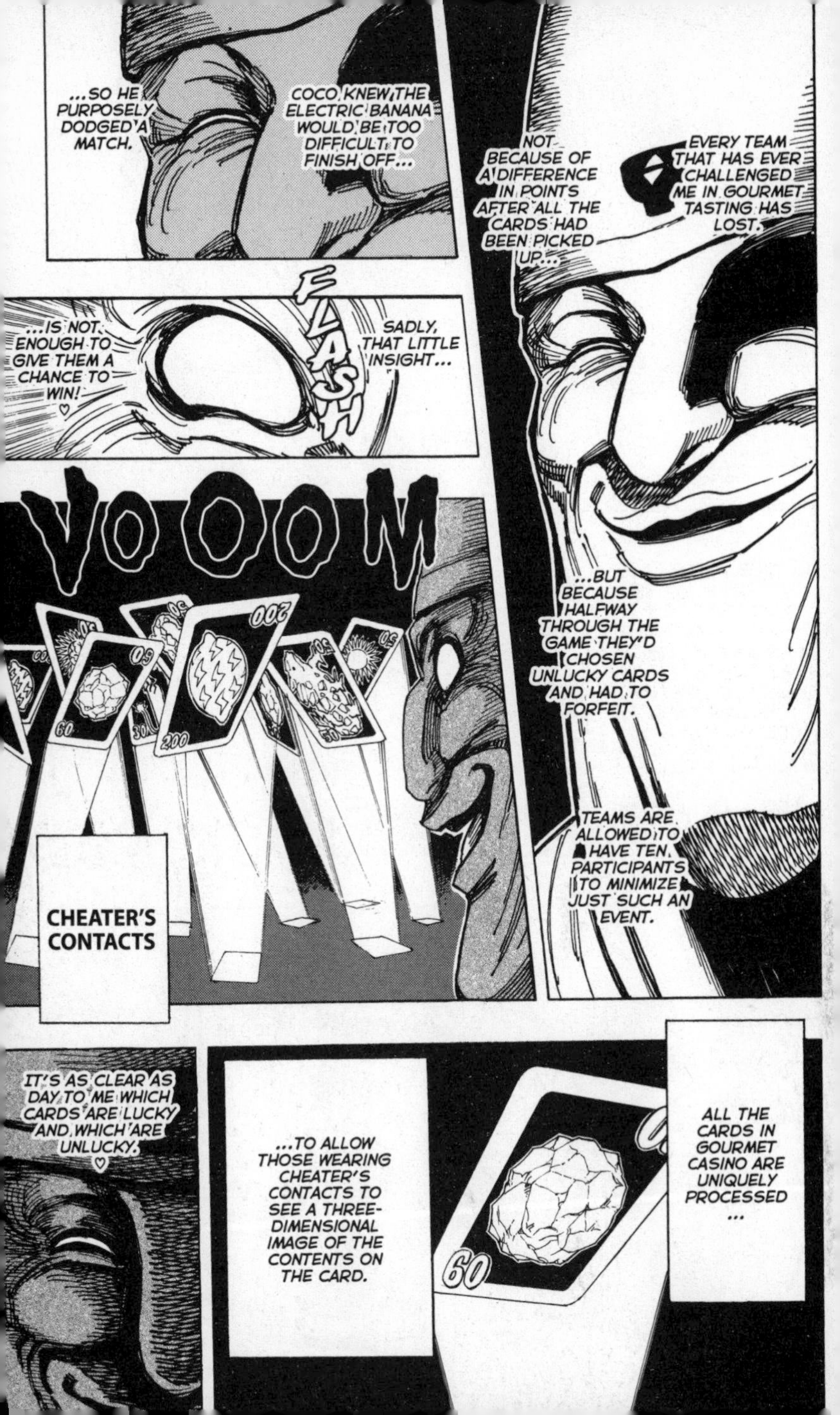
EVERY TEAM THAT HAS EVER CHALLENGED ME IN GOURMET TASTING HAS LOST.
NOT BECAUSE OF A DIFFERENCE IN POINTS AFTER ALL THE CARDS HAD BEEN PICKED UP...
...BUT BECAUSE HALFWAY THROUGH THE GAME THEY'D CHOSEN UNLUCKY CARDS AND HAD TO FORFEIT.
TEAMS ARE ALLOWED TO HAVE TEN PARTICIPANTS TO MINIMIZE JUST SUCH AN EVENT.
COCO KNEW THE ELECTRIC BANANA WOULD BE TOO DIFFICULT TO FINISH OFF...
...SO HE PURPOSELY DODGED A MATCH.
SADLY, THAT LITTLE INSIGHT...
FLASH
...IS NOT ENOUGH TO GIVE THEM A CHANCE TO WIN! ♡
VOOOM
CHEATER'S CONTACTS
ALL THE CARDS IN GOURMET CASINO ARE UNIQUELY PROCESSED ...
...TO ALLOW THOSE WEARING CHEATER'S CONTACTS TO SEE A THREE-DIMENSIONAL IMAGE OF THE CONTENTS ON THE CARD.
60
IT'S AS CLEAR AS DAY TO ME WHICH CARDS ARE LUCKY AND WHICH ARE UNLUCKY. ♡

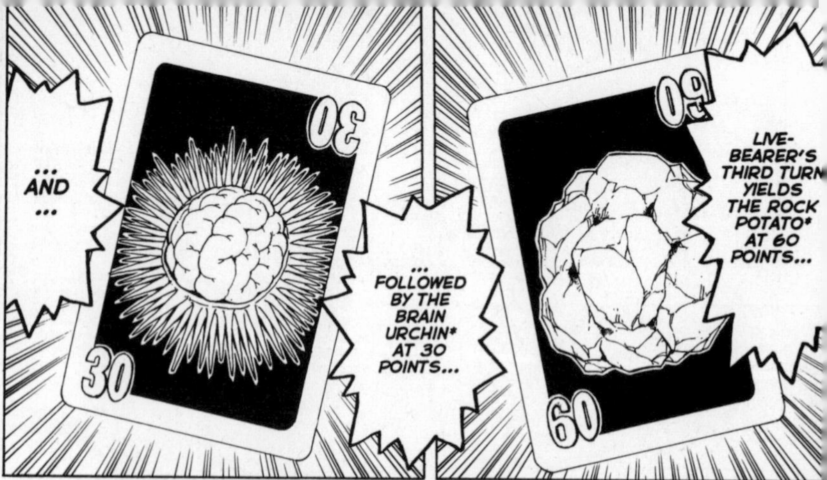
60
LIVE-BEARER'S THIRD TURN YIELDS THE ROCK POTATO* AT 60 POINTS...
60
30
... FOLLOWED BY THE BRAIN URCHIN* AT 30 POINTS...
30
... AND ...

*ROCK POTATO SUBMITTED BY JUNICHI UEOKAN FROM SHIZUOKA; BRAIN URCHIN SUBMITTED BY MAKI KASAI FROM FUKUOKA!

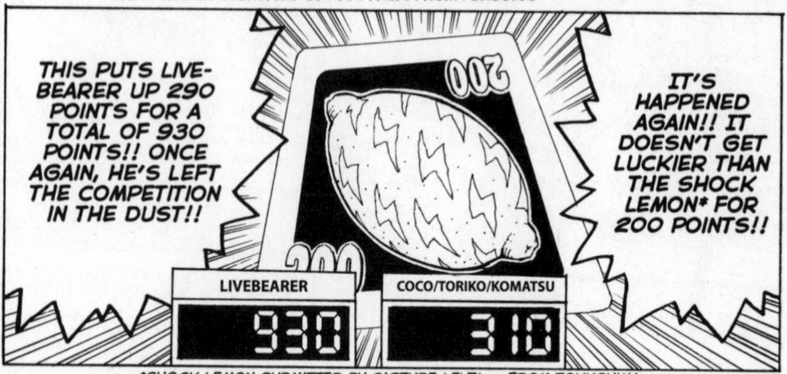
IT'S HAPPENED AGAIN!! IT DOESN'T GET LUCKIER THAN THE SHOCK LEMON* FOR 200 POINTS!!
200
THIS PUTS LIVE-BEARER UP 290 POINTS FOR A TOTAL OF 930 POINTS!! ONCE AGAIN, HE'S LEFT THE COMPETITION IN THE DUST!!
COCO/TORIKO/KOMATSU
310
LIVEBEARER
930

*SHOCK LEMON SUBMITTED BY CAPTURE LEVEL ∞ FROM TOKUSHIMA; DRAGONFIRE SUBMITTED BY JURAKI FROM NARA!

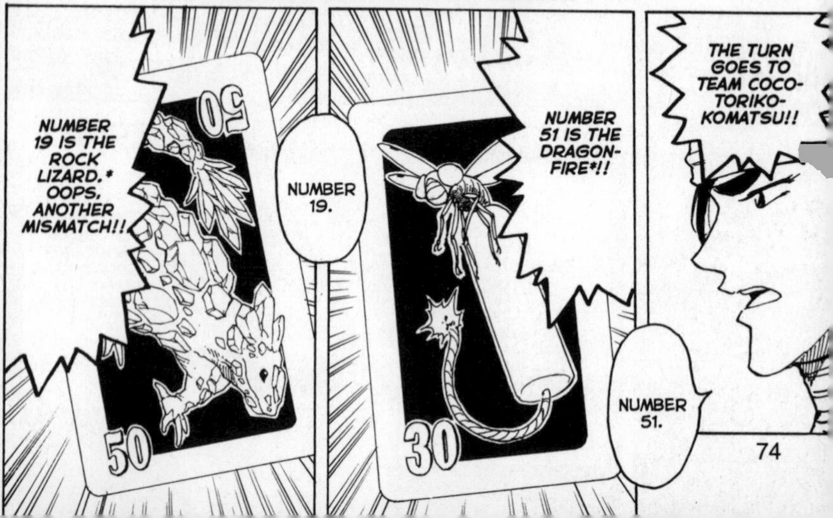
THE TURN GOES TO TEAM COCO-TORIKO-KOMATSU!!
NUMBER 51.
NUMBER 51 IS THE DRAGON-FIRE*!!
30
NUMBER 19.
50
NUMBER 19 IS THE ROCK LIZARD.* OOPS, ANOTHER MISMATCH!!
50

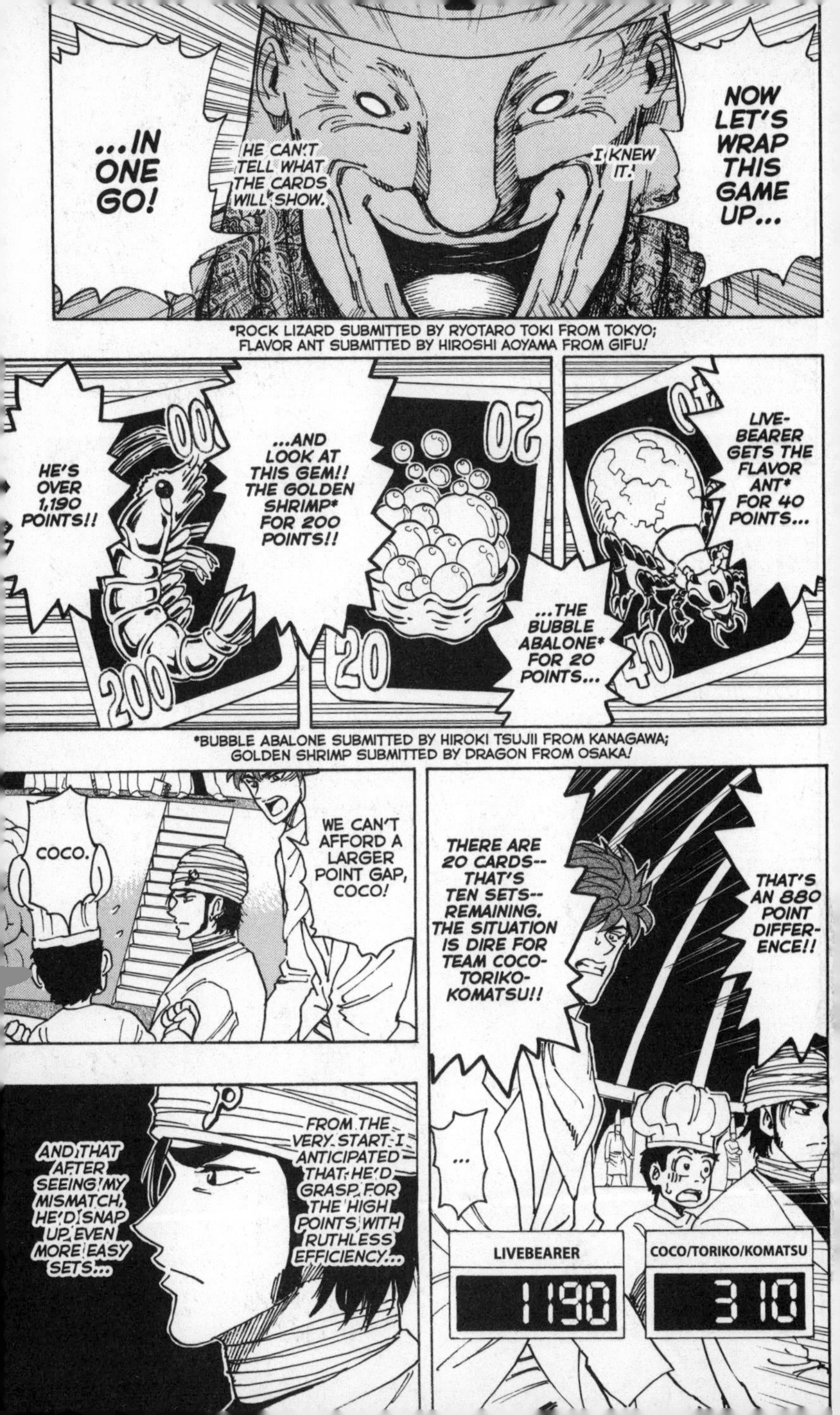
NOW LET'S WRAP THIS GAME UP...
I KNEW IT.
HE CAN'T TELL WHAT THE CARDS WILL SHOW.
...IN ONE GO!
*ROCK LIZARD SUBMITTED BY RYOTARO TOKI FROM TOKYO; FLAVOR ANT SUBMITTED BY HIROSHI AOYAMA FROM GIFU!
LIVE-BEARER GETS THE FLAVOR ANT* FOR 40 POINTS...
...THE BUBBLE ABALONE* FOR 20 POINTS...
...AND LOOK AT THIS GEM!! THE GOLDEN SHRIMP* FOR 200 POINTS!!
HE'S OVER 1,190 POINTS!!
*BUBBLE ABALONE SUBMITTED BY HIROKI TSUJII FROM KANAGAWA; GOLDEN SHRIMP SUBMITTED BY DRAGON FROM OSAKA!
THAT'S AN 880 POINT DIFFERENCE!!
THERE ARE 20 CARDS--THAT'S TEN SETS--REMAINING. THE SITUATION IS DIRE FOR TEAM COCO-TORIKO-KOMATSU!!
...
LIVEBEARER
1190
COCO/TORIKO/KOMATSU
310
WE CAN'T AFFORD A LARGER POINT GAP, COCO!
COCO.
FROM THE VERY START I ANTICIPATED THAT HE'D GRASP FOR THE HIGH POINTS WITH RUTHLESS EFFICIENCY...
AND THAT AFTER SEEING MY MISMATCH, HE'D SNAP UP EVEN MORE EASY SETS...

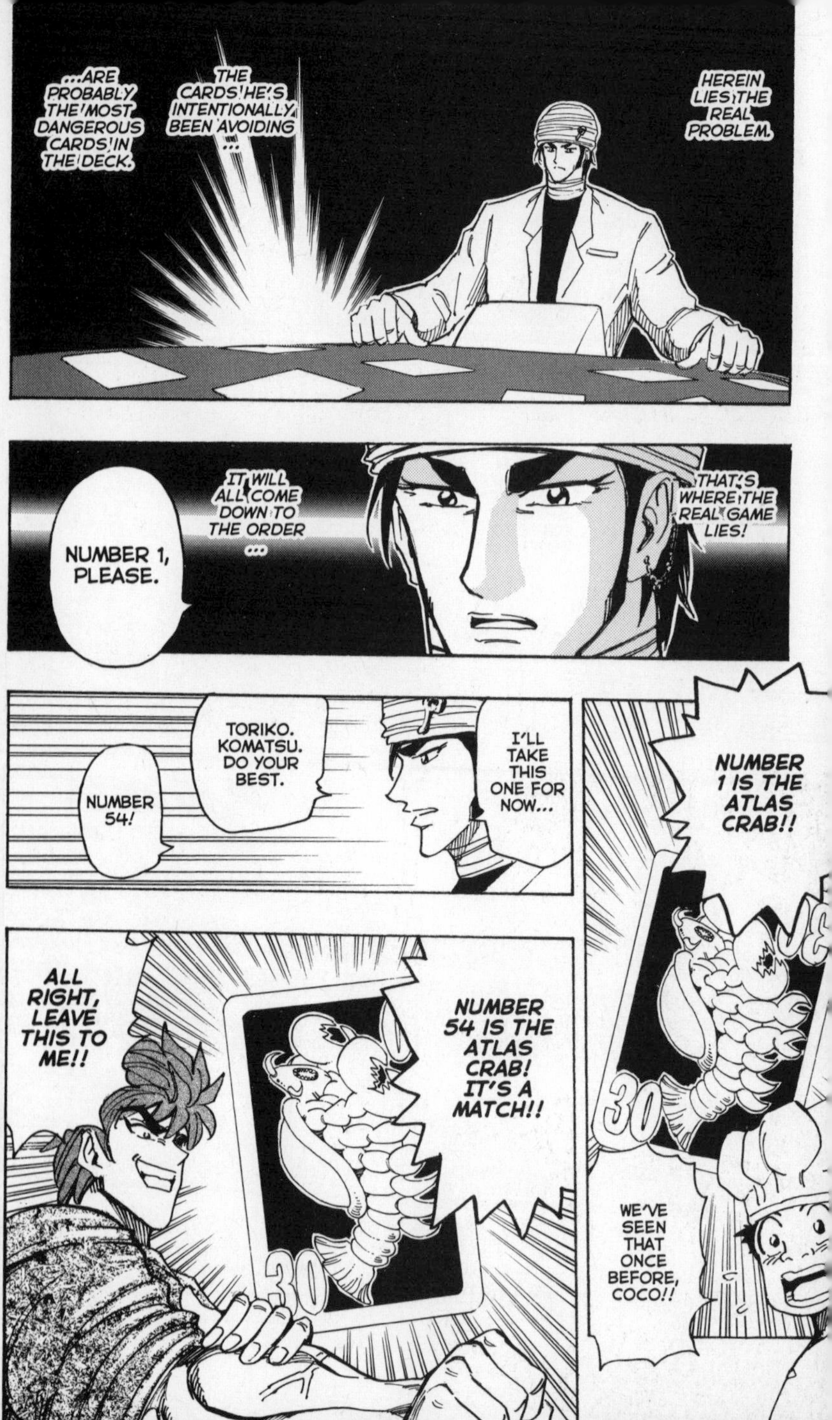
HEREIN LIES THE REAL PROBLEM.
THE CARDS HE'S INTENTIONALLY BEEN AVOIDING...
...ARE PROBABLY THE MOST DANGEROUS CARDS IN THE DECK.
THAT'S WHERE THE REAL GAME LIES!
IT WILL ALL COME DOWN TO THE ORDER...
NUMBER 1, PLEASE.
NUMBER 1 IS THE ATLAS CRAB!!
WE'VE SEEN THAT ONCE BEFORE, COCO!!
I'LL TAKE THIS ONE FOR NOW...
TORIKO. KOMATSU. DO YOUR BEST.
NUMBER 54!
NUMBER 54 IS THE ATLAS CRAB! IT'S A MATCH!!
ALL RIGHT, LEAVE THIS TO ME!!

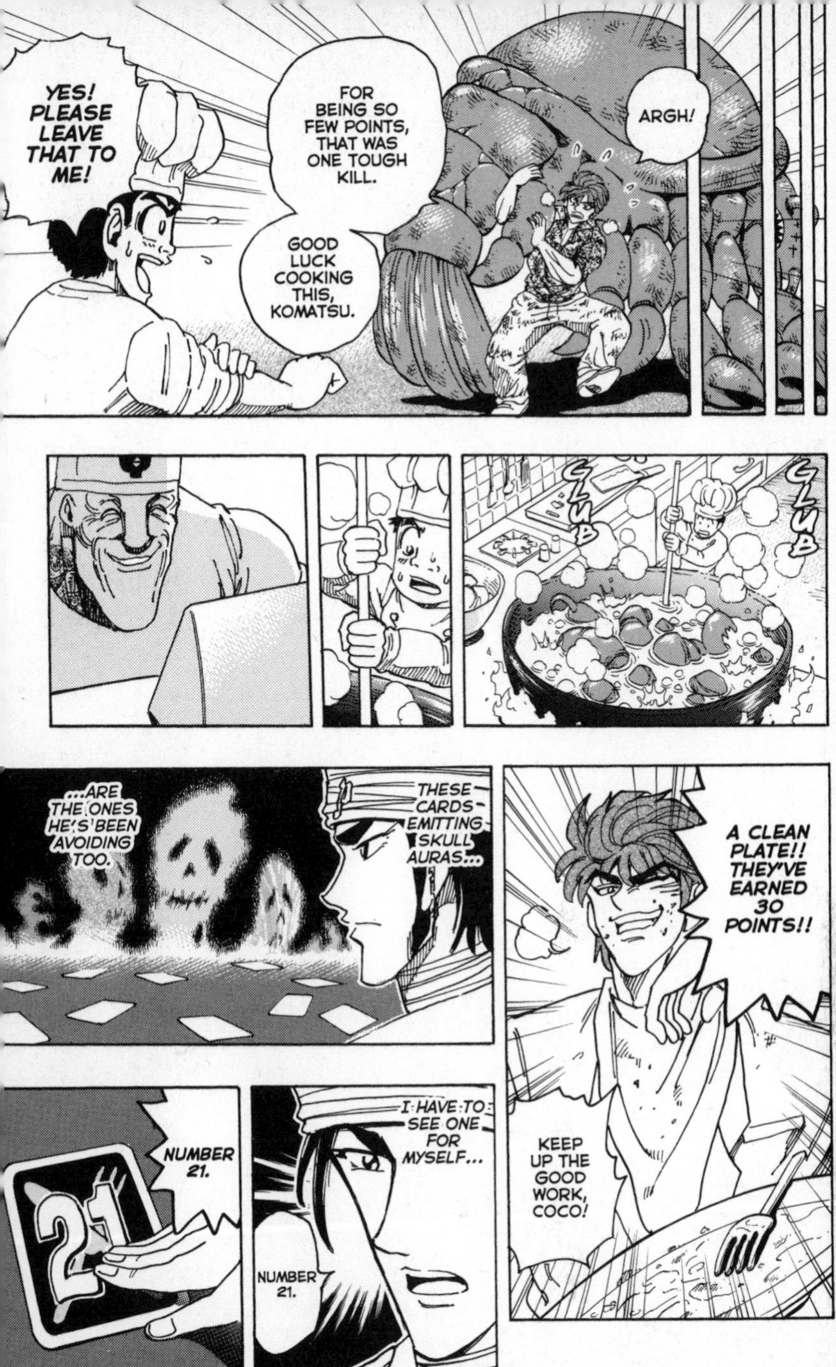
ARGH!
FOR BEING SO FEW POINTS, THAT WAS ONE TOUGH KILL.
GOOD LUCK COOKING THIS, KOMATSU.
YES! PLEASE LEAVE THAT TO ME!
GLUB
GLUB
A CLEAN PLATE!! THEY'VE EARNED 30 POINTS!!
KEEP UP THE GOOD WORK, COCO!
THESE CARDS EMITTING SKULL AURAS...
...ARE THE ONES HE'S BEEN AVOIDING TOO.
I HAVE TO SEE ONE FOR MYSELF...
NUMBER 21.
NUMBER 21.
21

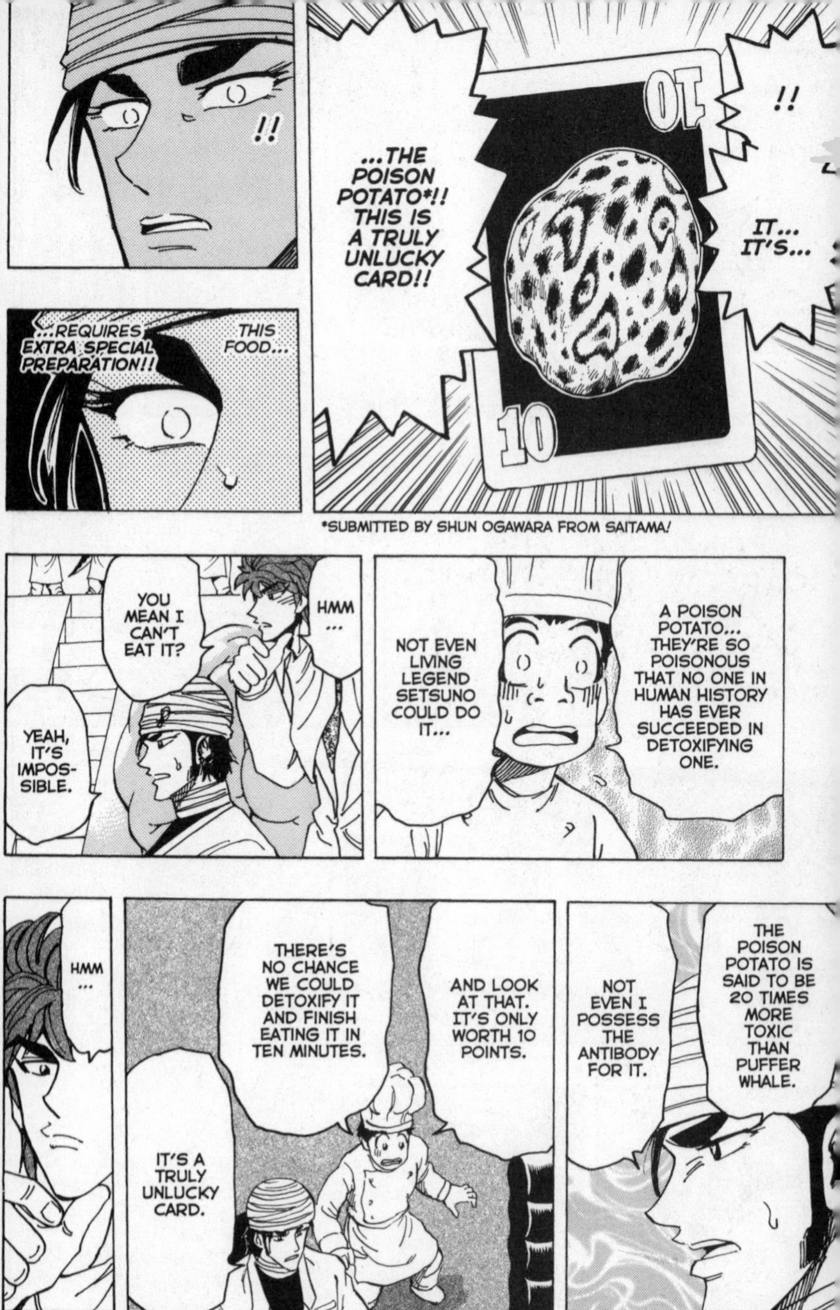
!!
IT... IT'S...
10
10
...THE POISON POTATO*!! THIS IS A TRULY UNLUCKY CARD!!
!!
THIS FOOD...
...REQUIRES EXTRA SPECIAL PREPARATION!!
A POISON POTATO... THEY'RE SO POISONOUS THAT NO ONE IN HUMAN HISTORY HAS EVER SUCCEEDED IN DETOXIFYING ONE.
NOT EVEN LIVING LEGEND SETSUNO COULD DO IT...
HMM ...
YOU MEAN I CAN'T EAT IT?
YEAH, IT'S IMPOSSIBLE.
THE POISON POTATO IS SAID TO BE 20 TIMES MORE TOXIC THAN PUFFER WHALE.
NOT EVEN I POSSESS THE ANTIBODY FOR IT.
AND LOOK AT THAT. IT'S ONLY WORTH 10 POINTS.
THERE'S NO CHANCE WE COULD DETOXIFY IT AND FINISH EATING IT IN TEN MINUTES.
IT'S A TRULY UNLUCKY CARD.
HMM ...

*SUBMITTED BY SHUN OGAWARA FROM SAITAMA!

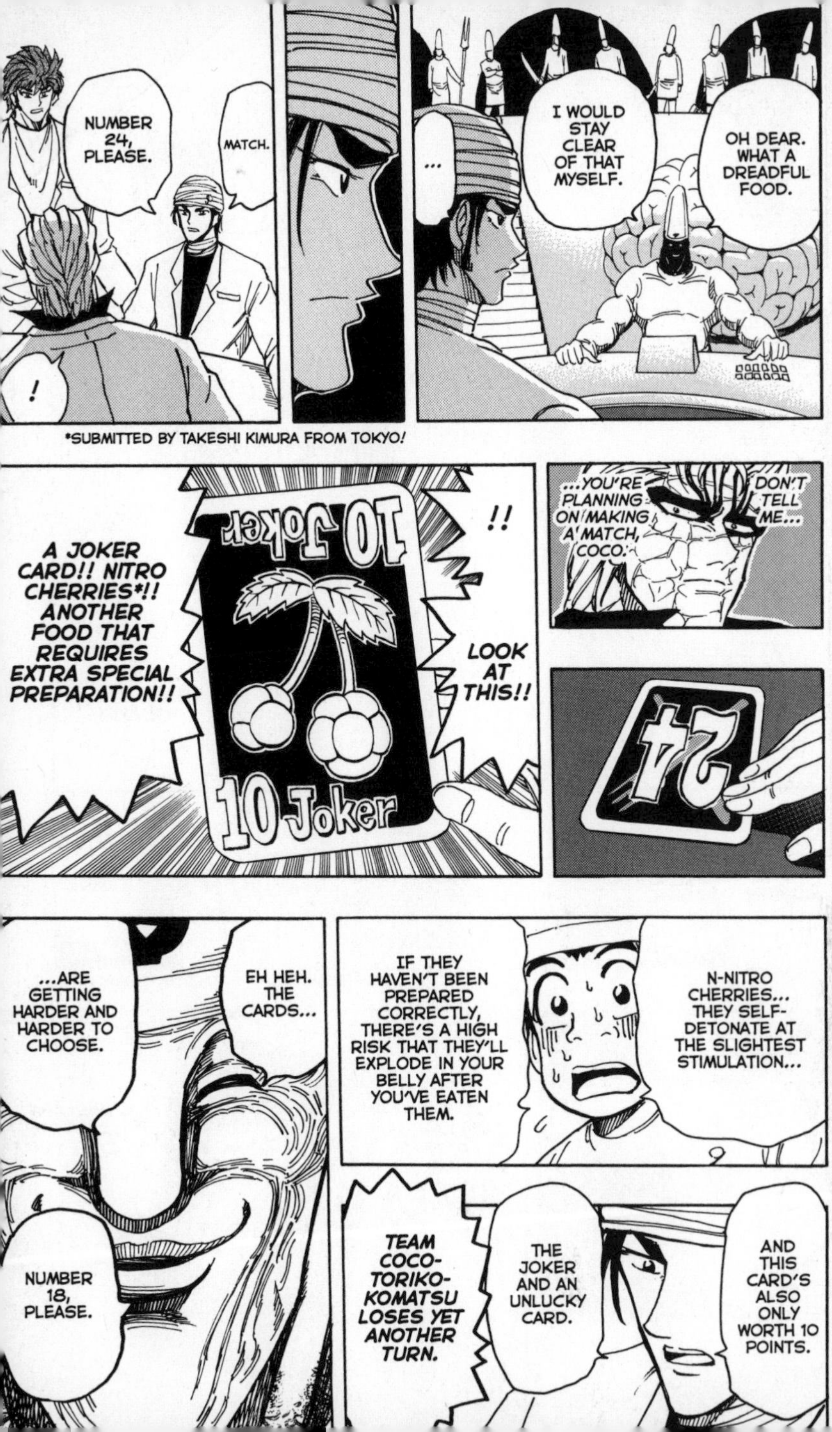
OH DEAR. WHAT A DREADFUL FOOD.
I WOULD STAY CLEAR OF THAT MYSELF.
...
MATCH.
NUMBER 24, PLEASE.
!
*SUBMITTED BY TAKESHI KIMURA FROM TOKYO!
DON'T TELL ME...
...YOU'RE PLANNING ON MAKING A MATCH, COCO.
24
!!
LOOK AT THIS!!
10 Joker
10 Joker
A JOKER CARD!! NITRO CHERRIES*!! ANOTHER FOOD THAT REQUIRES EXTRA SPECIAL PREPARATION!!
N-NITRO CHERRIES... THEY SELF-DETONATE AT THE SLIGHTEST STIMULATION...
IF THEY HAVEN'T BEEN PREPARED CORRECTLY, THERE'S A HIGH RISK THAT THEY'LL EXPLODE IN YOUR BELLY AFTER YOU'VE EATEN THEM.
AND THIS CARD'S ALSO ONLY WORTH 10 POINTS.
THE JOKER AND AN UNLUCKY CARD.
TEAM COCO-TORIKO-KOMATSU LOSES YET ANOTHER TURN.
EH HEH. THE CARDS...
...ARE GETTING HARDER AND HARDER TO CHOOSE.
NUMBER 18, PLEASE.

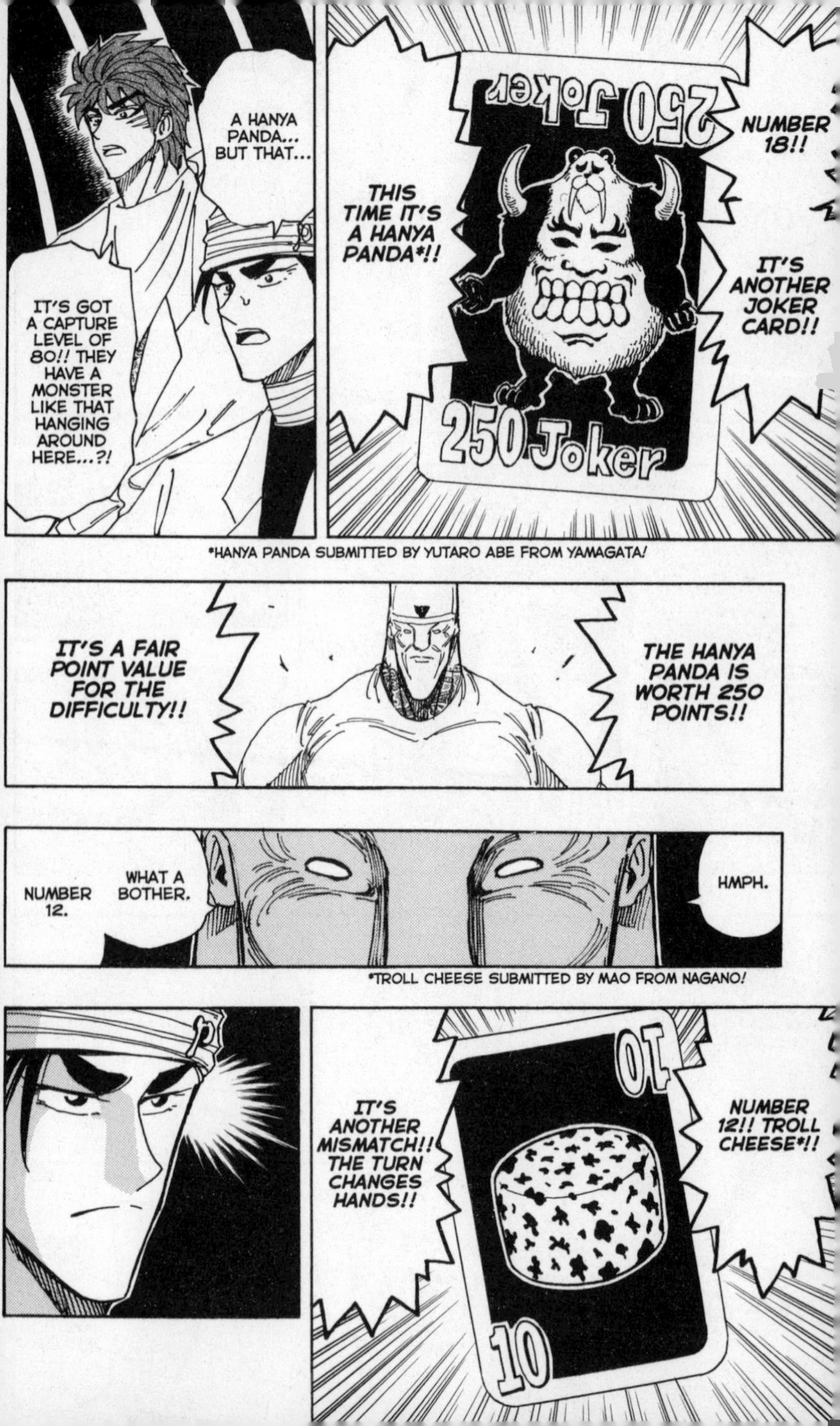
250 Joker
NUMBER 18!!
IT'S ANOTHER JOKER CARD!!
THIS TIME IT'S A HANYA PANDA*!!
250 Joker
A HANYA PANDA... BUT THAT...
IT'S GOT A CAPTURE LEVEL OF 80!! THEY HAVE A MONSTER LIKE THAT HANGING AROUND HERE...?!
*HANYA PANDA SUBMITTED BY YUTARO ABE FROM YAMAGATA!
THE HANYA PANDA IS WORTH 250 POINTS!!
IT'S A FAIR POINT VALUE FOR THE DIFFICULTY!!
HMPH.
WHAT A BOTHER.
NUMBER 12.
*TROLL CHEESE SUBMITTED BY MAO FROM NAGANO!
10
NUMBER 12!! TROLL CHEESE*!!
IT'S ANOTHER MISMATCH!! THE TURN CHANGES HANDS!!
10

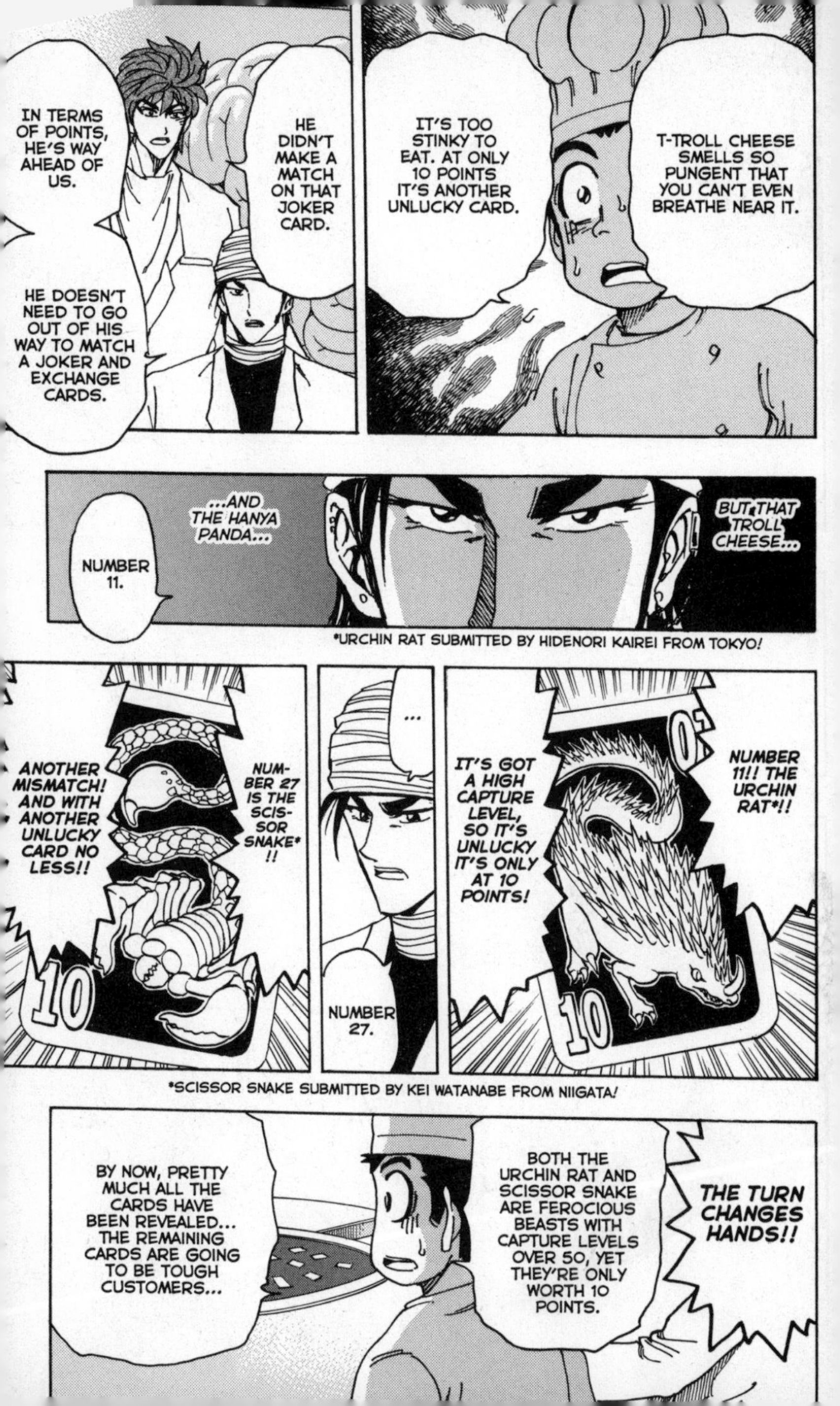
T-TROLL CHEESE SMELLS SO PUNGENT THAT YOU CAN'T EVEN BREATHE NEAR IT.
IT'S TOO STINKY TO EAT. AT ONLY 10 POINTS IT'S ANOTHER UNLUCKY CARD.
HE DIDN'T MAKE A MATCH ON THAT JOKER CARD.
IN TERMS OF POINTS, HE'S WAY AHEAD OF US.
HE DOESN'T NEED TO GO OUT OF HIS WAY TO MATCH A JOKER AND EXCHANGE CARDS.
BUT THAT TROLL CHEESE...
...AND THE HANYA PANDA...
NUMBER 11.
NUMBER 11!! THE URCHIN RAT*!!
10
IT'S GOT A HIGH CAPTURE LEVEL, SO IT'S UNLUCKY IT'S ONLY AT 10 POINTS!
...
NUMBER 27.
NUM-BER 27 IS THE SCIS-SOR SNAKE* !!
ANOTHER MISMATCH! AND WITH ANOTHER UNLUCKY CARD NO LESS!!
10
THE TURN CHANGES HANDS!!
BOTH THE URCHIN RAT AND SCISSOR SNAKE ARE FEROCIOUS BEASTS WITH CAPTURE LEVELS OVER 50, YET THEY'RE ONLY WORTH 10 POINTS.
BY NOW, PRETTY MUCH ALL THE CARDS HAVE BEEN REVEALED... THE REMAINING CARDS ARE GOING TO BE TOUGH CUSTOMERS...

*URCHIN RAT SUBMITTED BY HIDENORI KAIREI FROM TOKYO!

*SCISSOR SNAKE SUBMITTED BY KEI WATANABE FROM NIIGATA!

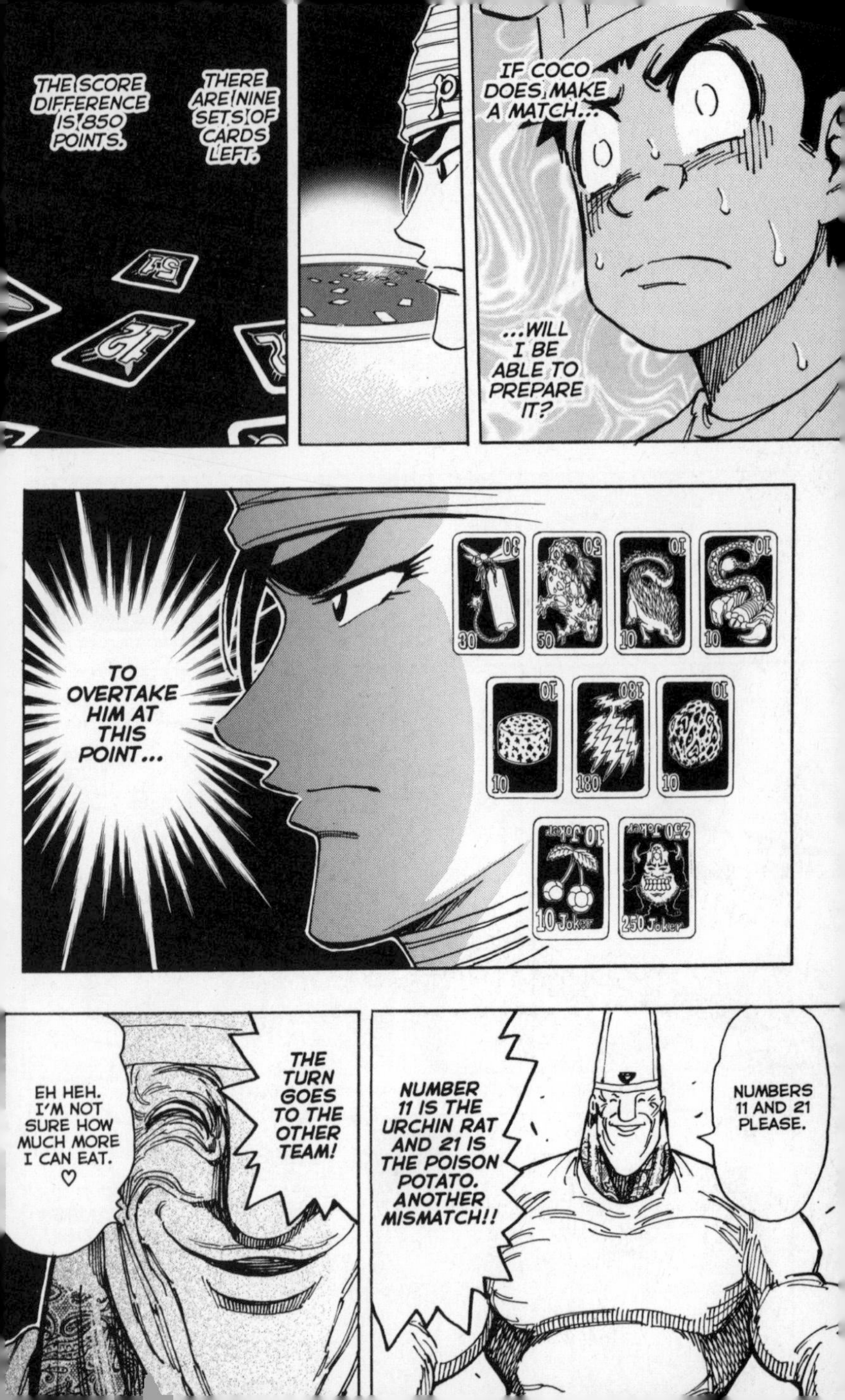
IF COCO DOES MAKE A MATCH...
...WILL I BE ABLE TO PREPARE IT?
THERE ARE NINE SETS OF CARDS LEFT.
THE SCORE DIFFERENCE IS 850 POINTS.
30
50
10
10
10
180
10
10 Joker
250 Joker
TO OVERTAKE HIM AT THIS POINT...
NUMBERS 11 AND 21 PLEASE.
NUMBER 11 IS THE URCHIN RAT AND 21 IS THE POISON POTATO. ANOTHER MISMATCH!!
THE TURN GOES TO THE OTHER TEAM!
EH HEH. I'M NOT SURE HOW MUCH MORE I CAN EAT. ♡

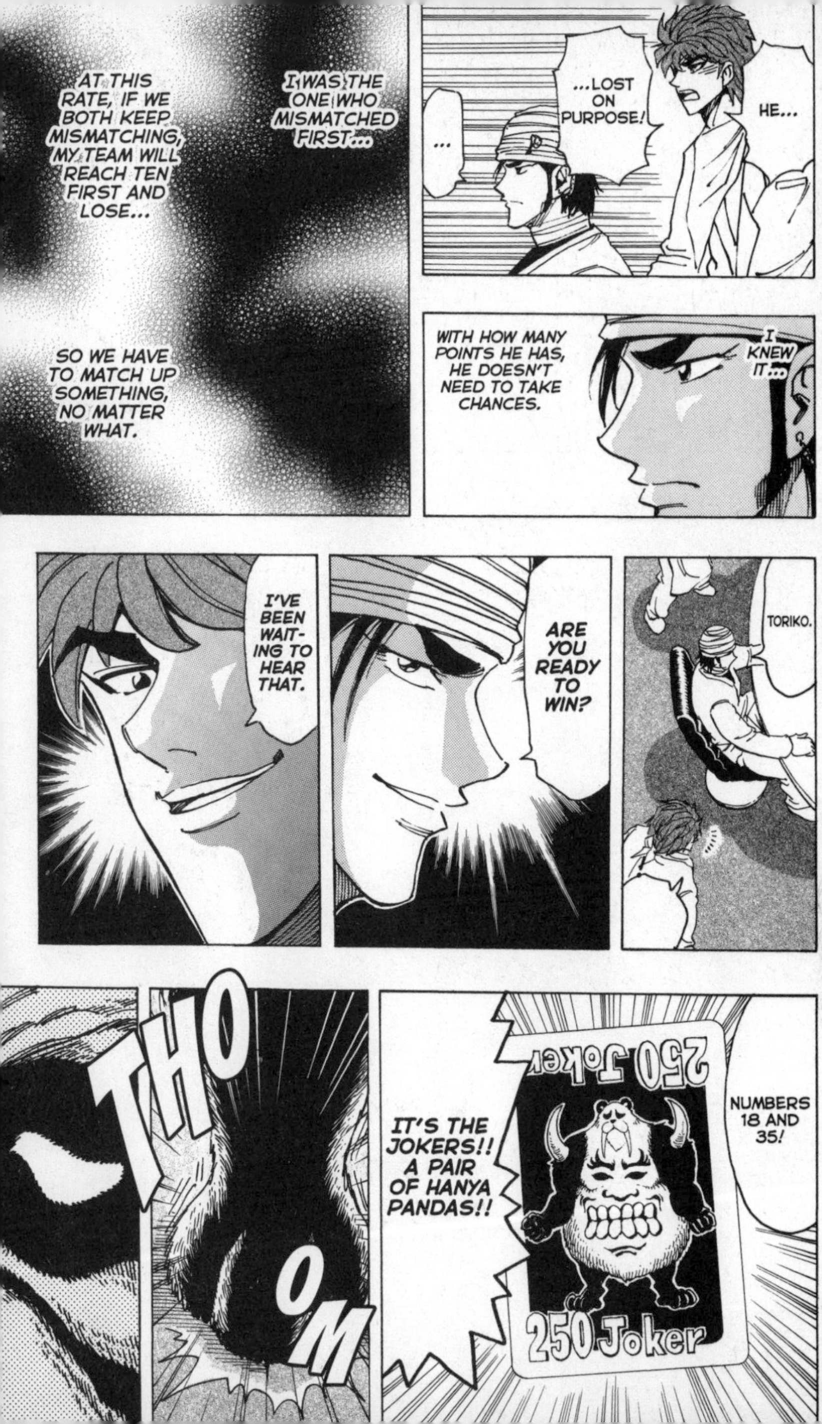
HE...
...LOST ON PURPOSE!
...
I KNEW IT...
WITH HOW MANY POINTS HE HAS, HE DOESN'T NEED TO TAKE CHANCES.
I WAS THE ONE WHO MISMATCHED FIRST...
AT THIS RATE, IF WE BOTH KEEP MISMATCHING, MY TEAM WILL REACH TEN FIRST AND LOSE...
SO WE HAVE TO MATCH UP SOMETHING, NO MATTER WHAT.
TORIKO.
ARE YOU READY TO WIN?
I'VE BEEN WAITING TO HEAR THAT.
NUMBERS 18 AND 35!
250 Joker
250 Joker
IT'S THE JOKERS!! A PAIR OF HANYA PANDAS!!
THOOM

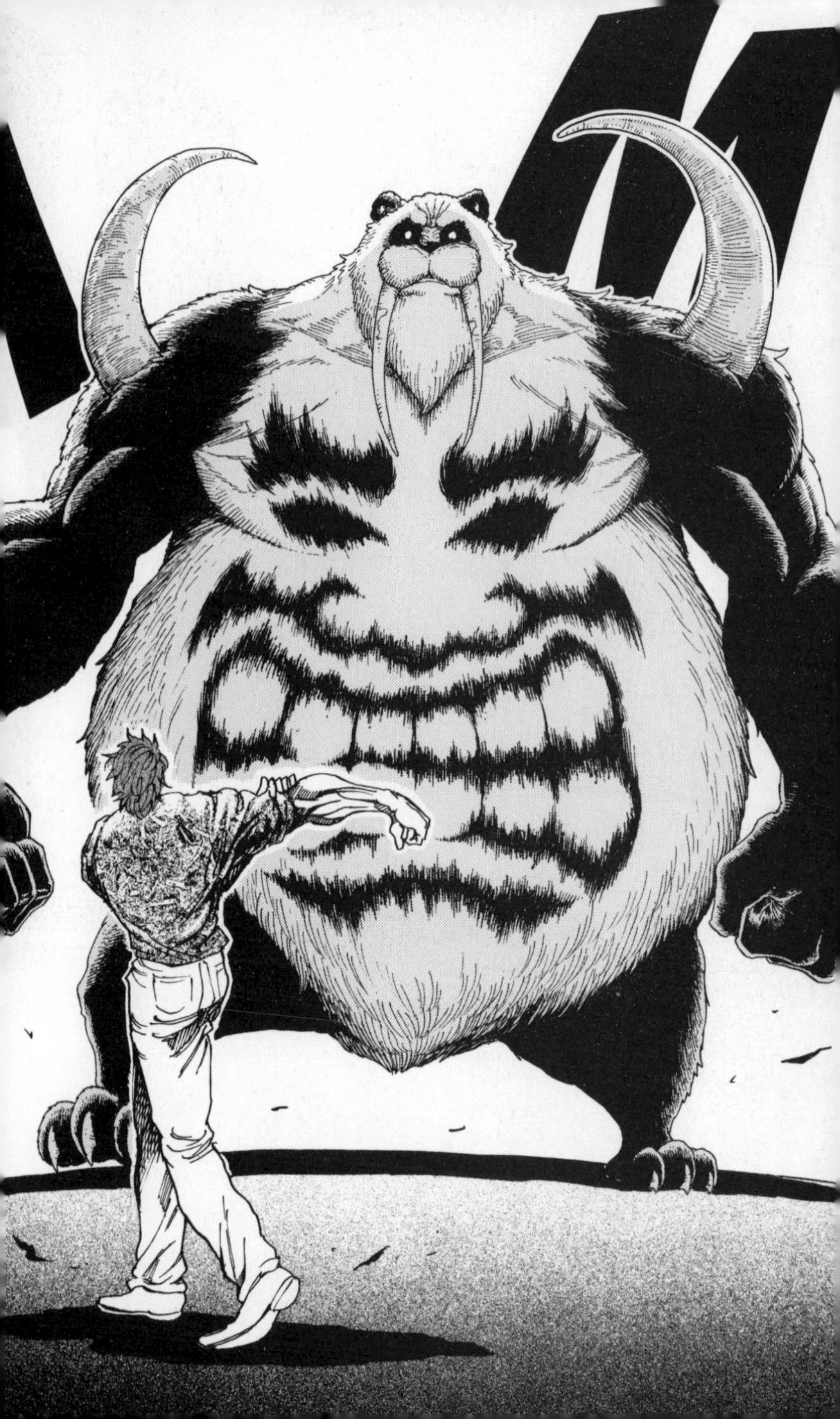

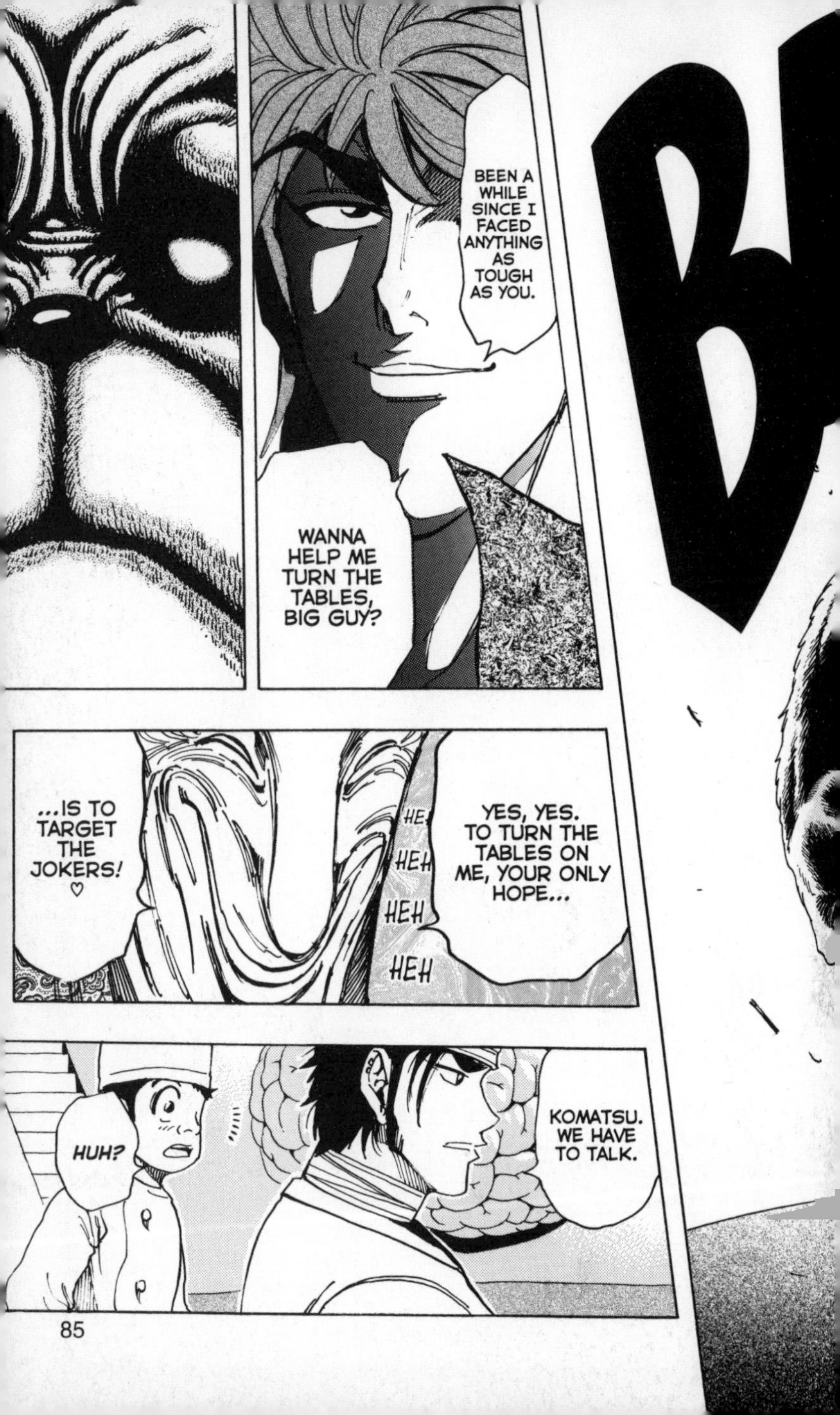
B
BEEN A WHILE SINCE I FACED ANYTHING AS TOUGH AS YOU.
WANNA HELP ME TURN THE TABLES, BIG GUY?
YES, YES. TO TURN THE TABLES ON ME, YOUR ONLY HOPE...
HE HEH HEH HEH
...IS TO TARGET THE JOKERS! ♡
KOMATSU. WE HAVE TO TALK.
HUH?

TORIKO

GOURMET CHECKLIST
Vol. 197

TIGER FANG
(MAMMAL)

CAPTURE LEVEL: 35
HABITAT: GOURMET PYRAMID
LENGTH: 8 METERS
HEIGHT: 3.5 METERS
WEIGHT: 10 TONS
PRICE: 100 G / 300 YEN; 100 G / 20,000 YEN (TONGUE)

TIGER FANG*
(MAMMAL)
CAPTURE LEVEL 35

SCALE

A CREATURE THAT RESIDES IN GOURMET PYRAMID'S LOWER LEVELS. ITS CLAWS ARE AS SHARP AS TORIKO'S KNIFE ATTACKS. BECAUSE IT LIVES IN SUCH A DARK ENVIRONMENT, IT HAS SUPERIOR HEARING. IT CAN EVEN HEAR THE FOOTSTEPS OF PREY TWO KILOMETERS AWAY! THE FUR ON ITS TAIL IS AS TOUGH AS A WHIP AND THE POWER OF ITS HIND LEGS IS SUCH THAT ONE KICK CAN PUNCH A CRATER INTO THE EARTH. IT WOULD BE NO EXAGGERATION TO SAY THAT ITS ENTIRE BODY IS A LETHAL WEAPON. BECAUSE THE TIGER FANG'S MUSCLES ARE SO SPRINGY, IT WOULD BE A GROSS OVERSTATEMENT TO SAY IT TASTES ANY GOOD. THE TONGUE, HOWEVER, IS PRETTY TASTY.

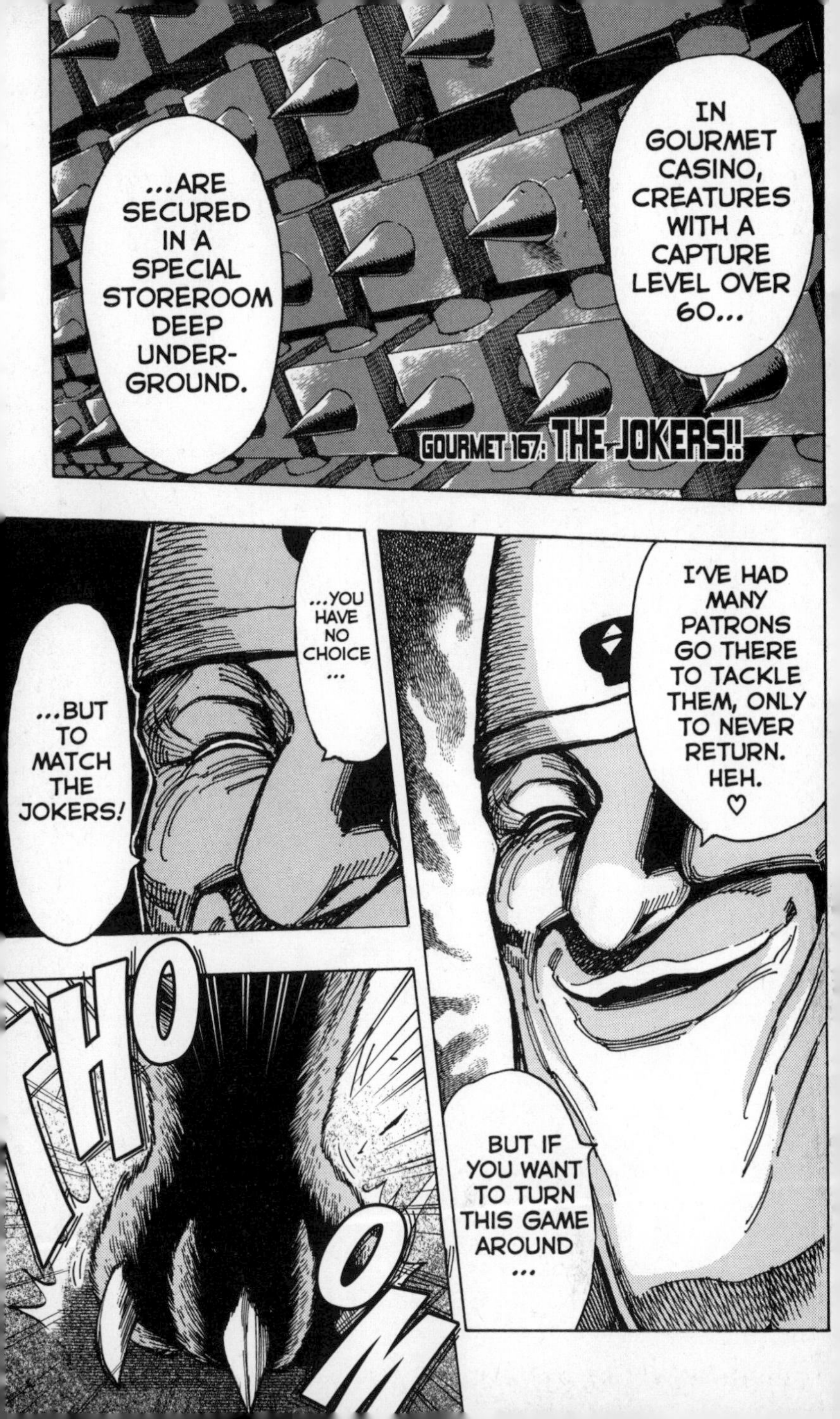
IN GOURMET CASINO, CREATURES WITH A CAPTURE LEVEL OVER 60...
...ARE SECURED IN A SPECIAL STOREROOM DEEP UNDERGROUND.
GOURMET 167: THE JOKERS!!
I'VE HAD MANY PATRONS GO THERE TO TACKLE THEM, ONLY TO NEVER RETURN. HEH. ♡
BUT IF YOU WANT TO TURN THIS GAME AROUND...
...YOU HAVE NO CHOICE...
...BUT TO MATCH THE JOKERS!
HOOM

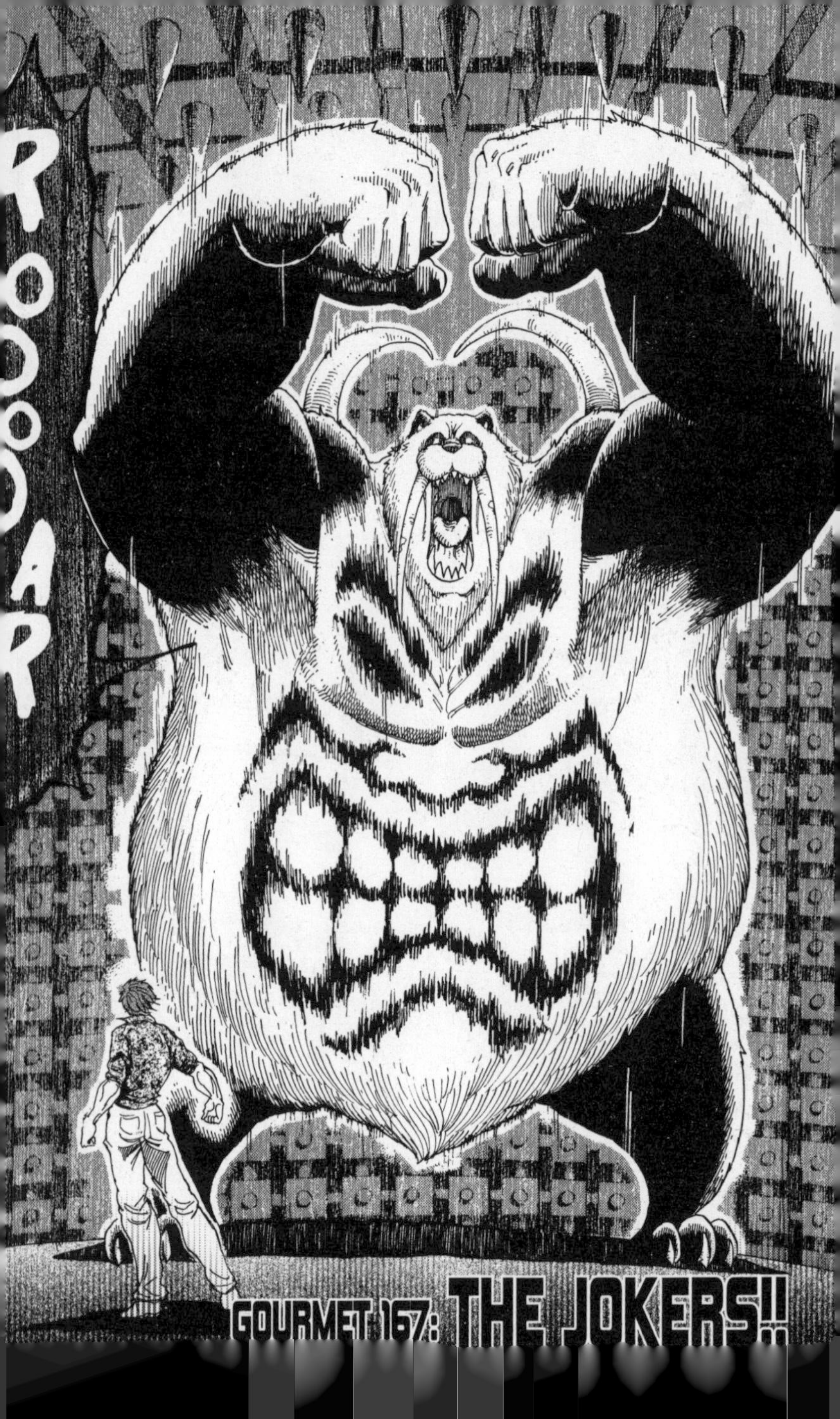
ROOOOAR
GOURMET 167: THE JOKERS!!

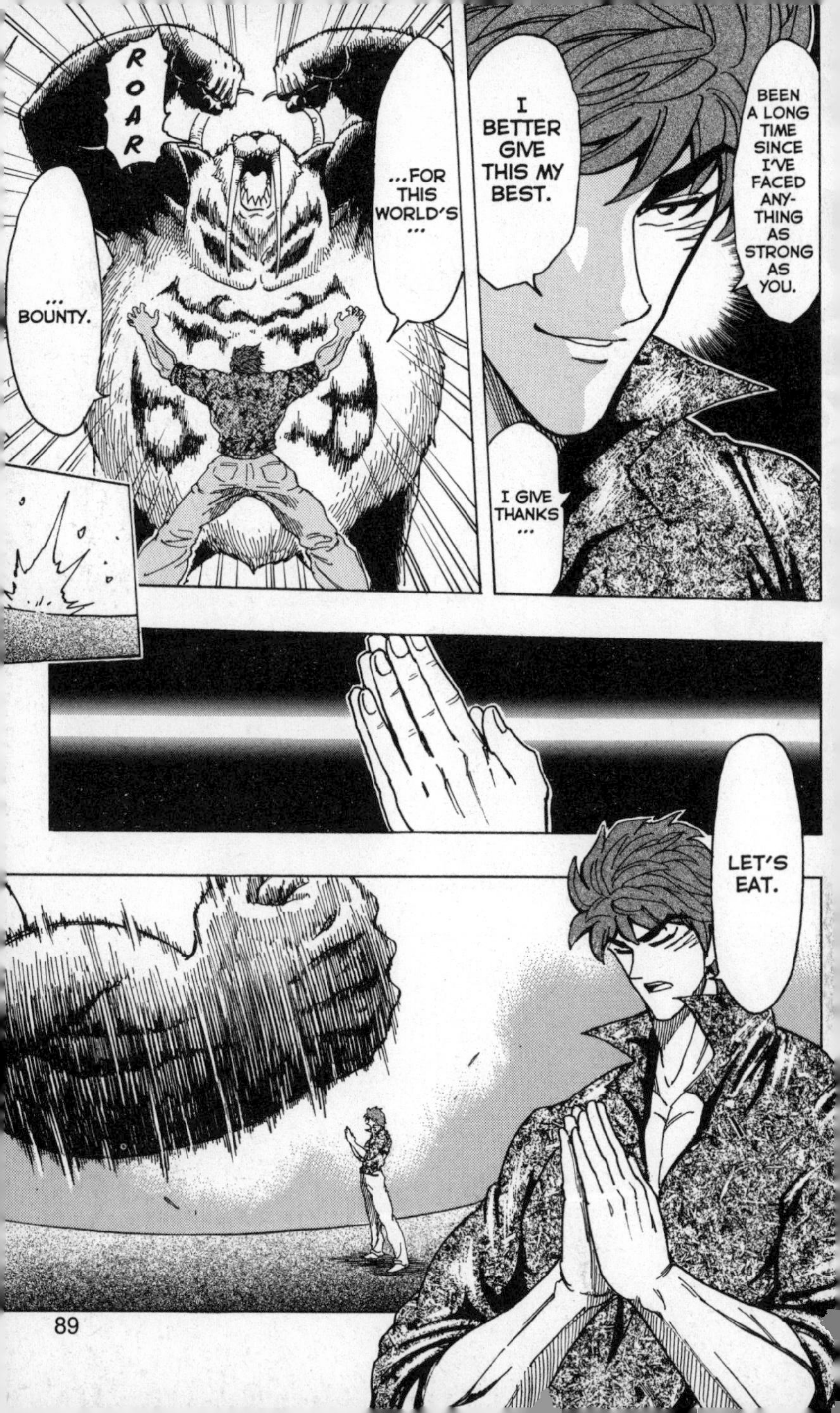
BEEN A LONG TIME SINCE I'VE FACED ANY-THING AS STRONG AS YOU.
I BETTER GIVE THIS MY BEST.
I GIVE THANKS...
ROAR
...FOR THIS WORLD'S...
...BOUNTY.
LET'S EAT.

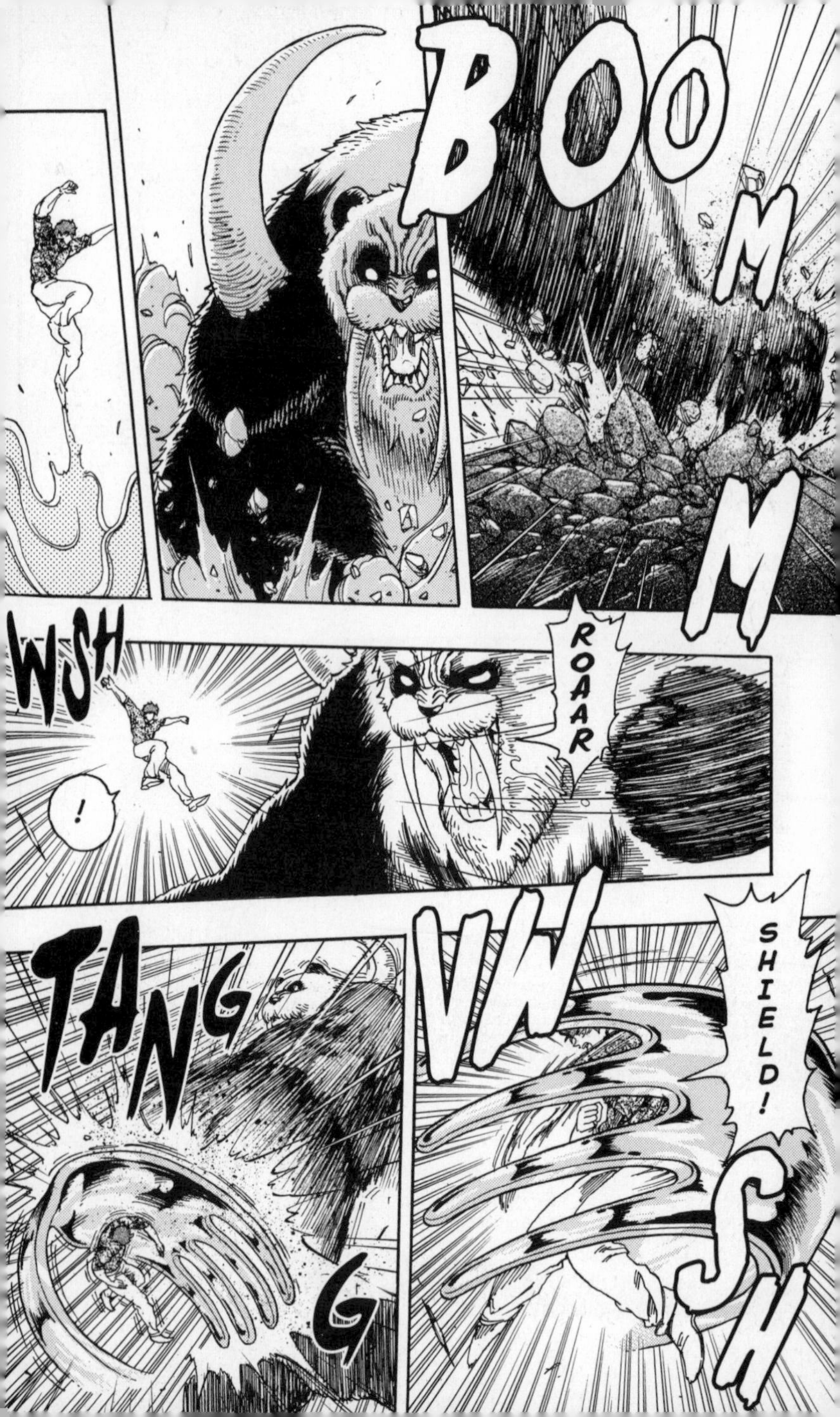
BOOMM
ROAAR
WSH
!
SHIELD!
VW
SH
TANGG

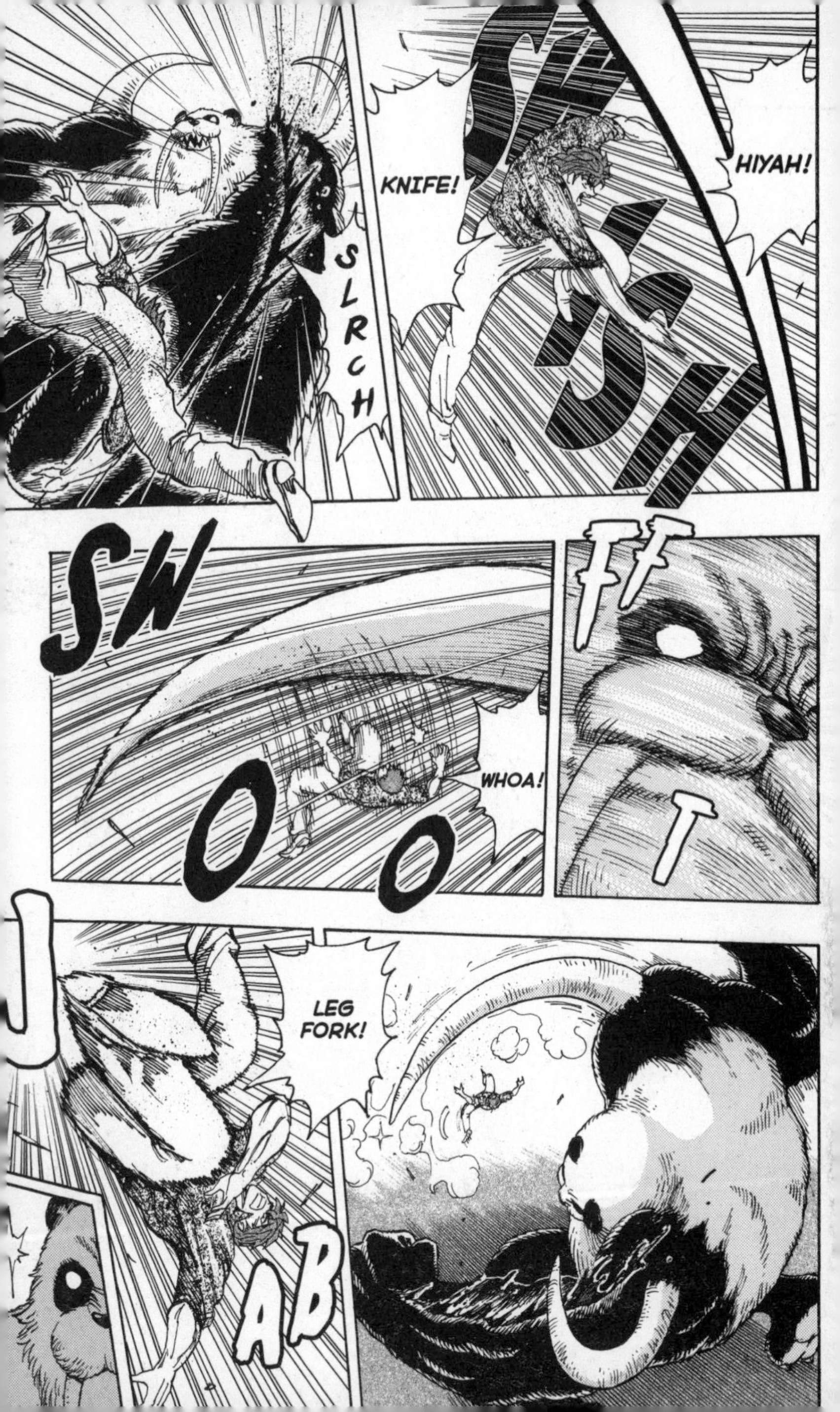
HIYAH!
KNIFE!
SLRCH
FFT
SWOO
WHOA!
LEG FORK!
JAB

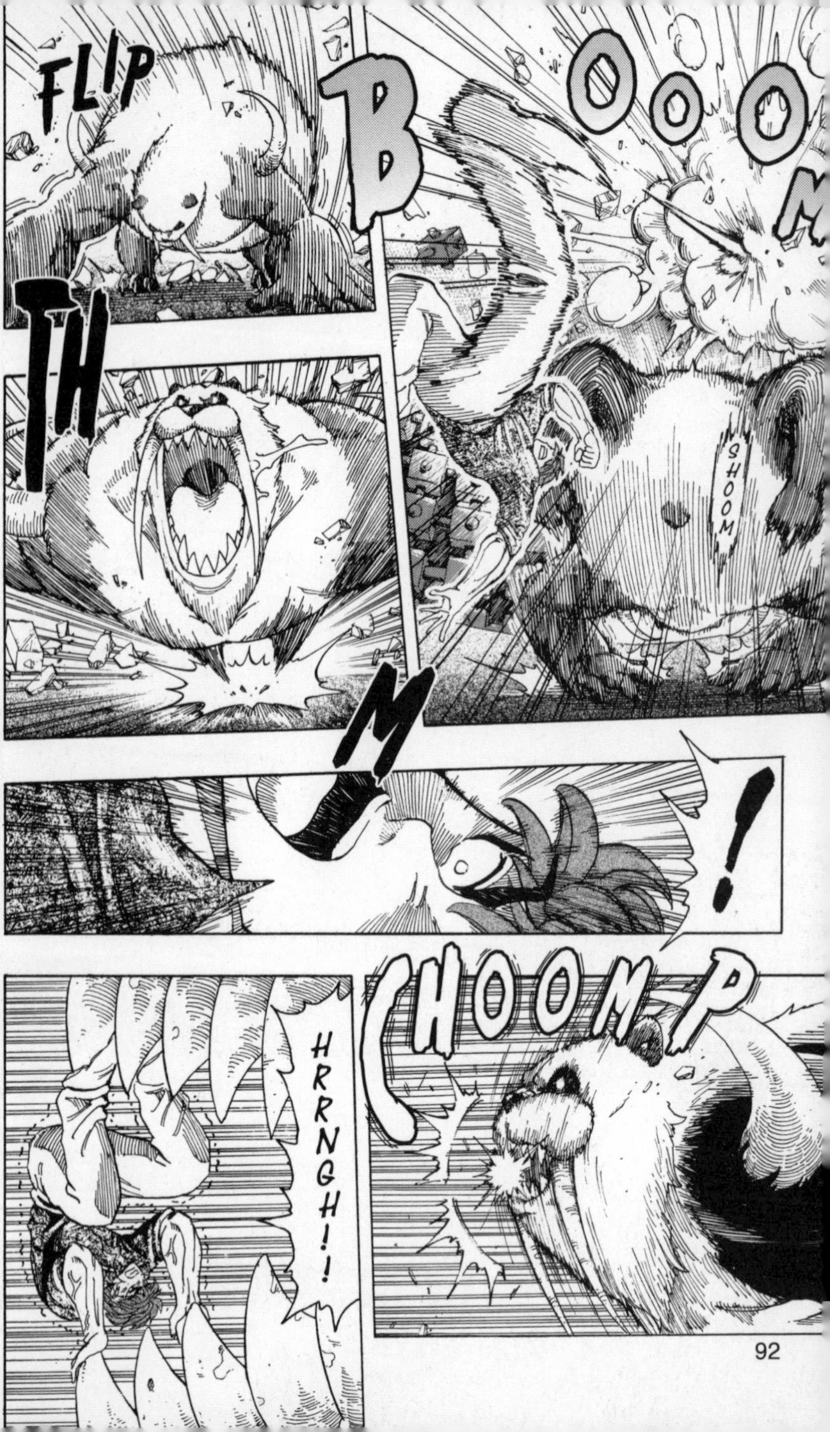
BOOOM
SHOOM
FLIP
TH
M
!
CHOOMP
HRRNGH!!

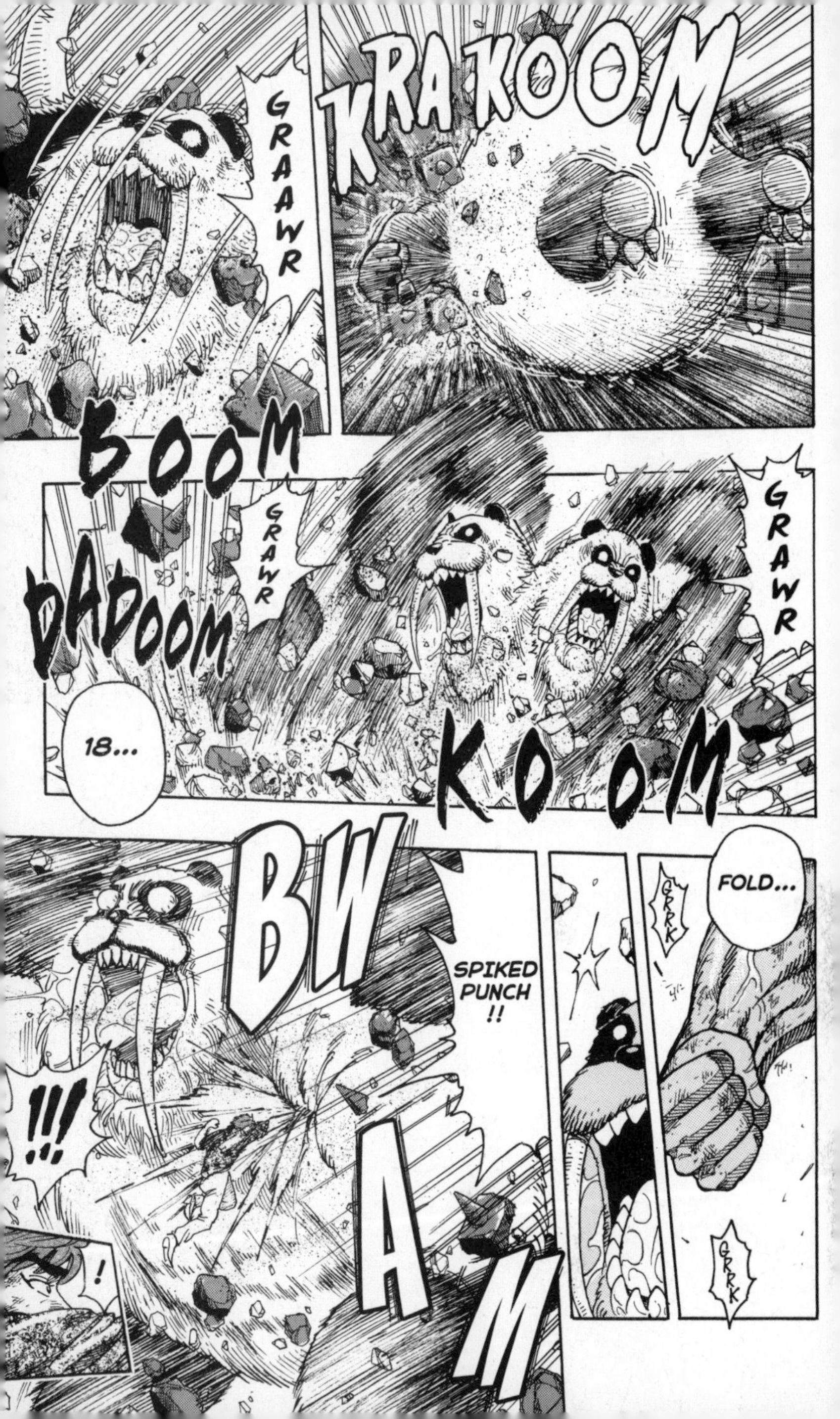

KRAKOOM
GRAAWR
GRAWR
GRAWR
BOOM
DADOOM
KOOM
18...
FOLD...
GRRK
GRRK
SPIKED PUNCH !!
BWAM
!!!
!

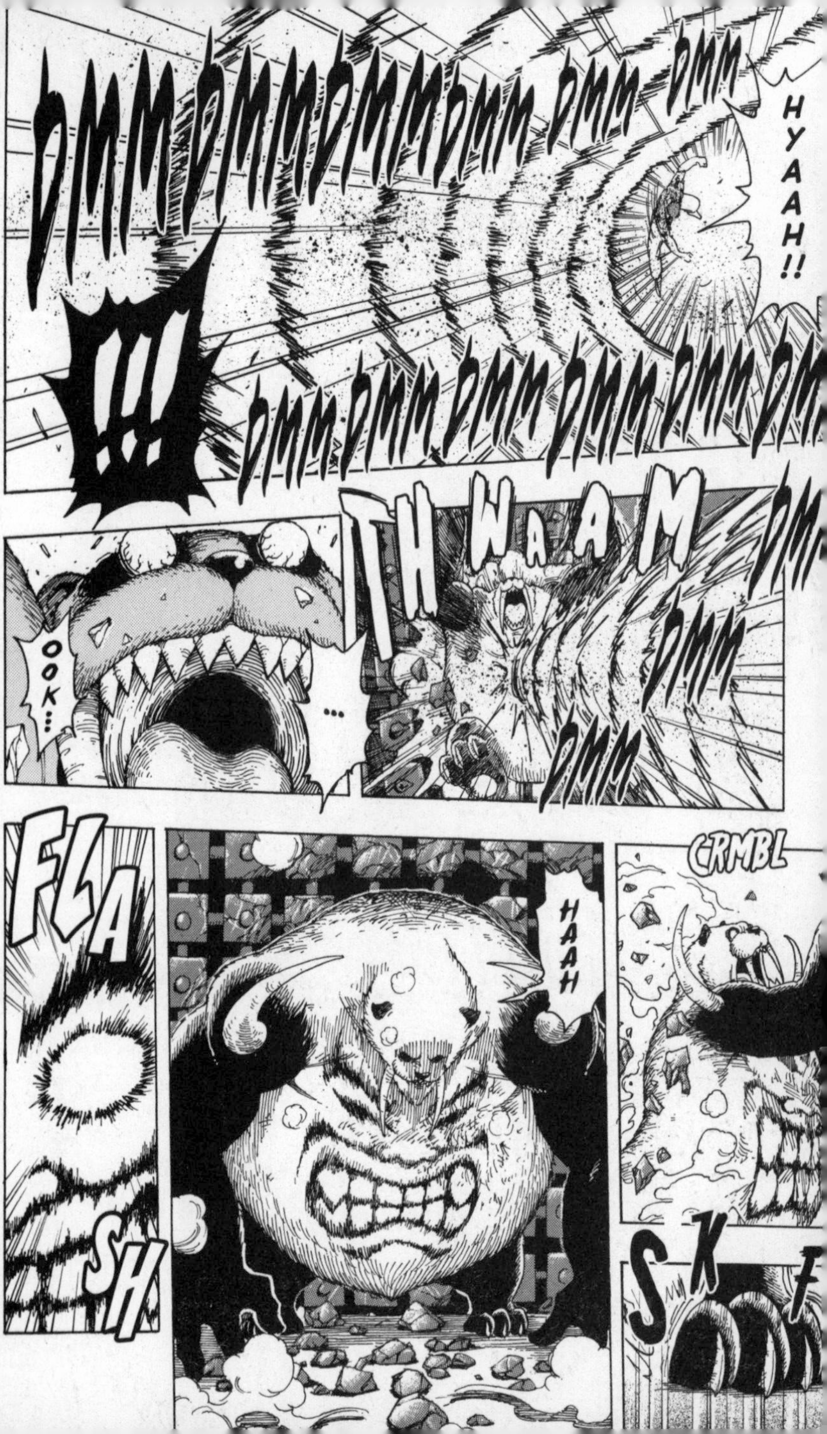
HYAAAH!!
DMM DMM DMM DMM DMM DMM
!!
DMM DMM DMM DMM DMM DMM
THWAAM
DMM DMM DMM DMM
OOK...
...
CRMBL
SK
HAAAH
FLASH

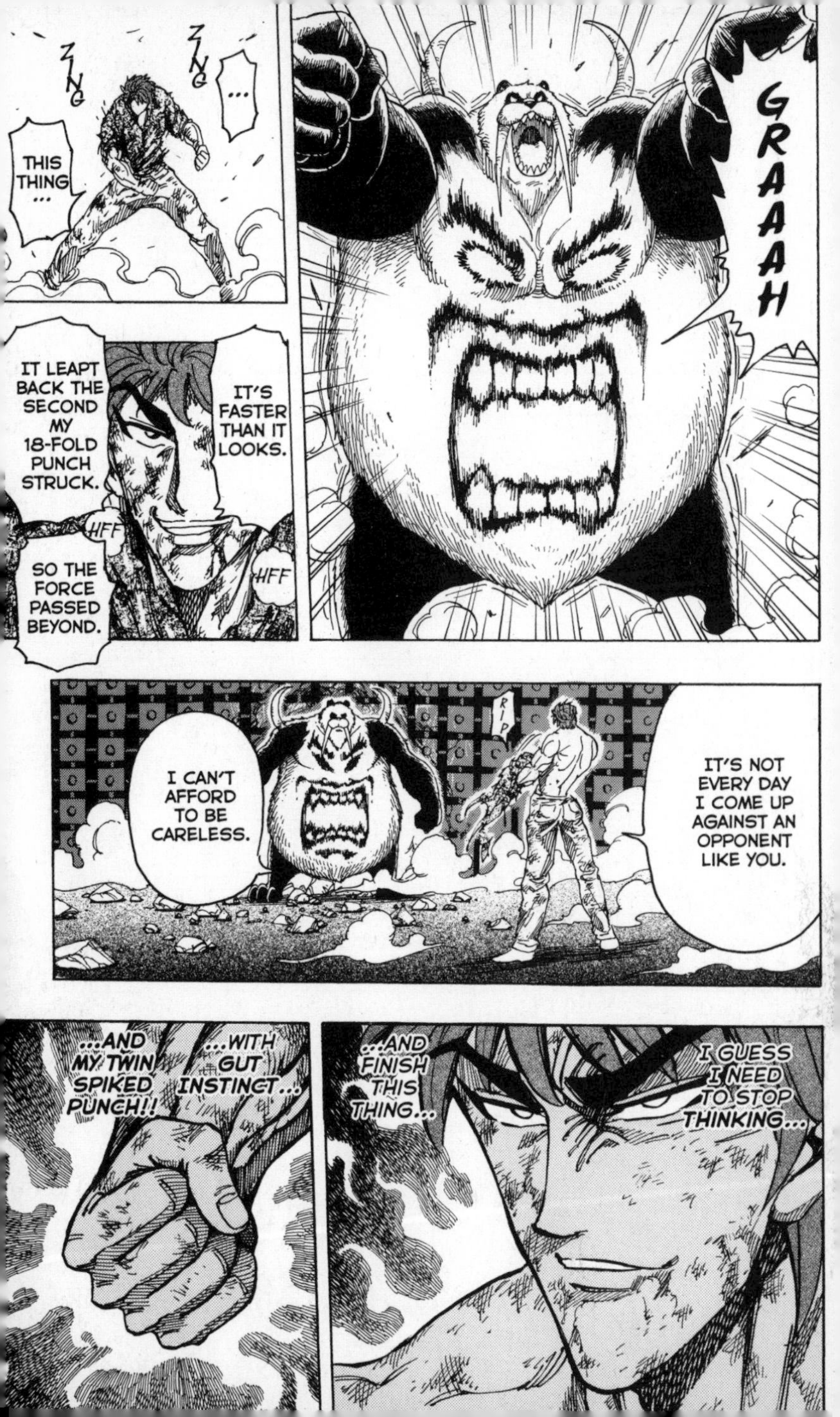
GRAAAAH
...
ZING
ZING
THIS THING...
IT'S FASTER THAN IT LOOKS.
IT LEAPT BACK THE SECOND MY 18-FOLD PUNCH STRUCK.
HFF
HFF
SO THE FORCE PASSED BEYOND.
IT'S NOT EVERY DAY I COME UP AGAINST AN OPPONENT LIKE YOU.
RIP
I CAN'T AFFORD TO BE CARELESS.
I GUESS I NEED TO STOP THINKING...
...AND FINISH THIS THING...
...WITH GUT INSTINCT...
...AND MY TWIN SPIKED PUNCH!!

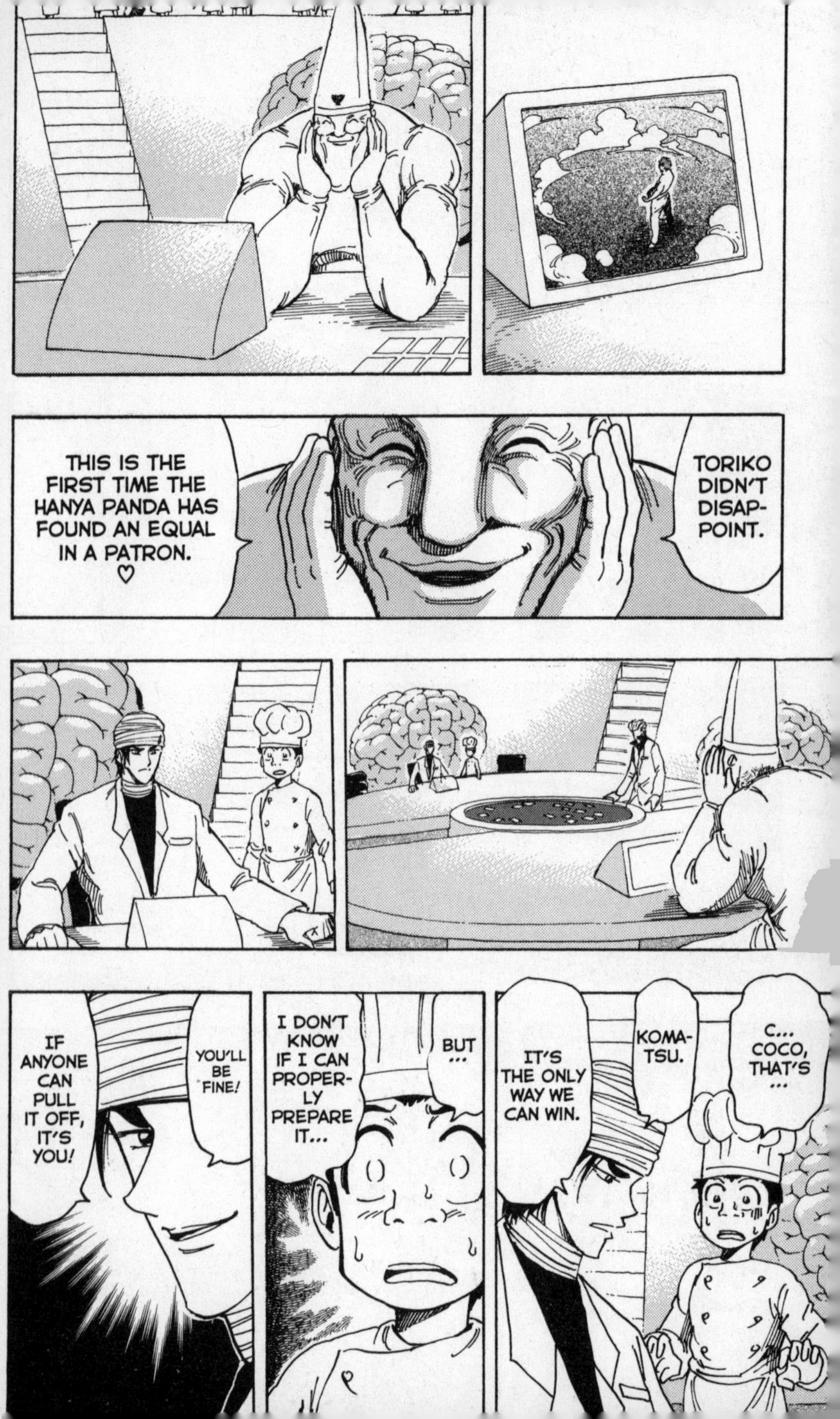
TORIKO DIDN'T DISAP-POINT.
THIS IS THE FIRST TIME THE HANYA PANDA HAS FOUND AN EQUAL IN A PATRON. ♡
C... COCO, THAT'S ...
KOMA-TSU.
IT'S THE ONLY WAY WE CAN WIN.
BUT ...
I DON'T KNOW IF I CAN PROPER-LY PREPARE IT...
YOU'LL BE FINE!
IF ANYONE CAN PULL IT OFF, IT'S YOU!

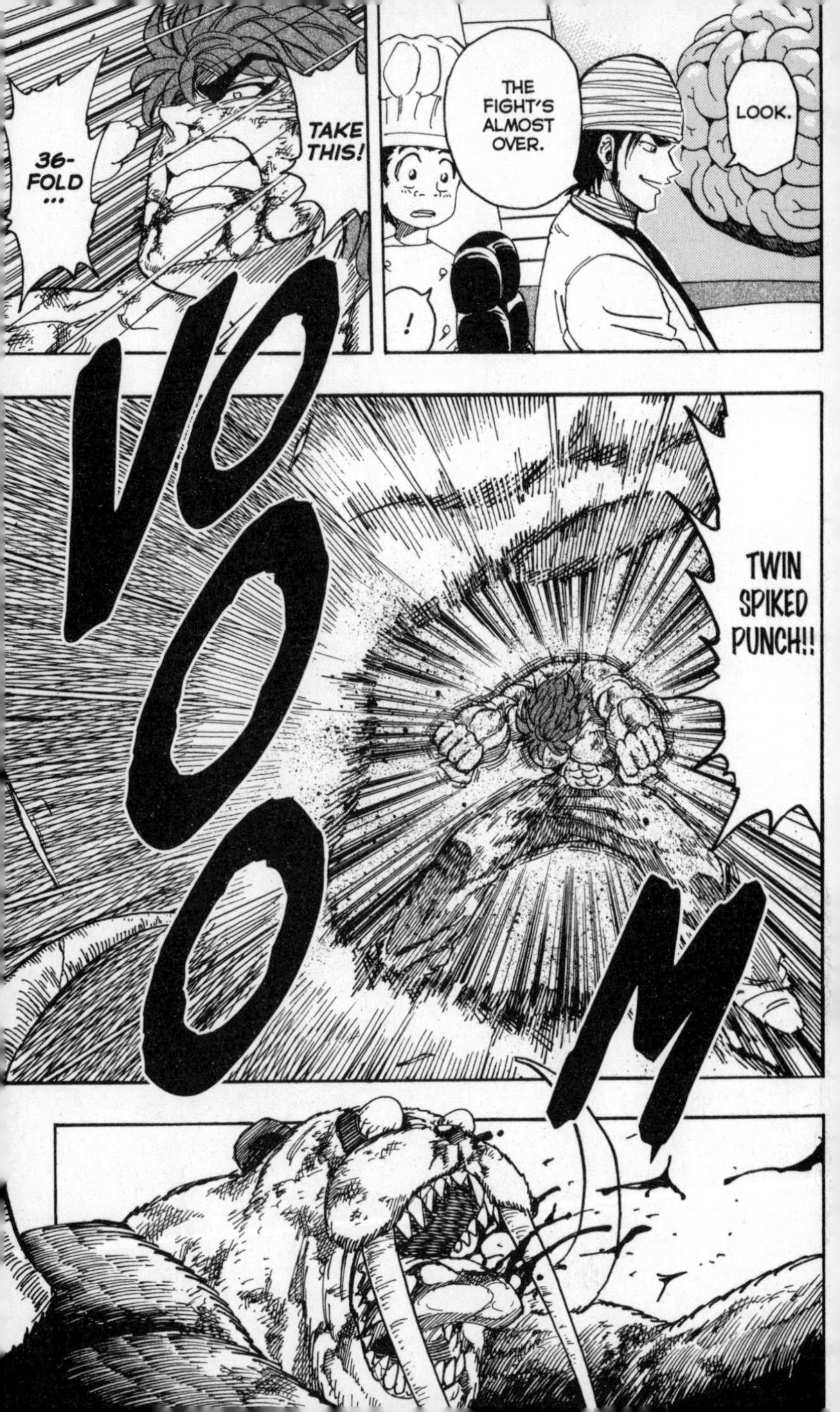
LOOK.
THE FIGHT'S ALMOST OVER.
!
TAKE THIS!
36-FOLD...
TWIN SPIKED PUNCH!!
SOOM

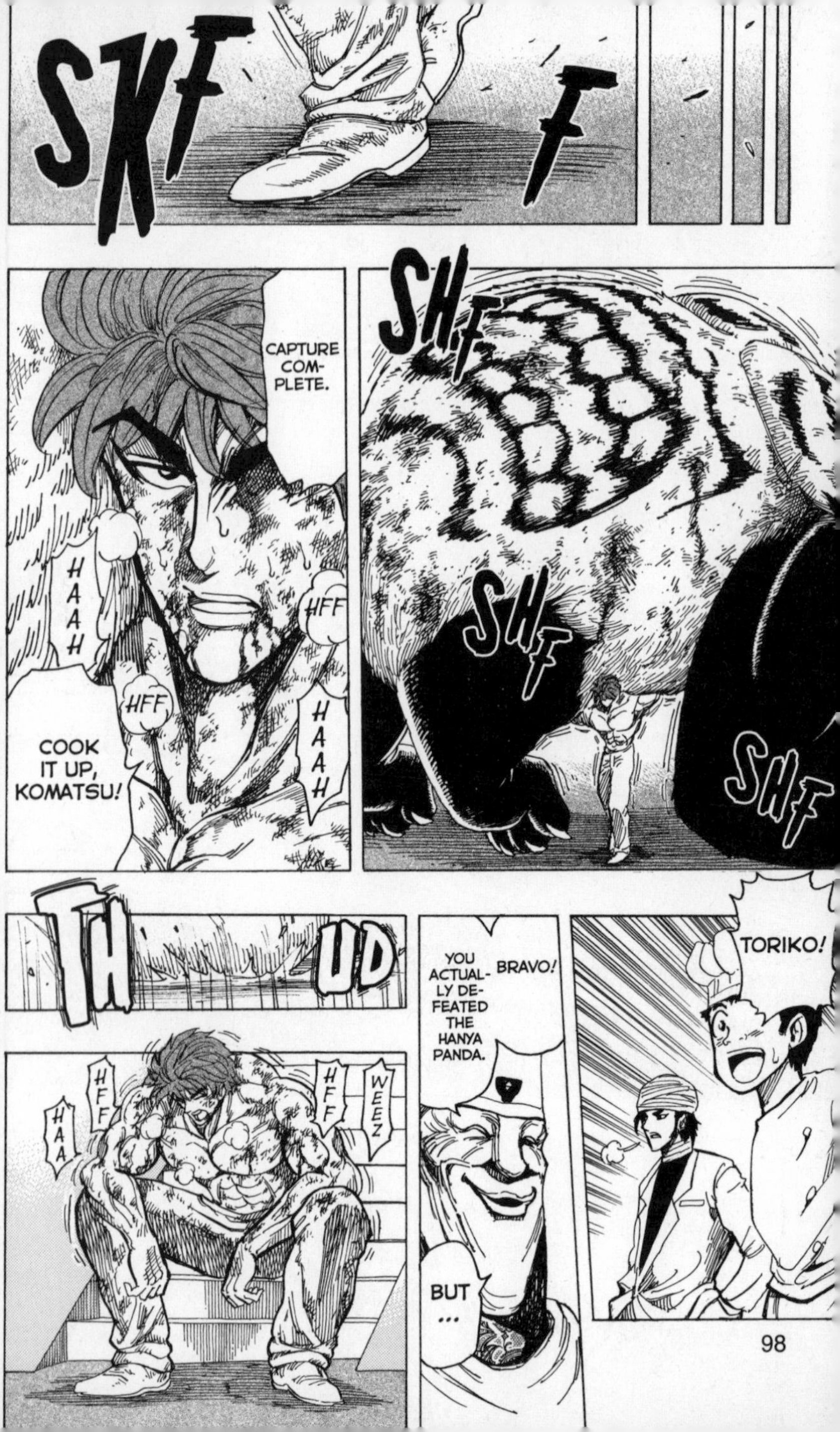
SKF
F
SHF
SHF
SHF
CAPTURE COMPLETE.
HAAAH
HFF
HFF
HAAAH
COOK IT UP, KOMATSU!
TORIKO!
BRAVO!
YOU ACTUALLY DEFEATED THE HANYA PANDA.
BUT...
THUD
WEEZ
HFF
HFF
HAA

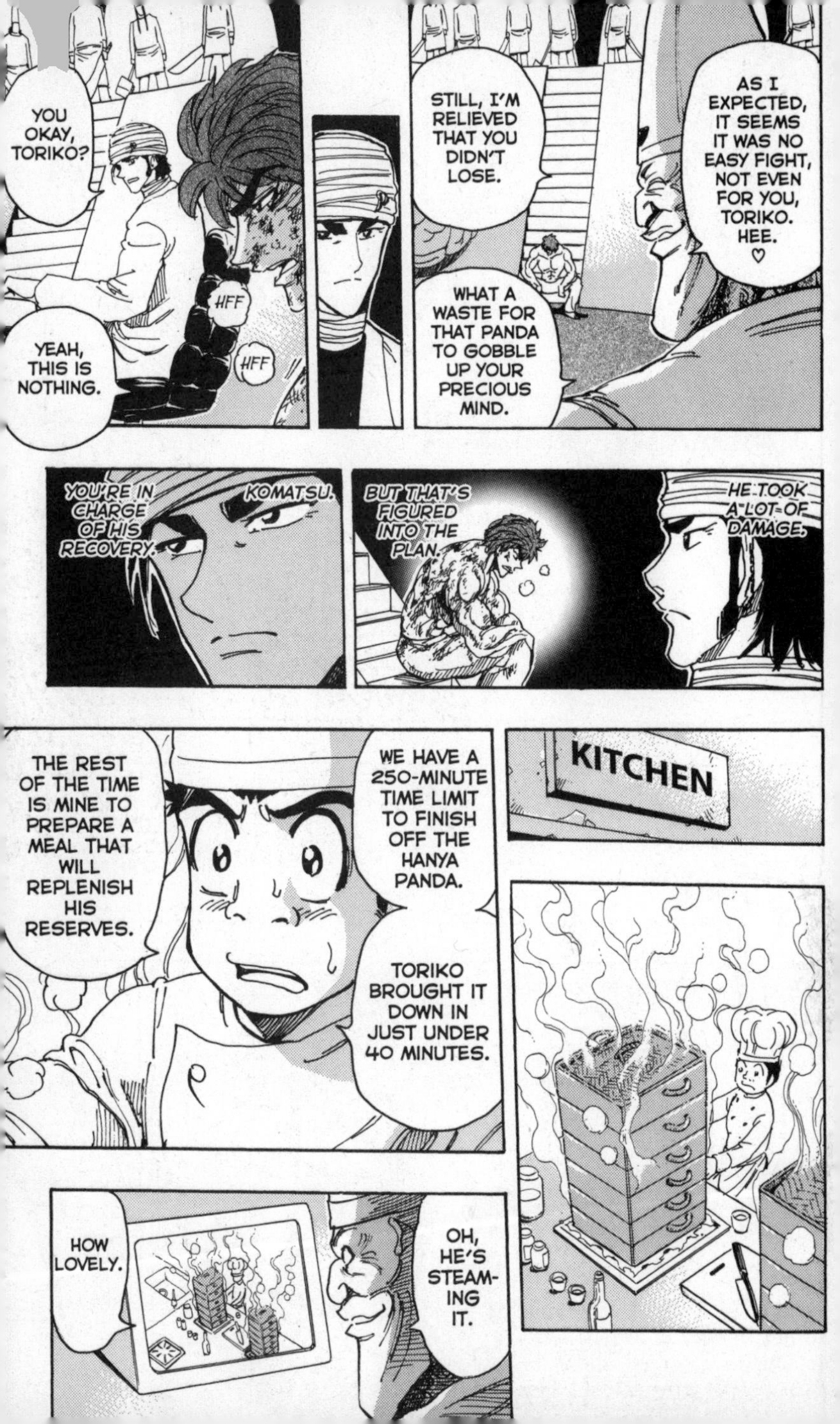
AS I EXPECTED, IT SEEMS IT WAS NO EASY FIGHT, NOT EVEN FOR YOU, TORIKO. HEE. ♡
STILL, I'M RELIEVED THAT YOU DIDN'T LOSE.
WHAT A WASTE FOR THAT PANDA TO GOBBLE UP YOUR PRECIOUS MIND.
YOU OKAY, TORIKO?
HFF
HFF
YEAH, THIS IS NOTHING.
HE TOOK A LOT OF DAMAGE.
BUT THAT'S FIGURED INTO THE PLAN.
KOMATSU.
YOU'RE IN CHARGE OF HIS RECOVERY.
KITCHEN
WE HAVE A 250-MINUTE TIME LIMIT TO FINISH OFF THE HANYA PANDA.
TORIKO BROUGHT IT DOWN IN JUST UNDER 40 MINUTES.
THE REST OF THE TIME IS MINE TO PREPARE A MEAL THAT WILL REPLENISH HIS RESERVES.
OH, HE'S STEAMING IT.
HOW LOVELY.

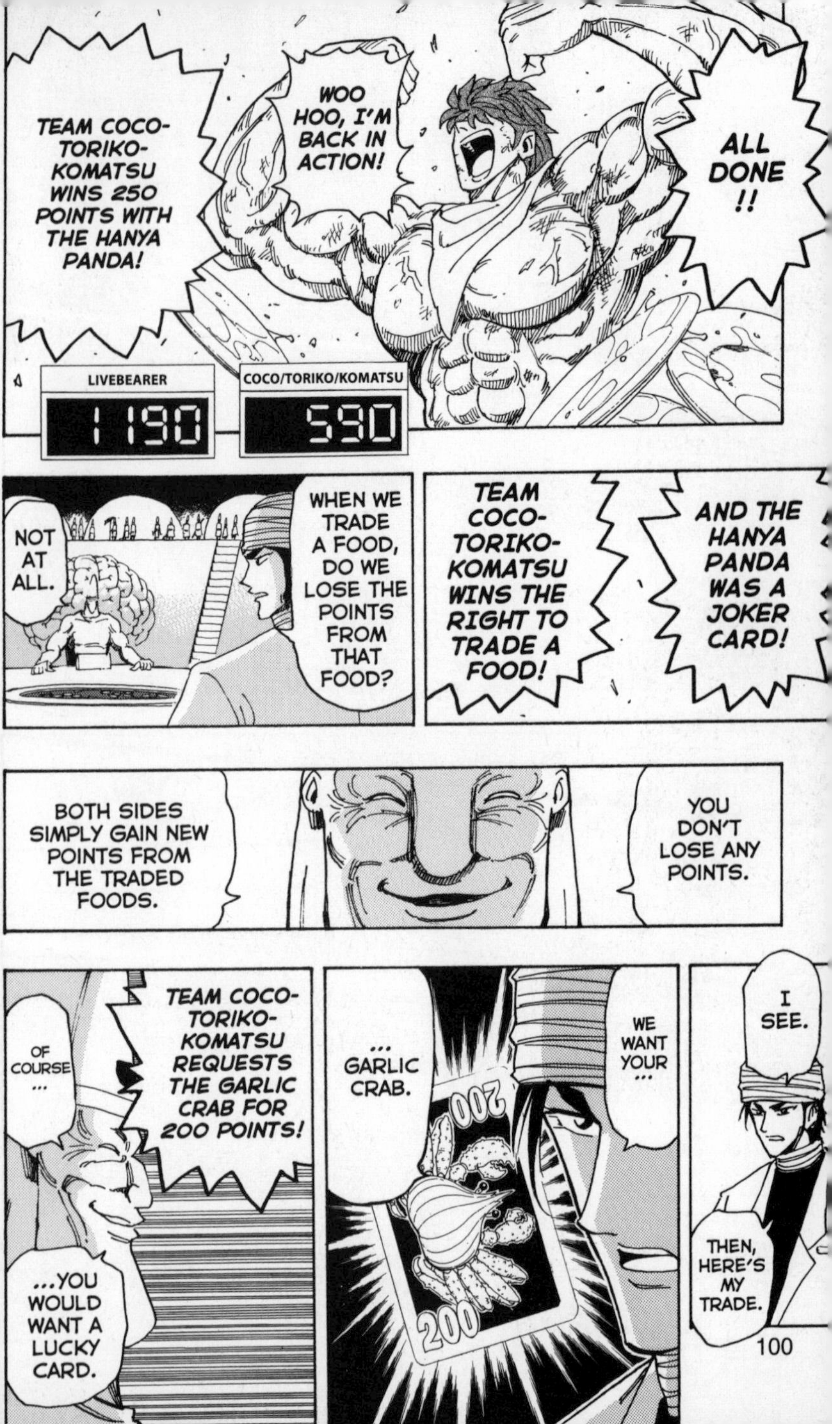
ALL DONE !!
WOO HOO, I'M BACK IN ACTION!
TEAM COCO-TORIKO-KOMATSU WINS 250 POINTS WITH THE HANYA PANDA!
LIVEBEARER
1190
COCO/TORIKO/KOMATSU
590
AND THE HANYA PANDA WAS A JOKER CARD!
TEAM COCO-TORIKO-KOMATSU WINS THE RIGHT TO TRADE A FOOD!
WHEN WE TRADE A FOOD, DO WE LOSE THE POINTS FROM THAT FOOD?
NOT AT ALL.
YOU DON'T LOSE ANY POINTS.
BOTH SIDES SIMPLY GAIN NEW POINTS FROM THE TRADED FOODS.
I SEE.
THEN, HERE'S MY TRADE.
WE WANT YOUR...
...GARLIC CRAB.
200
200
TEAM COCO-TORIKO-KOMATSU REQUESTS THE GARLIC CRAB FOR 200 POINTS!
OF COURSE...
...YOU WOULD WANT A LUCKY CARD.

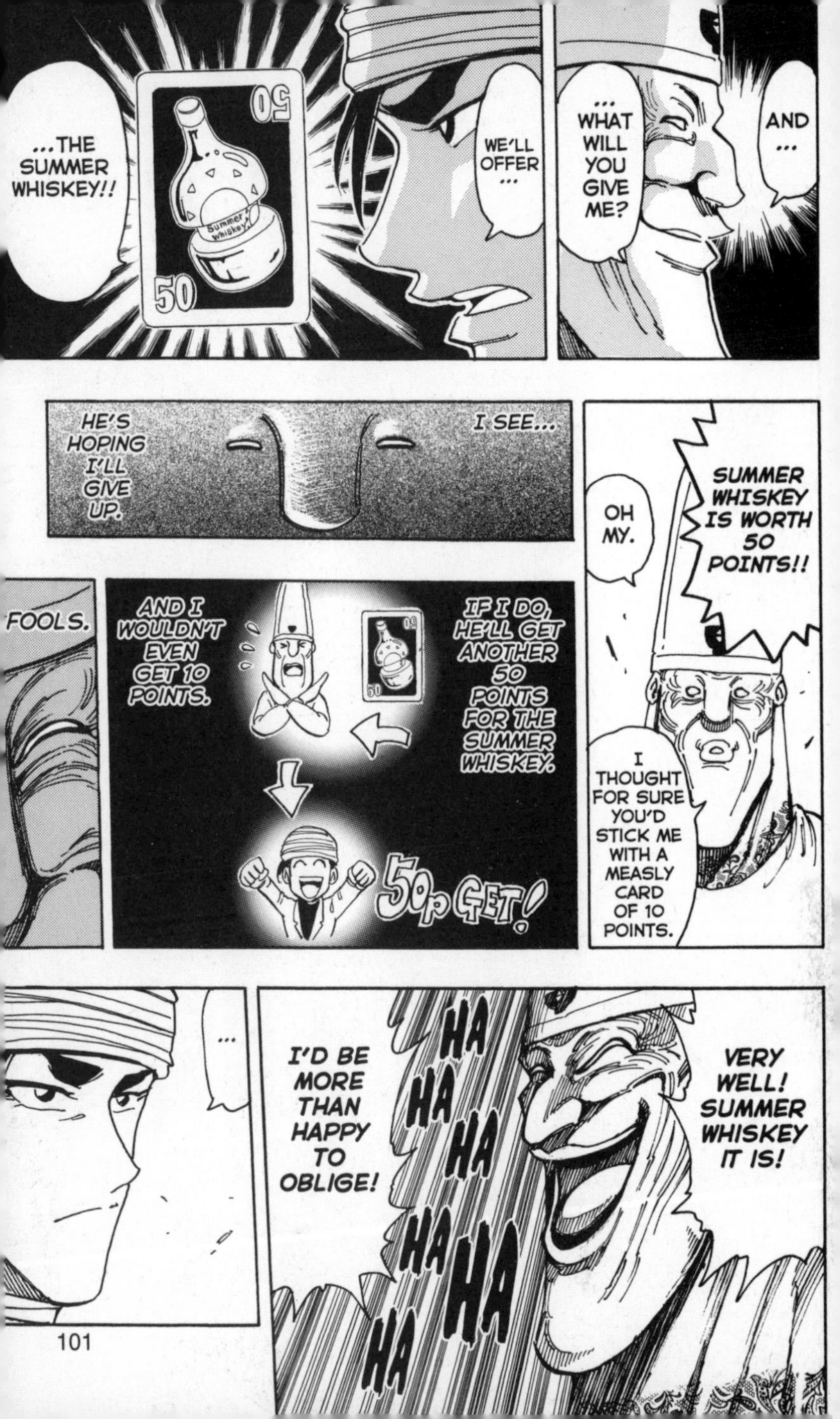
AND...
...WHAT WILL YOU GIVE ME?
WE'LL OFFER...
...THE SUMMER WHISKEY!!
50
Summer Whiskey
50
SUMMER WHISKEY IS WORTH 50 POINTS!!
OH MY.
I THOUGHT FOR SURE YOU'D STICK ME WITH A MEASLY CARD OF 10 POINTS.
I SEE...
HE'S HOPING I'LL GIVE UP.
IF I DO, HE'LL GET ANOTHER 50 POINTS FOR THE SUMMER WHISKEY.
AND I WOULDN'T EVEN GET 10 POINTS.
50p GET!
FOOLS.
VERY WELL! SUMMER WHISKEY IT IS!
HA HA HA HA HA HA HA HA HA
I'D BE MORE THAN HAPPY TO OBLIGE!
...

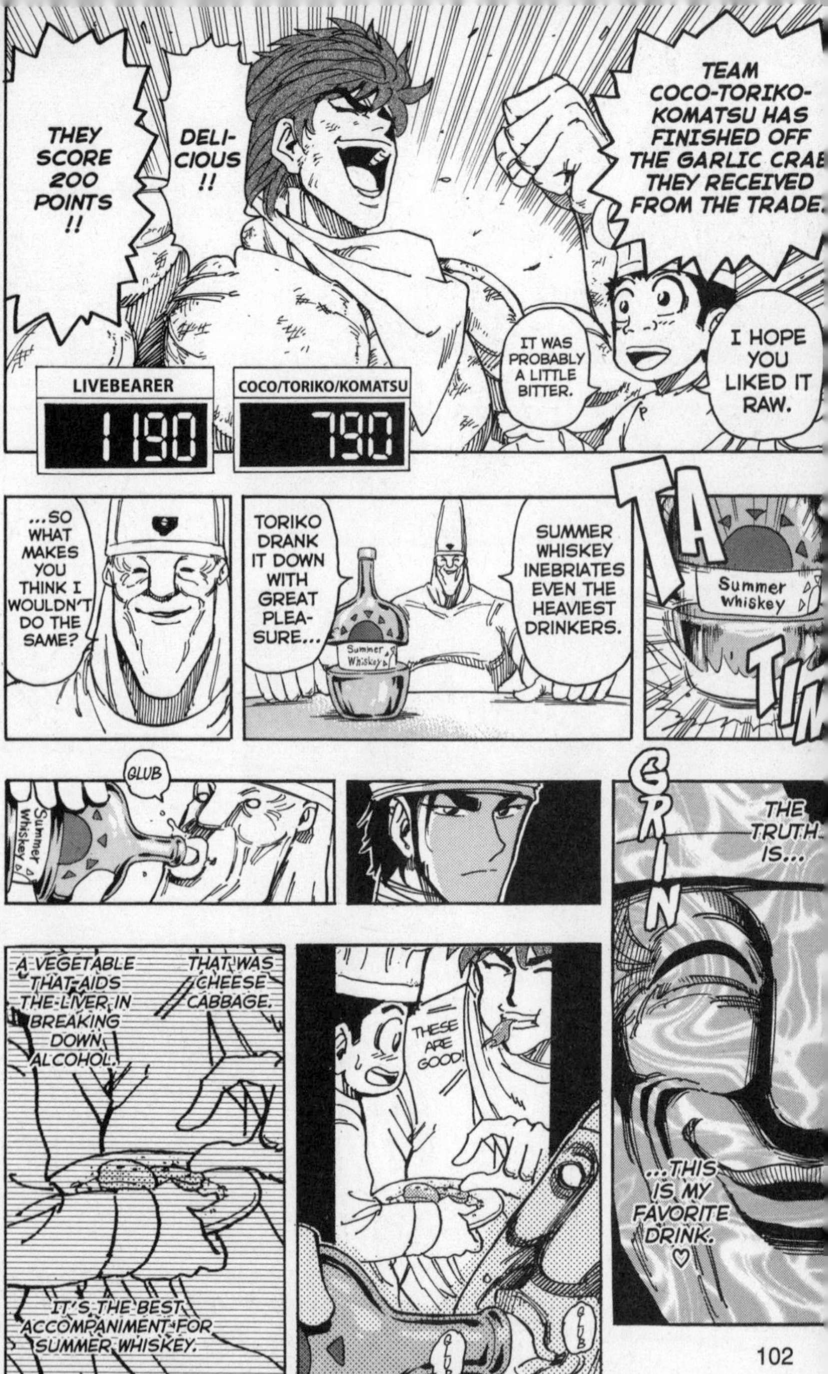
TEAM COCO-TORIKO-KOMATSU HAS FINISHED OFF THE GARLIC CRAB THEY RECEIVED FROM THE TRADE.
DELI-CIOUS !!
THEY SCORE 200 POINTS !!
I HOPE YOU LIKED IT RAW.
IT WAS PROBABLY A LITTLE BITTER.
LIVEBEARER
1190
COCO/TORIKO/KOMATSU
790
TA
Summer Whiskey
TIN
SUMMER WHISKEY INEBRIATES EVEN THE HEAVIEST DRINKERS.
TORIKO DRANK IT DOWN WITH GREAT PLEA-SURE...
Summer Whiskey
...SO WHAT MAKES YOU THINK I WOULDN'T DO THE SAME?
GRIN
THE TRUTH IS...
GLUB
Summer Whiskey
...THIS IS MY FAVORITE DRINK. ♡
THESE ARE GOOD!
GLUB
GLUB
THAT WAS CHEESE CABBAGE.
A VEGETABLE THAT AIDS THE LIVER IN BREAKING DOWN ALCOHOL.
IT'S THE BEST ACCOMPANIMENT FOR SUMMER WHISKEY.

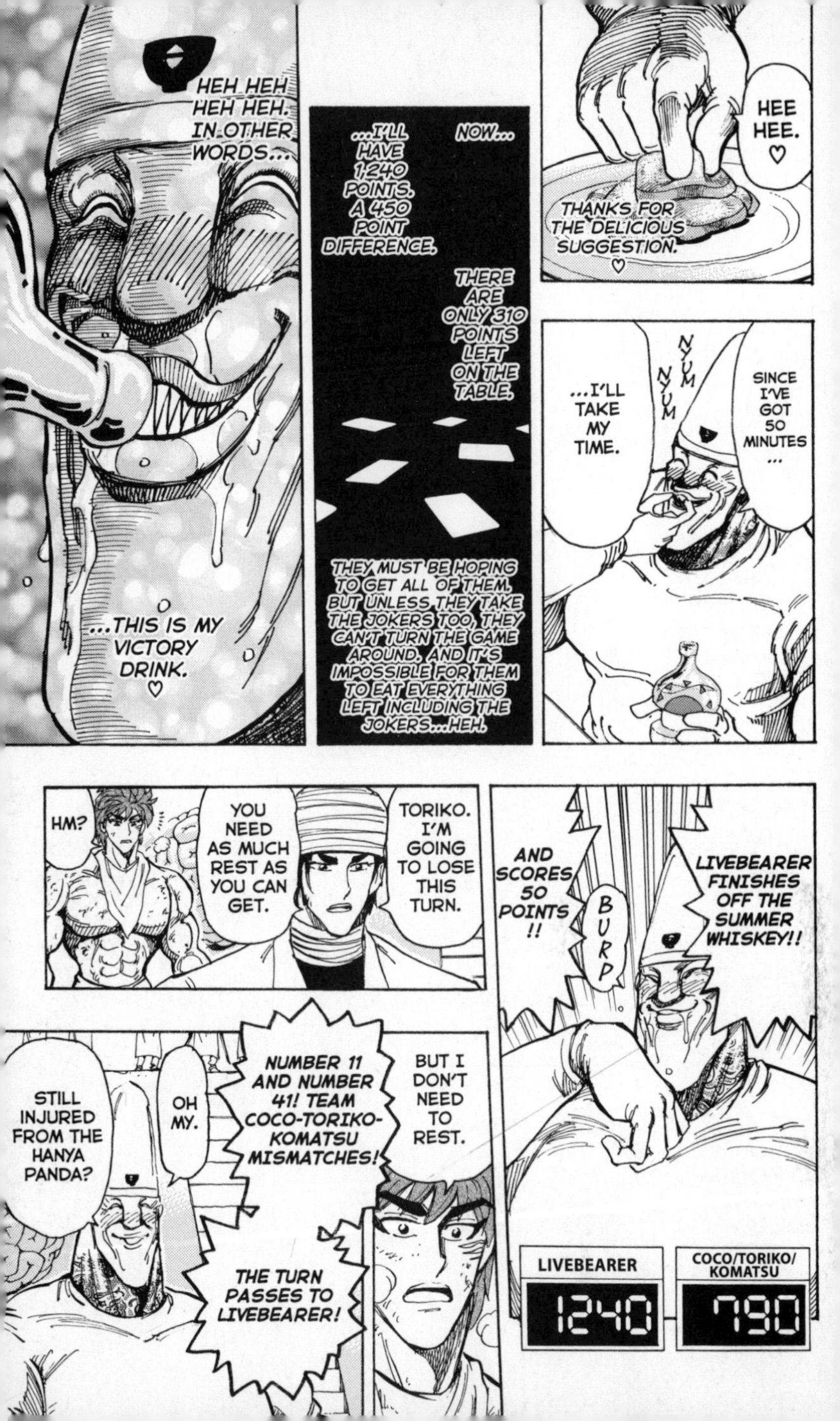
HEE HEE. ♡
THANKS FOR THE DELICIOUS SUGGESTION. ♡
SINCE I'VE GOT 50 MINUTES...
NYUM NYUM
...I'LL TAKE MY TIME.
NOW...
...I'LL HAVE 1,240 POINTS. A 450 POINT DIFFERENCE.
THERE ARE ONLY 310 POINTS LEFT ON THE TABLE.
THEY MUST BE HOPING TO GET ALL OF THEM, BUT UNLESS THEY TAKE THE JOKERS TOO, THEY CAN'T TURN THE GAME AROUND. AND IT'S IMPOSSIBLE FOR THEM TO EAT EVERYTHING LEFT INCLUDING THE JOKERS...HEH.
HEH HEH HEH HEH. IN OTHER WORDS...
...THIS IS MY VICTORY DRINK. ♡
LIVEBEARER FINISHES OFF THE SUMMER WHISKEY!!
BURP
AND SCORES 50 POINTS!!
LIVEBEARER
1240
COCO/TORIKO/KOMATSU
790
TORIKO. I'M GOING TO LOSE THIS TURN.
YOU NEED AS MUCH REST AS YOU CAN GET.
HM?
BUT I DON'T NEED TO REST.
NUMBER 11 AND NUMBER 41! TEAM COCO-TORIKO-KOMATSU MISMATCHES!
OH MY.
STILL INJURED FROM THE HANYA PANDA?
THE TURN PASSES TO LIVEBEARER!

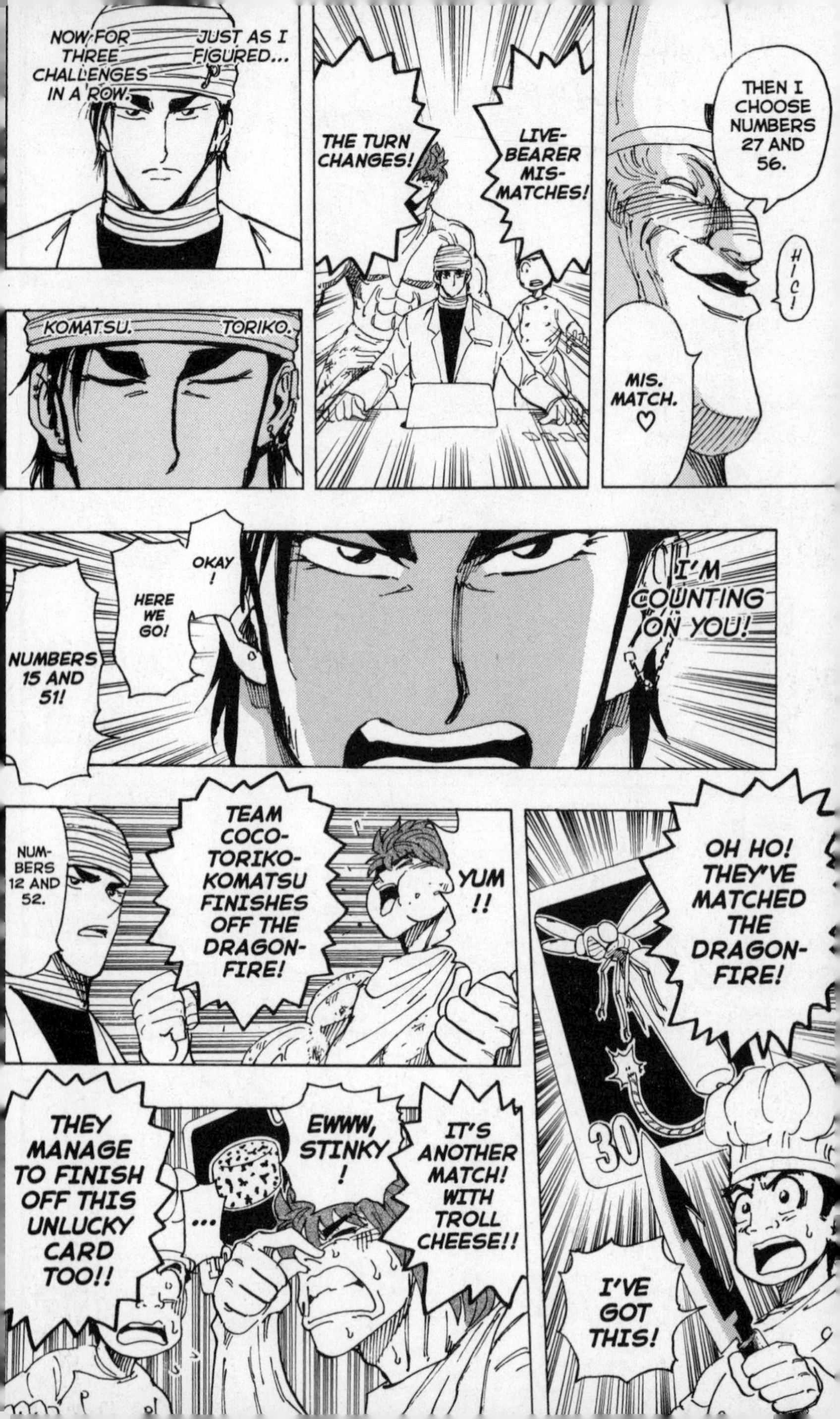
THEN I CHOOSE NUMBERS 27 AND 56.
HIC!
MIS. MATCH. ♥
LIVE-BEARER MIS-MATCHES!
THE TURN CHANGES!
JUST AS I FIGURED...
NOW FOR THREE CHALLENGES IN A ROW.
TORIKO.
KOMATSU.
I'M COUNTING ON YOU!
OKAY!
HERE WE GO!
NUMBERS 15 AND 51!
OH HO! THEY'VE MATCHED THE DRAGON-FIRE!
30
I'VE GOT THIS!
YUM!!
TEAM COCO-TORIKO-KOMATSU FINISHES OFF THE DRAGON-FIRE!
NUMBERS 12 AND 52.
IT'S ANOTHER MATCH! WITH TROLL CHEESE!!
EWWW, STINKY!
...
THEY MANAGE TO FINISH OFF THIS UNLUCKY CARD TOO!!

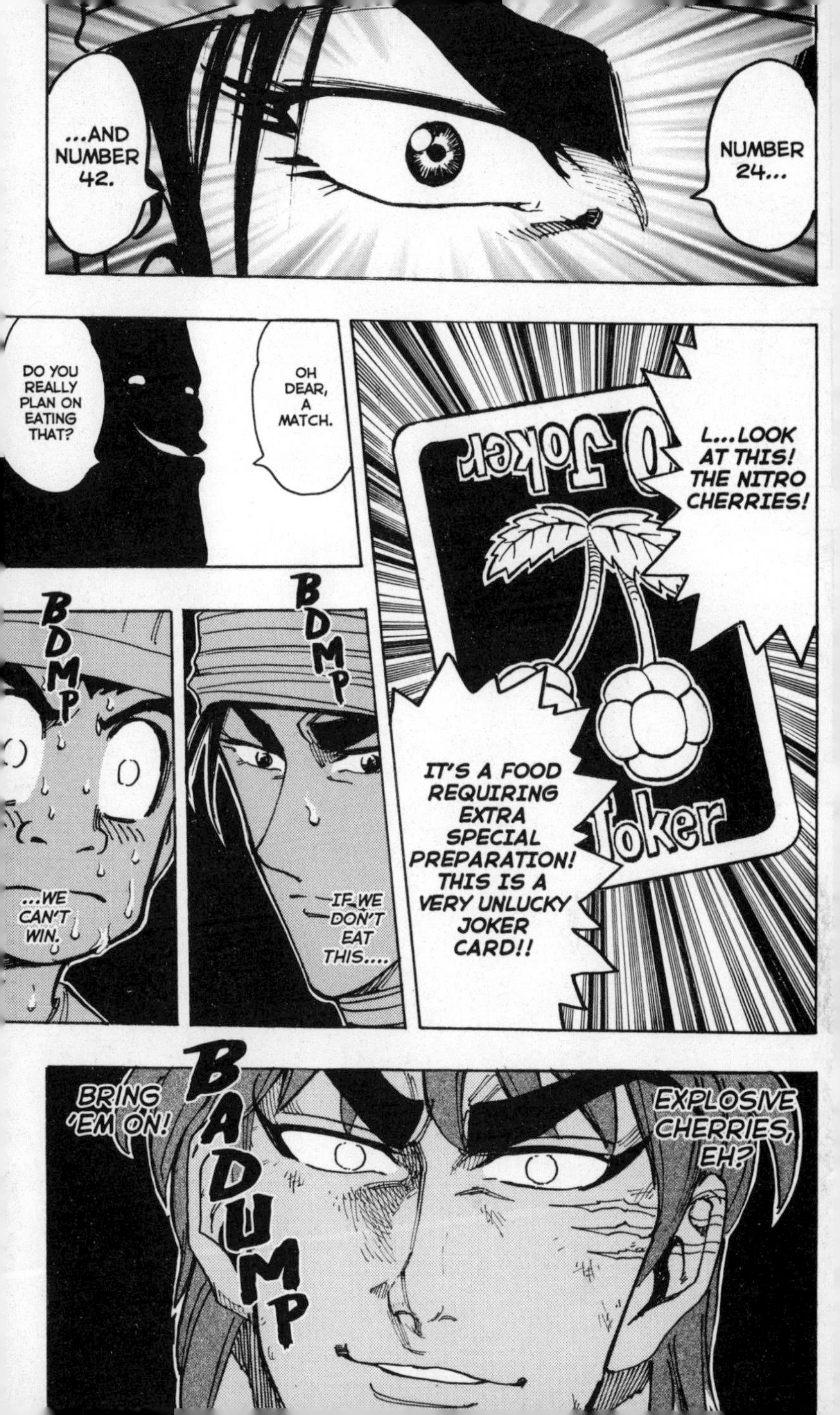
NUMBER 24...
...AND NUMBER 42.
L...LOOK AT THIS! THE NITRO CHERRIES!
Joker
Joker
IT'S A FOOD REQUIRING EXTRA SPECIAL PREPARATION! THIS IS A VERY UNLUCKY JOKER CARD!!
OH DEAR, A MATCH.
DO YOU REALLY PLAN ON EATING THAT?
BDMP
IF WE DON'T EAT THIS....
BDMP
...WE CAN'T WIN.
EXPLOSIVE CHERRIES, EH?
BADUMP
BRING 'EM ON!

GOURMET 168: COCO'S AIM!!

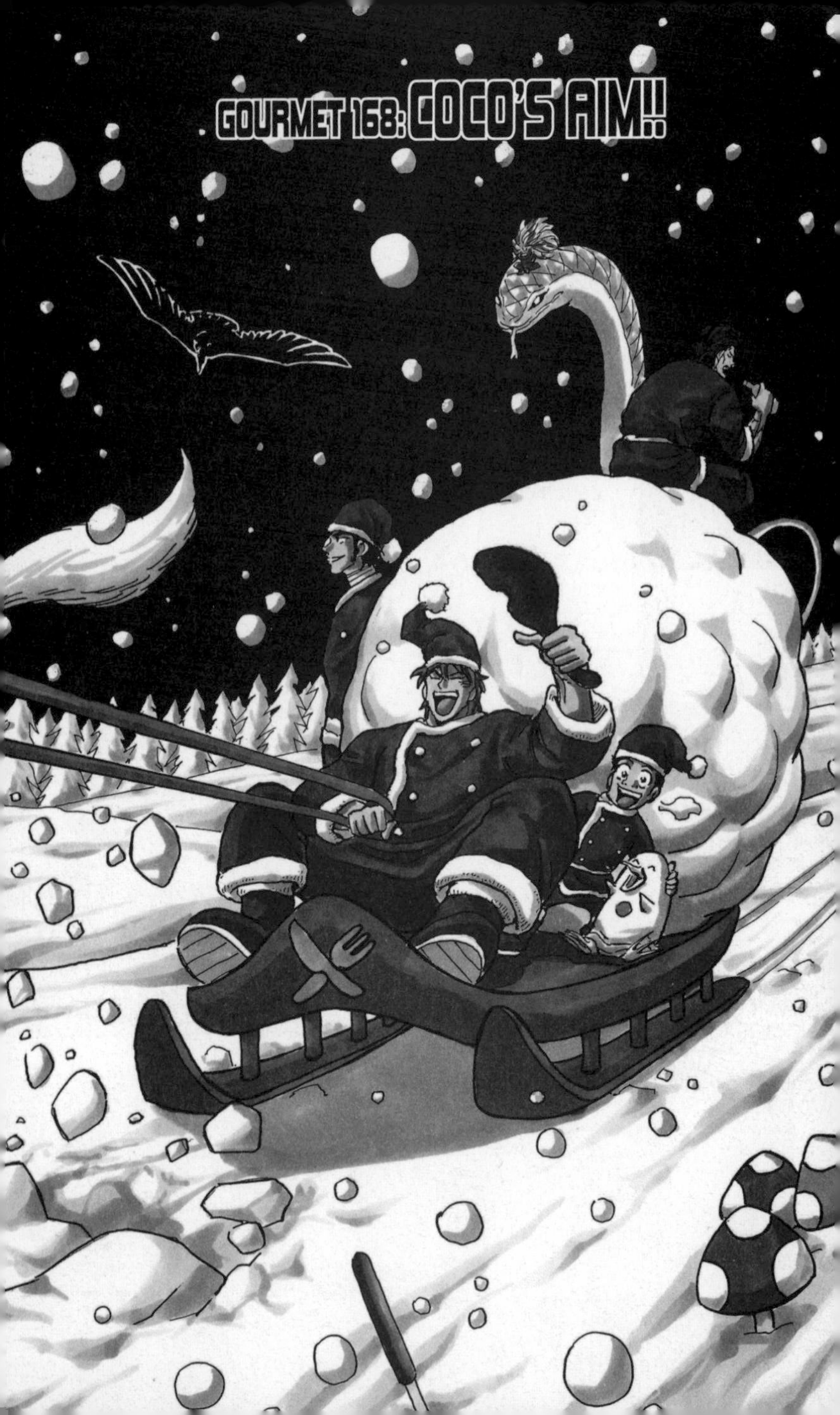

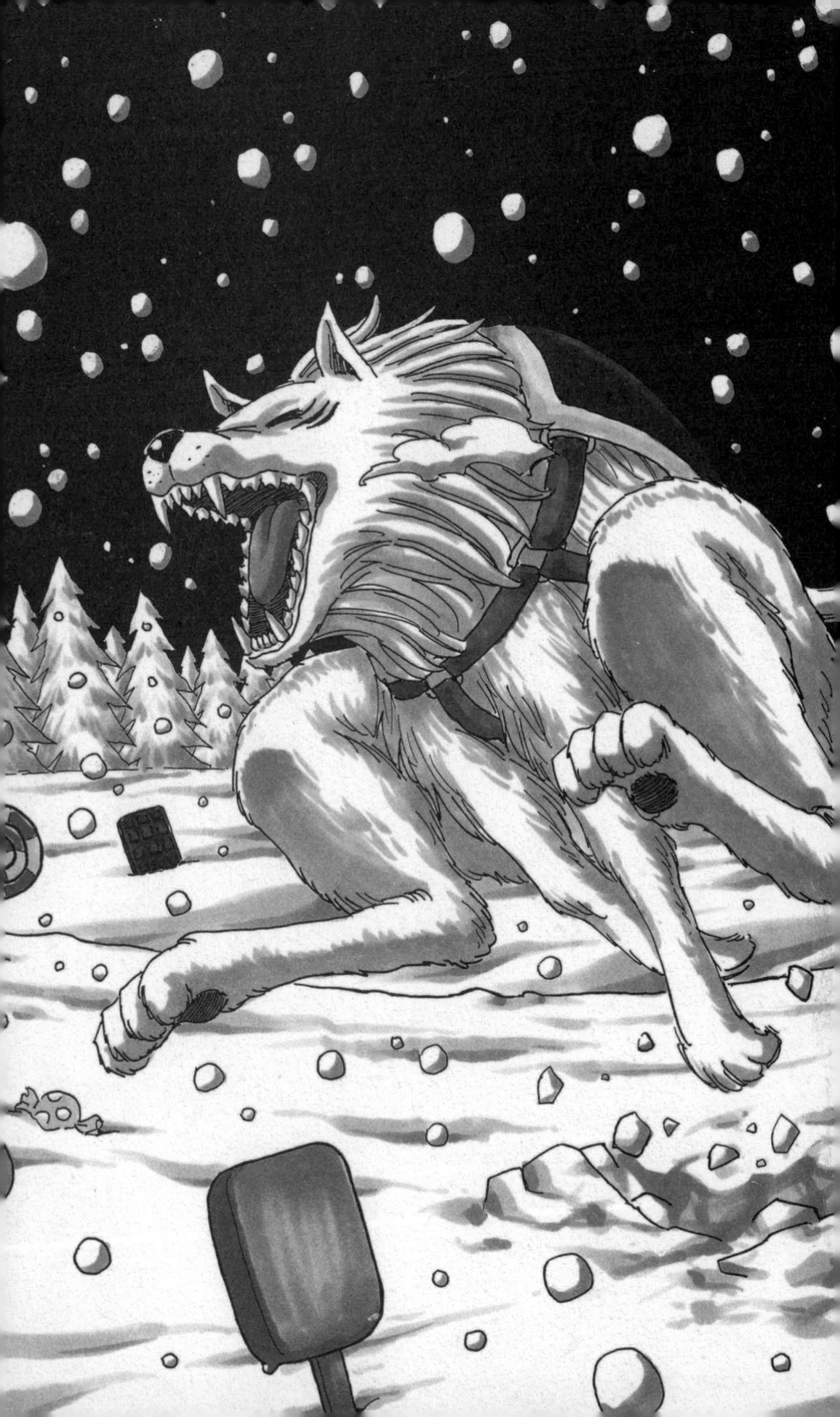

TORIKO

GOURMET CHECKLIST
Vol. 198

MIMIC BAGWORM
(INSECT)

CAPTURE LEVEL: 12
HABITAT: GOURMET PYRAMID
LENGTH: 60 CM
HEIGHT: ---
WEIGHT: 32 KG
PRICE: TYPICALLY NOT FIT FOR CONSUMPTION, BUT WITH SPECIAL PREPARATION CAN BE 100 G / 10,000 YEN

SCALE

AN INSECT THAT NESTS IN THE WALLS OF GOURMET PYRAMID. IT TYPICALLY KEEPS ITS MOUTH CLOSED TO MIMIC THE BAGWORM, BUT WHEN PREY DRAWS NEAR, ITS GAPING MAW POPS OPEN. MUCH LIKE THE OTHER CREATURES IN GOURMET PYRAMID, THE MIMIC BAGWORM IS NOT FIT FOR CONSUMPTION UNLESS CAPTURED IN A SPECIFIC WAY. THEN IT'S SHOCKINGLY DELICIOUS.

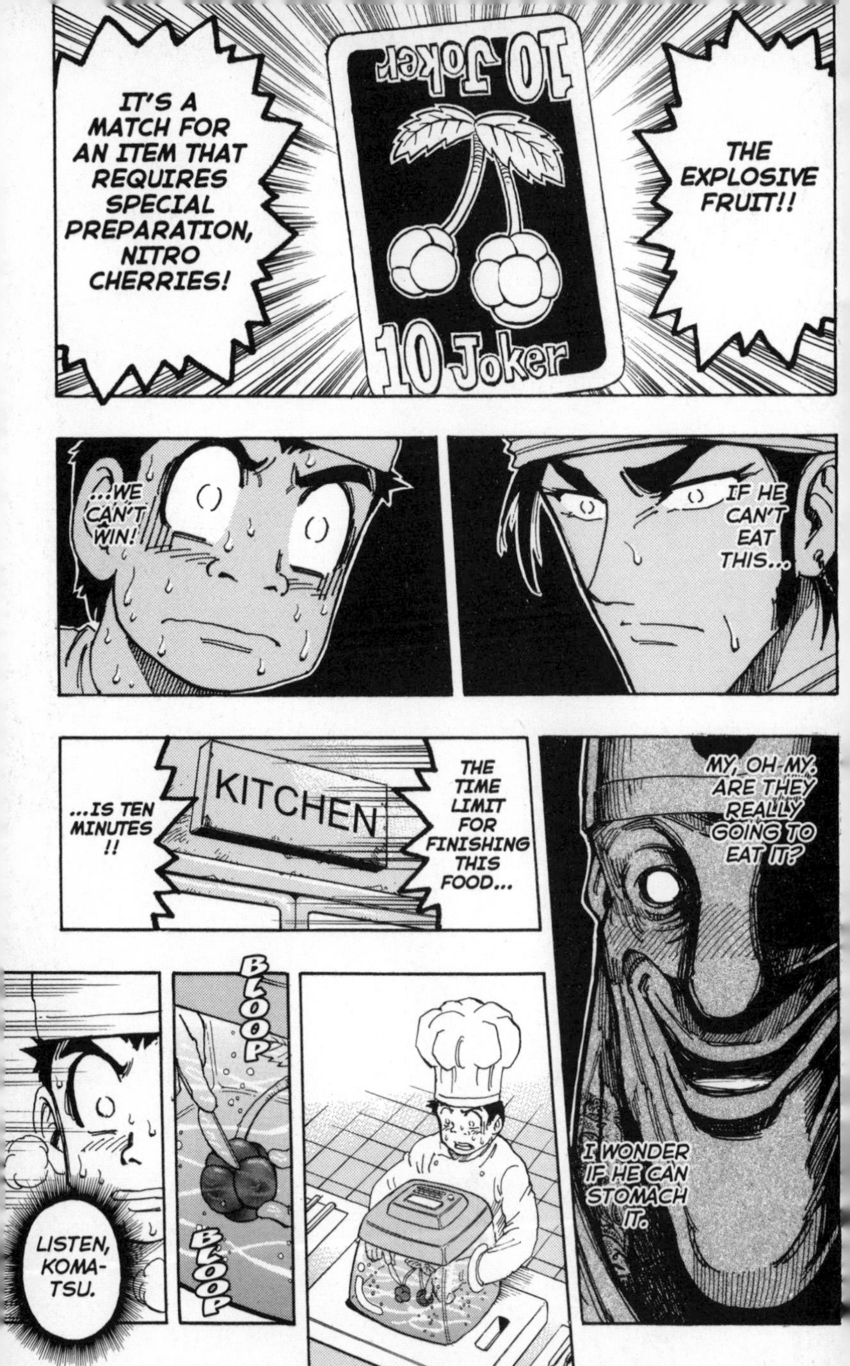
THE EXPLOSIVE FRUIT!!
10 Joker
10 Joker
IT'S A MATCH FOR AN ITEM THAT REQUIRES SPECIAL PREPARATION, NITRO CHERRIES!
IF HE CAN'T EAT THIS...
...WE CAN'T WIN!
MY, OH MY. ARE THEY REALLY GOING TO EAT IT?
I WONDER IF HE CAN STOMACH IT.
THE TIME LIMIT FOR FINISHING THIS FOOD...
KITCHEN
...IS TEN MINUTES!!
BLOOP
BLOOP
LISTEN, KOMATSU.

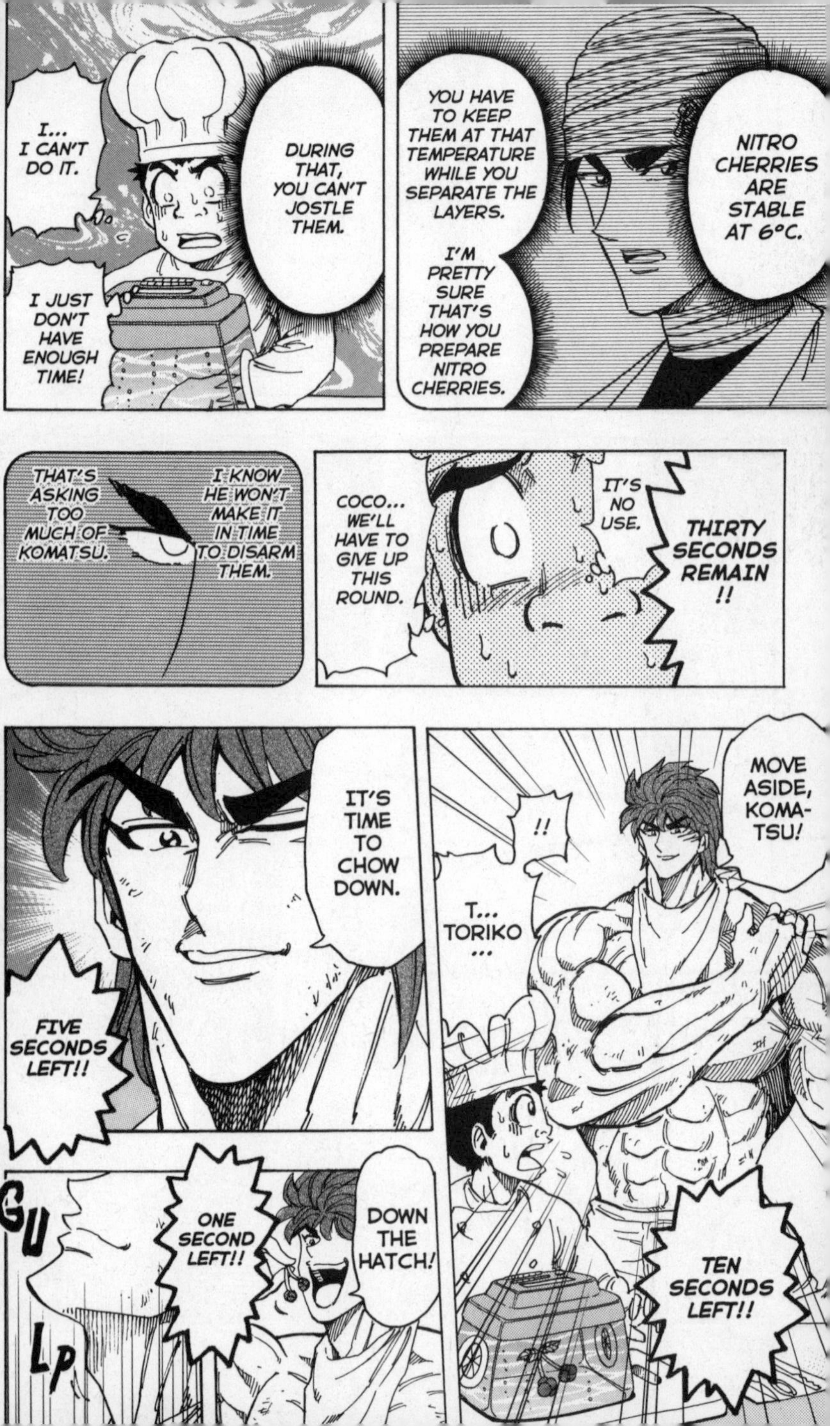
NITRO CHERRIES ARE STABLE AT 6°C.
YOU HAVE TO KEEP THEM AT THAT TEMPERATURE WHILE YOU SEPARATE THE LAYERS.
I'M PRETTY SURE THAT'S HOW YOU PREPARE NITRO CHERRIES.
DURING THAT, YOU CAN'T JOSTLE THEM.
I... I CAN'T DO IT.
I JUST DON'T HAVE ENOUGH TIME!
THIRTY SECONDS REMAIN!!
IT'S NO USE.
COCO... WE'LL HAVE TO GIVE UP THIS ROUND.
I KNOW HE WON'T MAKE IT IN TIME TO DISARM THEM.
THAT'S ASKING TOO MUCH OF KOMATSU.
MOVE ASIDE, KOMATSU!
!!
T... TORIKO...
TEN SECONDS LEFT!!
IT'S TIME TO CHOW DOWN.
FIVE SECONDS LEFT!!
DOWN THE HATCH!
ONE SECOND LEFT!!
GULP

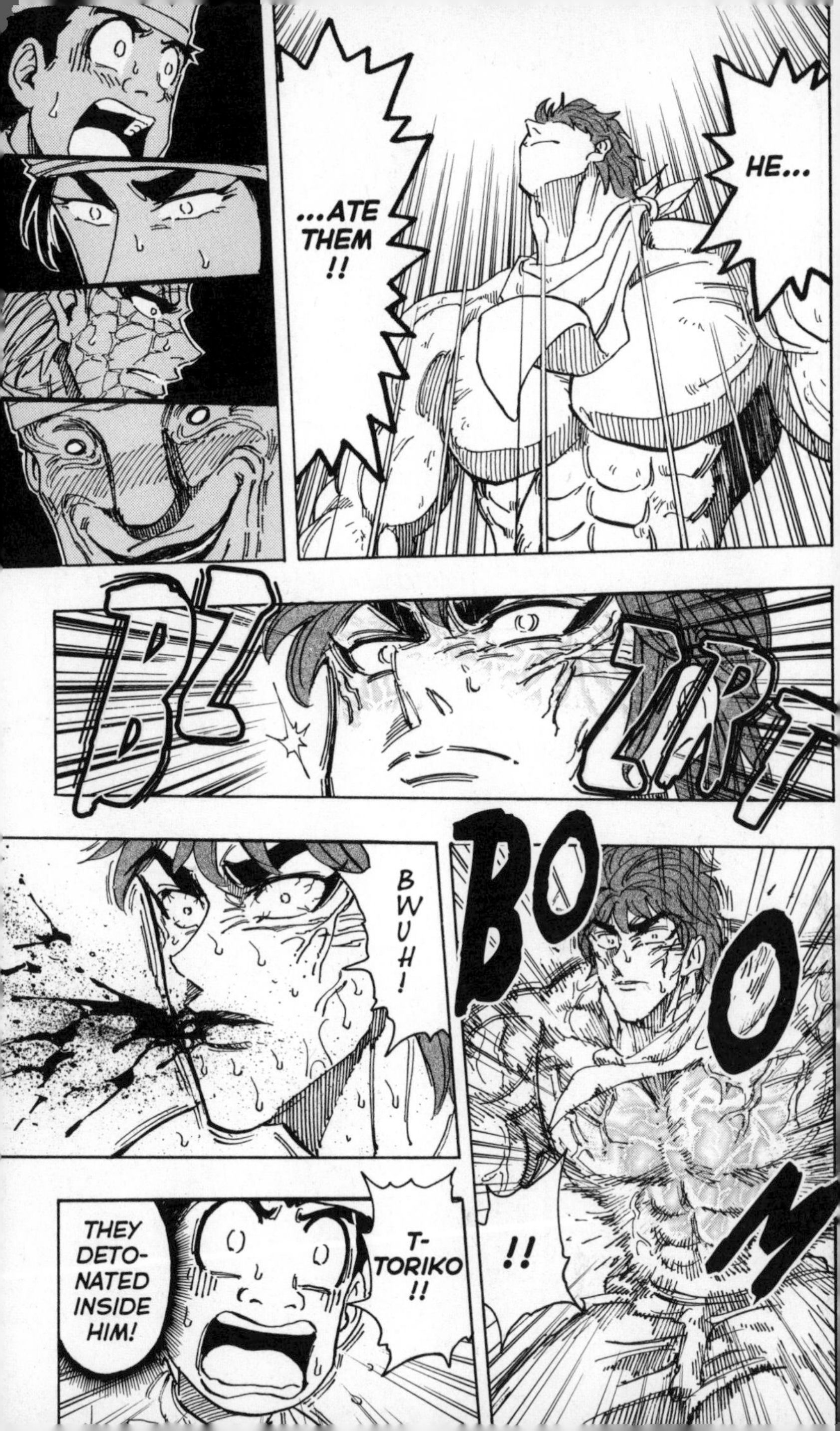
HE...
...ATE THEM !!
BZZRT
BOOM
BWUH!
!!
T-TORIKO!!
THEY DETONATED INSIDE HIM!

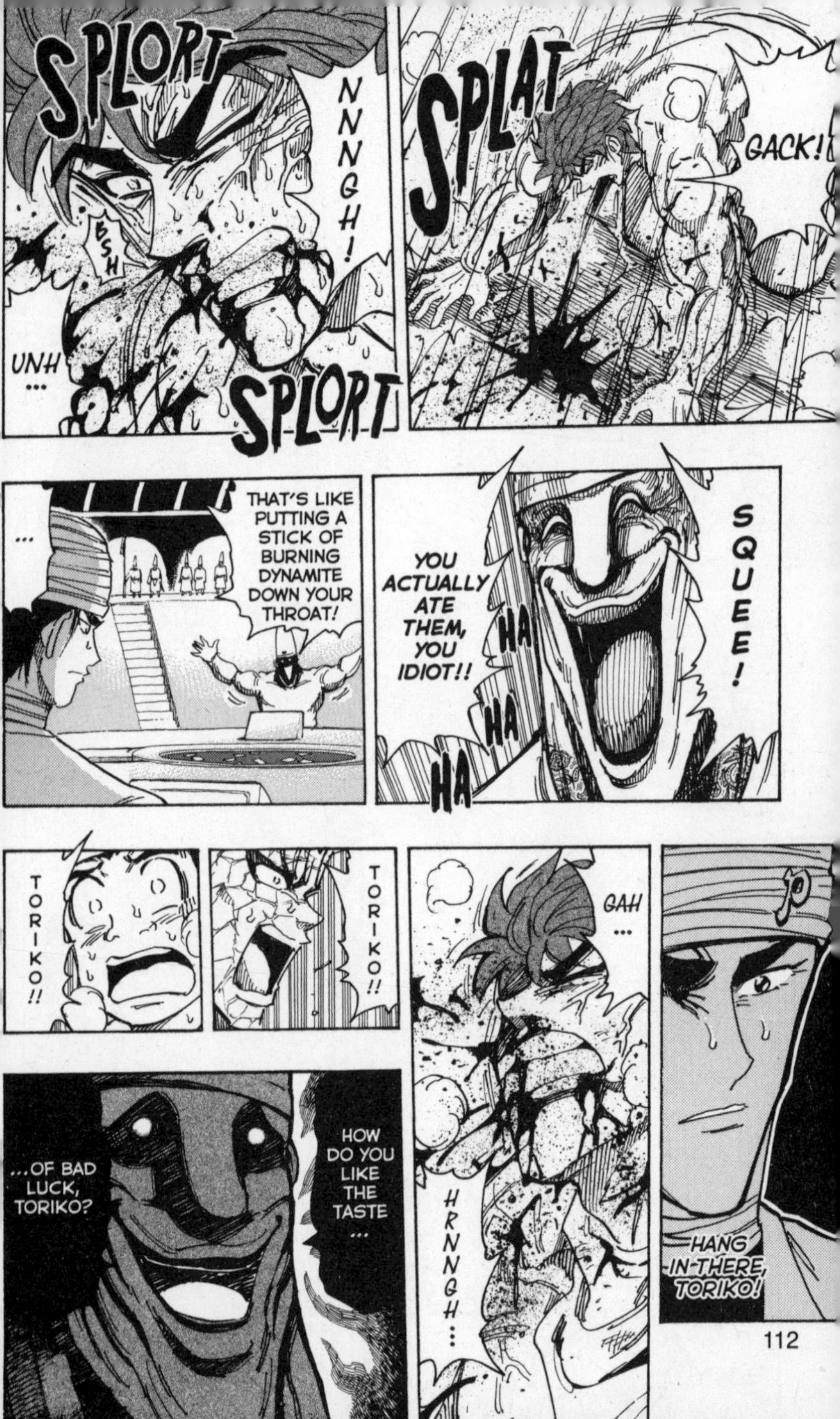

SPLAT
GACK!
SPLORT
NNNNGH!
BSH
UNH...
SPLORT
SQUEEE!
YOU ACTUALLY ATE THEM, YOU IDIOT!!
HA HA HA
THAT'S LIKE PUTTING A STICK OF BURNING DYNAMITE DOWN YOUR THROAT!
...
HANG IN THERE, TORIKO!
GAH...
HRNNNGH...
TORIKO!!
TORIKO!!
HOW DO YOU LIKE THE TASTE...
...OF BAD LUCK, TORIKO?

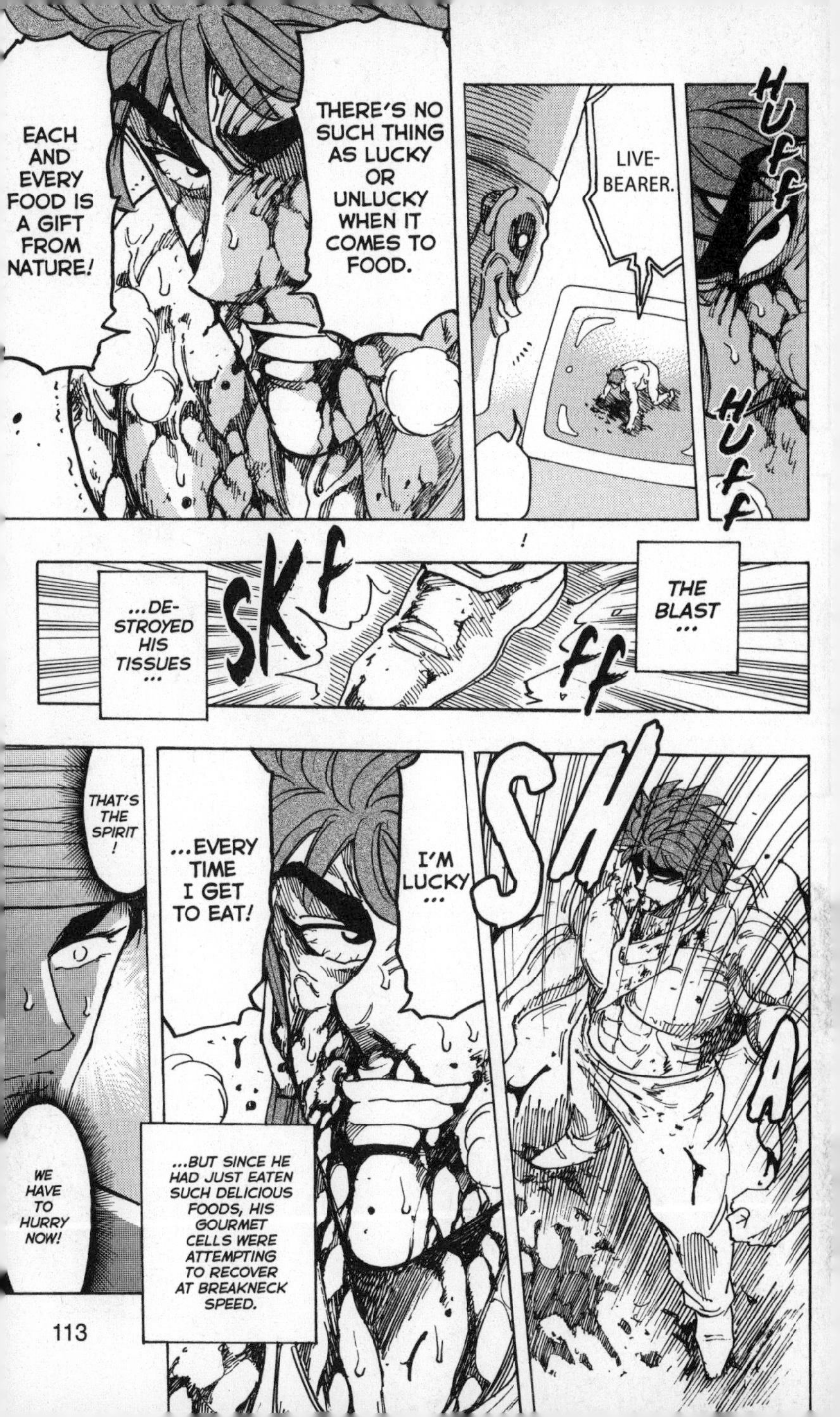
HUFF HUFF
LIVE-BEARER.
THERE'S NO SUCH THING AS LUCKY OR UNLUCKY WHEN IT COMES TO FOOD.
EACH AND EVERY FOOD IS A GIFT FROM NATURE!
THE BLAST...
SKFFF
...DE-STROYED HIS TISSUES...
I'M LUCKY...
...EVERY TIME I GET TO EAT!
...BUT SINCE HE HAD JUST EATEN SUCH DELICIOUS FOODS, HIS GOURMET CELLS WERE ATTEMPTING TO RECOVER AT BREAKNECK SPEED.
THAT'S THE SPIRIT!
WE HAVE TO HURRY NOW!

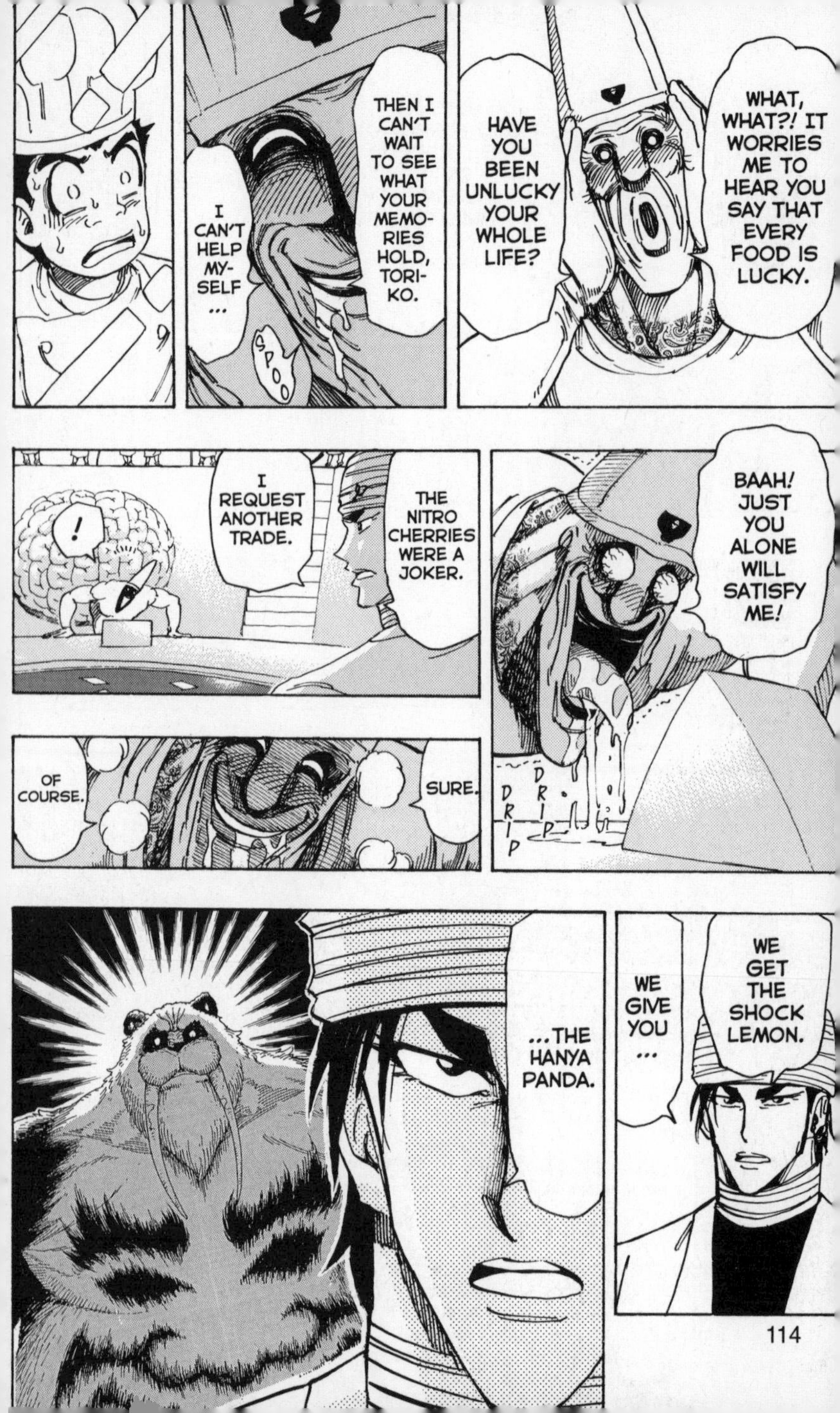
WHAT, WHAT?! IT WORRIES ME TO HEAR YOU SAY THAT EVERY FOOD IS LUCKY.
HAVE YOU BEEN UNLUCKY YOUR WHOLE LIFE?
THEN I CAN'T WAIT TO SEE WHAT YOUR MEMORIES HOLD, TORIKO.
I CAN'T HELP MYSELF...
SPOO
BAAH! JUST YOU ALONE WILL SATISFY ME!
DRIP DRIP
THE NITRO CHERRIES WERE A JOKER.
I REQUEST ANOTHER TRADE.
!
SURE.
OF COURSE.
WE GET THE SHOCK LEMON.
WE GIVE YOU...
...THE HANYA PANDA.

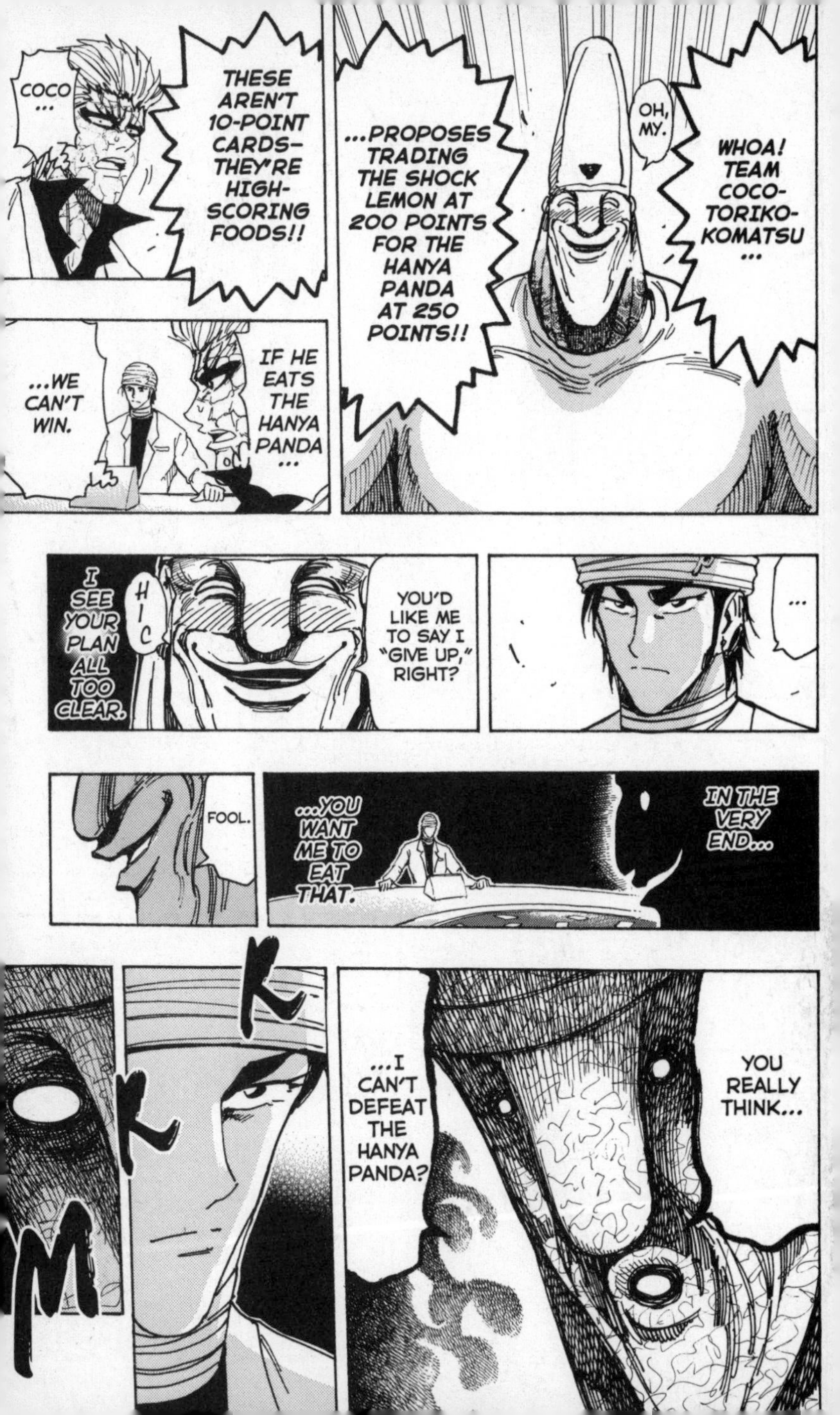
WHOA! TEAM COCO-TORIKO-KOMATSU...
OH, MY.
...PROPOSES TRADING THE SHOCK LEMON AT 200 POINTS FOR THE HANYA PANDA AT 250 POINTS!!
THESE AREN'T 10-POINT CARDS—THEY'RE HIGH-SCORING FOODS!!
COCO...
IF HE EATS THE HANYA PANDA...
...WE CAN'T WIN.
...
YOU'D LIKE ME TO SAY I "GIVE UP," RIGHT?
HIC
I SEE YOUR PLAN ALL TOO CLEAR.
IN THE VERY END...
...YOU WANT ME TO EAT THAT.
FOOL.
YOU REALLY THINK...
...I CAN'T DEFEAT THE HANYA PANDA?
K
K
M

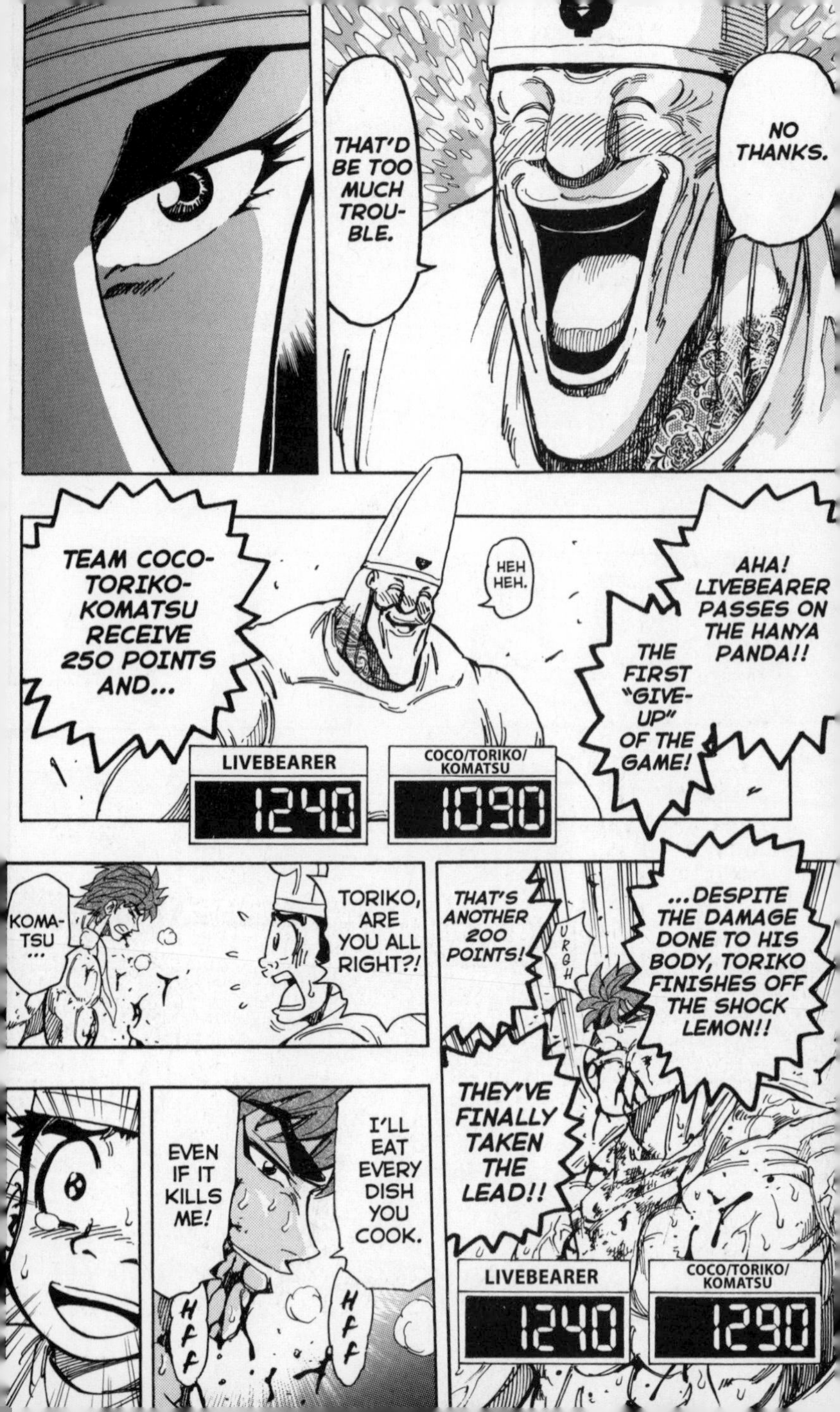
NO THANKS.
THAT'D BE TOO MUCH TROUBLE.
AHA! LIVEBEARER PASSES ON THE HANYA PANDA!!
THE FIRST "GIVE-UP" OF THE GAME!
HEH HEH.
TEAM COCO-TORIKO-KOMATSU RECEIVE 250 POINTS AND...
LIVEBEARER
1240
COCO/TORIKO/KOMATSU
1090
...DESPITE THE DAMAGE DONE TO HIS BODY, TORIKO FINISHES OFF THE SHOCK LEMON!!
URGH
THAT'S ANOTHER 200 POINTS!
THEY'VE FINALLY TAKEN THE LEAD!!
LIVEBEARER
1240
COCO/TORIKO/KOMATSU
1290
TORIKO, ARE YOU ALL RIGHT?!
KOMATSU...
I'LL EAT EVERY DISH YOU COOK.
HFF
EVEN IF IT KILLS ME!
HFF

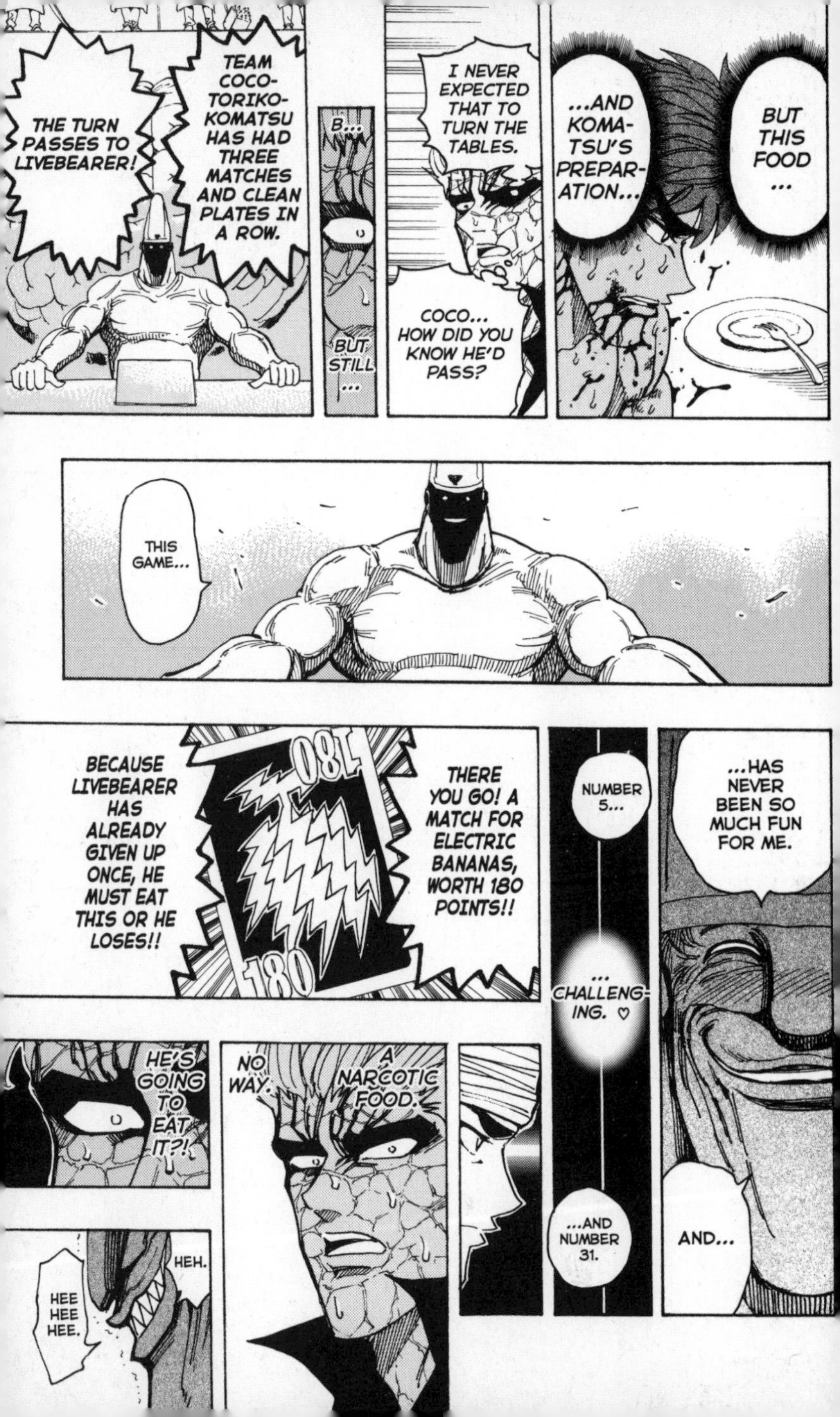
BUT THIS FOOD...
...AND KOMATSU'S PREPARATION...
I NEVER EXPECTED THAT TO TURN THE TABLES.
COCO... HOW DID YOU KNOW HE'D PASS?
B...
BUT STILL...
TEAM COCO-TORIKO-KOMATSU HAS HAD THREE MATCHES AND CLEAN PLATES IN A ROW.
THE TURN PASSES TO LIVEBEARER!
THIS GAME...
...HAS NEVER BEEN SO MUCH FUN FOR ME.
AND...
NUMBER 5...
...CHALLENGING. ♡
...AND NUMBER 31.
THERE YOU GO! A MATCH FOR ELECTRIC BANANAS, WORTH 180 POINTS!!
180
180
BECAUSE LIVEBEARER HAS ALREADY GIVEN UP ONCE, HE MUST EAT THIS OR HE LOSES!!
A NARCOTIC FOOD.
NO WAY.
HE'S GOING TO EAT IT?!
HEH.
HEE HEE HEE.

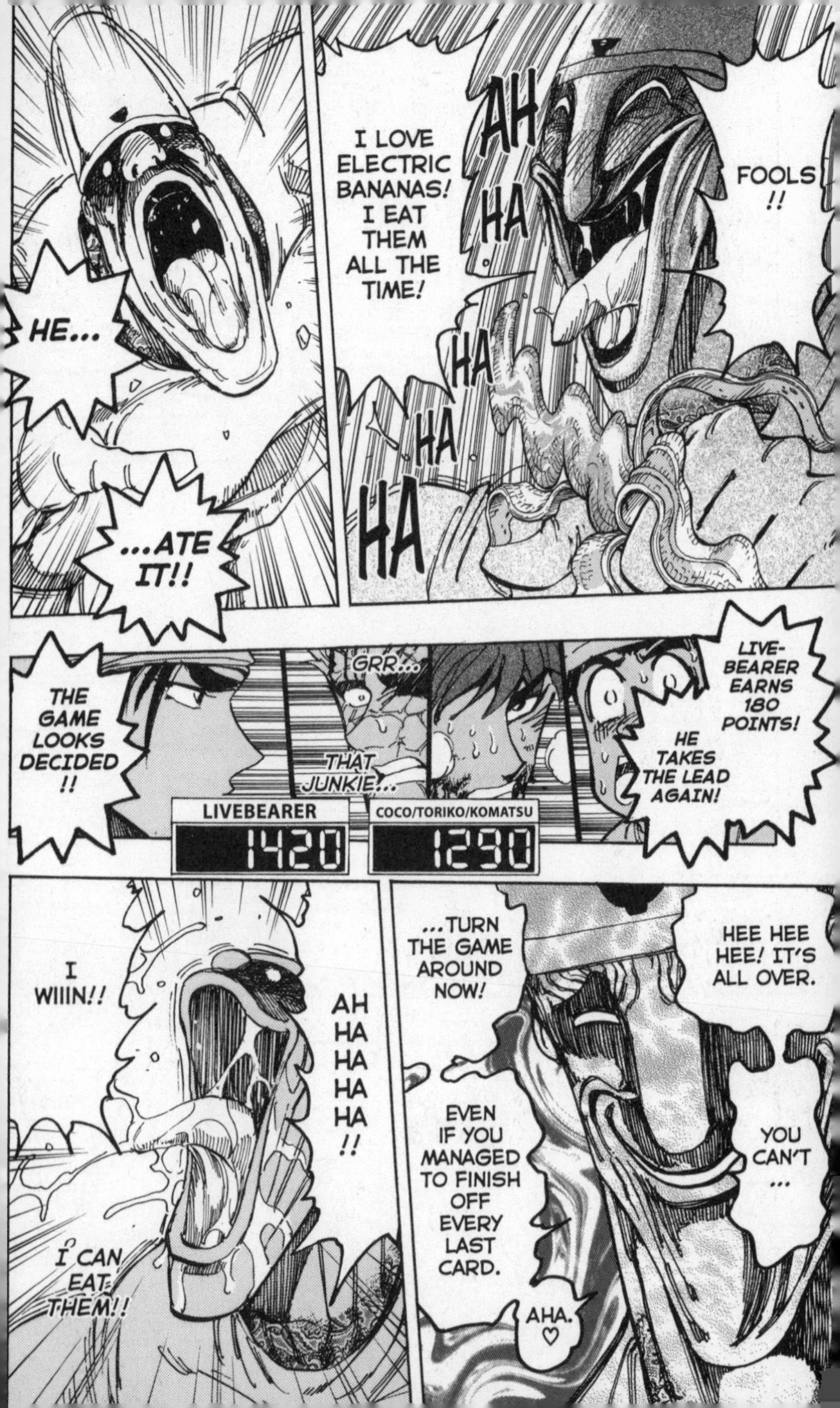
FOOLS !!
AH HA
I LOVE ELECTRIC BANANAS! I EAT THEM ALL THE TIME!
HA HA HA
HE...
...ATE IT!!
LIVE-BEARER EARNS 180 POINTS!
HE TAKES THE LEAD AGAIN!
GRR...
THAT JUNKIE...
THE GAME LOOKS DECIDED !!
LIVEBEARER 1420
COCO/TORIKO/KOMATSU 1290
HEE HEE HEE! IT'S ALL OVER.
YOU CAN'T ...
...TURN THE GAME AROUND NOW!
EVEN IF YOU MANAGED TO FINISH OFF EVERY LAST CARD.
AHA. ♡
AH HA HA HA HA !!
I WIIIN!!
I CAN EAT THEM!!

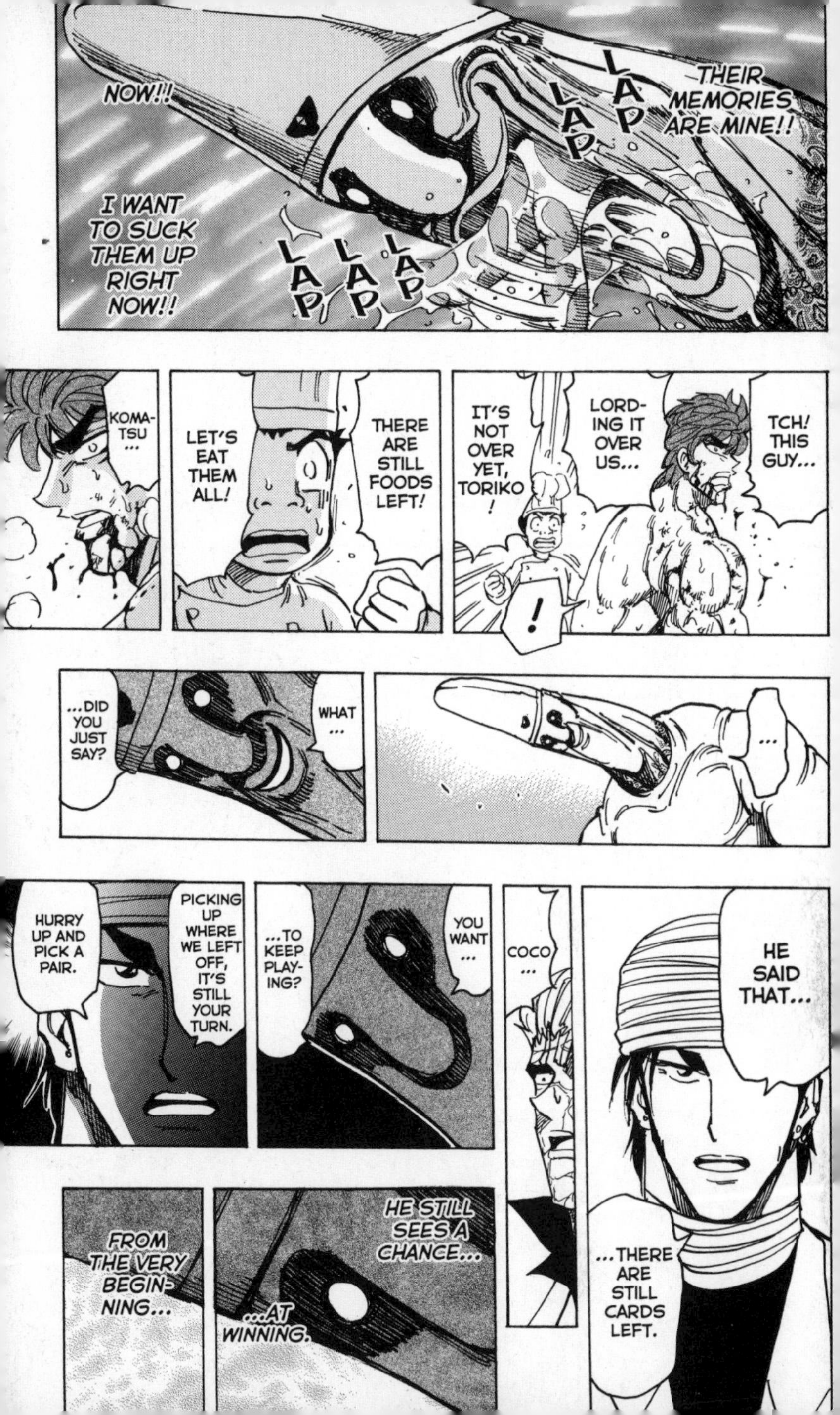
THEIR MEMORIES ARE MINE!!
LAP LAP
NOW!!
I WANT TO SUCK THEM UP RIGHT NOW!!
LAP LAP LAP
TCH! THIS GUY...
LORD-ING IT OVER US...
IT'S NOT OVER YET, TORIKO!
!
THERE ARE STILL FOODS LEFT!
LET'S EAT THEM ALL!
KOMA-TSU...
...
WHAT...
...DID YOU JUST SAY?
HE SAID THAT...
...THERE ARE STILL CARDS LEFT.
COCO...
YOU WANT...
...TO KEEP PLAY-ING?
PICKING UP WHERE WE LEFT OFF, IT'S STILL YOUR TURN.
HURRY UP AND PICK A PAIR.
HE STILL SEES A CHANCE...
...AT WINNING.
FROM THE VERY BEGIN-NING...

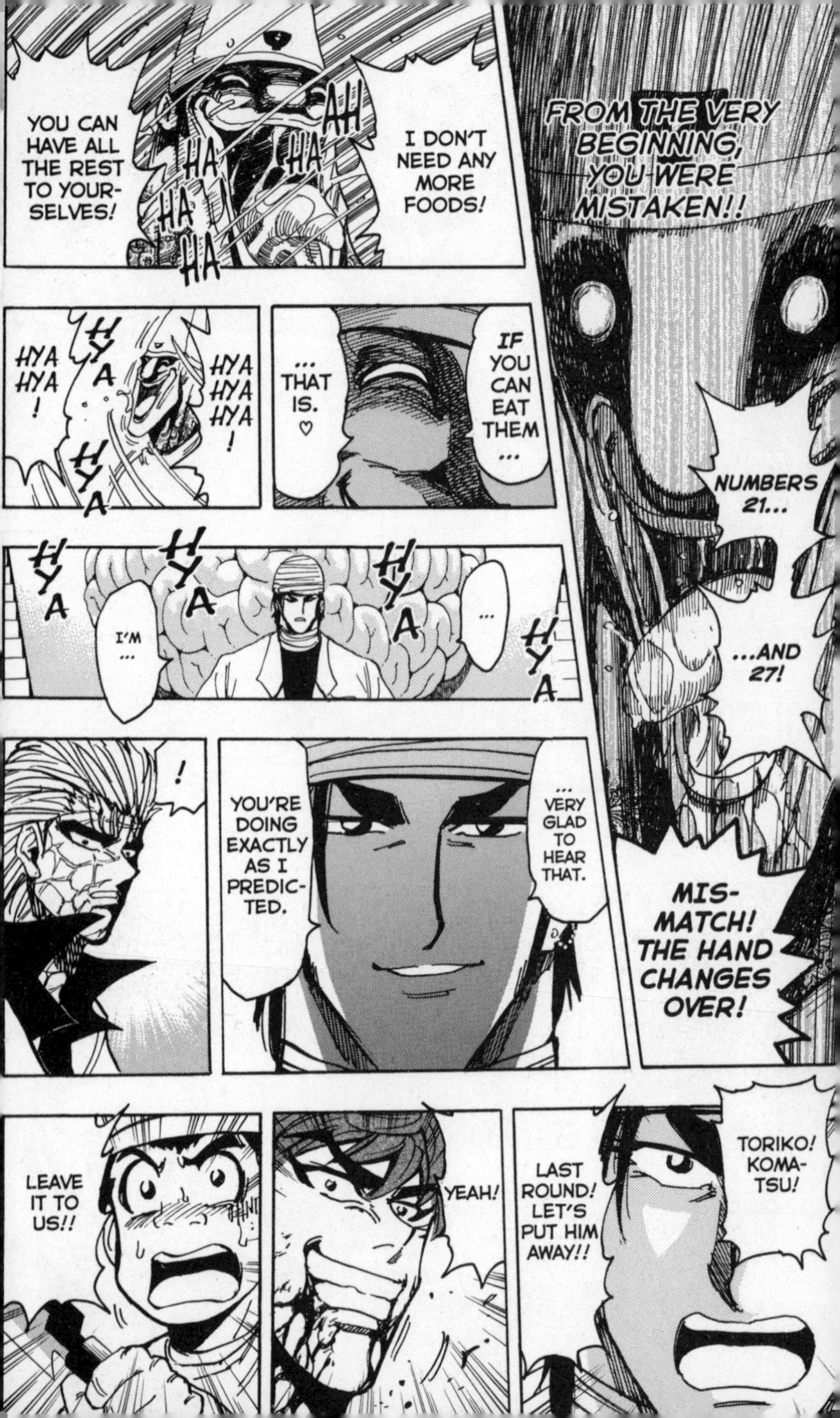
FROM THE VERY BEGINNING, YOU WERE MISTAKEN!!
NUMBERS 21...
...AND 27!
MIS-MATCH! THE HAND CHANGES OVER!
AH HA HA HA HA HA
I DON'T NEED ANY MORE FOODS!
YOU CAN HAVE ALL THE REST TO YOUR-SELVES!
IF YOU CAN EAT THEM ...
... THAT IS. ♡
HYA HYA HYA!
HYA
HYA HYA!
HYA
HYA
HYA
...
HYA
I'M ...
HYA
... VERY GLAD TO HEAR THAT.
YOU'RE DOING EXACTLY AS I PREDIC-TED.
!
TORIKO! KOMA-TSU!
LAST ROUND! LET'S PUT HIM AWAY!!
YEAH!
LEAVE IT TO US!!

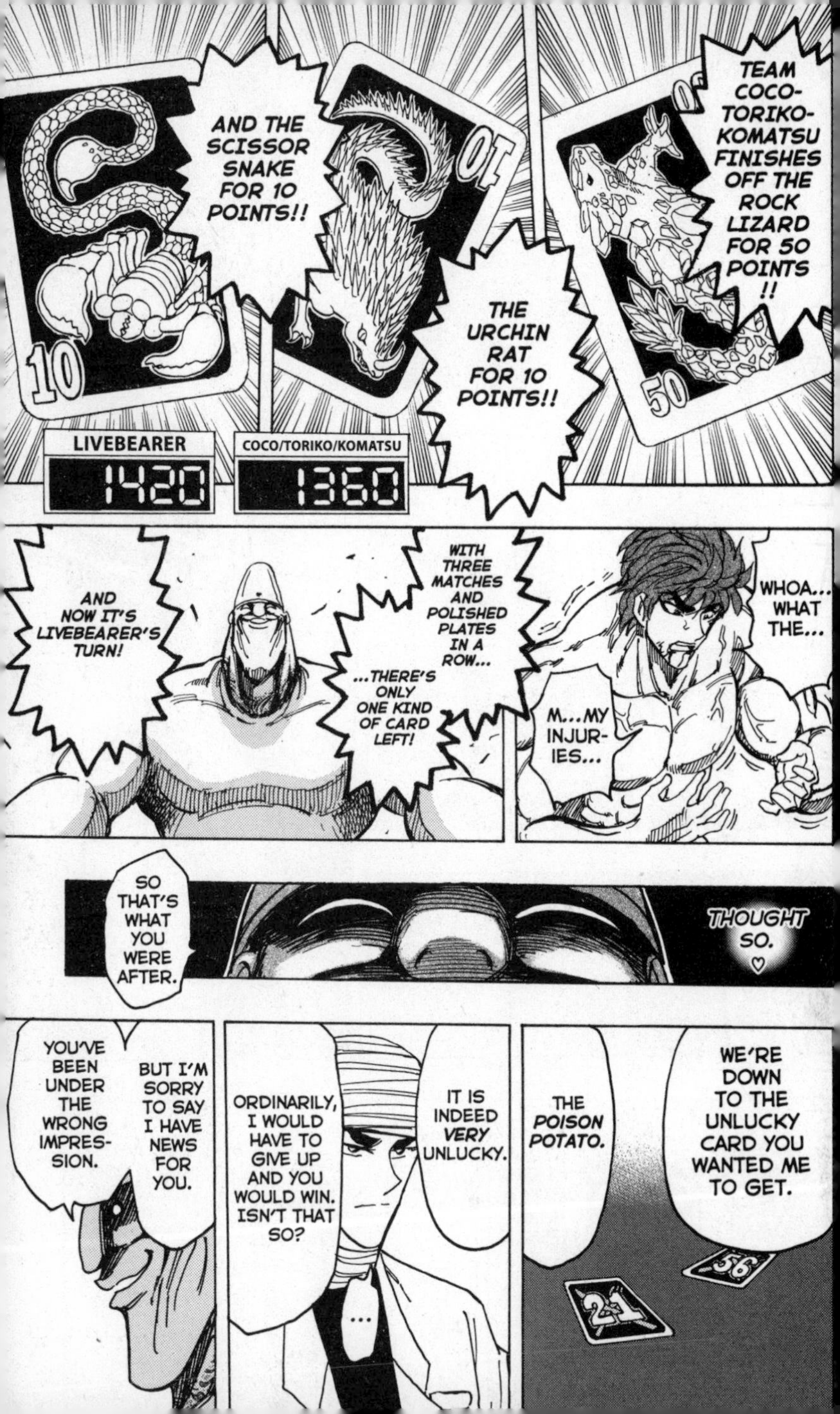
TEAM COCO-TORIKO-KOMATSU FINISHES OFF THE ROCK LIZARD FOR 50 POINTS!!
50
THE URCHIN RAT FOR 10 POINTS!!
10
AND THE SCISSOR SNAKE FOR 10 POINTS!!
10
LIVEBEARER
1420
COCO/TORIKO/KOMATSU
1360
WHOA... WHAT THE...
M...MY INJURIES...
WITH THREE MATCHES AND POLISHED PLATES IN A ROW...
...THERE'S ONLY ONE KIND OF CARD LEFT!
AND NOW IT'S LIVEBEARER'S TURN!
THOUGHT SO. ♡
SO THAT'S WHAT YOU WERE AFTER.
WE'RE DOWN TO THE UNLUCKY CARD YOU WANTED ME TO GET.
THE POISON POTATO.
56
21
IT IS INDEED VERY UNLUCKY.
ORDINARILY, I WOULD HAVE TO GIVE UP AND YOU WOULD WIN. ISN'T THAT SO?
...
BUT I'M SORRY TO SAY I HAVE NEWS FOR YOU.
YOU'VE BEEN UNDER THE WRONG IMPRESSION.

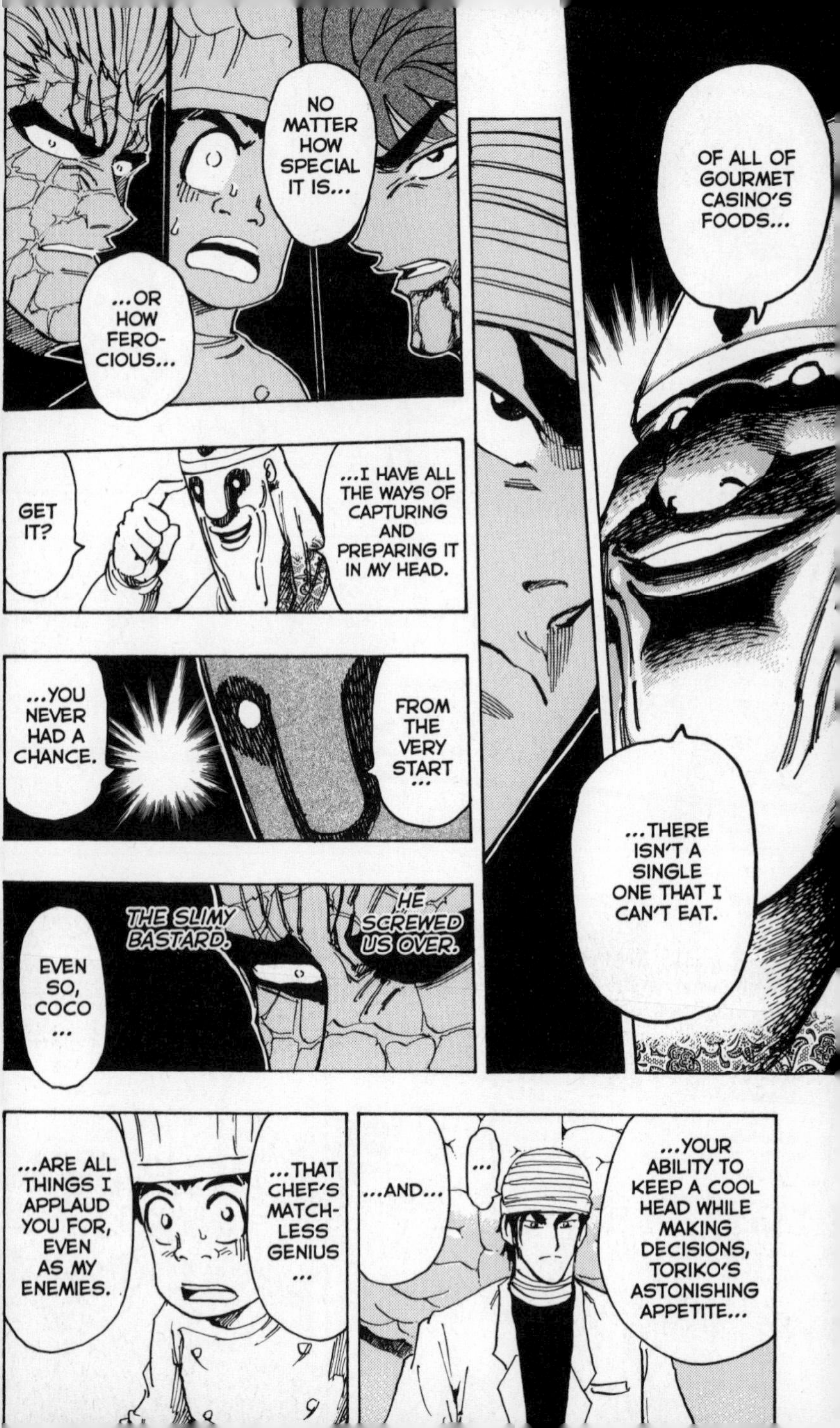

OF ALL OF GOURMET CASINO'S FOODS...
...THERE ISN'T A SINGLE ONE THAT I CAN'T EAT.
NO MATTER HOW SPECIAL IT IS...
...OR HOW FEROCIOUS...
...I HAVE ALL THE WAYS OF CAPTURING AND PREPARING IT IN MY HEAD.
GET IT?
FROM THE VERY START...
...YOU NEVER HAD A CHANCE.
HE SCREWED US OVER.
THE SLIMY BASTARD.
EVEN SO, COCO...
...YOUR ABILITY TO KEEP A COOL HEAD WHILE MAKING DECISIONS, TORIKO'S ASTONISHING APPETITE...
...
...AND...
...THAT CHEF'S MATCHLESS GENIUS...
...ARE ALL THINGS I APPLAUD YOU FOR, EVEN AS MY ENEMIES.

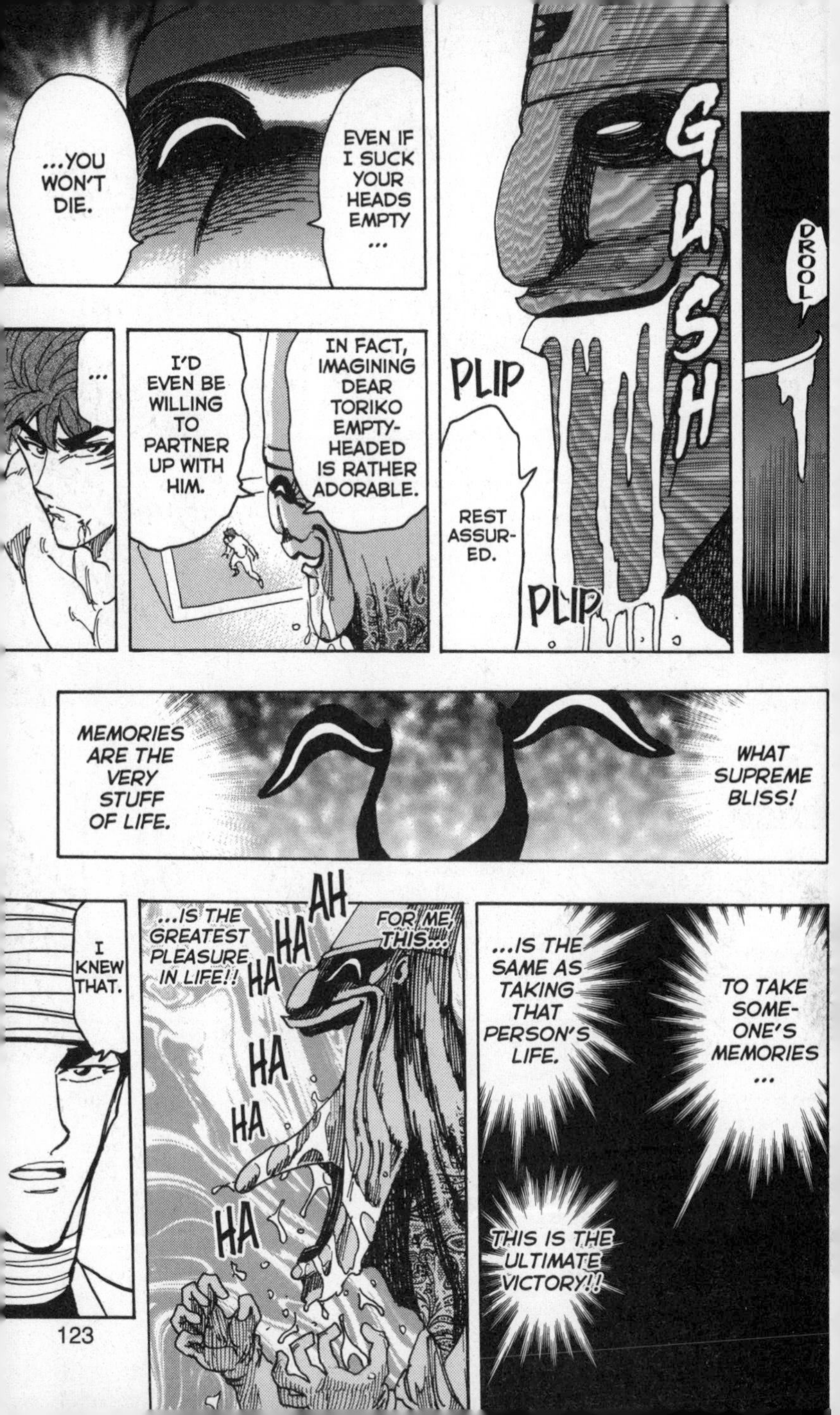
DROOL
GUSH
PLIP
REST ASSURED.
PLIP
EVEN IF I SUCK YOUR HEADS EMPTY...
...YOU WON'T DIE.
IN FACT, IMAGINING DEAR TORIKO EMPTY-HEADED IS RATHER ADORABLE.
I'D EVEN BE WILLING TO PARTNER UP WITH HIM.
...
WHAT SUPREME BLISS!
MEMORIES ARE THE VERY STUFF OF LIFE.
TO TAKE SOMEONE'S MEMORIES...
...IS THE SAME AS TAKING THAT PERSON'S LIFE.
THIS IS THE ULTIMATE VICTORY!!
FOR ME, THIS...
AH
HA
HA
HA
HA
HA
HA
...IS THE GREATEST PLEASURE IN LIFE!!
I KNEW THAT.

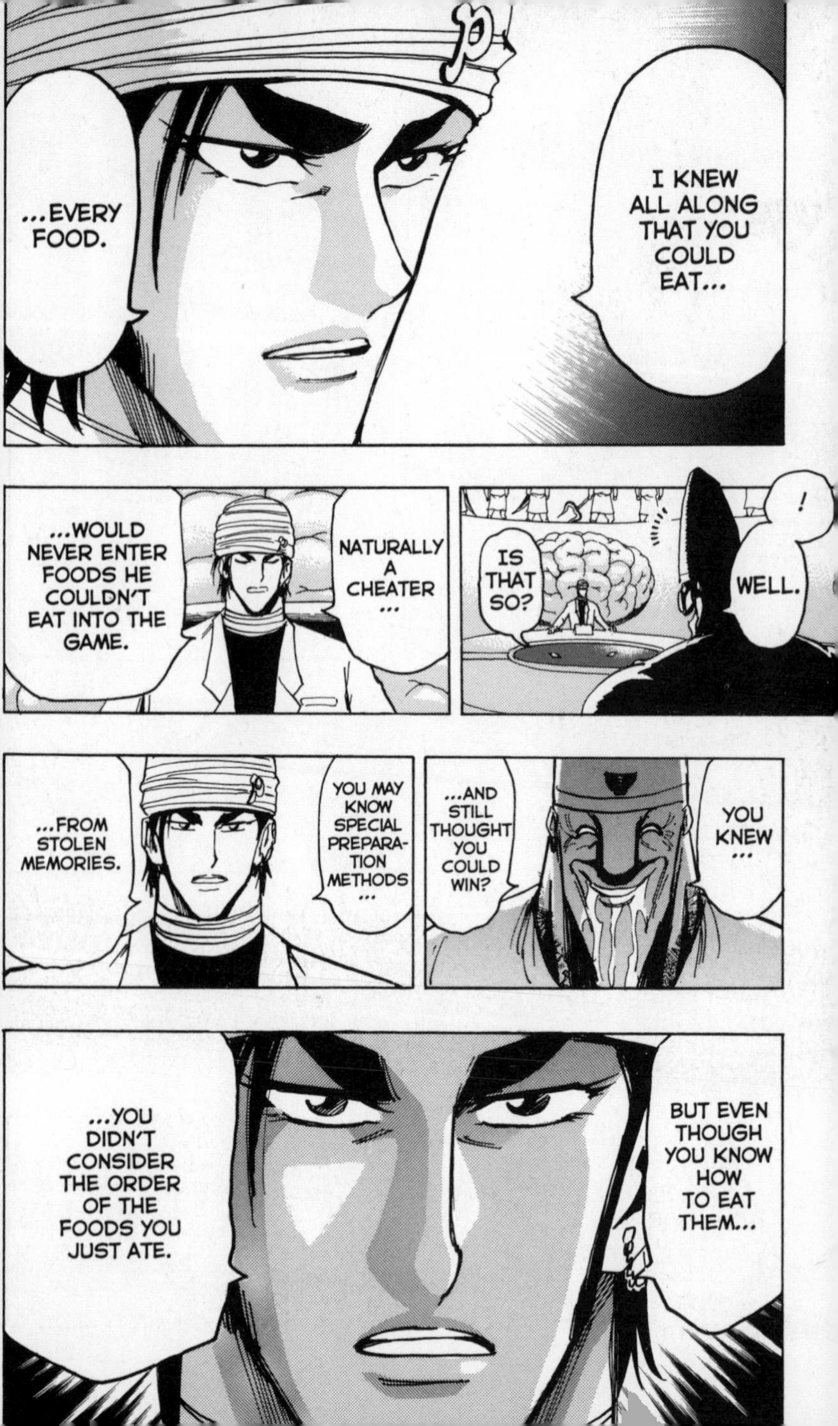
I KNEW ALL ALONG THAT YOU COULD EAT...
...EVERY FOOD.
!
WELL.
IS THAT SO?
NATURALLY A CHEATER...
...WOULD NEVER ENTER FOODS HE COULDN'T EAT INTO THE GAME.
YOU KNEW...
...AND STILL THOUGHT YOU COULD WIN?
YOU MAY KNOW SPECIAL PREPARATION METHODS...
...FROM STOLEN MEMORIES.
BUT EVEN THOUGH YOU KNOW HOW TO EAT THEM...
...YOU DIDN'T CONSIDER THE ORDER OF THE FOODS YOU JUST ATE.

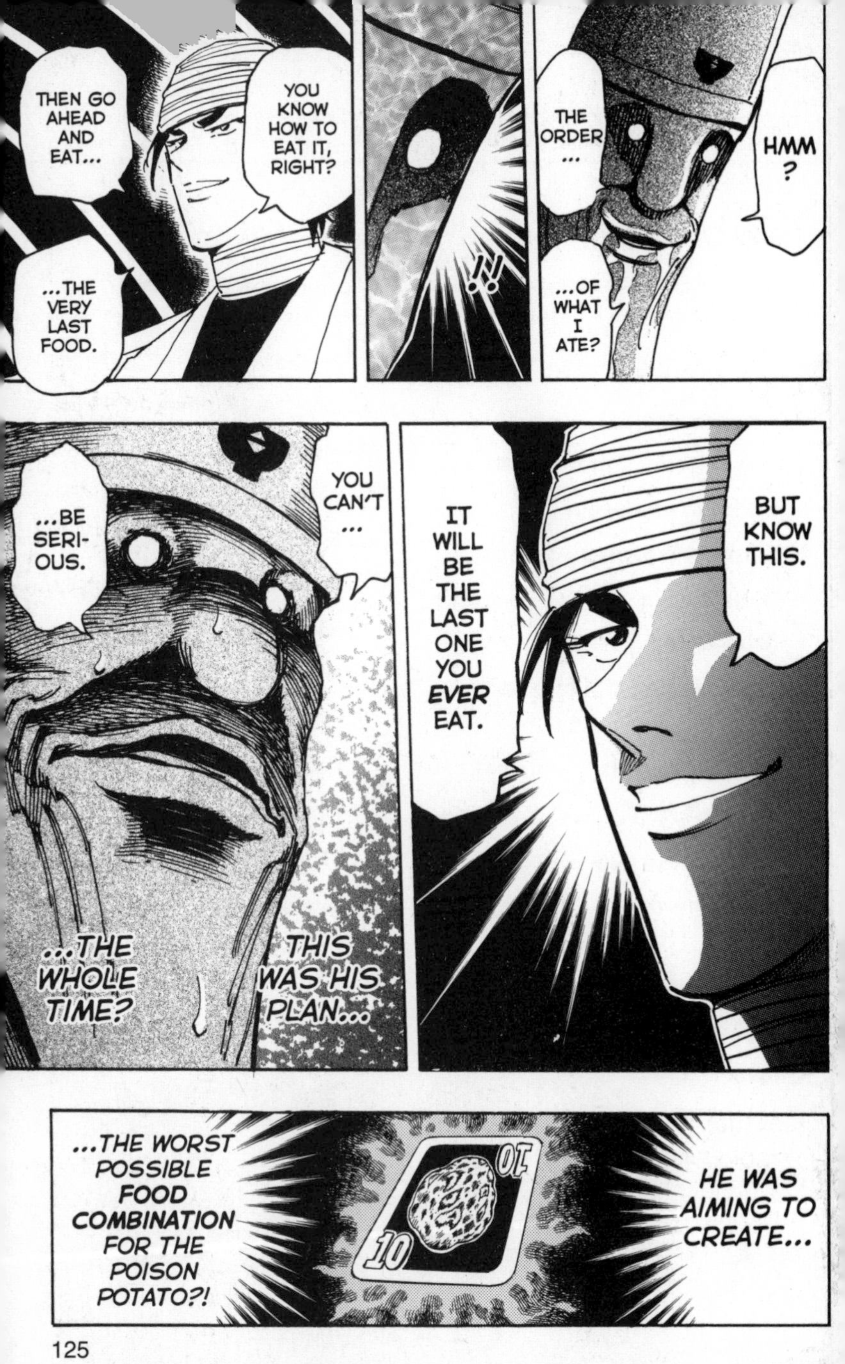
HMM?
THE ORDER...
...OF WHAT I ATE?
!!
YOU KNOW HOW TO EAT IT, RIGHT?
THEN GO AHEAD AND EAT...
...THE VERY LAST FOOD.
BUT KNOW THIS.
IT WILL BE THE LAST ONE YOU *EVER* EAT.
YOU CAN'T...
...BE SERIOUS.
THIS WAS HIS PLAN...
...THE WHOLE TIME?
HE WAS AIMING TO CREATE...
...THE WORST POSSIBLE FOOD COMBINATION FOR THE POISON POTATO?!
10
10

"GOURMET TASTING" STANDINGS

VS

Team Coco/Toriko/Komatsu

(Acquired Cards & Points)

Card	Points
◎Cherry Apple	10 Points
◎Smashroom	20 Points
◎Watermelon Clam	10 Points
◎Pudding Mountain	150 Points
◎Summer Whiskey	50 Points
◎Bullet Acorn	70 Points
◎Atlas Crab	30 Points
◎Hanya Panda (Joker)	250 Points
+ Garlic Crab	200 Points
◎Dragonfire	30 Points
◎Troll Cheese (Joker)	10 Points
◎Nitro Cherry	10 Points
+ Shock Lemon	200 Points
+ Hanya Panda	250 Points
◎Rock Lizard	50 Points
◎Urchin Rat	10 Points
◎Scissor Snake	10 Points

TOTAL 1,360 Points

Team Livebearer

(Acquired Cards & Points)

Card	Points
◎ Sausage Worm	50 Points
◎ Man-Faced Mushroom	70 Points
◎ Melon Egg	100 Points
◎ Rockadillo	70 Points
◎ River Styx Poison Lizard	150 Points
◎ Garlic Crab	200 Points
◎ Rock Potato	60 Points
◎ Brain Urchin	30 Points
◎ Shock Lemon	200 Points
◎ Flavor Ant	40 Points
◎ Bubble Abalone	20 Points
◎ Golden Shrimp	200 Points
◎ Summer Whiskey	50 Points
◎ Electric Banana	180 Points

TOTAL 1,420 Points

LIVEBEARER IS IN THE LEAD BY 60 POINTS AND THE REMAINING CARD, THE POISON POTATO, IS ONLY 10 POINTS. IT'S LIVEBEARER'S TURN NOW.

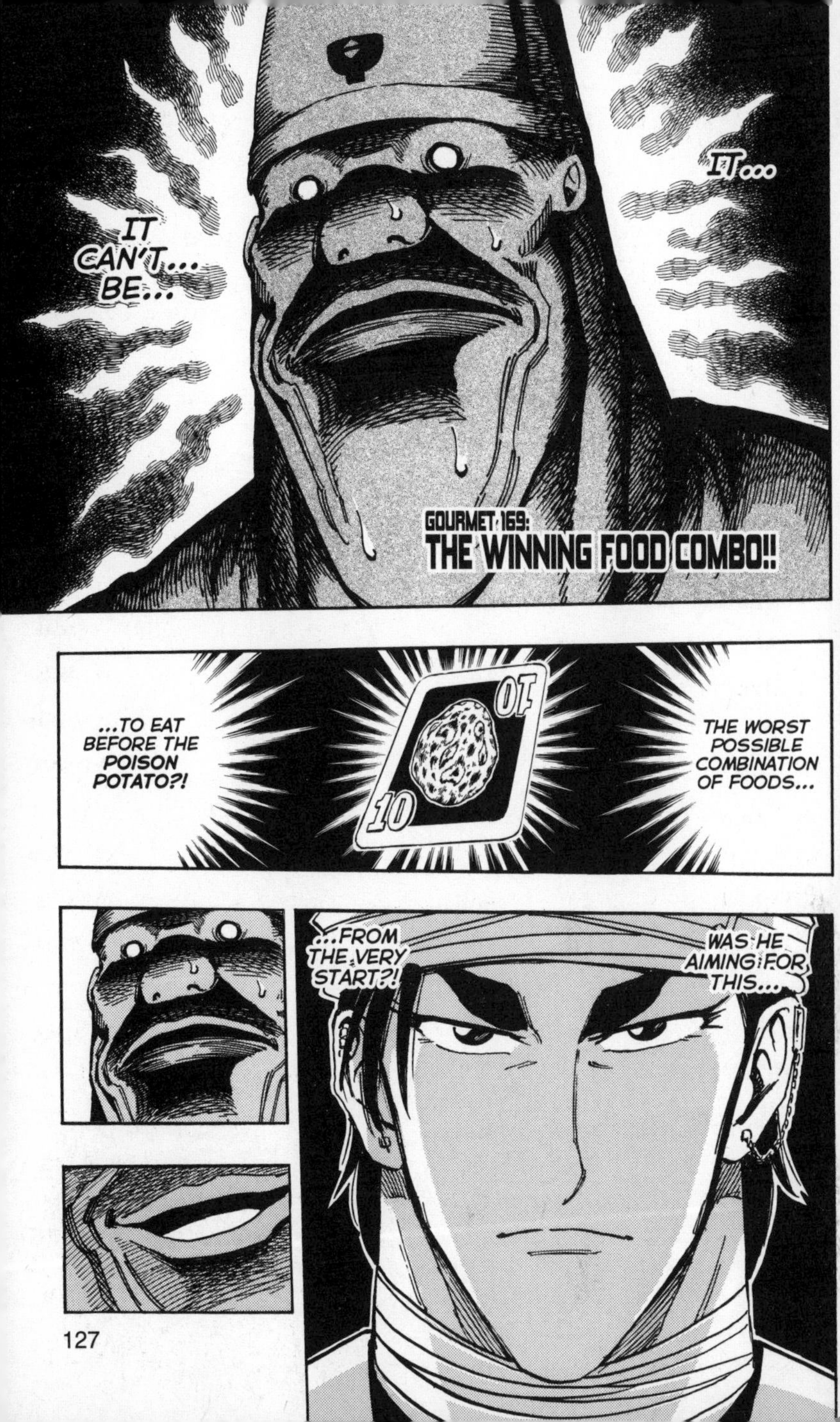
IT...
IT CAN'T... BE...
GOURMET 169:
THE WINNING FOOD COMBO!!
THE WORST POSSIBLE COMBINATION OF FOODS...
10
10
...TO EAT BEFORE THE POISON POTATO?!
WAS HE AIMING FOR THIS...
...FROM THE VERY START?!

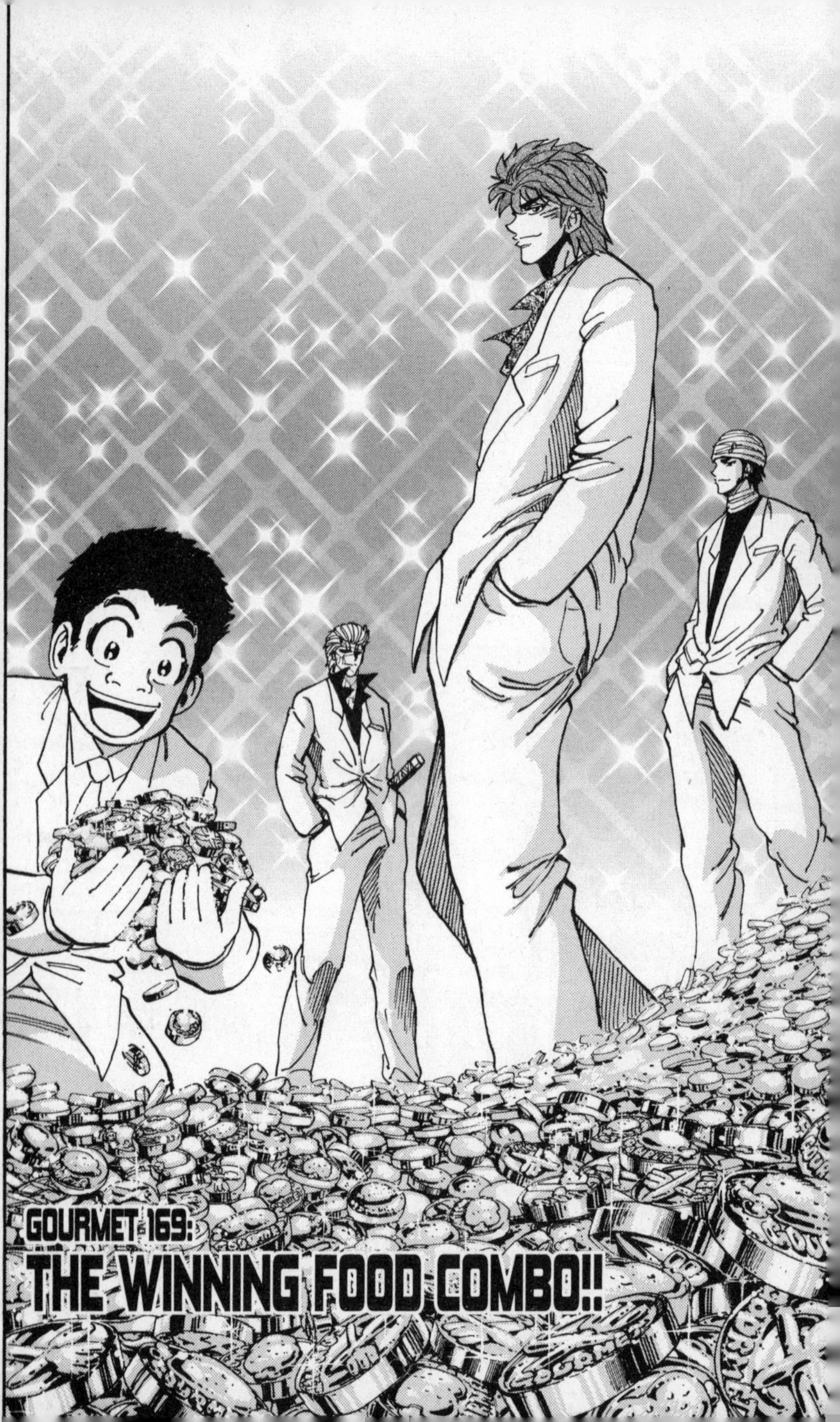
GOURMET 169:
THE WINNING FOOD COMBO!!

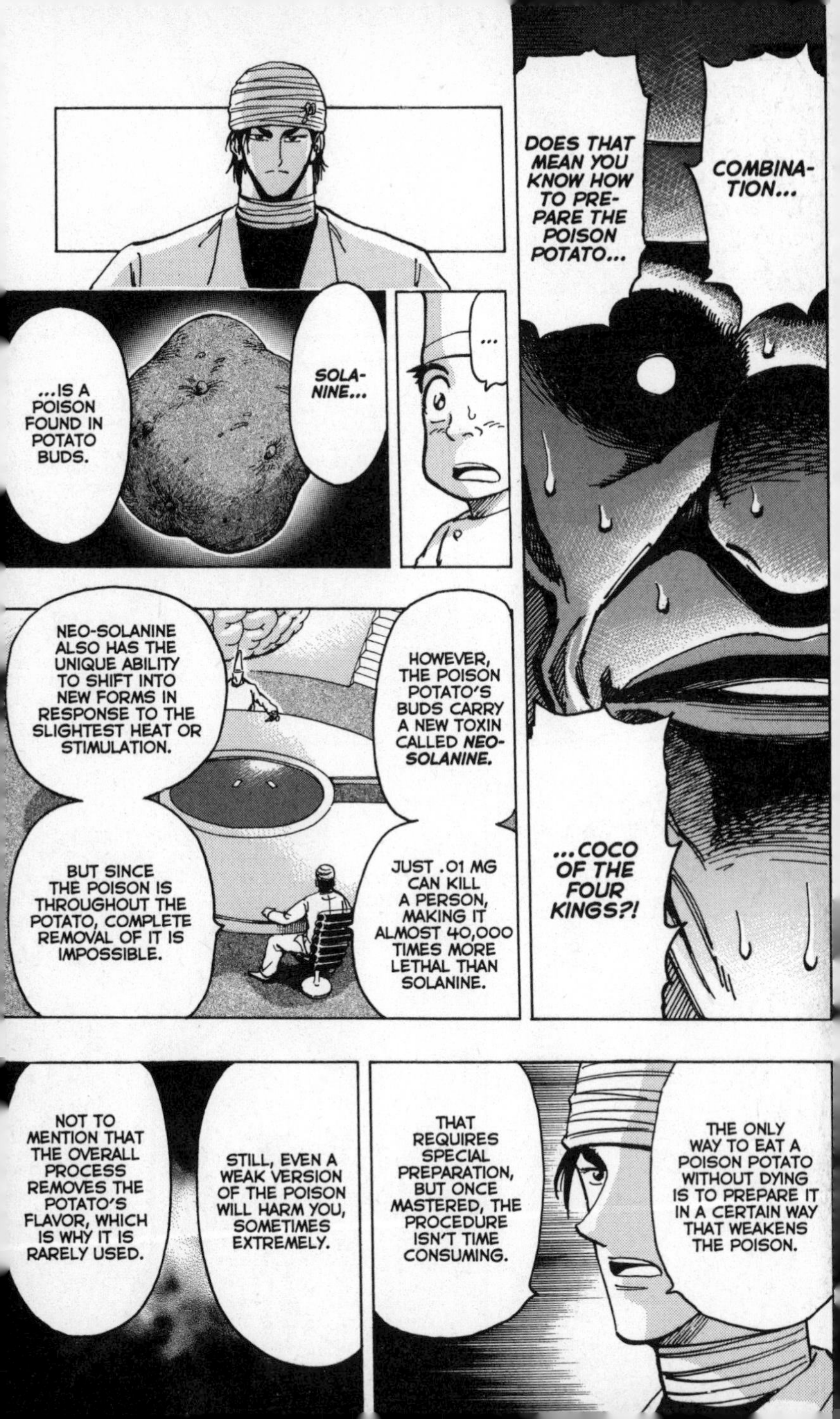
COMBINATION...
DOES THAT MEAN YOU KNOW HOW TO PREPARE THE POISON POTATO...
...COCO OF THE FOUR KINGS?!
...
SOLANINE...
...IS A POISON FOUND IN POTATO BUDS.
HOWEVER, THE POISON POTATO'S BUDS CARRY A NEW TOXIN CALLED *NEO-SOLANINE.*
JUST .01 MG CAN KILL A PERSON, MAKING IT ALMOST 40,000 TIMES MORE LETHAL THAN SOLANINE.
NEO-SOLANINE ALSO HAS THE UNIQUE ABILITY TO SHIFT INTO NEW FORMS IN RESPONSE TO THE SLIGHTEST HEAT OR STIMULATION.
BUT SINCE THE POISON IS THROUGHOUT THE POTATO, COMPLETE REMOVAL OF IT IS IMPOSSIBLE.
THE ONLY WAY TO EAT A POISON POTATO WITHOUT DYING IS TO PREPARE IT IN A CERTAIN WAY THAT WEAKENS THE POISON.
THAT REQUIRES SPECIAL PREPARATION, BUT ONCE MASTERED, THE PROCEDURE ISN'T TIME CONSUMING.
STILL, EVEN A WEAK VERSION OF THE POISON WILL HARM YOU, SOMETIMES EXTREMELY.
NOT TO MENTION THAT THE OVERALL PROCESS REMOVES THE POTATO'S FLAVOR, WHICH IS WHY IT IS RARELY USED.

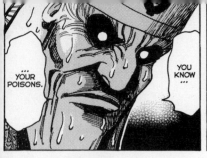

YOU KNOW ...
... YOUR POISONS.
IT'S WELL KNOWN THAT YOU BUY AND SELL EXPENSIVE MEMORY DATA ON THE BLACK MARKET.
YOU PROBABLY HAD NO TROUBLE OBTAINING THE SAFE PREPARATION METHOD.
HOWEVER, EVEN THE WEAKENED POISON CAN HAVE POWERFUL EFFECTS DEPENDING ON THE FOOD IT'S PAIRED WITH.
YOUR HIGH-PRICED DATA DIDN'T INCLUDE THAT INFORMATION, DID IT?
OH, IT DID... THE ANTIGENS IN CRUSTACEANS, THE ALCOHOL IN SUMMER WHISKEY...
...AND THE NARCOTICS IN *ELECTRIC BANANAS...*
200
...WILL REACT POORLY WITH THE POISON POTATO, RESULTING IN SEVERE SIDE EFFECTS.
180
180
GOLDEN SHRIMP, SUMMER WHISKEY, AND ELECTRIC BANANAS... WHEN DID THIS ORDER...
... COME TO YOU?
AFTER YOU ATE THE GOLDEN SHRIMP.
IT WAS THEN THAT I RECALLED THE POISON POTATO.

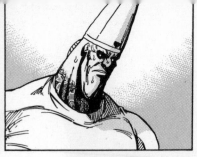

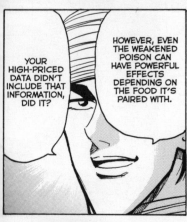

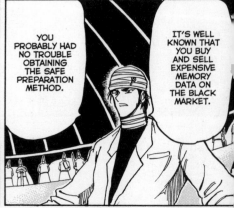

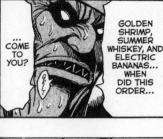

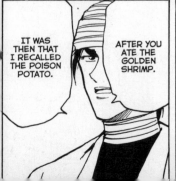

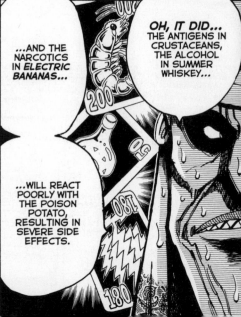

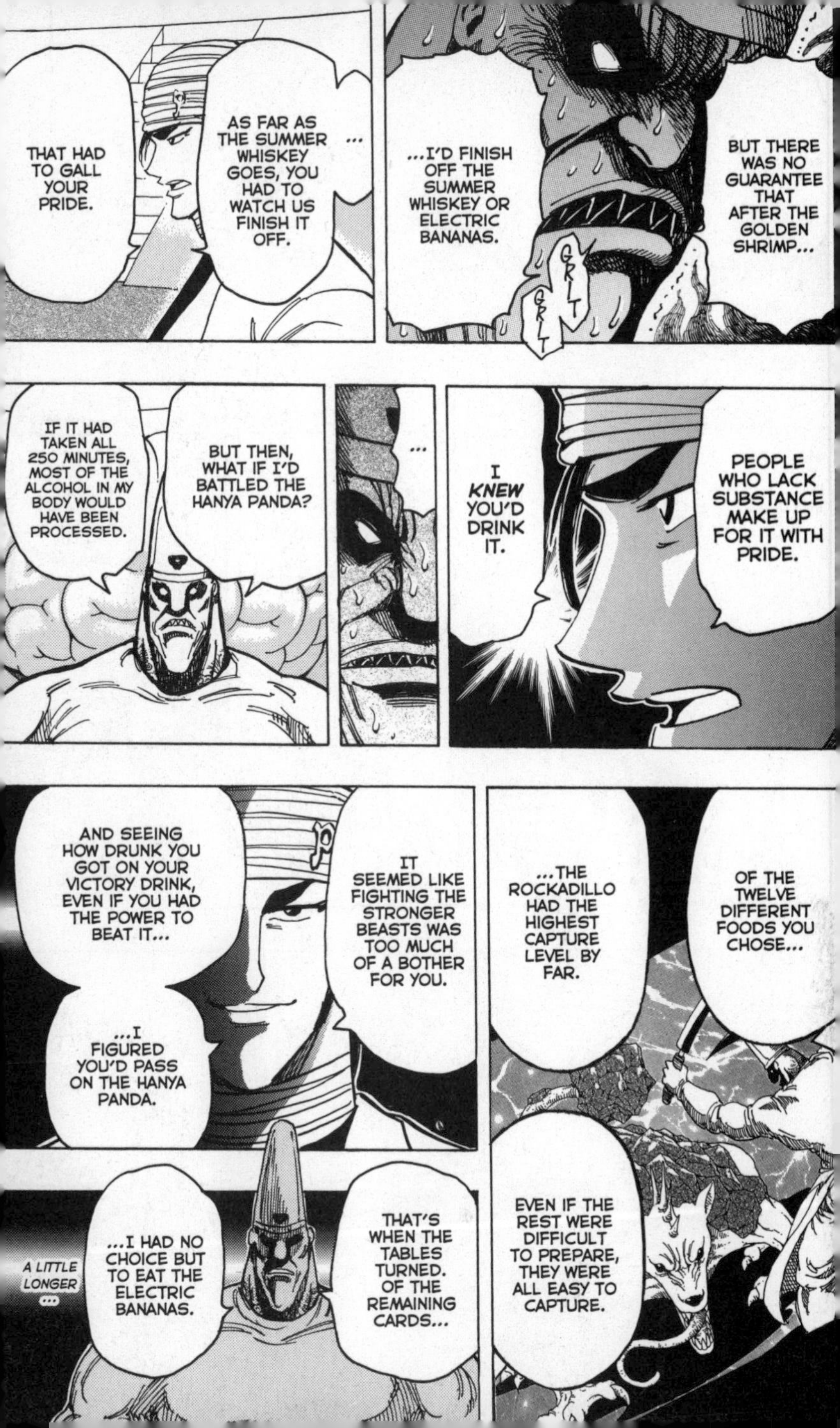
BUT THERE WAS NO GUARANTEE THAT AFTER THE GOLDEN SHRIMP...
...I'D FINISH OFF THE SUMMER WHISKEY OR ELECTRIC BANANAS.
GRLT GRLT
...
AS FAR AS THE SUMMER WHISKEY GOES, YOU HAD TO WATCH US FINISH IT OFF.
THAT HAD TO GALL YOUR PRIDE.
PEOPLE WHO LACK SUBSTANCE MAKE UP FOR IT WITH PRIDE.
I *KNEW* YOU'D DRINK IT.
...
BUT THEN, WHAT IF I'D BATTLED THE HANYA PANDA?
IF IT HAD TAKEN ALL 250 MINUTES, MOST OF THE ALCOHOL IN MY BODY WOULD HAVE BEEN PROCESSED.
OF THE TWELVE DIFFERENT FOODS YOU CHOSE...
...THE ROCKADILLO HAD THE HIGHEST CAPTURE LEVEL BY FAR.
EVEN IF THE REST WERE DIFFICULT TO PREPARE, THEY WERE ALL EASY TO CAPTURE.
IT SEEMED LIKE FIGHTING THE STRONGER BEASTS WAS TOO MUCH OF A BOTHER FOR YOU.
AND SEEING HOW DRUNK YOU GOT ON YOUR VICTORY DRINK, EVEN IF YOU HAD THE POWER TO BEAT IT...
...I FIGURED YOU'D PASS ON THE HANYA PANDA.
THAT'S WHEN THE TABLES TURNED. OF THE REMAINING CARDS...
...I HAD NO CHOICE BUT TO EAT THE ELECTRIC BANANAS.
A LITTLE LONGER...

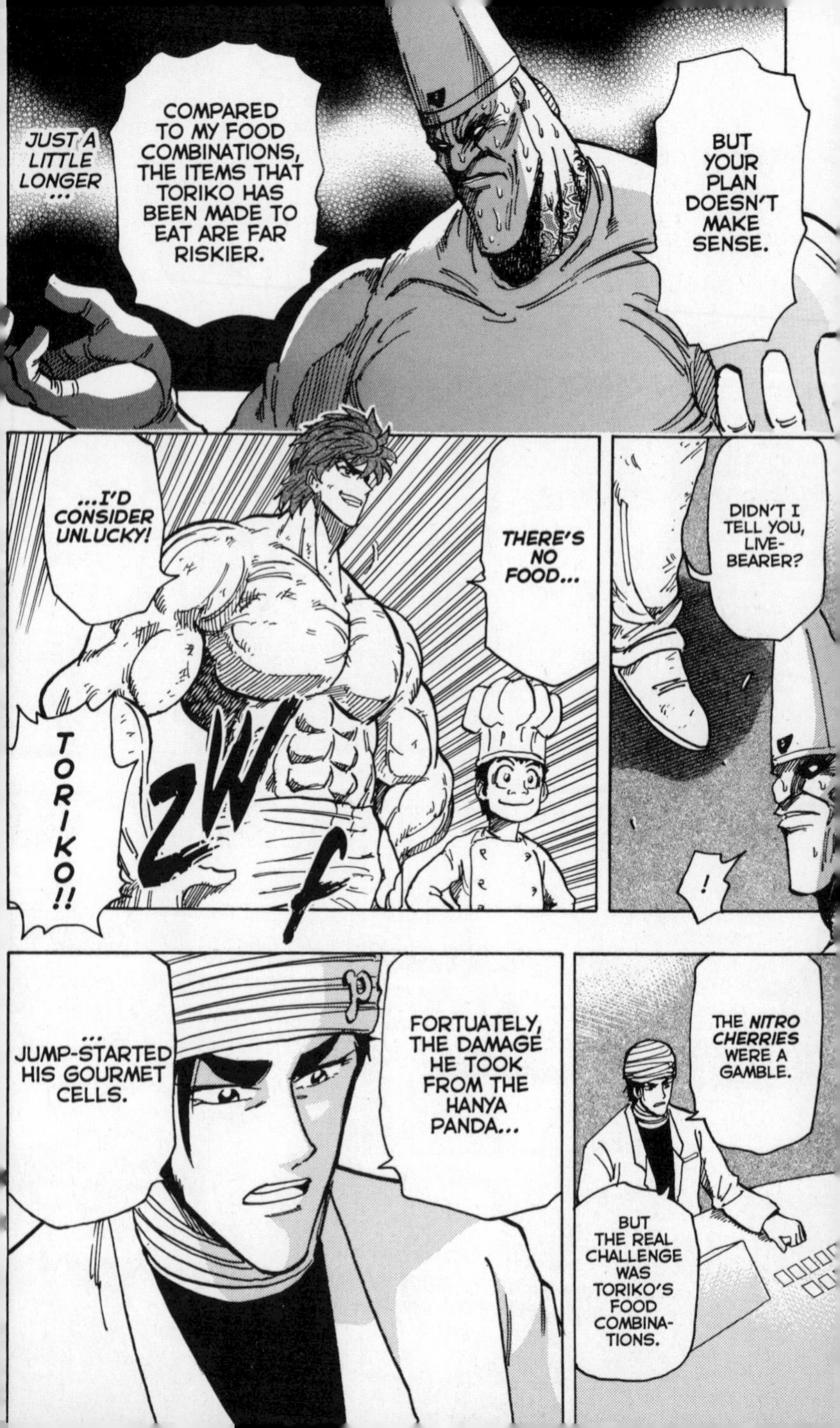
BUT YOUR PLAN DOESN'T MAKE SENSE.
COMPARED TO MY FOOD COMBINATIONS, THE ITEMS THAT TORIKO HAS BEEN MADE TO EAT ARE FAR RISKIER.
JUST A LITTLE LONGER...
DIDN'T I TELL YOU, LIVE-BEARER?
!
THERE'S NO FOOD...
...I'D CONSIDER UNLUCKY!
TORIKO!!
ZWF
THE NITRO CHERRIES WERE A GAMBLE.
BUT THE REAL CHALLENGE WAS TORIKO'S FOOD COMBINA-TIONS.
FORTUATELY, THE DAMAGE HE TOOK FROM THE HANYA PANDA...
...JUMP-STARTED HIS GOURMET CELLS.

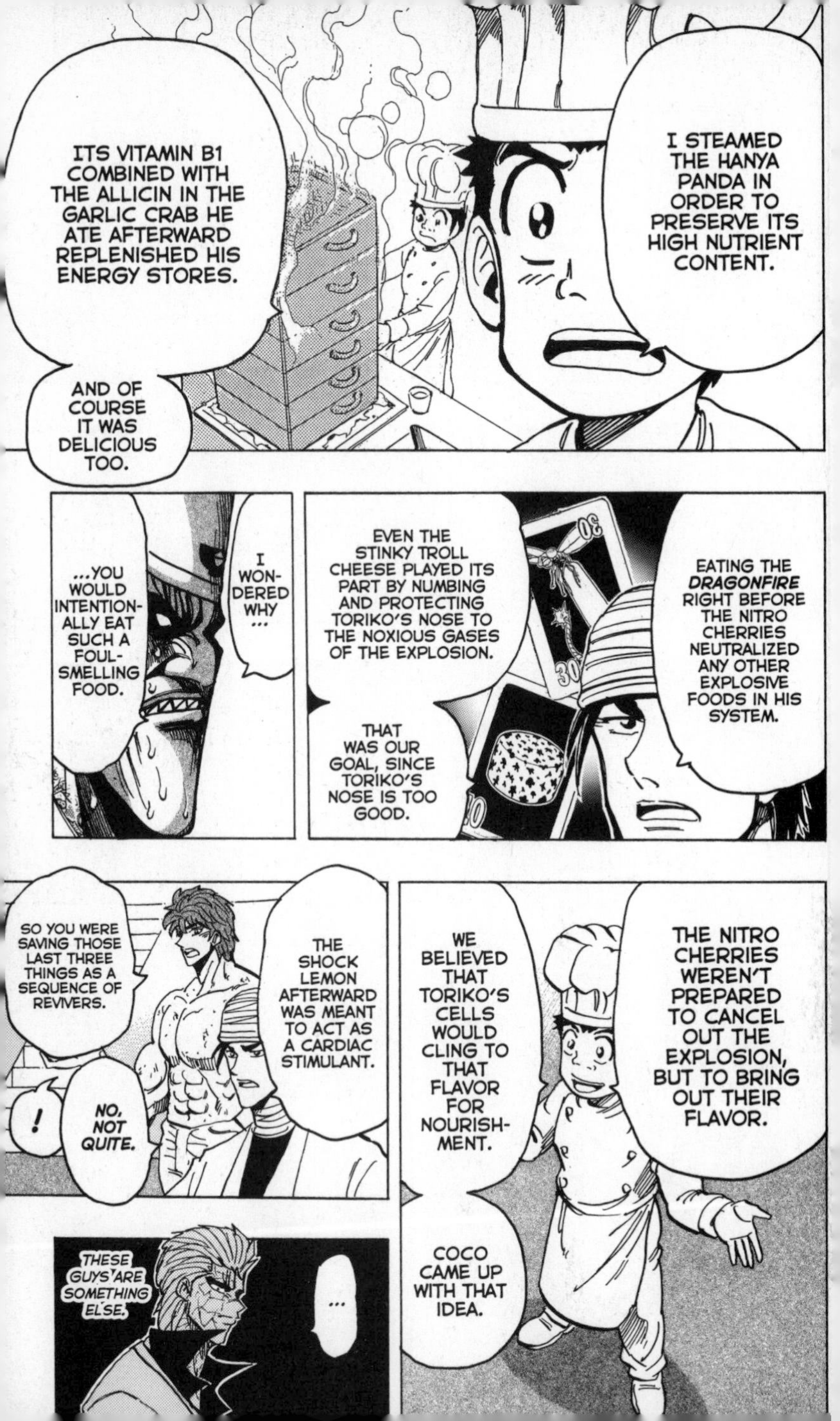
I STEAMED THE HANYA PANDA IN ORDER TO PRESERVE ITS HIGH NUTRIENT CONTENT.
ITS VITAMIN B1 COMBINED WITH THE ALLICIN IN THE GARLIC CRAB HE ATE AFTERWARD REPLENISHED HIS ENERGY STORES.
AND OF COURSE IT WAS DELICIOUS TOO.
EATING THE *DRAGONFIRE* RIGHT BEFORE THE NITRO CHERRIES NEUTRALIZED ANY OTHER EXPLOSIVE FOODS IN HIS SYSTEM.
EVEN THE STINKY TROLL CHEESE PLAYED ITS PART BY NUMBING AND PROTECTING TORIKO'S NOSE TO THE NOXIOUS GASES OF THE EXPLOSION.
THAT WAS OUR GOAL, SINCE TORIKO'S NOSE IS TOO GOOD.
I WONDERED WHY...
...YOU WOULD INTENTIONALLY EAT SUCH A FOUL-SMELLING FOOD.
THE NITRO CHERRIES WEREN'T PREPARED TO CANCEL OUT THE EXPLOSION, BUT TO BRING OUT THEIR FLAVOR.
WE BELIEVED THAT TORIKO'S CELLS WOULD CLING TO THAT FLAVOR FOR NOURISHMENT.
COCO CAME UP WITH THAT IDEA.
THE SHOCK LEMON AFTERWARD WAS MEANT TO ACT AS A CARDIAC STIMULANT.
SO YOU WERE SAVING THOSE LAST THREE THINGS AS A SEQUENCE OF REVIVERS.
!
NO, NOT QUITE.
...
THESE GUYS ARE SOMETHING ELSE.

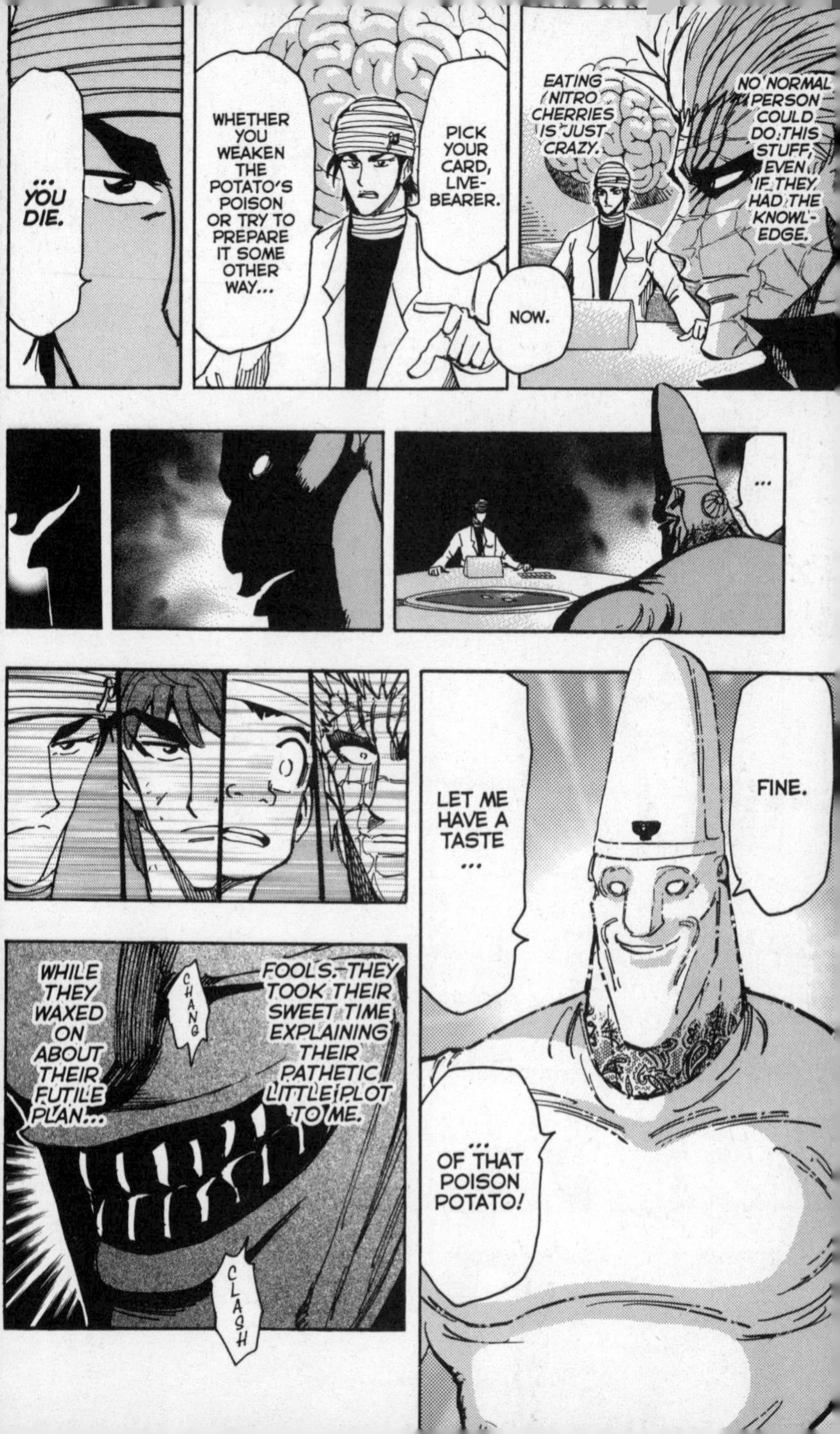
NO NORMAL PERSON COULD DO THIS STUFF, EVEN IF THEY HAD THE KNOWL-EDGE.
EATING NITRO CHERRIES IS JUST CRAZY.
PICK YOUR CARD, LIVE-BEARER.
NOW.
WHETHER YOU WEAKEN THE POTATO'S POISON OR TRY TO PREPARE IT SOME OTHER WAY...
... YOU DIE.
...
FINE.
LET ME HAVE A TASTE ...
... OF THAT POISON POTATO!
FOOLS. THEY TOOK THEIR SWEET TIME EXPLAINING THEIR PATHETIC LITTLE PLOT TO ME.
CHANG
WHILE THEY WAXED ON ABOUT THEIR FUTILE PLAN...
CLASH

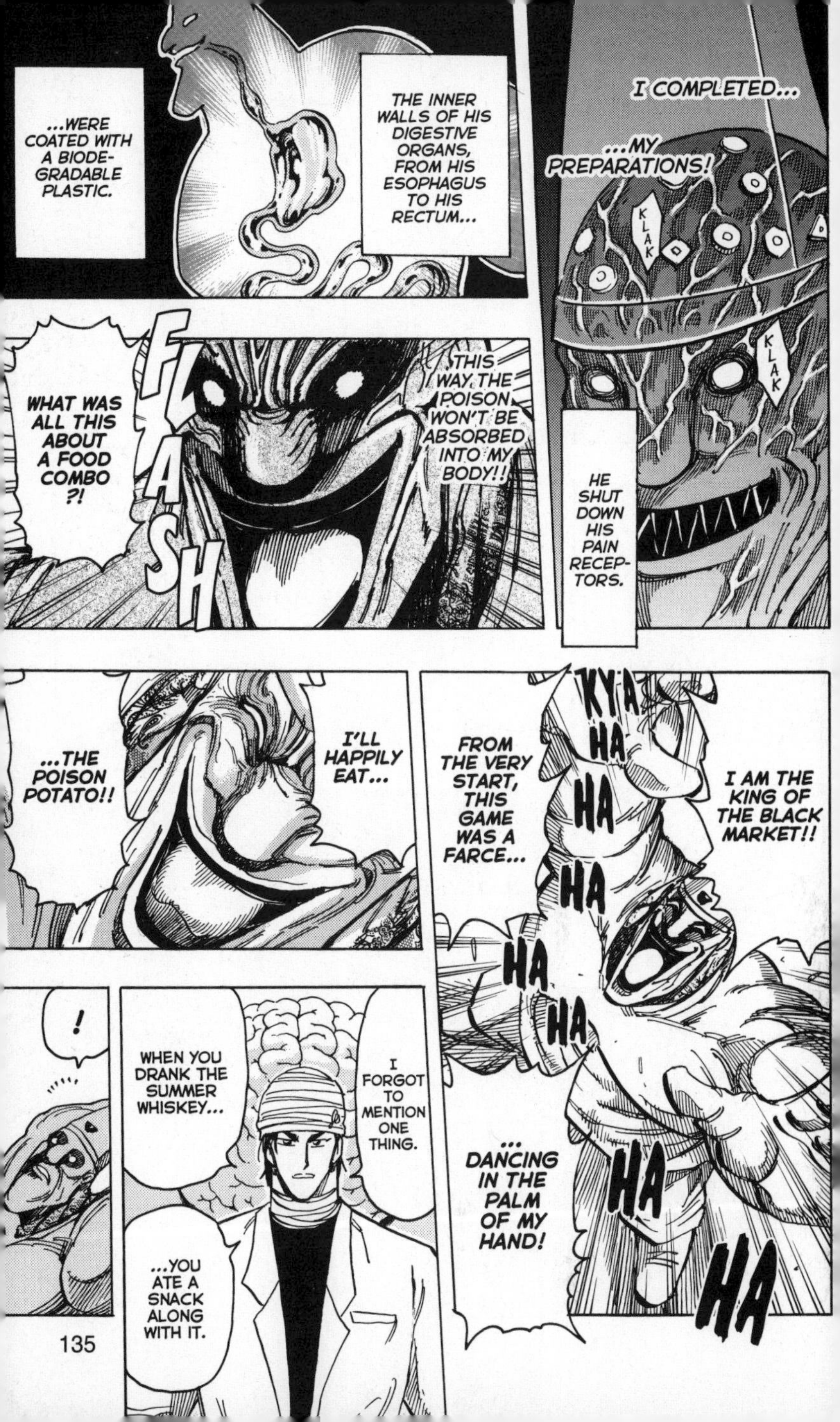
I COMPLETED...
...MY PREPARATIONS!
KLAK
KLAK
HE SHUT DOWN HIS PAIN RECEPTORS.
THE INNER WALLS OF HIS DIGESTIVE ORGANS, FROM HIS ESOPHAGUS TO HIS RECTUM...
...WERE COATED WITH A BIODEGRADABLE PLASTIC.
THIS WAY THE POISON WON'T BE ABSORBED INTO MY BODY!!
FLASH
WHAT WAS ALL THIS ABOUT A FOOD COMBO?!
I AM THE KING OF THE BLACK MARKET!!
KYAHAHAHAHAHAHAHAHA
FROM THE VERY START, THIS GAME WAS A FARCE...
...DANCING IN THE PALM OF MY HAND!
I'LL HAPPILY EAT...
...THE POISON POTATO!!
I FORGOT TO MENTION ONE THING.
WHEN YOU DRANK THE SUMMER WHISKEY...
...YOU ATE A SNACK ALONG WITH IT.
!

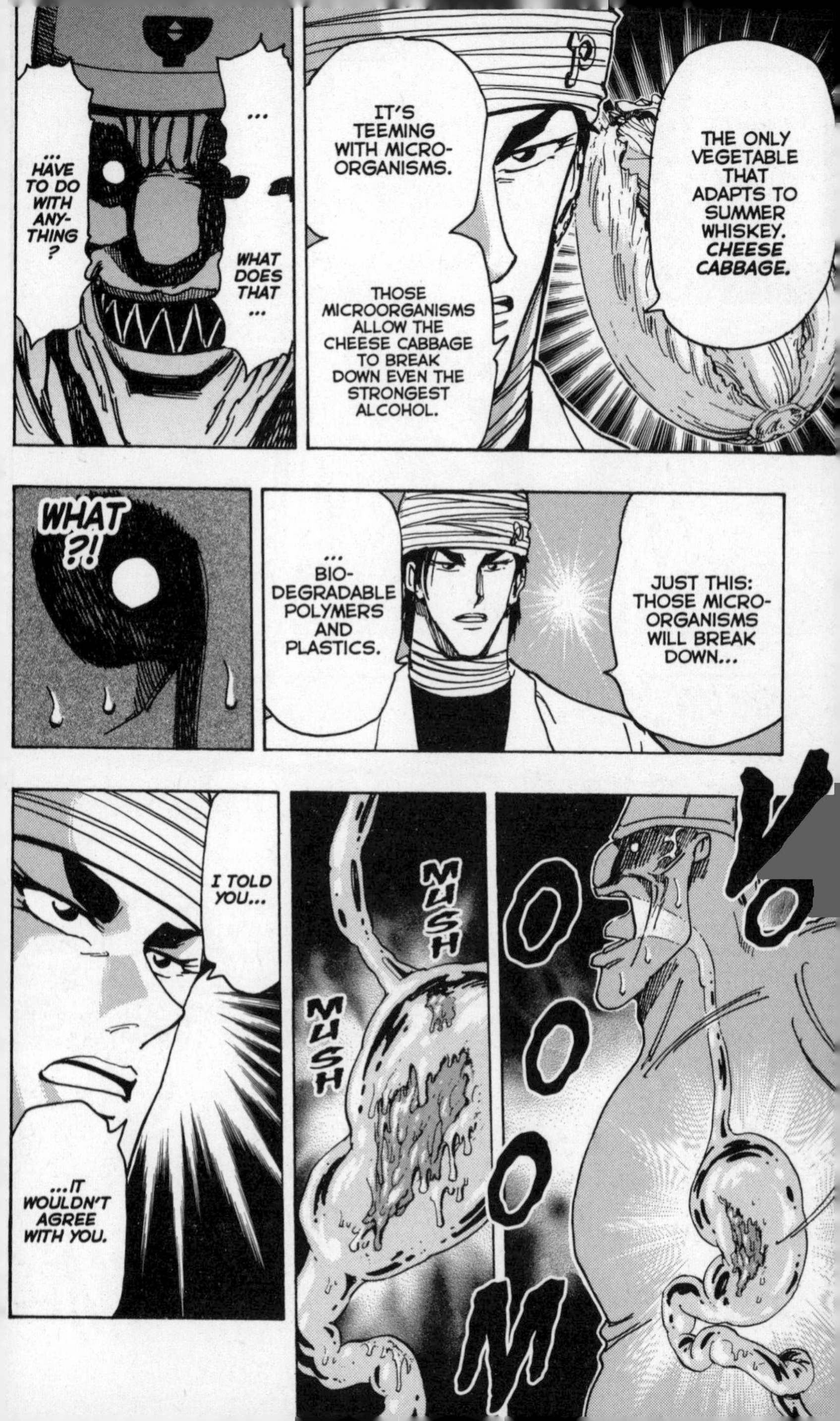
THE ONLY VEGETABLE THAT ADAPTS TO SUMMER WHISKEY. *CHEESE CABBAGE.*
IT'S TEEMING WITH MICRO-ORGANISMS.
THOSE MICROORGANISMS ALLOW THE CHEESE CABBAGE TO BREAK DOWN EVEN THE STRONGEST ALCOHOL.
...
WHAT DOES THAT ...
... HAVE TO DO WITH ANYTHING ?
JUST THIS: THOSE MICRO-ORGANISMS WILL BREAK DOWN...
... BIO-DEGRADABLE POLYMERS AND PLASTICS.
WHAT ?!
VOOOOM
MUSH
MUSH
I TOLD YOU...
...IT WOULDN'T AGREE WITH YOU.

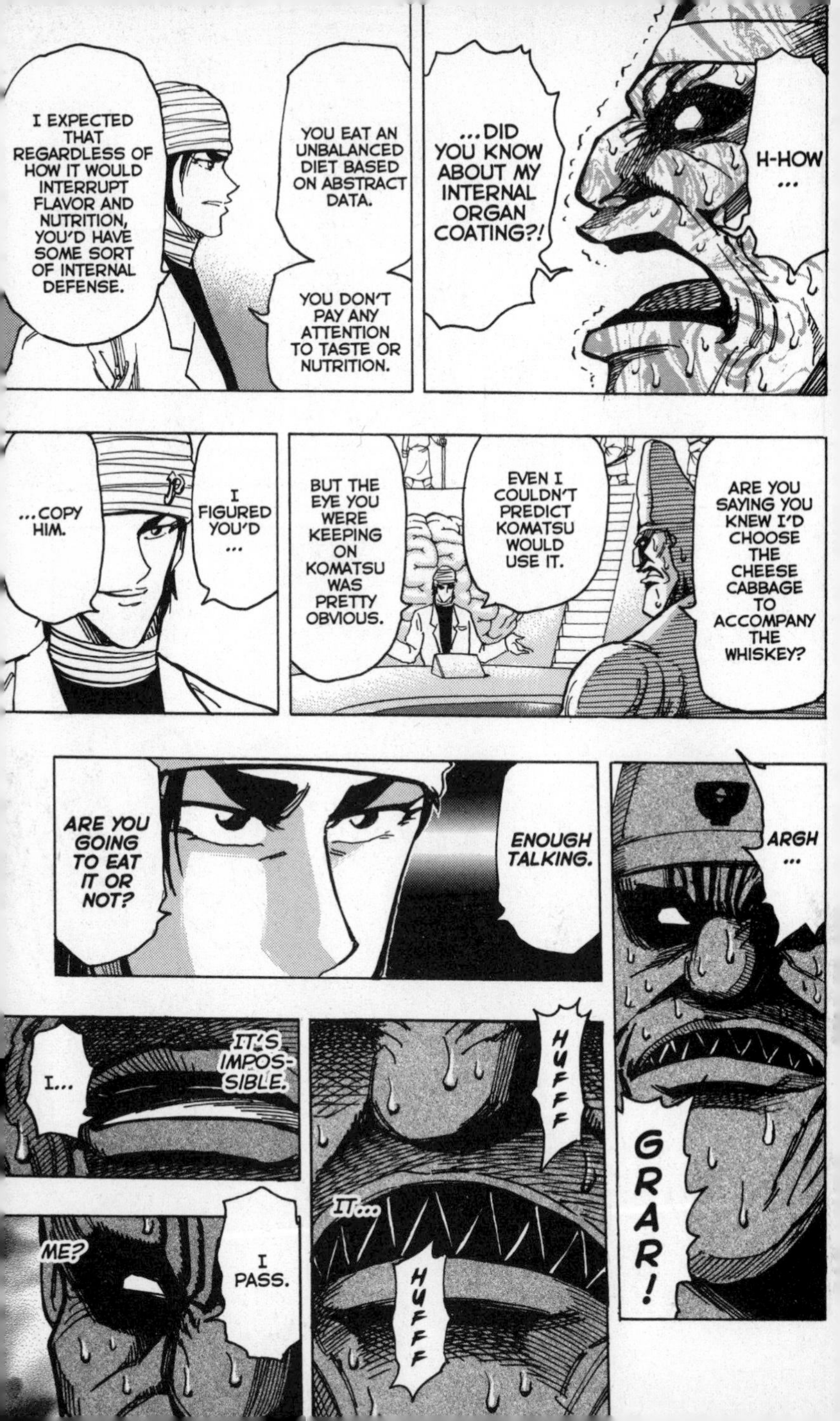
H-HOW ...
...DID YOU KNOW ABOUT MY INTERNAL ORGAN COATING?!
YOU EAT AN UNBALANCED DIET BASED ON ABSTRACT DATA.
YOU DON'T PAY ANY ATTENTION TO TASTE OR NUTRITION.
I EXPECTED THAT REGARDLESS OF HOW IT WOULD INTERRUPT FLAVOR AND NUTRITION, YOU'D HAVE SOME SORT OF INTERNAL DEFENSE.
ARE YOU SAYING YOU KNEW I'D CHOOSE THE CHEESE CABBAGE TO ACCOMPANY THE WHISKEY?
EVEN I COULDN'T PREDICT KOMATSU WOULD USE IT.
BUT THE EYE YOU WERE KEEPING ON KOMATSU WAS PRETTY OBVIOUS.
I FIGURED YOU'D ...
...COPY HIM.
ARGH ...
GRAR!
ENOUGH TALKING.
ARE YOU GOING TO EAT IT OR NOT?
HUFFF
IT...
HUFFF
IT'S IMPOSSIBLE.
I...
ME?
I PASS.

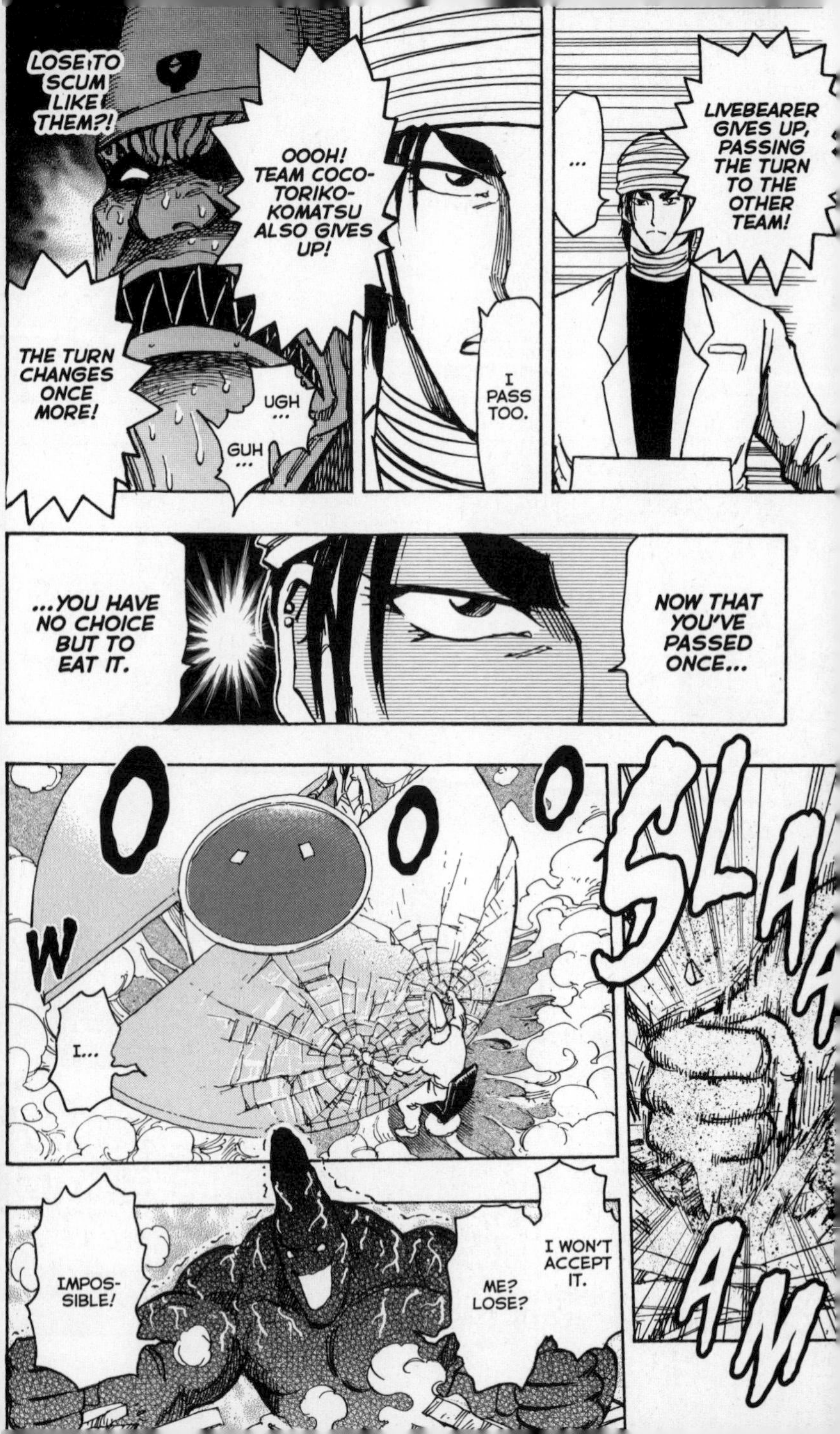
LIVEBEARER GIVES UP, PASSING THE TURN TO THE OTHER TEAM!
...
OOOH! TEAM COCO-TORIKO-KOMATSU ALSO GIVES UP!
I PASS TOO.
LOSE TO SCUM LIKE THEM?!
UGH...
GUH...
THE TURN CHANGES ONCE MORE!
NOW THAT YOU'VE PASSED ONCE...
...YOU HAVE NO CHOICE BUT TO EAT IT.
SLAAAM
WOOOO
I...
I WON'T ACCEPT IT.
ME? LOSE?
IMPOS-SIBLE!

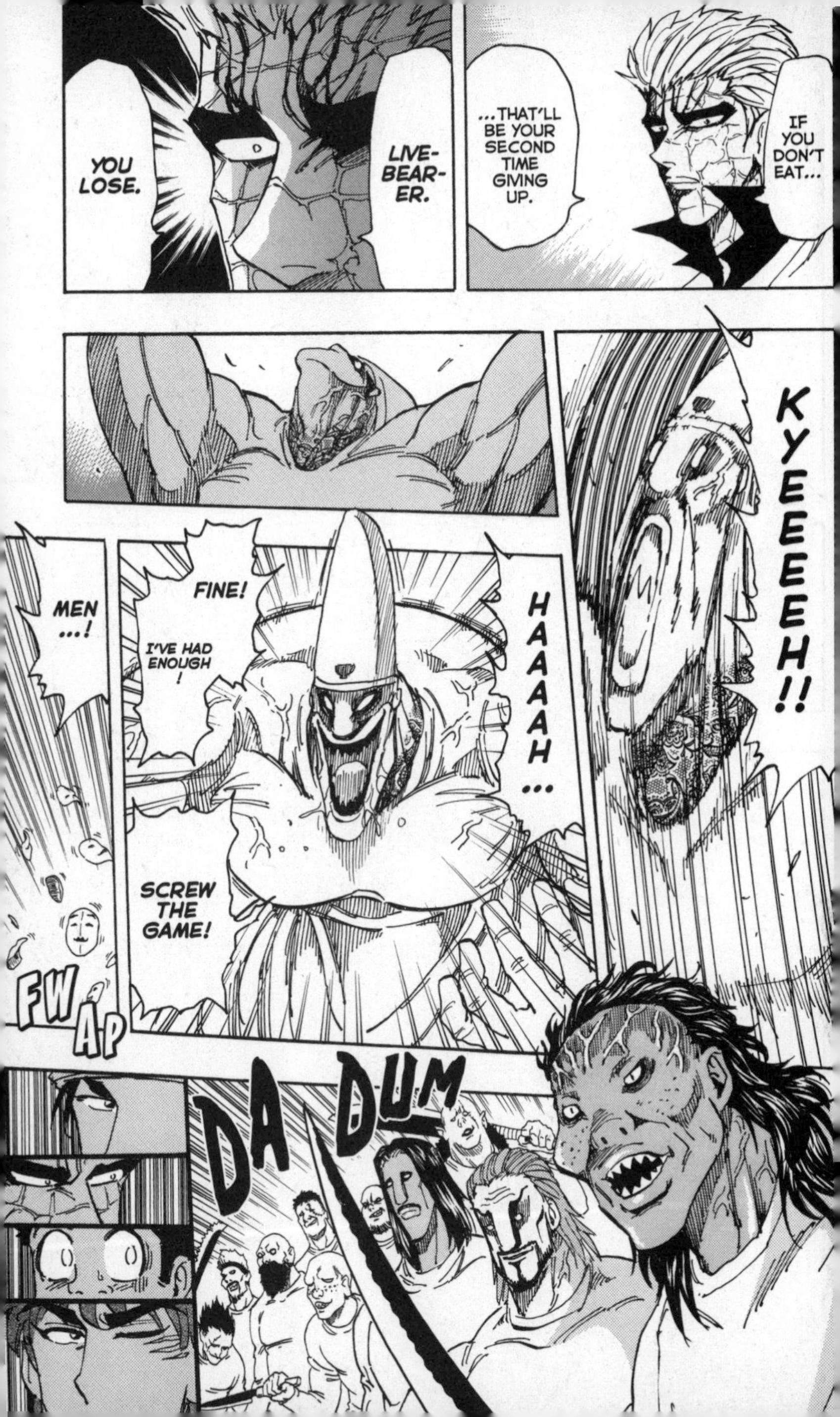
IF YOU DON'T EAT...
...THAT'LL BE YOUR SECOND TIME GIVING UP.
LIVE-BEARER.
YOU LOSE.
KYEEEEEH!!
HAAAAH...
FINE!
I'VE HAD ENOUGH!
SCREW THE GAME!
MEN...!
FWAP
DA DUM

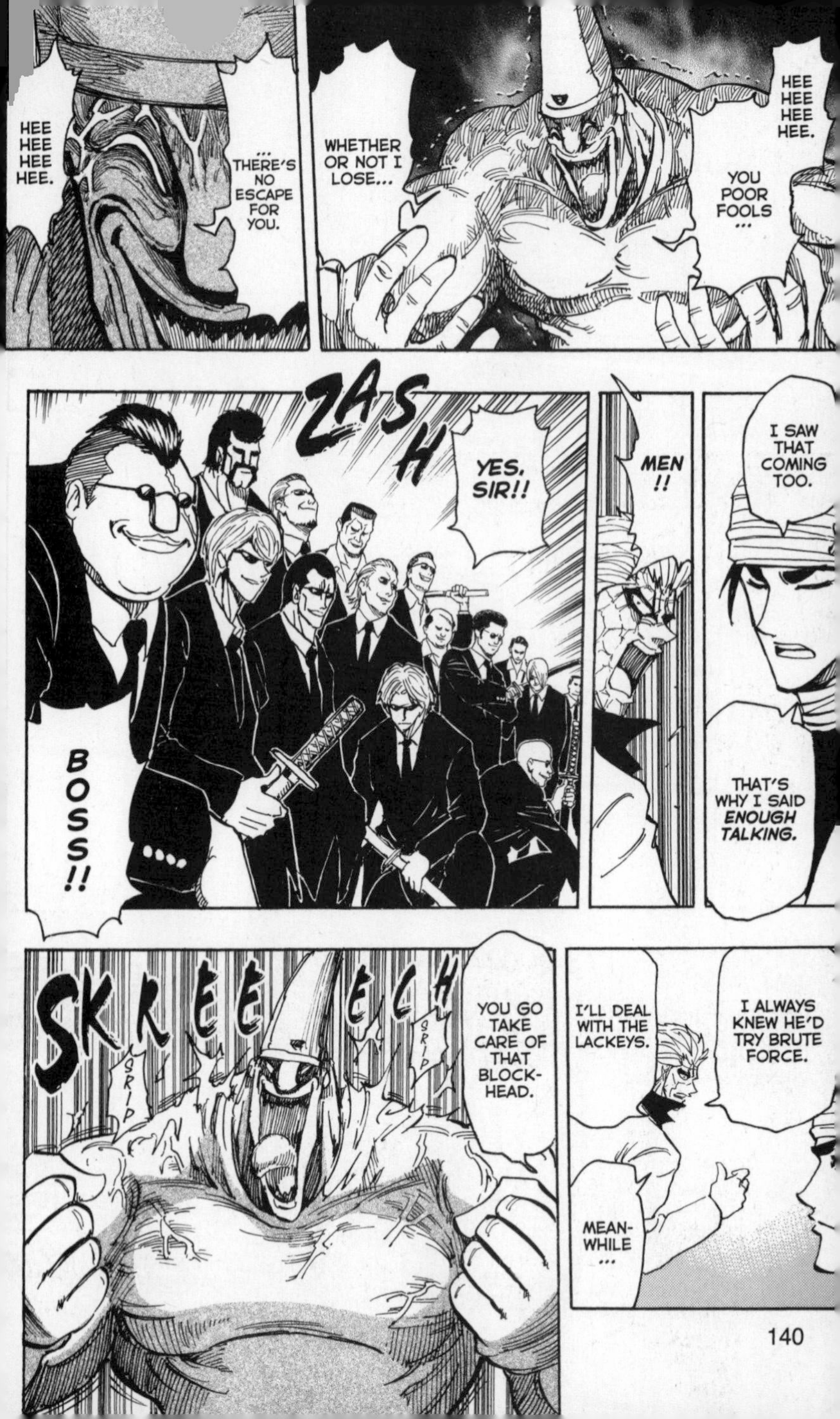
HEE HEE HEE HEE.
YOU POOR FOOLS...
WHETHER OR NOT I LOSE...
...THERE'S NO ESCAPE FOR YOU.
HEE HEE HEE HEE.
I SAW THAT COMING TOO.
THAT'S WHY I SAID *ENOUGH TALKING.*
MEN!!
YES, SIR!!
ZASH
BOSS!!
I ALWAYS KNEW HE'D TRY BRUTE FORCE.
I'LL DEAL WITH THE LACKEYS.
YOU GO TAKE CARE OF THAT BLOCK-HEAD.
MEAN-WHILE...
SKREEECH
SRIP
SRIP

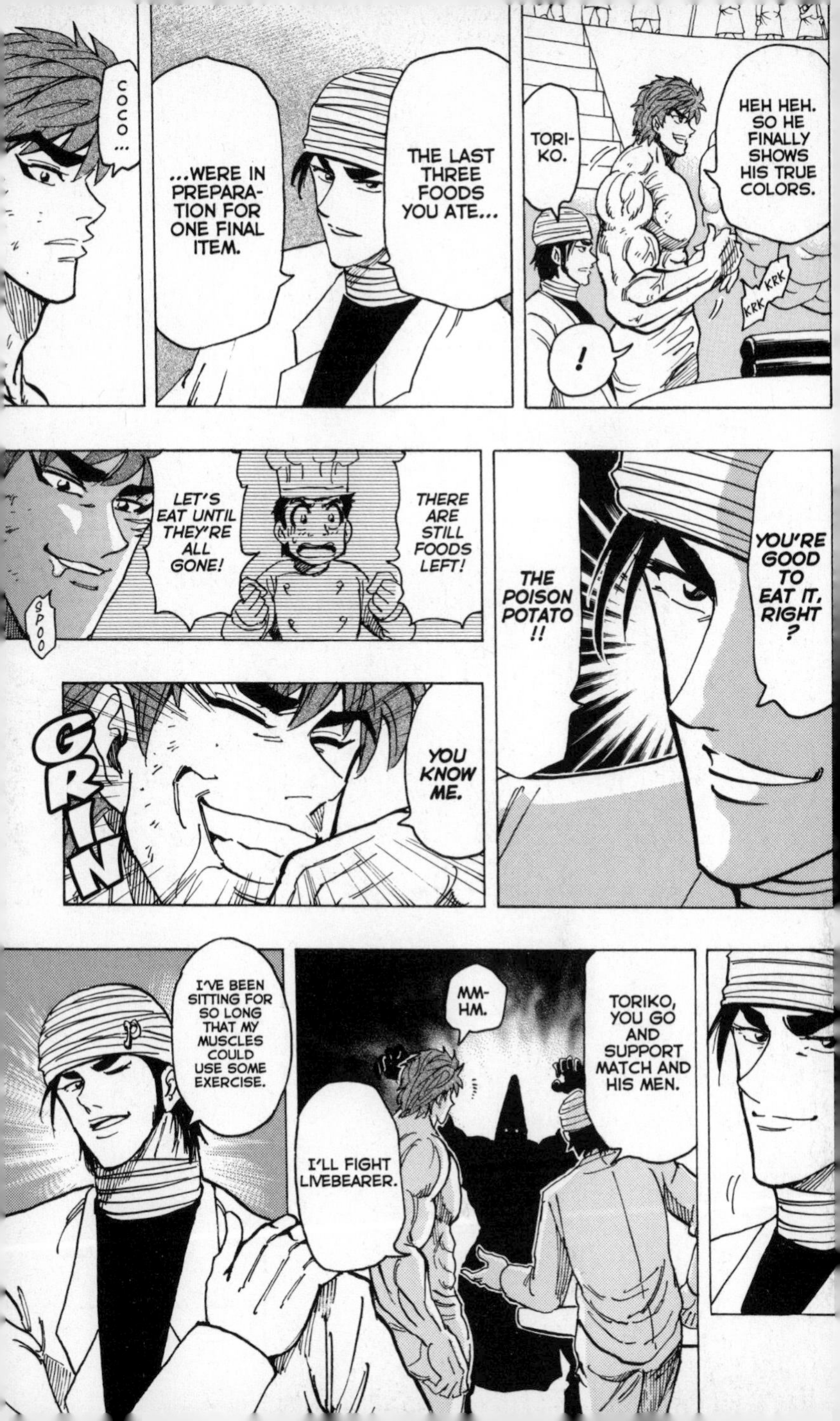
HEH HEH. SO HE FINALLY SHOWS HIS TRUE COLORS.
TORI-KO.
KRK KRK
!
THE LAST THREE FOODS YOU ATE...
...WERE IN PREPARATION FOR ONE FINAL ITEM.
COCO...
YOU'RE GOOD TO EAT IT, RIGHT?
THE POISON POTATO!!
THERE ARE STILL FOODS LEFT!
LET'S EAT UNTIL THEY'RE ALL GONE!
SPOO
YOU KNOW ME.
GRIN
TORIKO, YOU GO AND SUPPORT MATCH AND HIS MEN.
MM-HM.
I'LL FIGHT LIVEBEARER.
I'VE BEEN SITTING FOR SO LONG THAT MY MUSCLES COULD USE SOME EXERCISE.

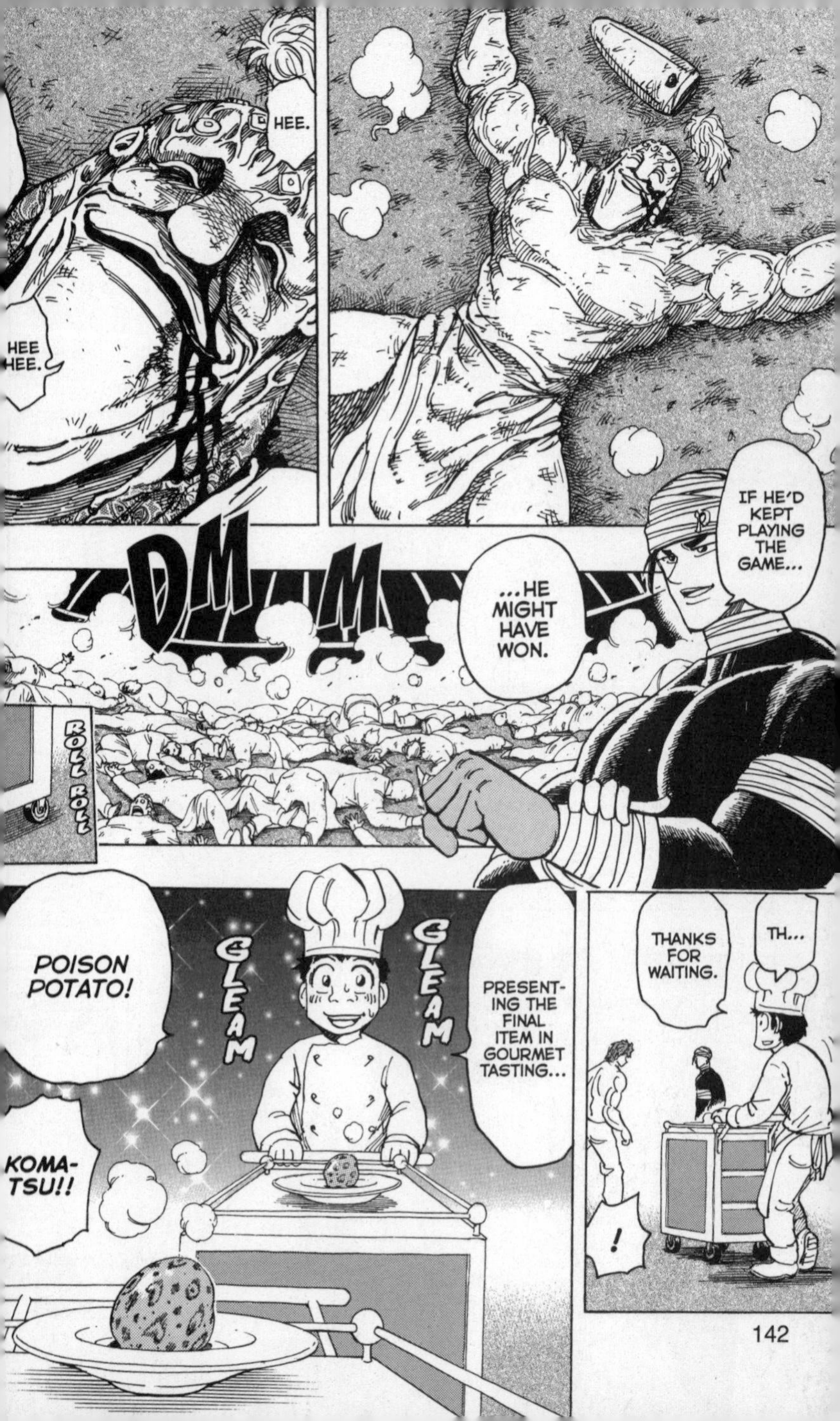
HEE.
HEE HEE.
IF HE'D KEPT PLAYING THE GAME...
...HE MIGHT HAVE WON.
DMM
ROLL ROLL
TH...
THANKS FOR WAITING.
!
PRESENT-ING THE FINAL ITEM IN GOURMET TASTING...
GLEAM GLEAM
POISON POTATO!
KOMA-TSU!!

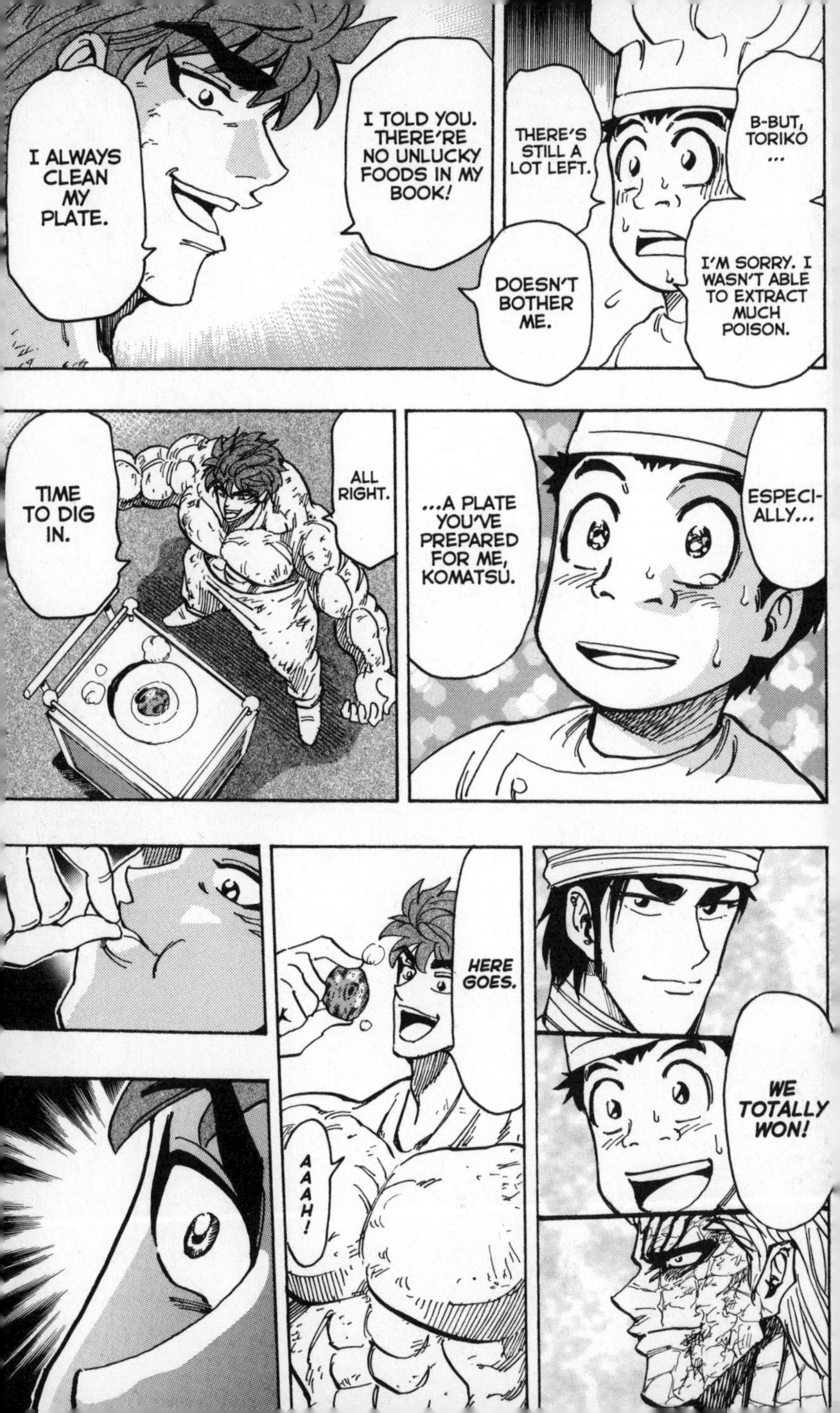
B-BUT, TORIKO ...
I'M SORRY. I WASN'T ABLE TO EXTRACT MUCH POISON.
THERE'S STILL A LOT LEFT.
DOESN'T BOTHER ME.
I TOLD YOU. THERE'RE NO UNLUCKY FOODS IN MY BOOK!
I ALWAYS CLEAN MY PLATE.
ESPECI-ALLY...
...A PLATE YOU'VE PREPARED FOR ME, KOMATSU.
ALL RIGHT.
TIME TO DIG IN.
WE TOTALLY WON!
HERE GOES.
AAAH!

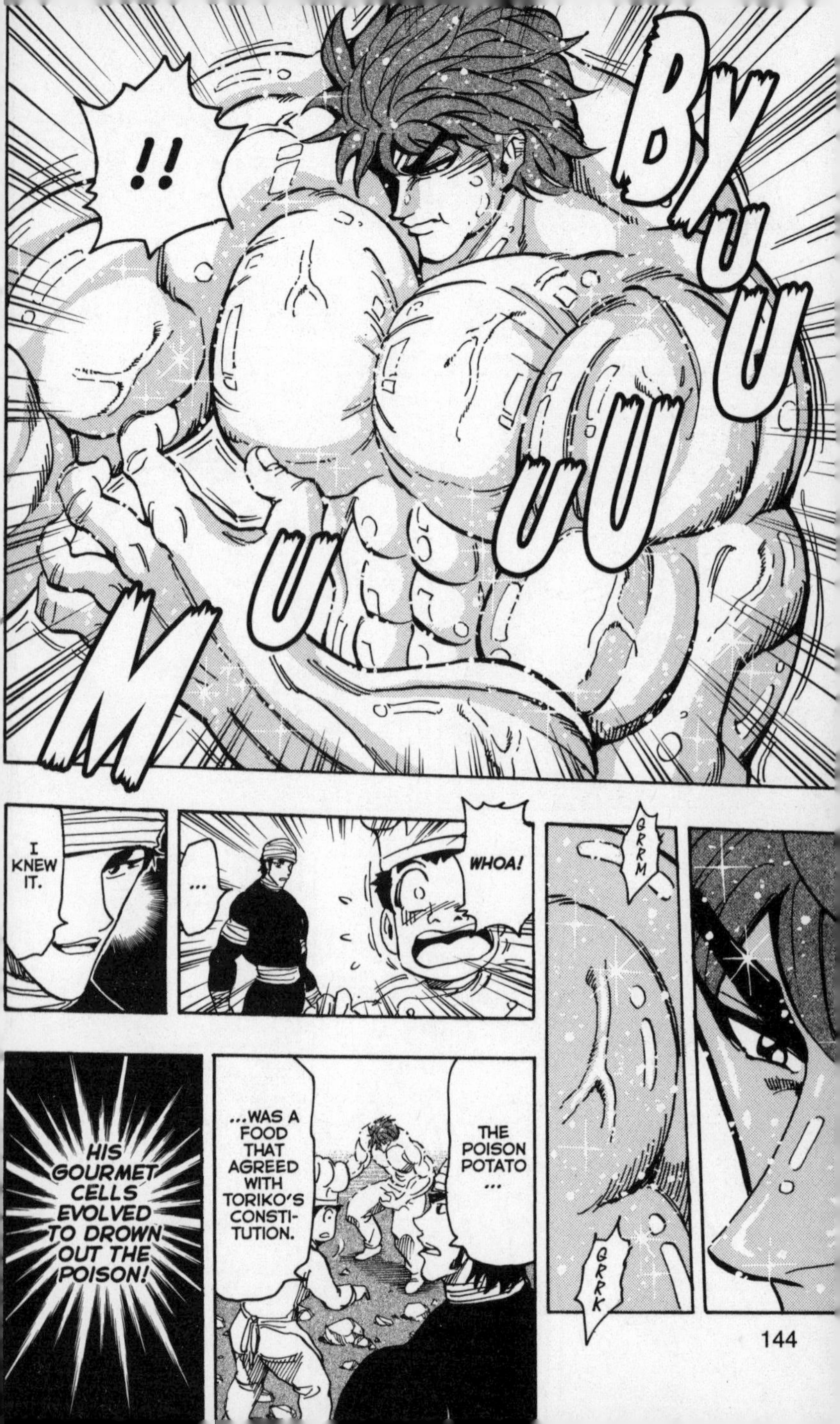
!!
BYUUUUUUM
GRRM
GRRK
WHOA!
...
I KNEW IT.
THE POISON POTATO...
...WAS A FOOD THAT AGREED WITH TORIKO'S CONSTITUTION.
HIS GOURMET CELLS EVOLVED TO DROWN OUT THE POISON!

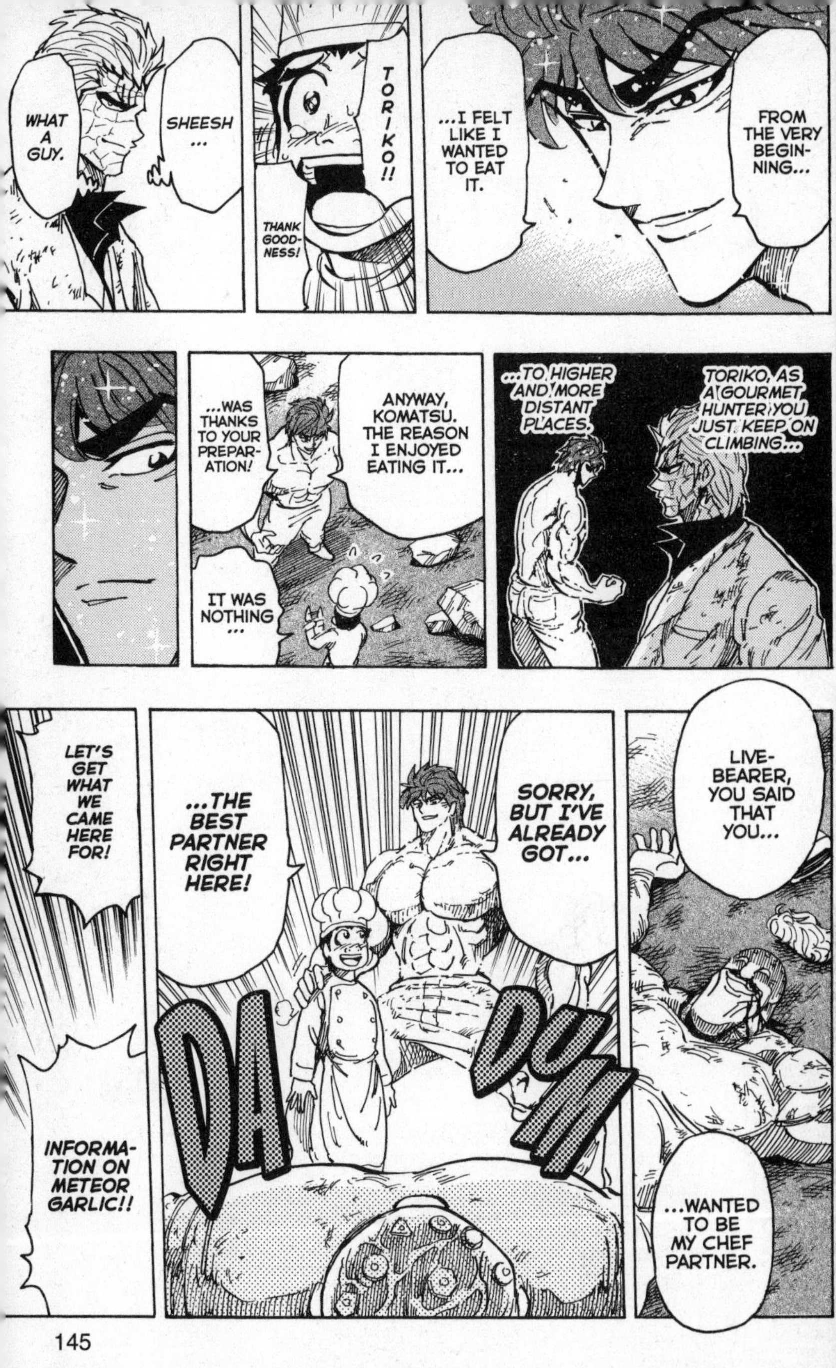
FROM THE VERY BEGINNING...
...I FELT LIKE I WANTED TO EAT IT.
TORIKO!!
THANK GOODNESS!
SHEESH...
WHAT A GUY.
TORIKO, AS A GOURMET HUNTER YOU JUST KEEP ON CLIMBING...
...TO HIGHER AND MORE DISTANT PLACES.
ANYWAY, KOMATSU. THE REASON I ENJOYED EATING IT...
...WAS THANKS TO YOUR PREPARATION!
IT WAS NOTHING...
LIVE-BEARER, YOU SAID THAT YOU...
...WANTED TO BE MY CHEF PARTNER.
SORRY, BUT I'VE ALREADY GOT...
...THE BEST PARTNER RIGHT HERE!
DA DUM
LET'S GET WHAT WE CAME HERE FOR!
INFORMATION ON METEOR GARLIC!!

TORIKO

GOURMET CHECKLIST

Vol. 199

EVIL HUNTER
(MAMMAL)

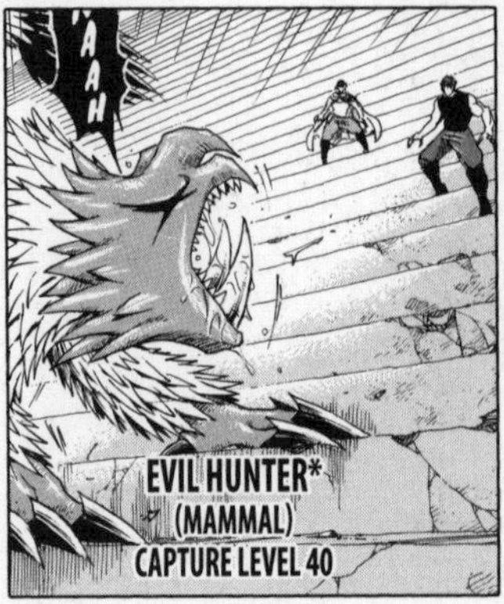
AAAH
EVIL HUNTER*
(MAMMAL)
CAPTURE LEVEL 40

CAPTURE LEVEL: 40

HABITAT: GOURMET PYRAMID

LENGTH: 7 METERS

HEIGHT: 3 METERS

WEIGHT: 8 TONS

PRICE: TYPICALLY NOT FIT FOR CONSUMPTION, BUT PREPARED CORRECTLY CAN BE 100 G / 25,000 YEN

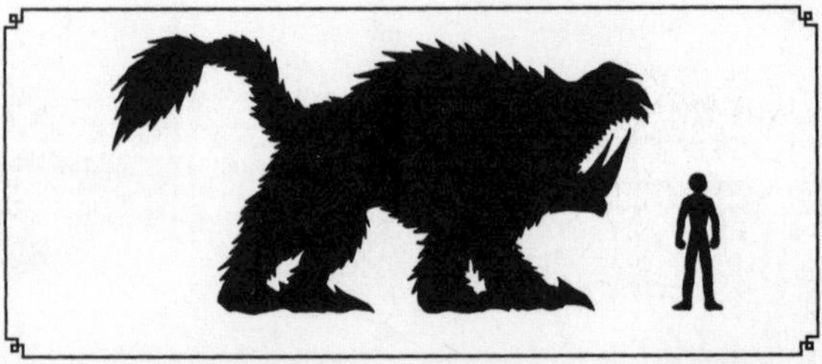

SCALE

A MONSTROUS MAMMAL THAT LIVES IN THE DARKEST DEPTHS OF GOURMET PYRAMID. ITS EYES ACTUALLY GLOW TO ILLUMINATE A PATH FOR IT THROUGH THE MURKY DARKNESS. THE EVIL HUNTER'S TEETH HOLD SUCH A STRONG POISON THAT ONCE BITTEN, ITS PREY DIES WITHIN MINUTES. NO PART OF THIS CREATURE IS PARTICULARLY PALATABLE, BUT LIKE THE MIMIC BAGWORM, IT TASTES BETTER WHEN PREPARED CORRECTLY.

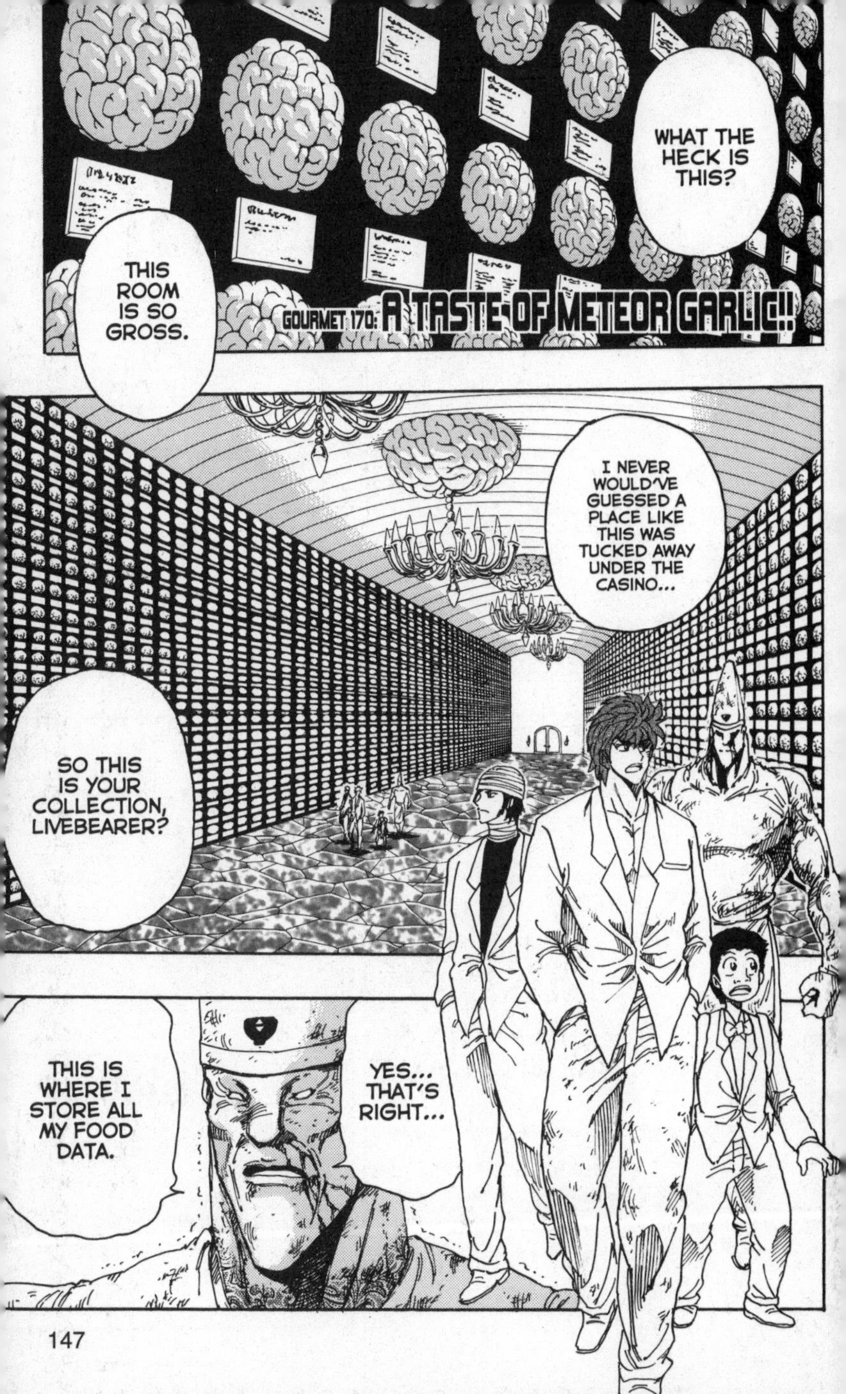
WHAT THE HECK IS THIS?
THIS ROOM IS SO GROSS.
GOURMET 170: A TASTE OF METEOR GARLIC!!
I NEVER WOULD'VE GUESSED A PLACE LIKE THIS WAS TUCKED AWAY UNDER THE CASINO...
SO THIS IS YOUR COLLECTION, LIVEBEARER?
YES... THAT'S RIGHT...
THIS IS WHERE I STORE ALL MY FOOD DATA.

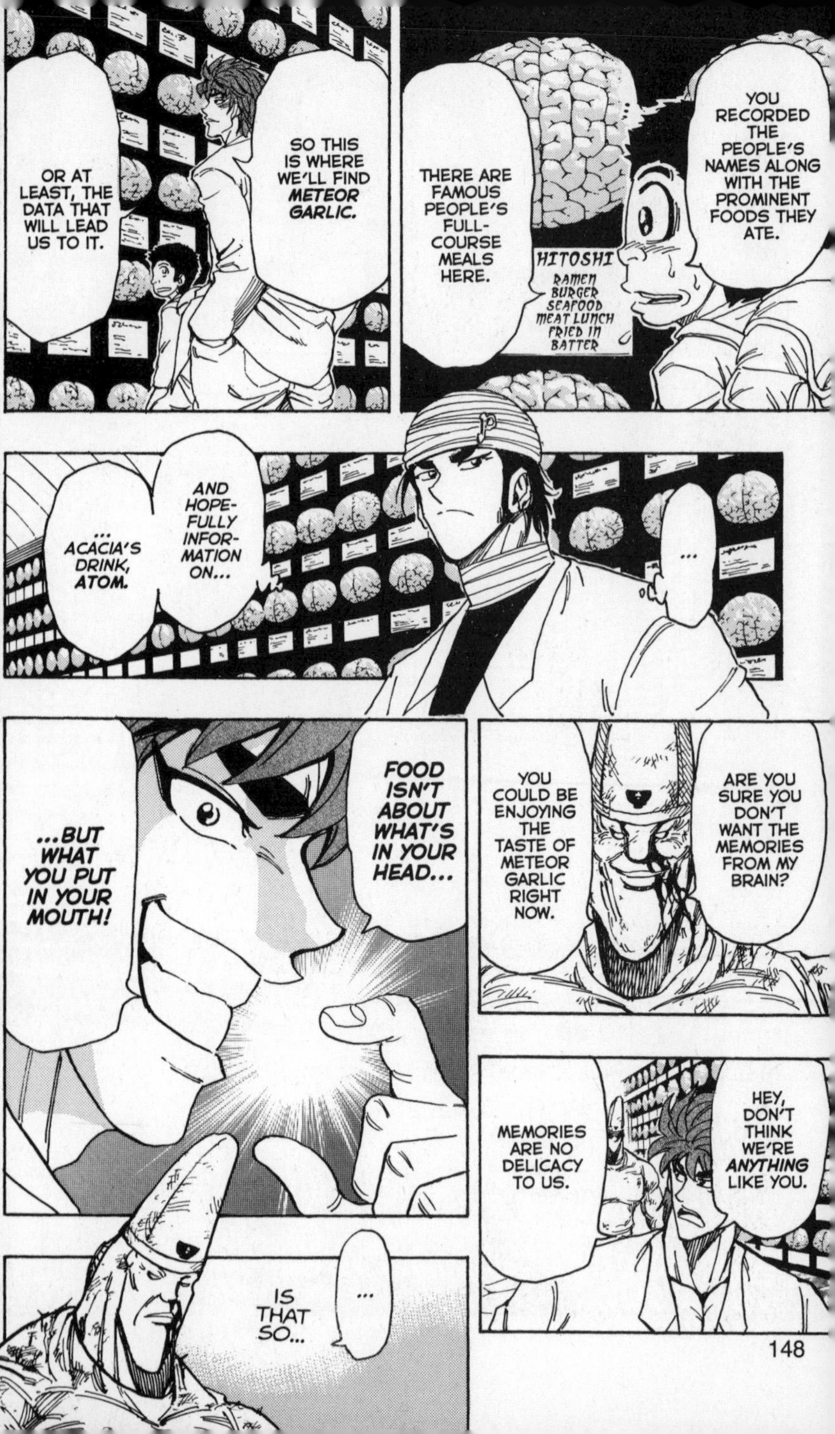

YOU RECORDED THE PEOPLE'S NAMES ALONG WITH THE PROMINENT FOODS THEY ATE.
...
THERE ARE FAMOUS PEOPLE'S FULL-COURSE MEALS HERE.
HITOSHI
RAMEN BURGER SEAFOOD MEAT LUNCH FRIED IN BATTER
SO THIS IS WHERE WE'LL FIND *METEOR GARLIC.*
OR AT LEAST, THE DATA THAT WILL LEAD US TO IT.
...
AND HOPEFULLY INFORMATION ON...
...ACACIA'S DRINK, ATOM.
ARE YOU SURE YOU DON'T WANT THE MEMORIES FROM MY BRAIN?
YOU COULD BE ENJOYING THE TASTE OF METEOR GARLIC RIGHT NOW.
HEY, DON'T THINK WE'RE *ANYTHING* LIKE YOU.
MEMORIES ARE NO DELICACY TO US.
FOOD ISN'T ABOUT WHAT'S IN YOUR HEAD...
...BUT WHAT YOU PUT IN YOUR MOUTH!
...
IS THAT SO...

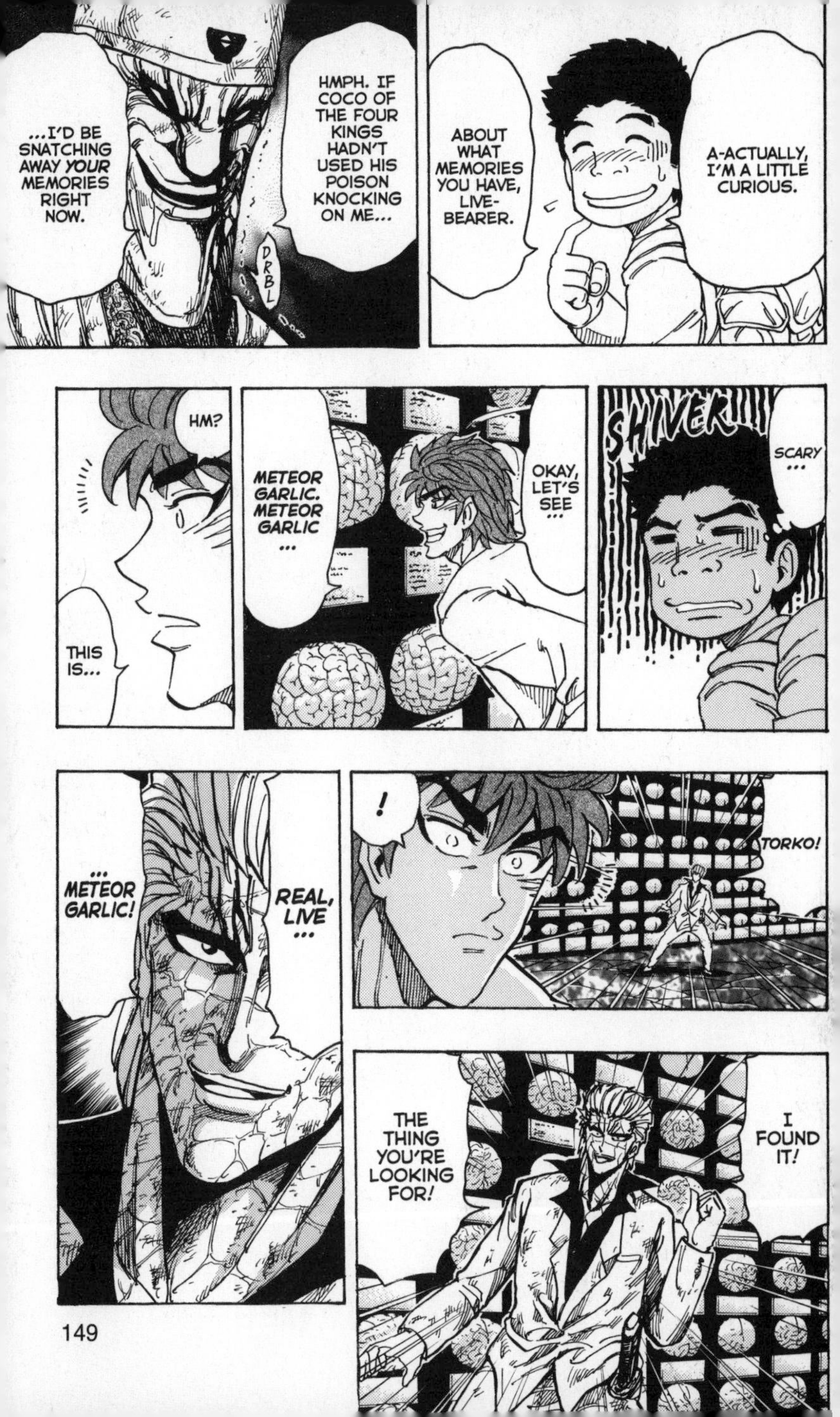
A-ACTUALLY, I'M A LITTLE CURIOUS.
ABOUT WHAT MEMORIES YOU HAVE, LIVE-BEARER.
HMPH. IF COCO OF THE FOUR KINGS HADN'T USED HIS POISON KNOCKING ON ME...
...I'D BE SNATCHING AWAY *YOUR* MEMORIES RIGHT NOW.
DRBL
SHIVER
SCARY...
OKAY, LET'S SEE...
METEOR GARLIC. METEOR GARLIC...
HM?
THIS IS...
TORKO!
!
I FOUND IT!
THE THING YOU'RE LOOKING FOR!
REAL, LIVE...
...METEOR GARLIC!

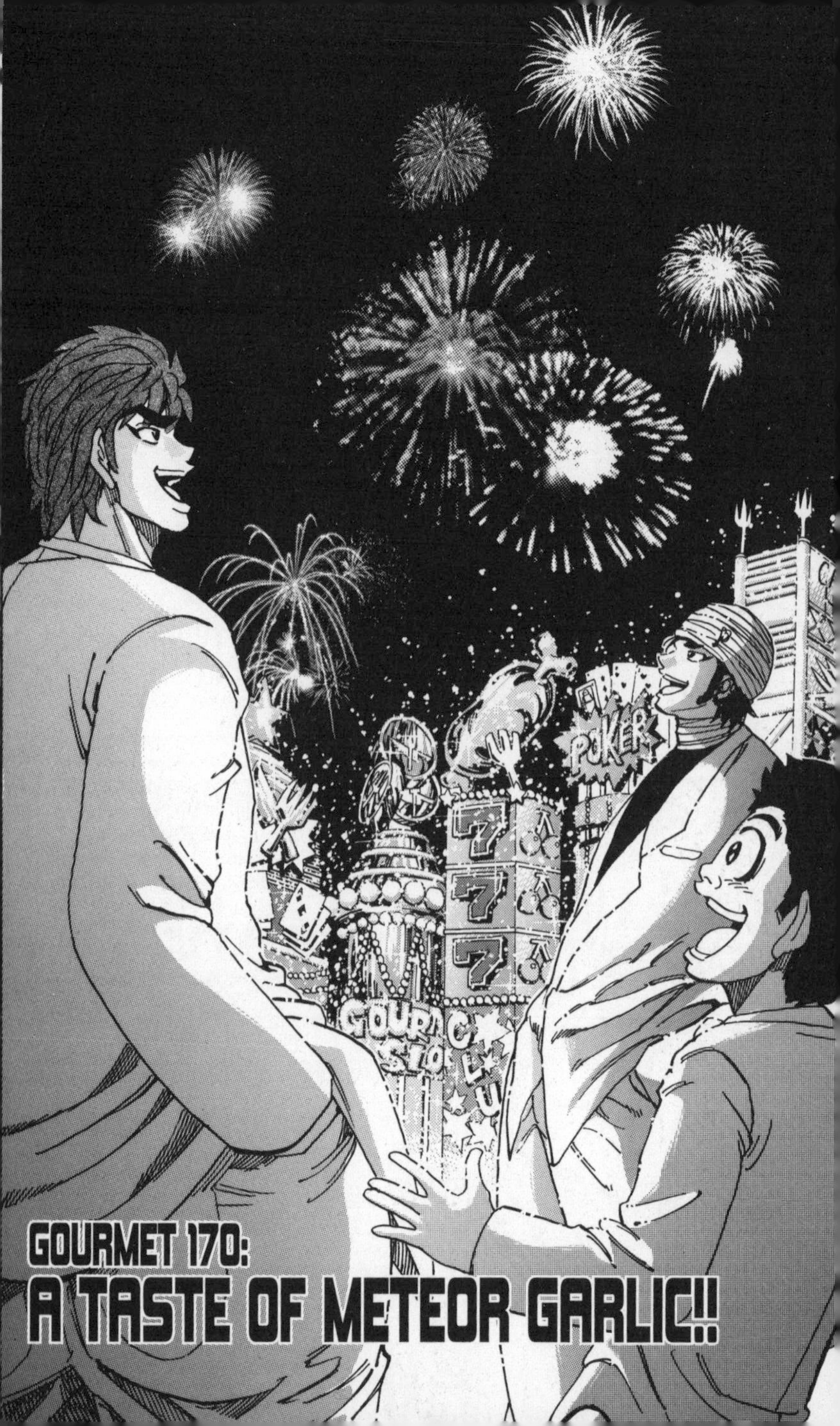
POKER

GOURMET 170:
A TASTE OF METEOR GARLIC!!

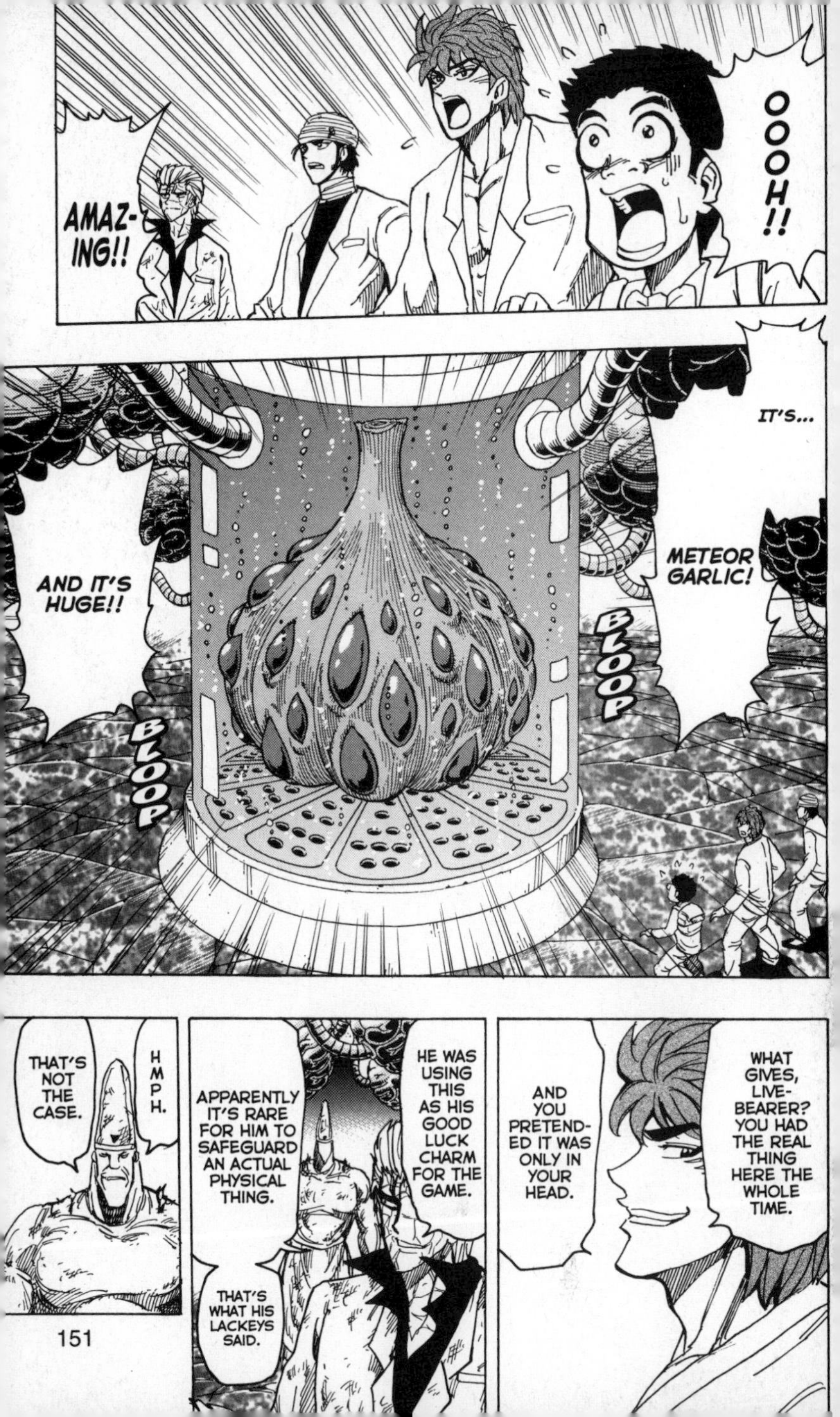
OOOH!!
AMAZ-ING!!
IT'S...
METEOR GARLIC!
BLOOP
AND IT'S HUGE!!
BLOOP
WHAT GIVES, LIVE-BEARER? YOU HAD THE REAL THING HERE THE WHOLE TIME.
AND YOU PRETEND-ED IT WAS ONLY IN YOUR HEAD.
HE WAS USING THIS AS HIS GOOD LUCK CHARM FOR THE GAME.
APPARENTLY IT'S RARE FOR HIM TO SAFEGUARD AN ACTUAL PHYSICAL THING.
THAT'S WHAT HIS LACKEYS SAID.
HMPH.
THAT'S NOT THE CASE.

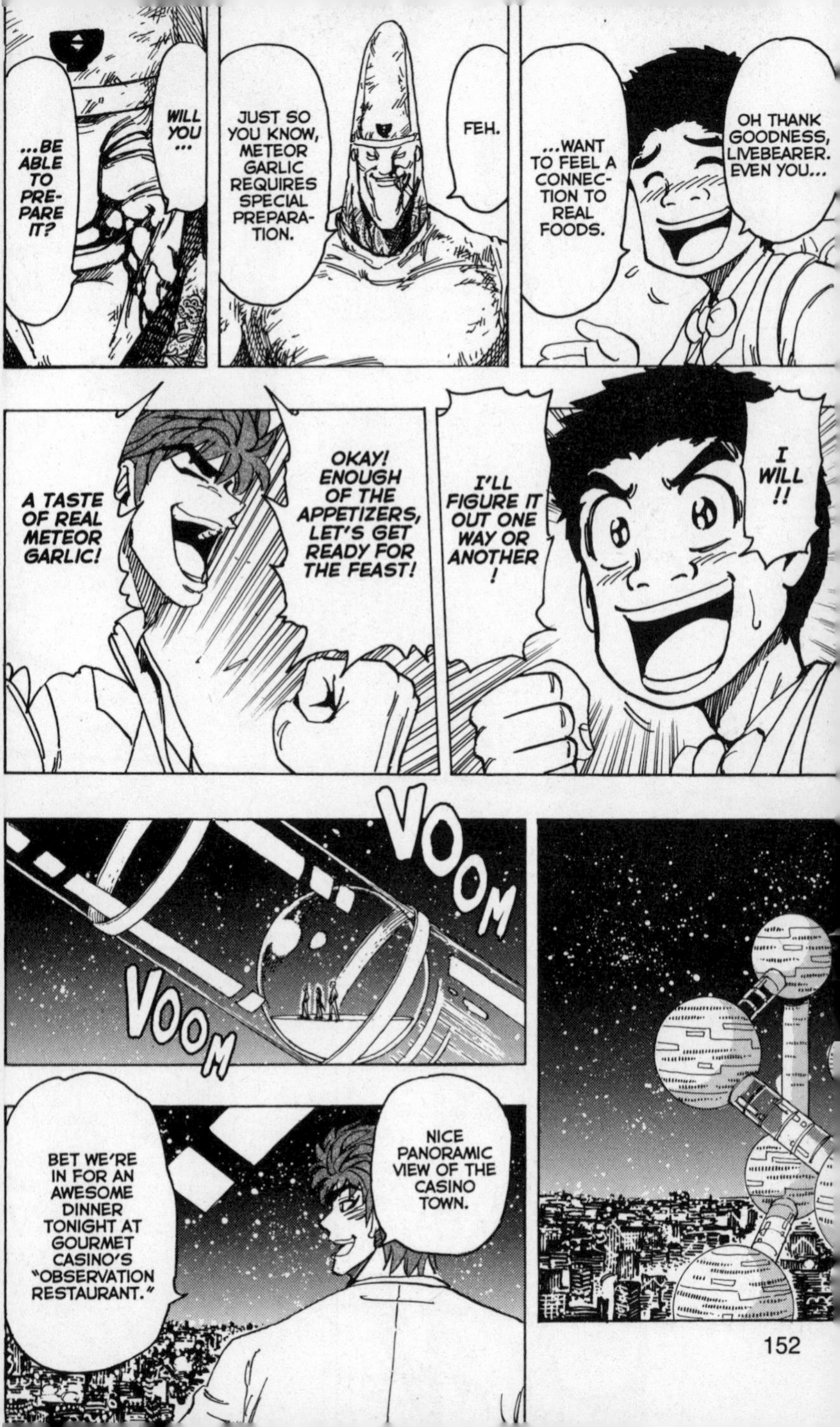
OH THANK GOODNESS, LIVEBEARER. EVEN YOU...
...WANT TO FEEL A CONNECTION TO REAL FOODS.
FEH.
JUST SO YOU KNOW, METEOR GARLIC REQUIRES SPECIAL PREPARATION.
WILL YOU ...
...BE ABLE TO PREPARE IT?
I WILL !!
I'LL FIGURE IT OUT ONE WAY OR ANOTHER !
OKAY! ENOUGH OF THE APPETIZERS, LET'S GET READY FOR THE FEAST!
A TASTE OF REAL METEOR GARLIC!
VOOM
VOOM
NICE PANORAMIC VIEW OF THE CASINO TOWN.
BET WE'RE IN FOR AN AWESOME DINNER TONIGHT AT GOURMET CASINO'S "OBSERVATION RESTAURANT."

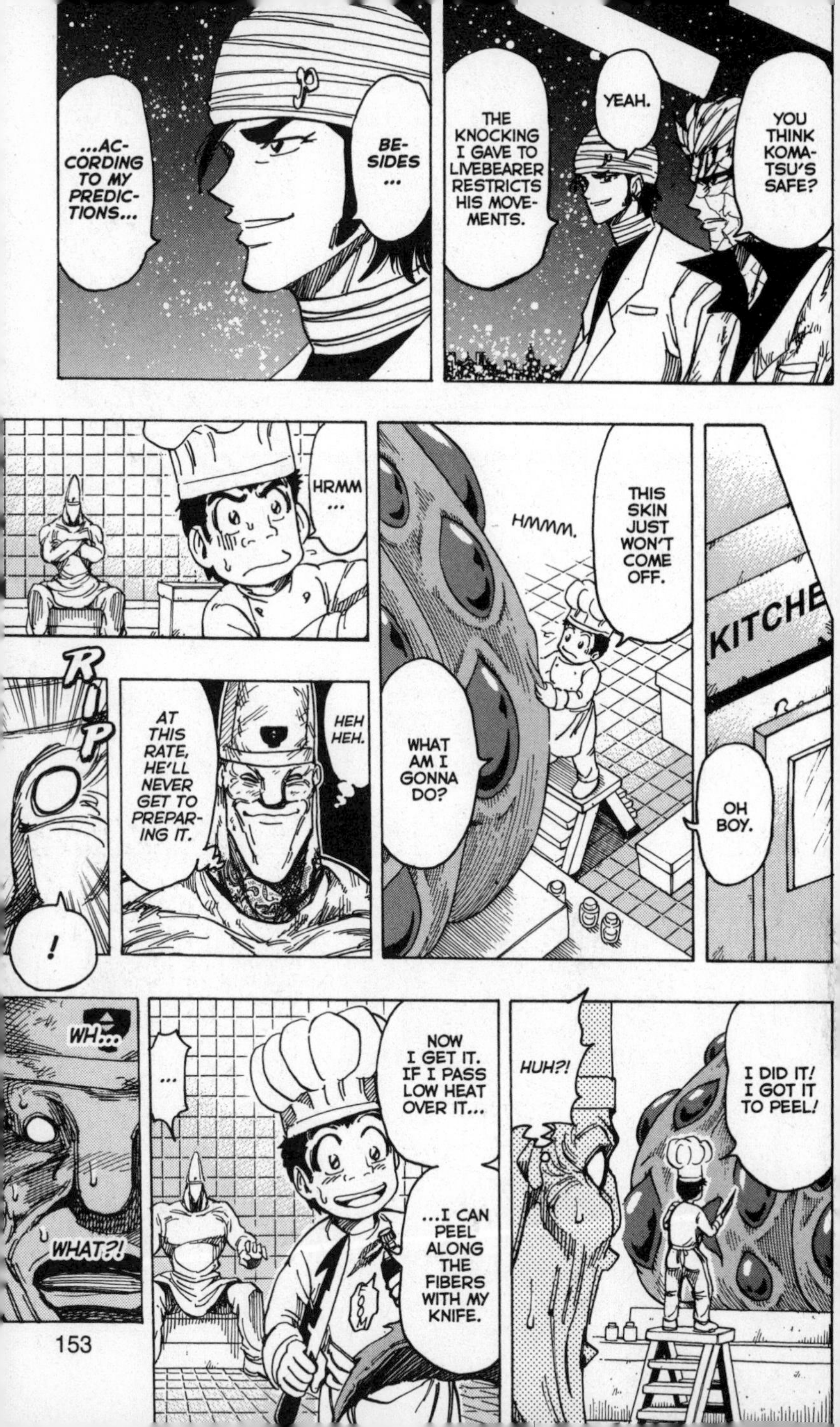
YOU THINK KOMATSU'S SAFE?
YEAH.
THE KNOCKING I GAVE TO LIVEBEARER RESTRICTS HIS MOVEMENTS.
BESIDES...
...ACCORDING TO MY PREDICTIONS...
KITCHE
OH BOY.
THIS SKIN JUST WON'T COME OFF.
HMMM.
WHAT AM I GONNA DO?
HRMM...
HEH HEH.
AT THIS RATE, HE'LL NEVER GET TO PREPARING IT.
RIP
!
I DID IT! I GOT IT TO PEEL!
HUH?!
NOW I GET IT. IF I PASS LOW HEAT OVER IT...
...I CAN PEEL ALONG THE FIBERS WITH MY KNIFE.
...
WH...
WHAT?!

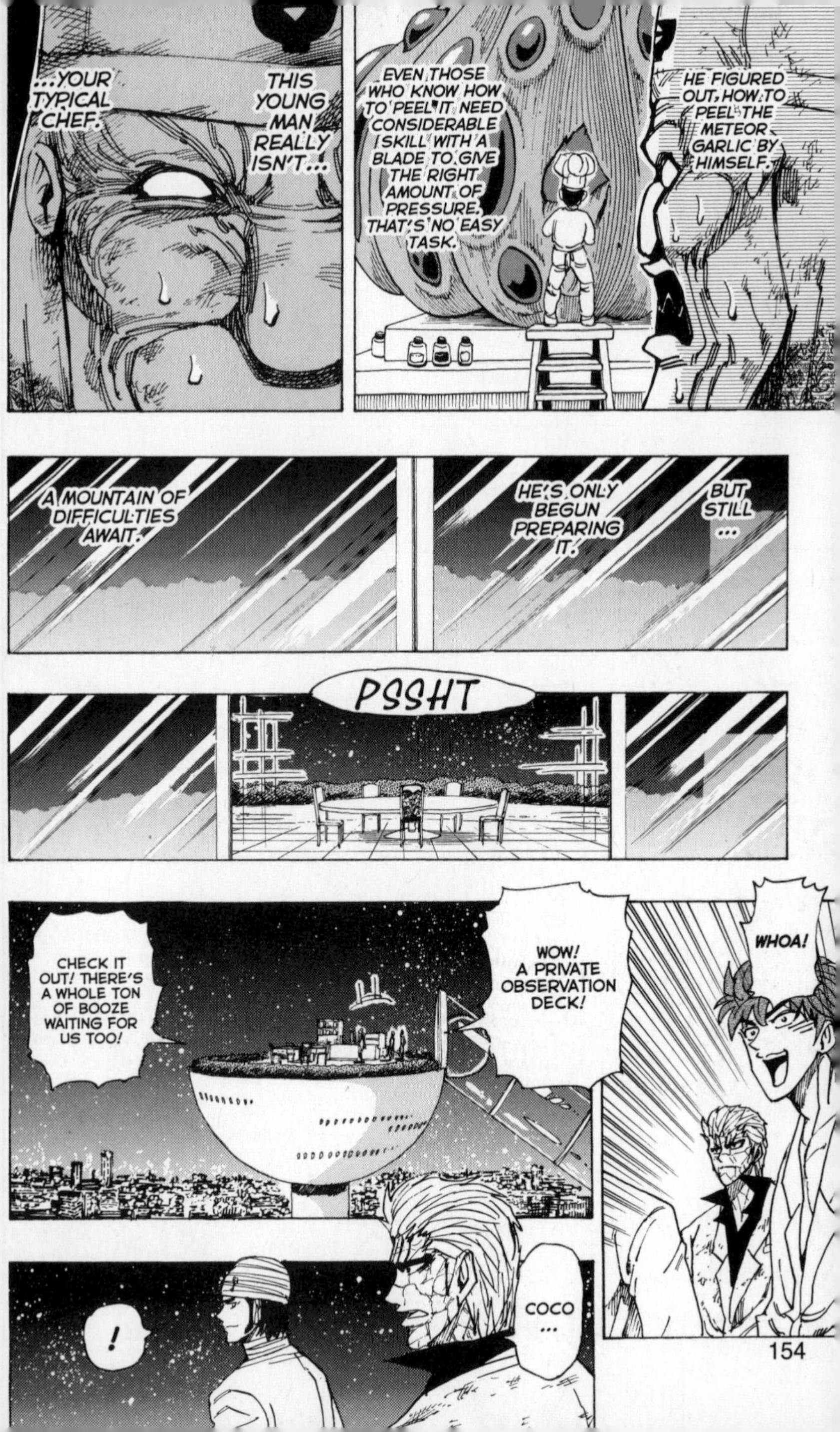
HE FIGURED OUT HOW TO PEEL THE METEOR GARLIC BY HIMSELF.
EVEN THOSE WHO KNOW HOW TO PEEL IT NEED CONSIDERABLE SKILL WITH A BLADE TO GIVE THE RIGHT AMOUNT OF PRESSURE. THAT'S NO EASY TASK.
THIS YOUNG MAN REALLY ISN'T...
...YOUR TYPICAL CHEF.
BUT STILL...
HE'S ONLY BEGUN PREPARING IT.
A MOUNTAIN OF DIFFICULTIES AWAIT.
PSSHT
WHOA!
WOW! A PRIVATE OBSERVATION DECK!
CHECK IT OUT! THERE'S A WHOLE TON OF BOOZE WAITING FOR US TOO!
COCO...
!

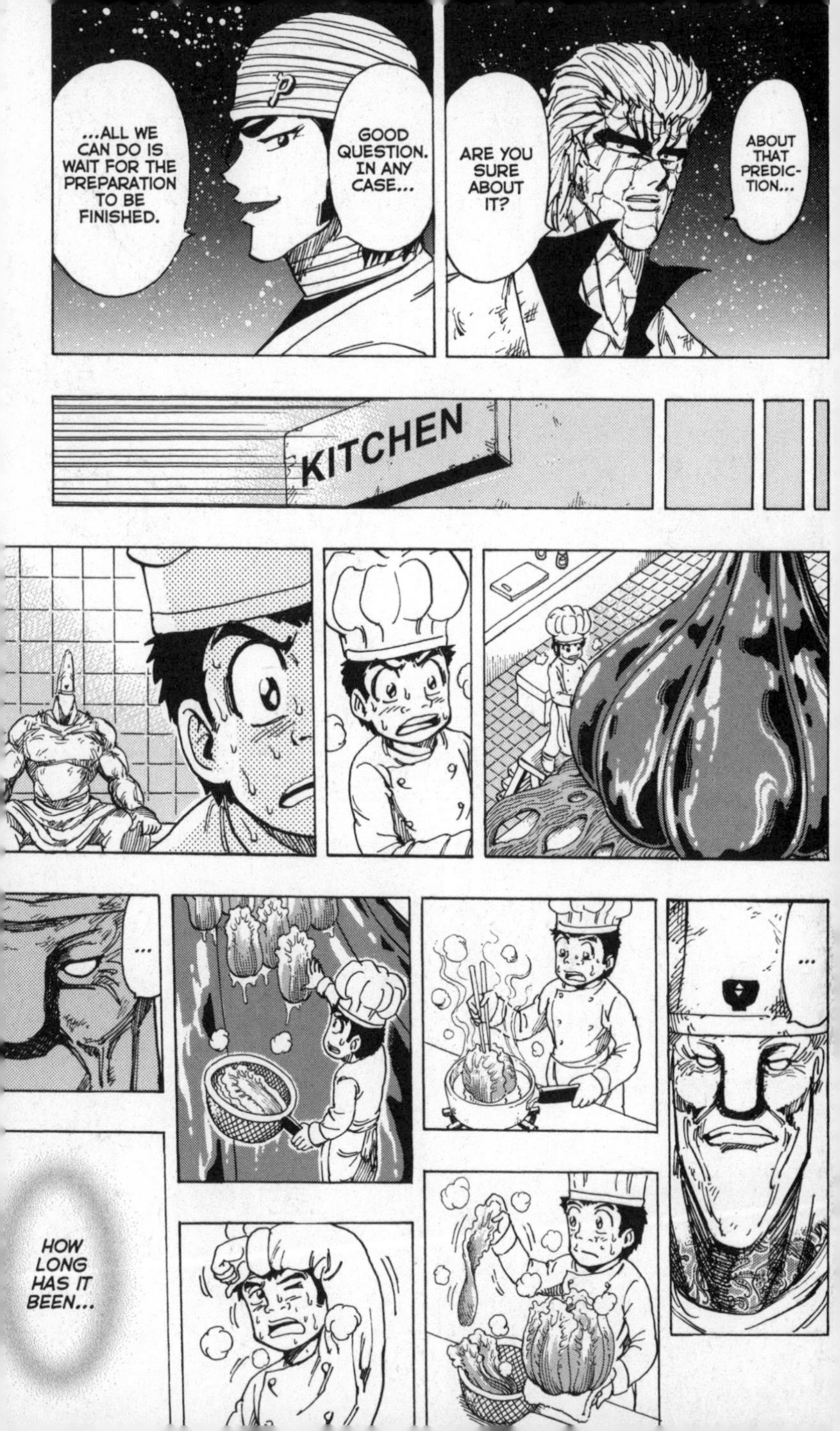
ABOUT THAT PREDIC-TION...
ARE YOU SURE ABOUT IT?
GOOD QUESTION. IN ANY CASE...
...ALL WE CAN DO IS WAIT FOR THE PREPARATION TO BE FINISHED.
KITCHEN
...
...
HOW LONG HAS IT BEEN...

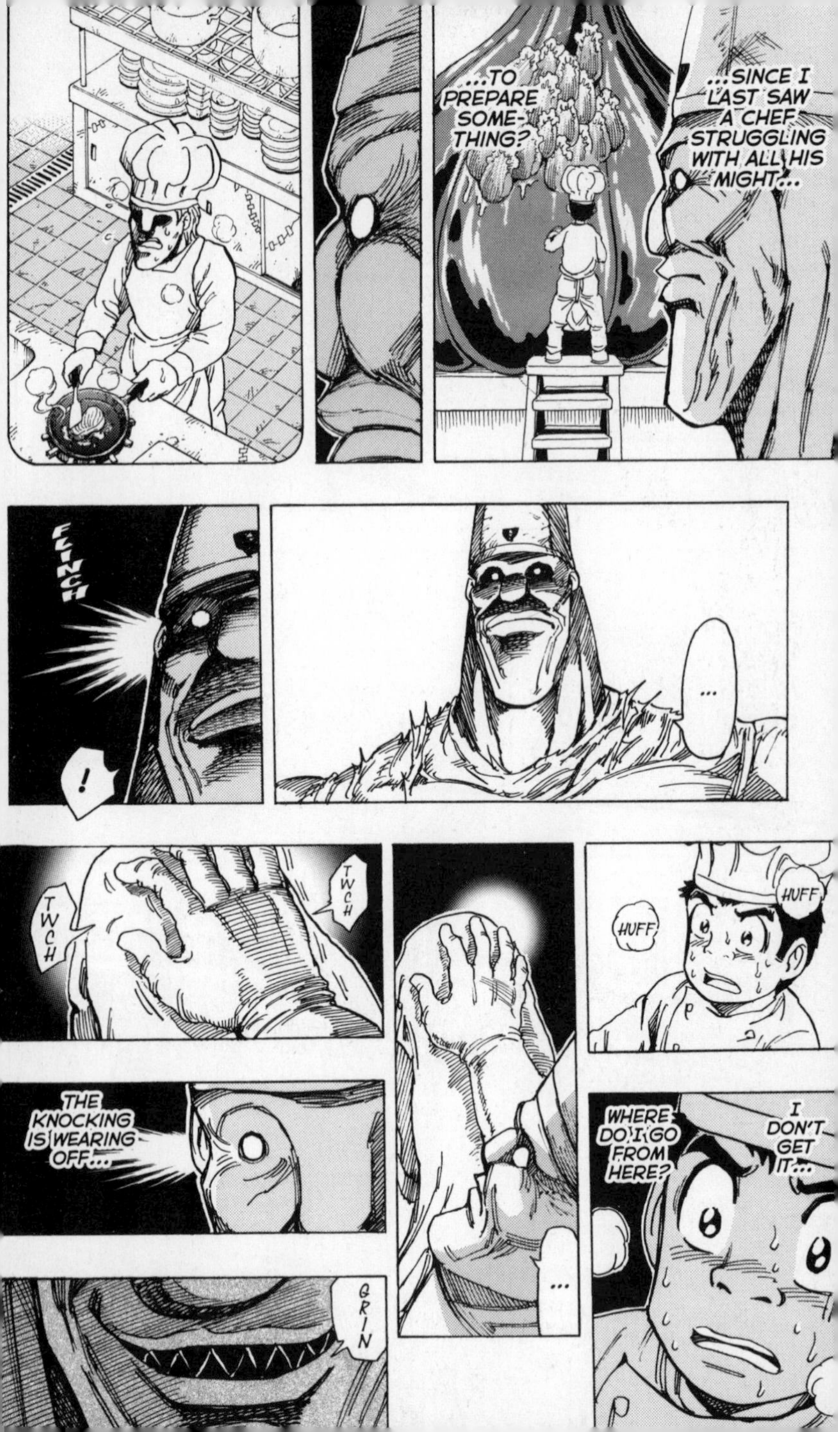
...SINCE I LAST SAW A CHEF STRUGGLING WITH ALL HIS MIGHT...
...TO PREPARE SOME-THING?
...
FLINCH
!
HUFF
HUFF
I DON'T GET IT...
WHERE DO I GO FROM HERE?
...
TWCH
TWCH
THE KNOCKING IS WEARING OFF...
GRIN

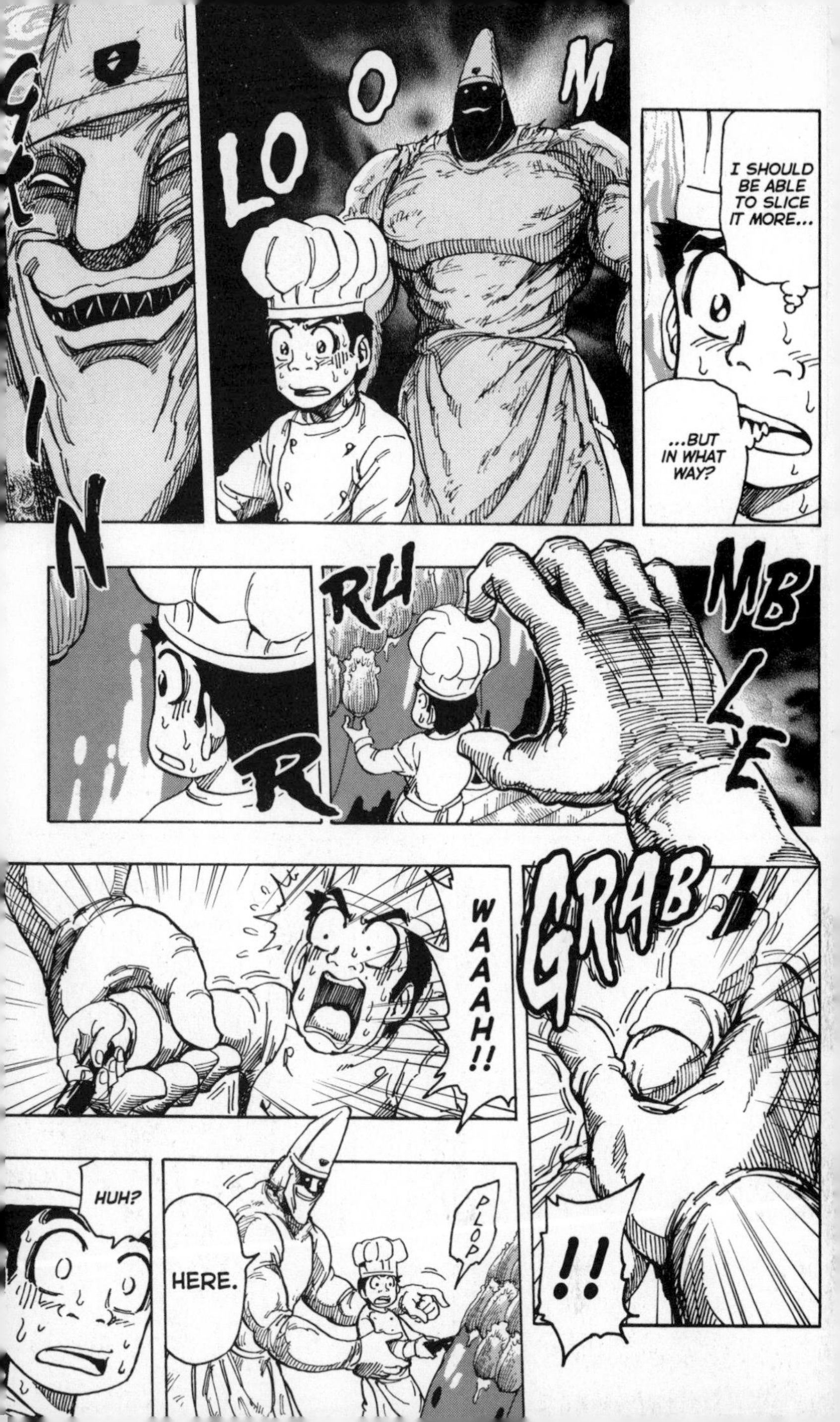

I SHOULD BE ABLE TO SLICE IT MORE...
...BUT IN WHAT WAY?
LOOM
RUMBLE
R
GRAB
WAAAAH!!
!!
PLOP
HERE.
HUH?

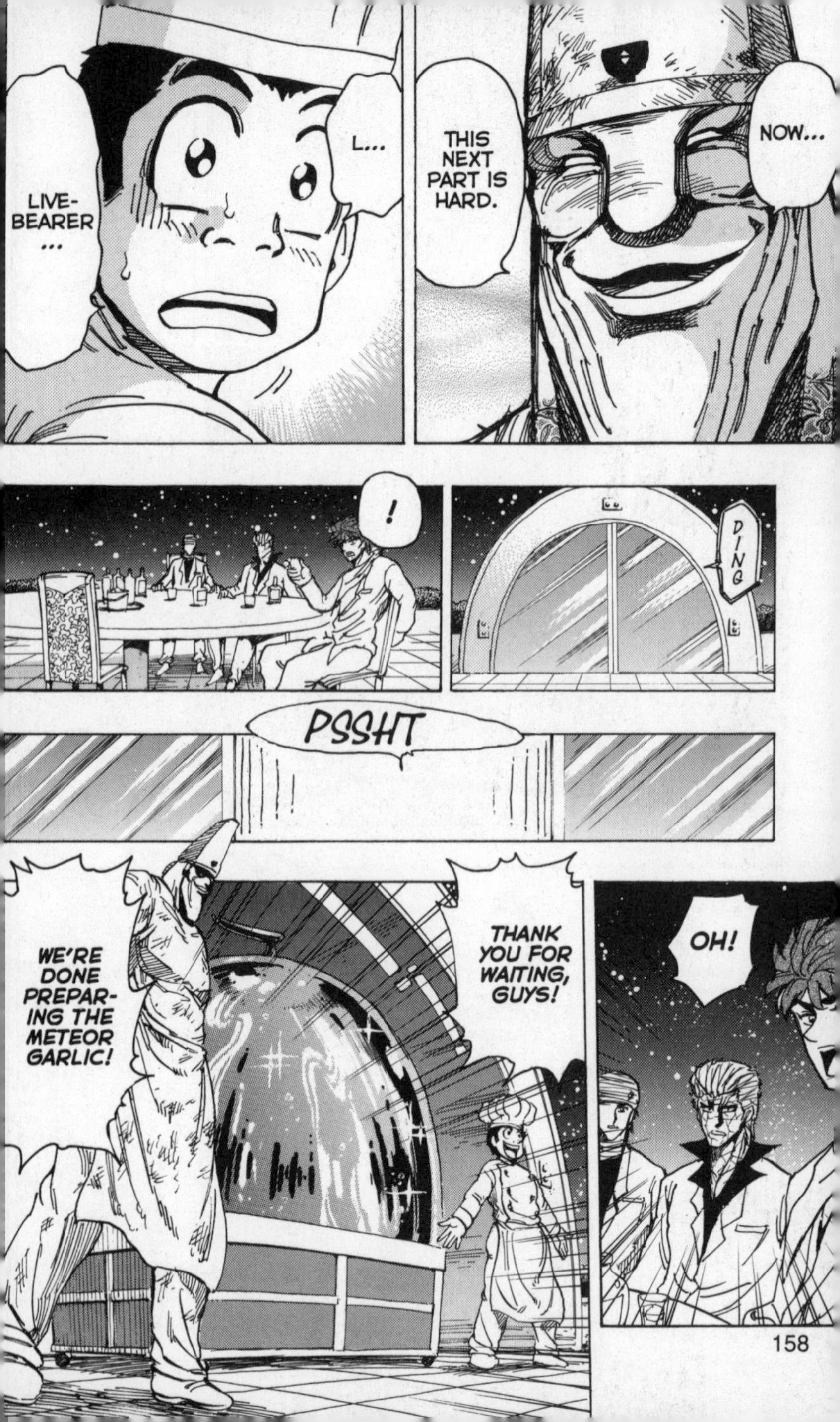
NOW...
THIS NEXT PART IS HARD.
L...
LIVE-BEARER...
DING
!
PSSHT
OH!
THANK YOU FOR WAITING, GUYS!
WE'RE DONE PREPARING THE METEOR GARLIC!

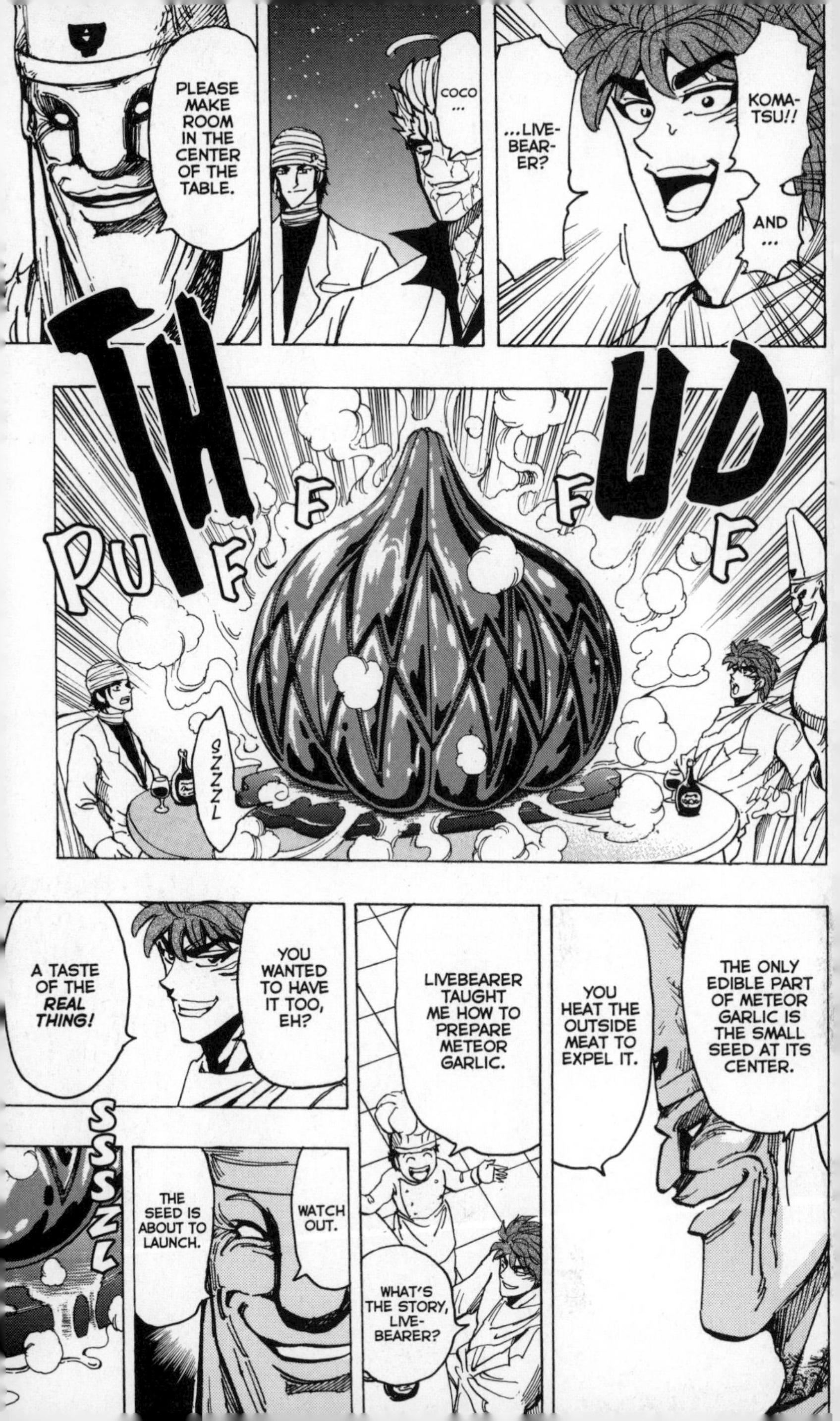
KOMA-TSU!!
...LIVE-BEAR-ER?
AND ...
COCO ...
PLEASE MAKE ROOM IN THE CENTER OF THE TABLE.
THUD
PUFF
PUFF
SZZZL
THE ONLY EDIBLE PART OF METEOR GARLIC IS THE SMALL SEED AT ITS CENTER.
YOU HEAT THE OUTSIDE MEAT TO EXPEL IT.
LIVEBEARER TAUGHT ME HOW TO PREPARE METEOR GARLIC.
WHAT'S THE STORY, LIVE-BEARER?
YOU WANTED TO HAVE IT TOO, EH?
A TASTE OF THE *REAL THING!*
SSSZZL
WATCH OUT.
THE SEED IS ABOUT TO LAUNCH.

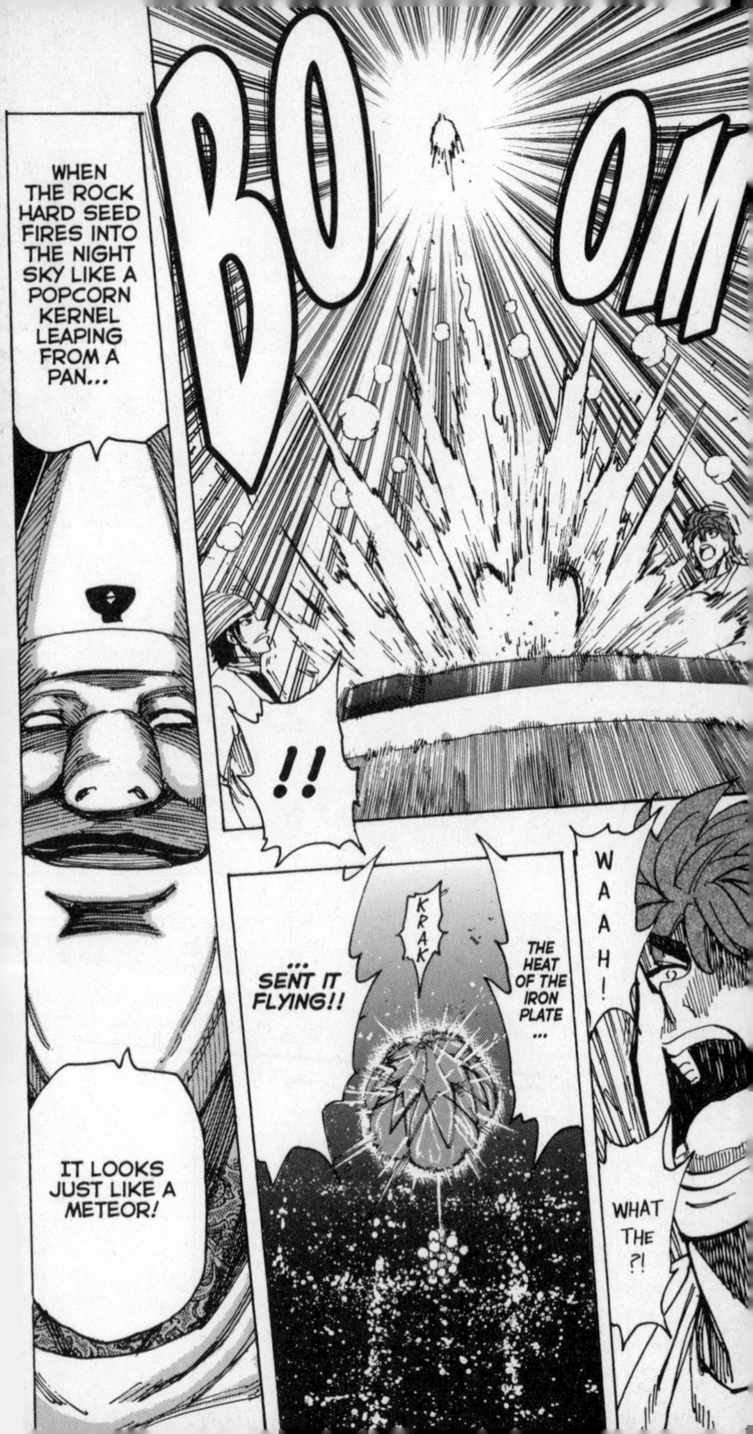
BO-OM
!!
WAAH!
WHAT THE ?!
KRAK
THE HEAT OF THE IRON PLATE ...
... SENT IT FLYING!!
WHEN THE ROCK HARD SEED FIRES INTO THE NIGHT SKY LIKE A POPCORN KERNEL LEAPING FROM A PAN...
IT LOOKS JUST LIKE A METEOR!

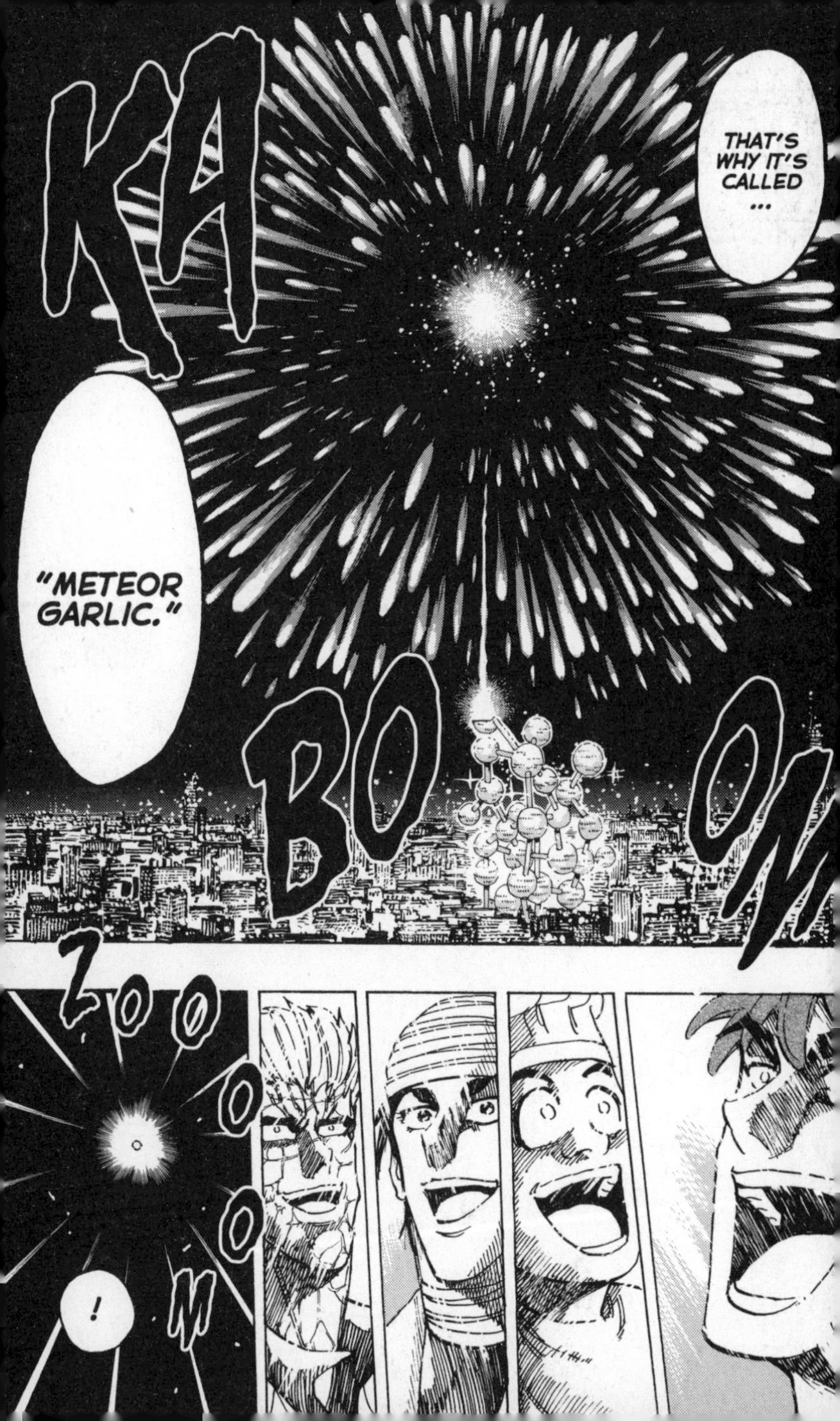
THAT'S WHY IT'S CALLED ...
KA
"METEOR GARLIC."
BOOM
ZOOOOM
!

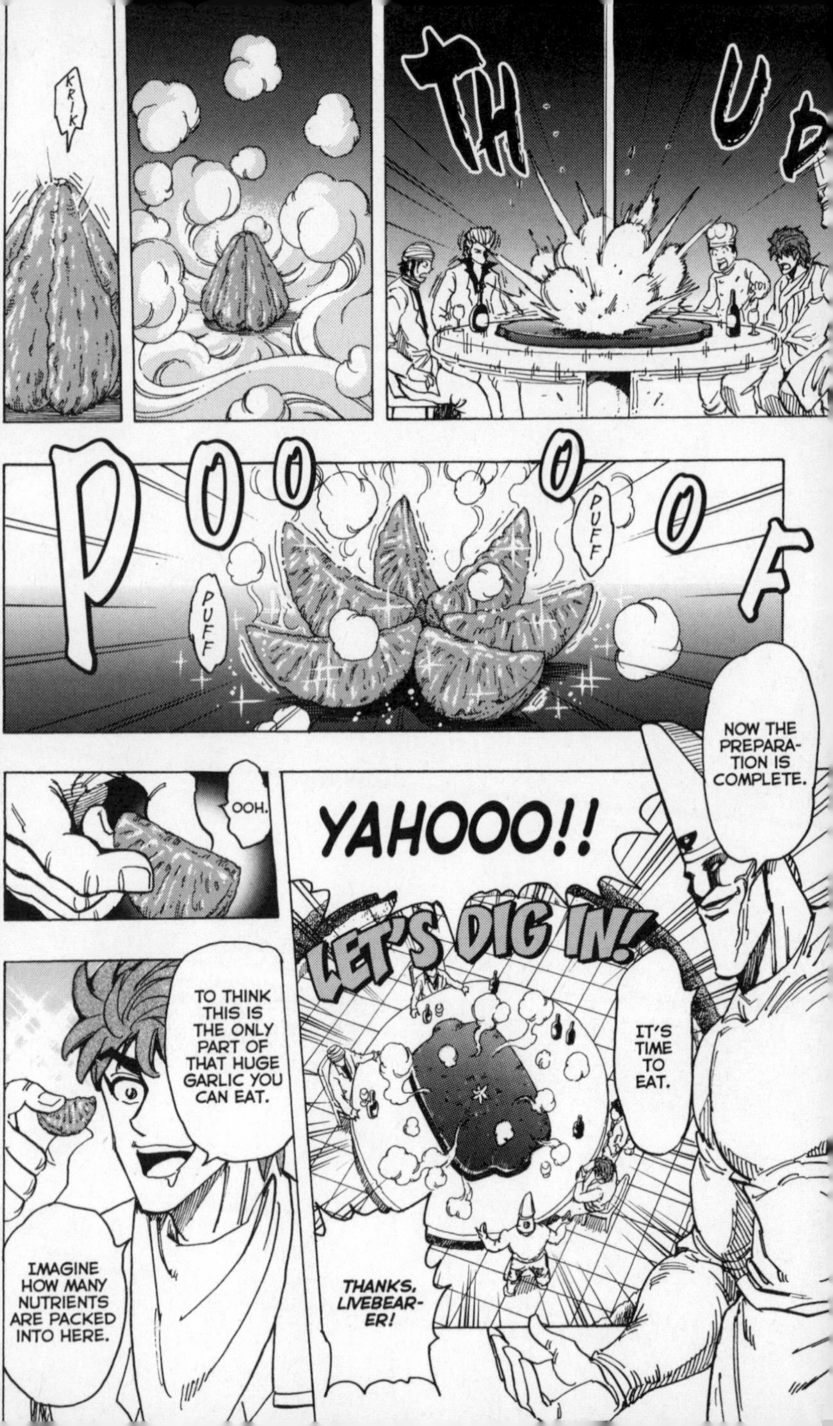
THUD
KRIK
POOOF
PUFF
PUFF
NOW THE PREPARA-TION IS COMPLETE.
YAHOOO!!
LET'S DIG IN!
IT'S TIME TO EAT.
THANKS, LIVEBEAR-ER!
OOH.
TO THINK THIS IS THE ONLY PART OF THAT HUGE GARLIC YOU CAN EAT.
IMAGINE HOW MANY NUTRIENTS ARE PACKED INTO HERE.

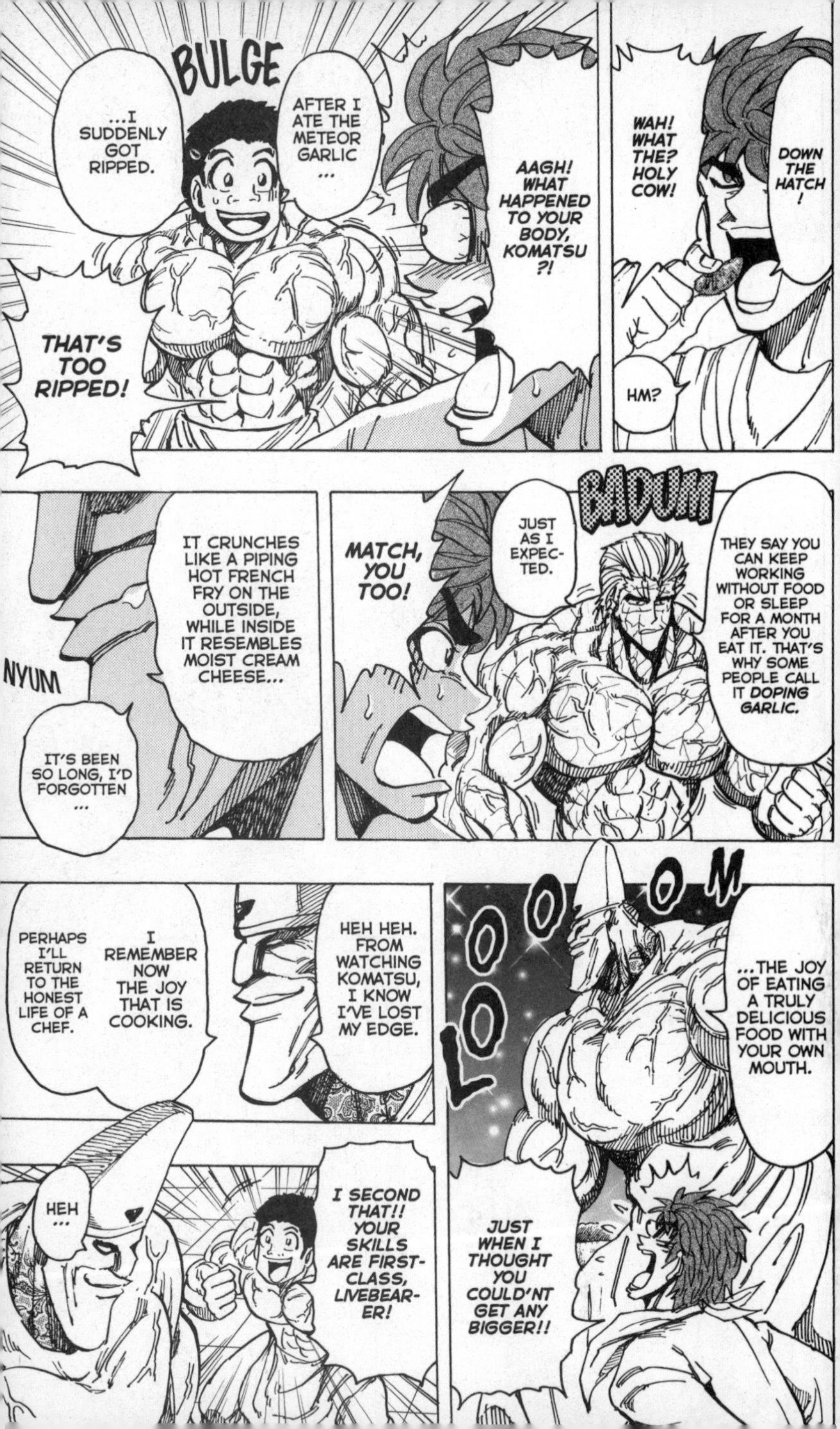
DOWN THE HATCH!
WAH! WHAT THE? HOLY COW!
HM?
AAGH! WHAT HAPPENED TO YOUR BODY, KOMATSU?!
AFTER I ATE THE METEOR GARLIC...
BULGE
...I SUDDENLY GOT RIPPED.
THAT'S TOO RIPPED!
BADUM
THEY SAY YOU CAN KEEP WORKING WITHOUT FOOD OR SLEEP FOR A MONTH AFTER YOU EAT IT. THAT'S WHY SOME PEOPLE CALL IT DOPING GARLIC.
JUST AS I EXPEC-TED.
MATCH, YOU TOO!
IT CRUNCHES LIKE A PIPING HOT FRENCH FRY ON THE OUTSIDE, WHILE INSIDE IT RESEMBLES MOIST CREAM CHEESE...
NYUM
IT'S BEEN SO LONG, I'D FORGOTTEN...
LOOOOM
...THE JOY OF EATING A TRULY DELICIOUS FOOD WITH YOUR OWN MOUTH.
JUST WHEN I THOUGHT YOU COULD'NT GET ANY BIGGER!!
HEH HEH. FROM WATCHING KOMATSU, I KNOW I'VE LOST MY EDGE.
I REMEMBER NOW THE JOY THAT IS COOKING.
PERHAPS I'LL RETURN TO THE HONEST LIFE OF A CHEF.
I SECOND THAT!! YOUR SKILLS ARE FIRST-CLASS, LIVEBEAR-ER!
HEH...

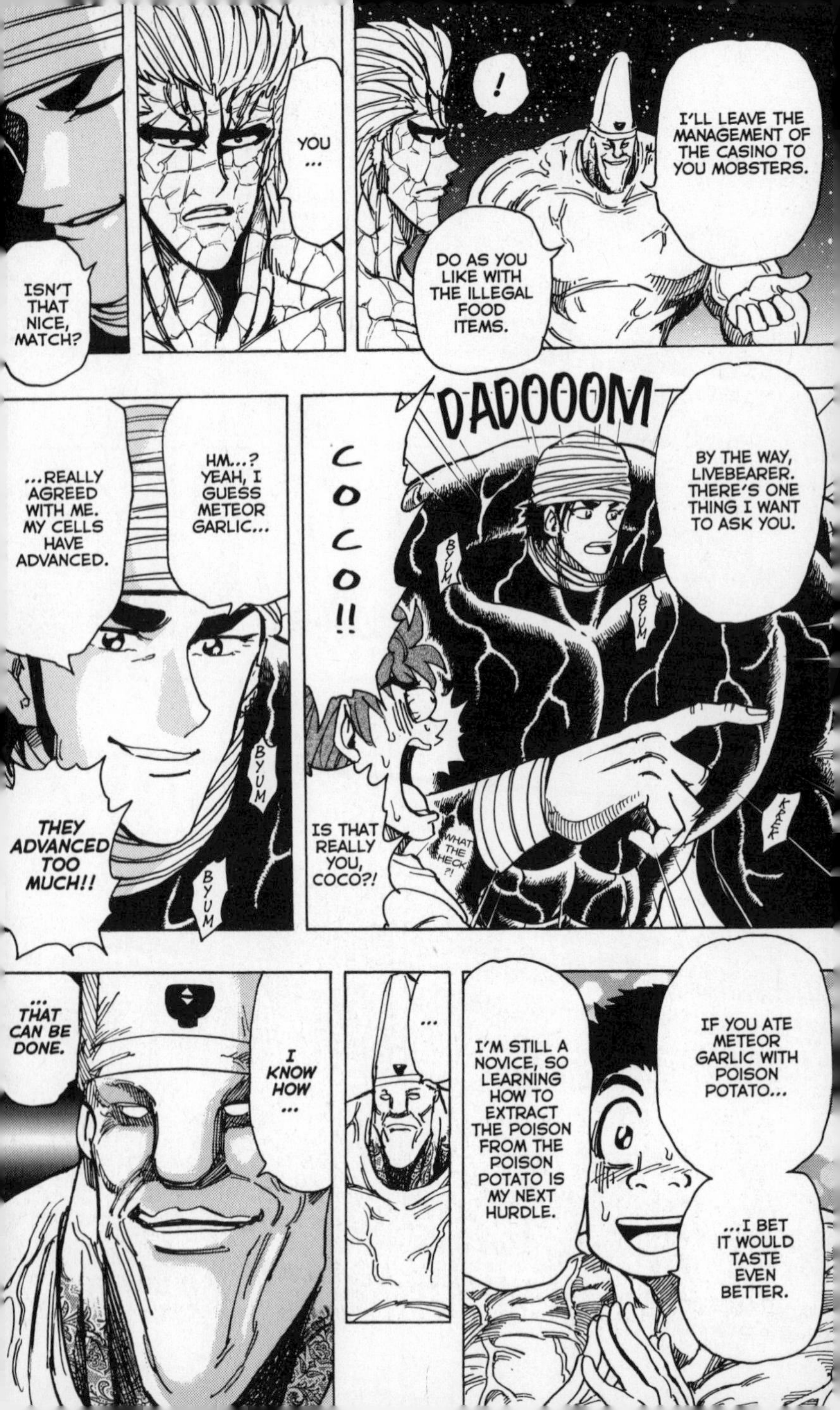
!
I'LL LEAVE THE MANAGEMENT OF THE CASINO TO YOU MOBSTERS.
DO AS YOU LIKE WITH THE ILLEGAL FOOD ITEMS.
YOU ...
ISN'T THAT NICE, MATCH?
DADOOOM
BY THE WAY, LIVEBEARER. THERE'S ONE THING I WANT TO ASK YOU.
COCO!!
BYUM
BYUM
KRAEK
IS THAT REALLY YOU, COCO?!
WHAT THE HECK?!
HM...? YEAH, I GUESS METEOR GARLIC...
...REALLY AGREED WITH ME. MY CELLS HAVE ADVANCED.
BYUM
THEY ADVANCED TOO MUCH!!
BYUM
IF YOU ATE METEOR GARLIC WITH POISON POTATO...
...I BET IT WOULD TASTE EVEN BETTER.
I'M STILL A NOVICE, SO LEARNING HOW TO EXTRACT THE POISON FROM THE POISON POTATO IS MY NEXT HURDLE.
...
I KNOW HOW ...
... THAT CAN BE DONE.

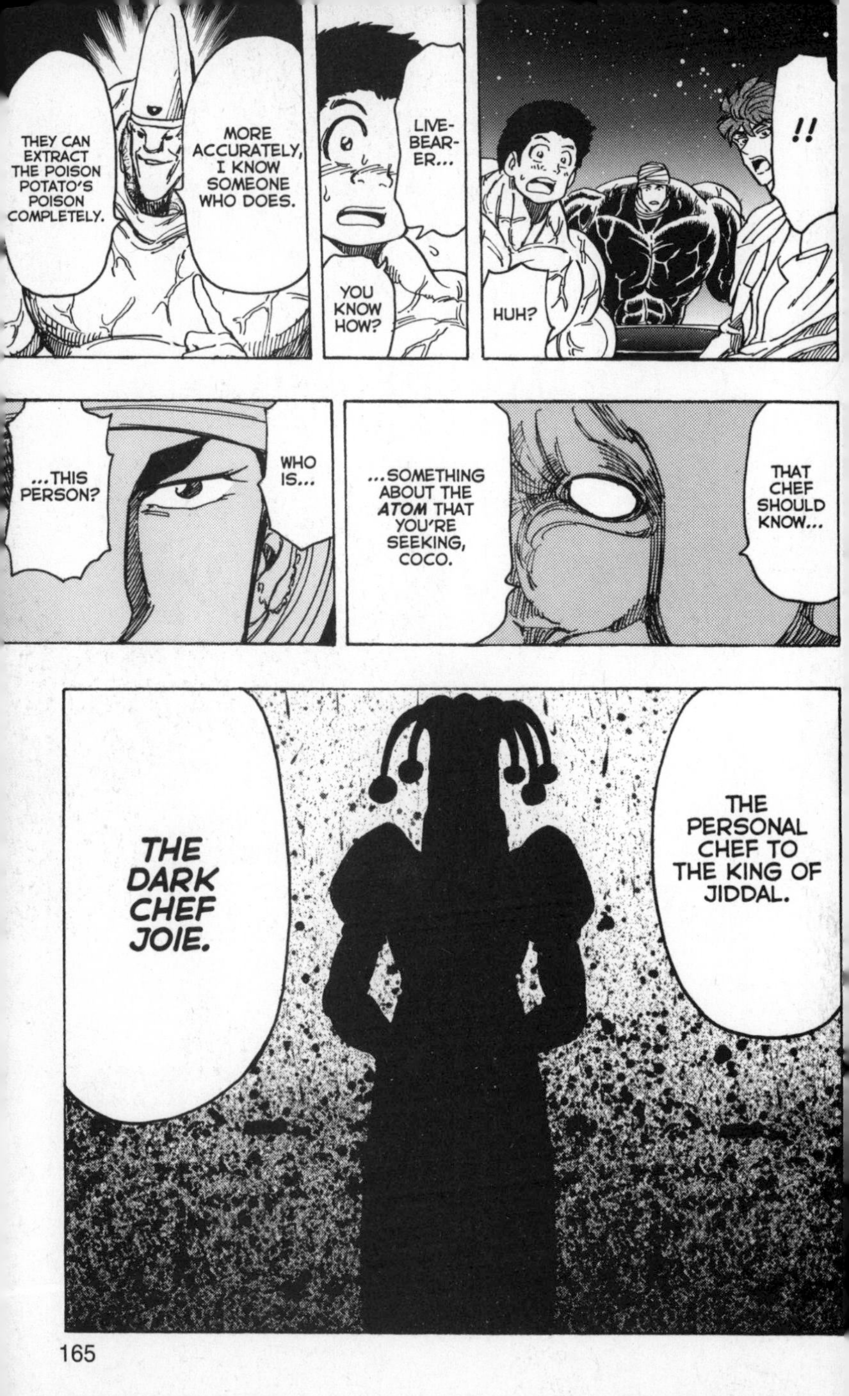
!!
HUH?
LIVE-BEARER...
YOU KNOW HOW?
MORE ACCURATELY, I KNOW SOMEONE WHO DOES.
THEY CAN EXTRACT THE POISON POTATO'S POISON COMPLETELY.
THAT CHEF SHOULD KNOW...
...SOMETHING ABOUT THE ATOM THAT YOU'RE SEEKING, COCO.
WHO IS...
...THIS PERSON?
THE PERSONAL CHEF TO THE KING OF JIDDAL.
THE DARK CHEF JOIE.

TORIKO

GOURMET CHECKLIST
Vol. 200

SALAMANDER SPHINX
(MAMMAL)

CAPTURE LEVEL: 92
HABITAT: GOURMET PYRAMID
LENGTH: 65 METERS
HEIGHT: 27 METERS
WEIGHT: 700 TONS
PRICE: 100 G OF MEAT /
30,000 YEN

SCALE

A MAMMAL THAT REIGNS SUPREME OVER GOURMET PYRAMID. THIS BIZARRE MONSTER HAS THE BODY OF A LION, WINGS ON ITS BACK, AND A SNAKE GROWING OUT OF ITS TAIL. ITS POWER, SPEED, AND COMBAT PROWESS ARE THE GREATEST OF ANY HUMAN WORLD CREATURE. IT STORES THE NUTRIENTS OF THE PREY IT'S EATEN AS DEXTROSE IN ITS TEAR DUCTS AND RELEASES THE MATURED TEARS ONLY ONCE A YEAR. THOSE TEARS ARE THE MELLOW COLA COVETED BY GOURMET HUNTERS THE WORLD OVER.

GOURMET 171: VICTOR OF THE AGE!!

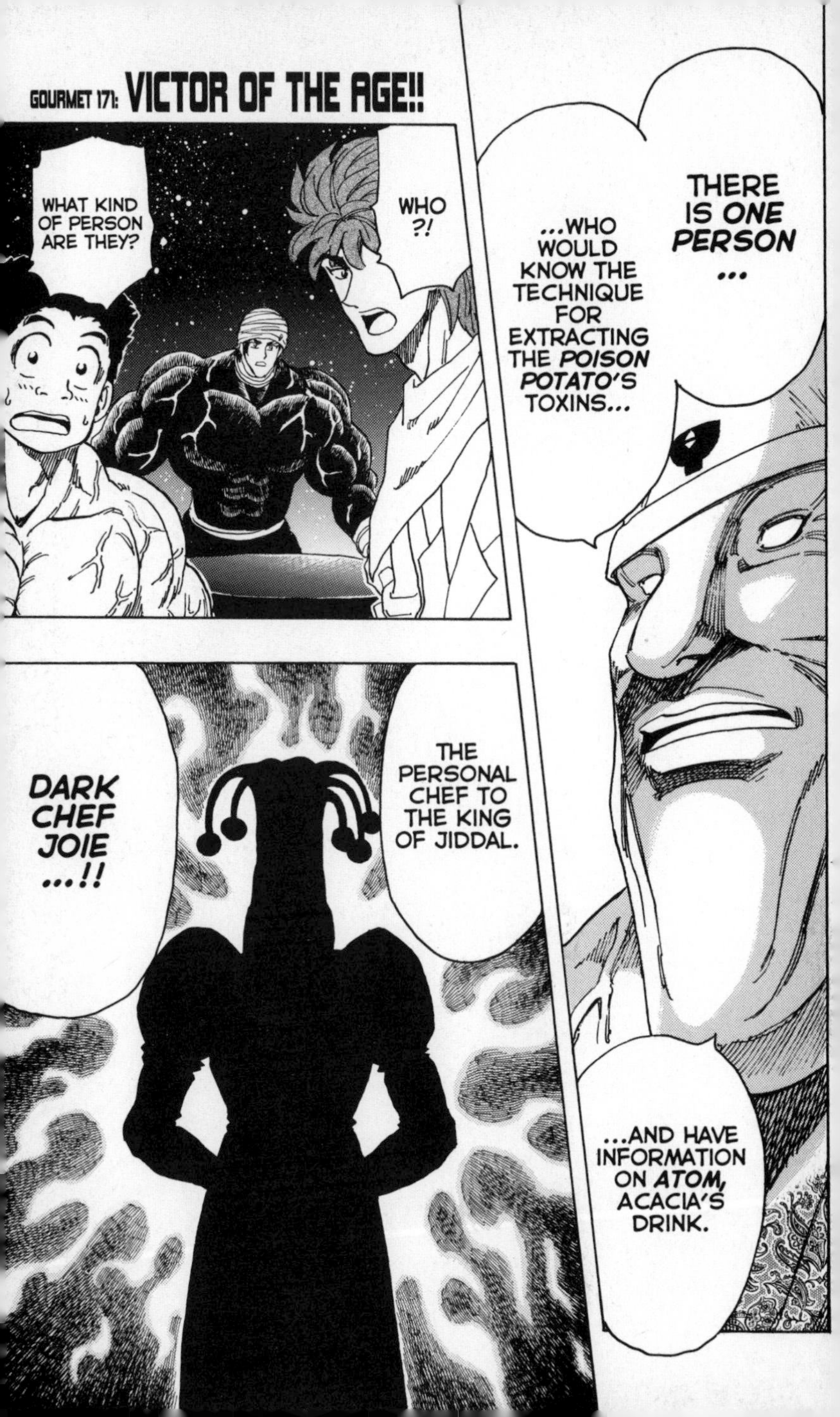

THERE IS *ONE PERSON* ...
...WHO WOULD KNOW THE TECHNIQUE FOR EXTRACTING THE *POISON POTATO*'S TOXINS...
...AND HAVE INFORMATION ON *ATOM*, ACACIA'S DRINK.
WHO ?!
WHAT KIND OF PERSON ARE THEY?
THE PERSONAL CHEF TO THE KING OF JIDDAL.
DARK CHEF JOIE ...!!

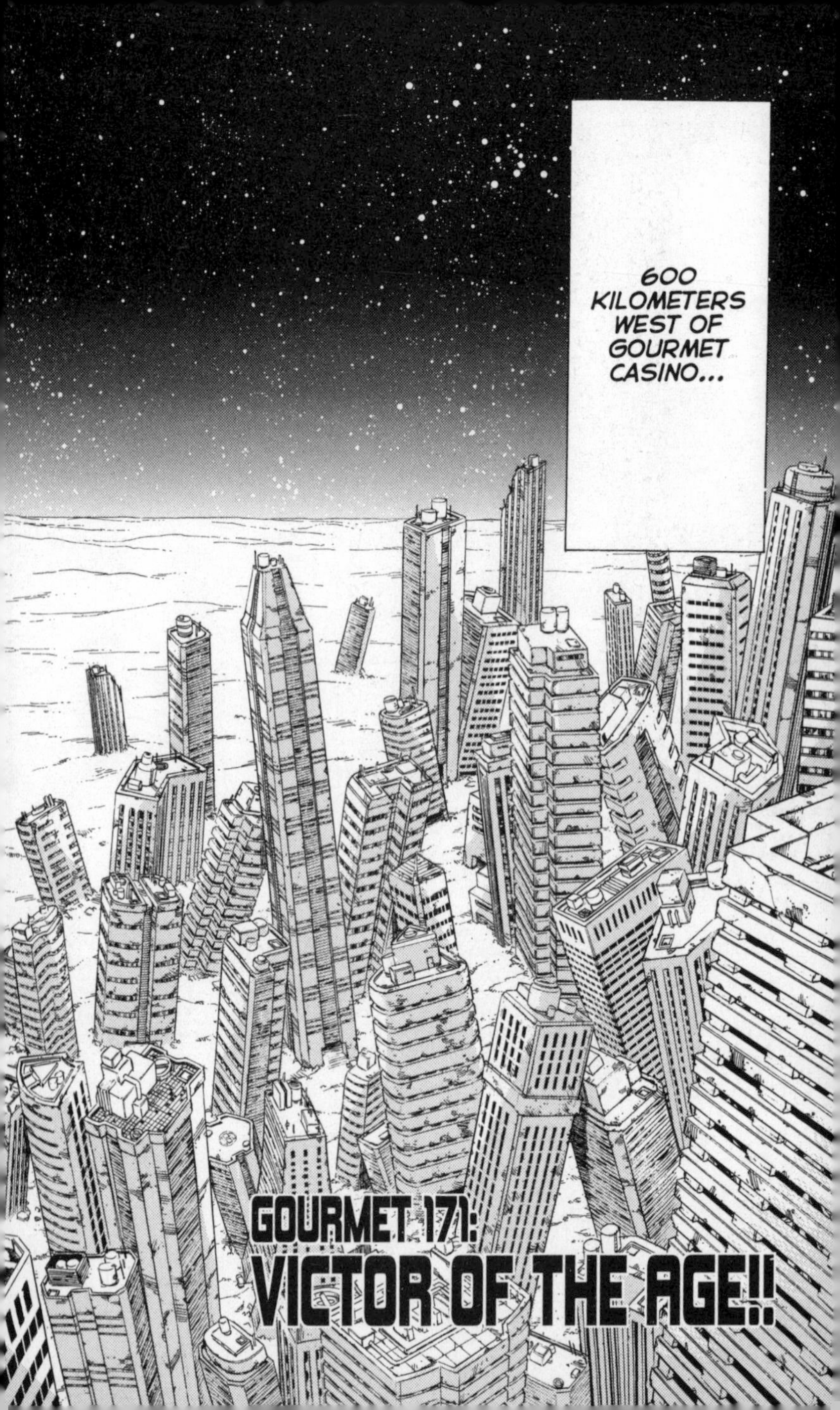
600 KILOMETERS WEST OF GOURMET CASINO...
GOURMET 171:
VICTOR OF THE AGE!!

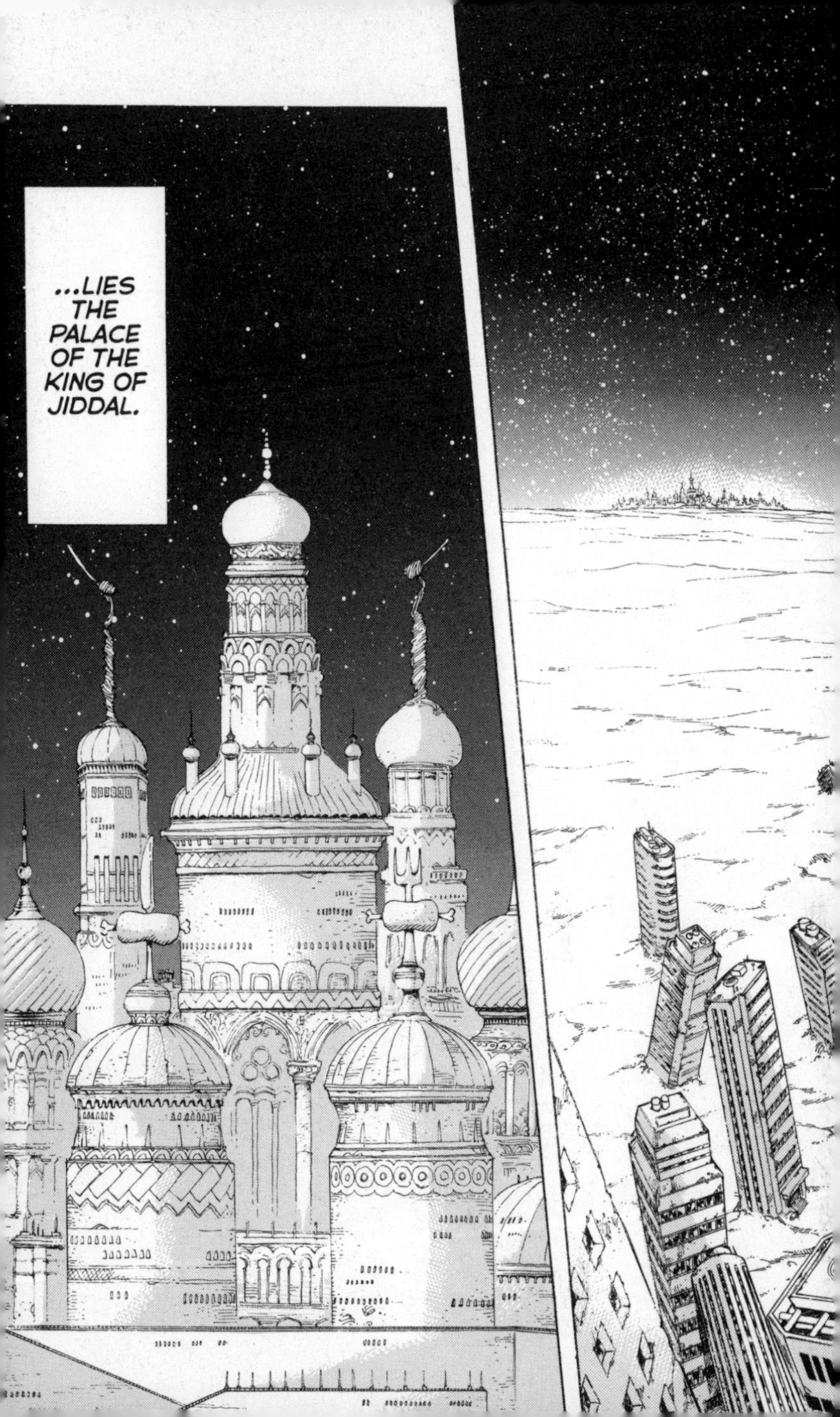
...LIES THE PALACE OF THE KING OF JIDDAL.

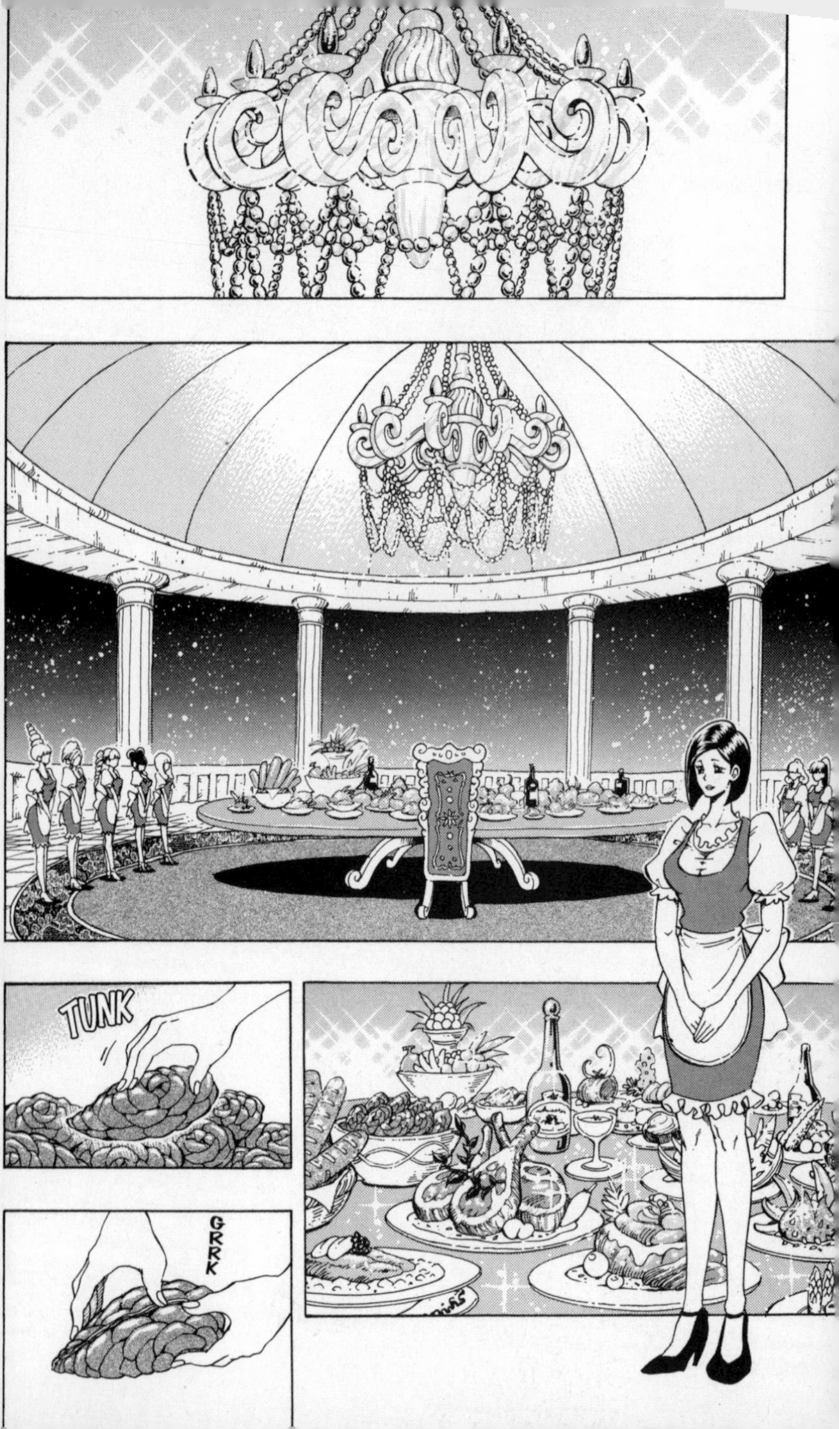
TUNK
GRRK

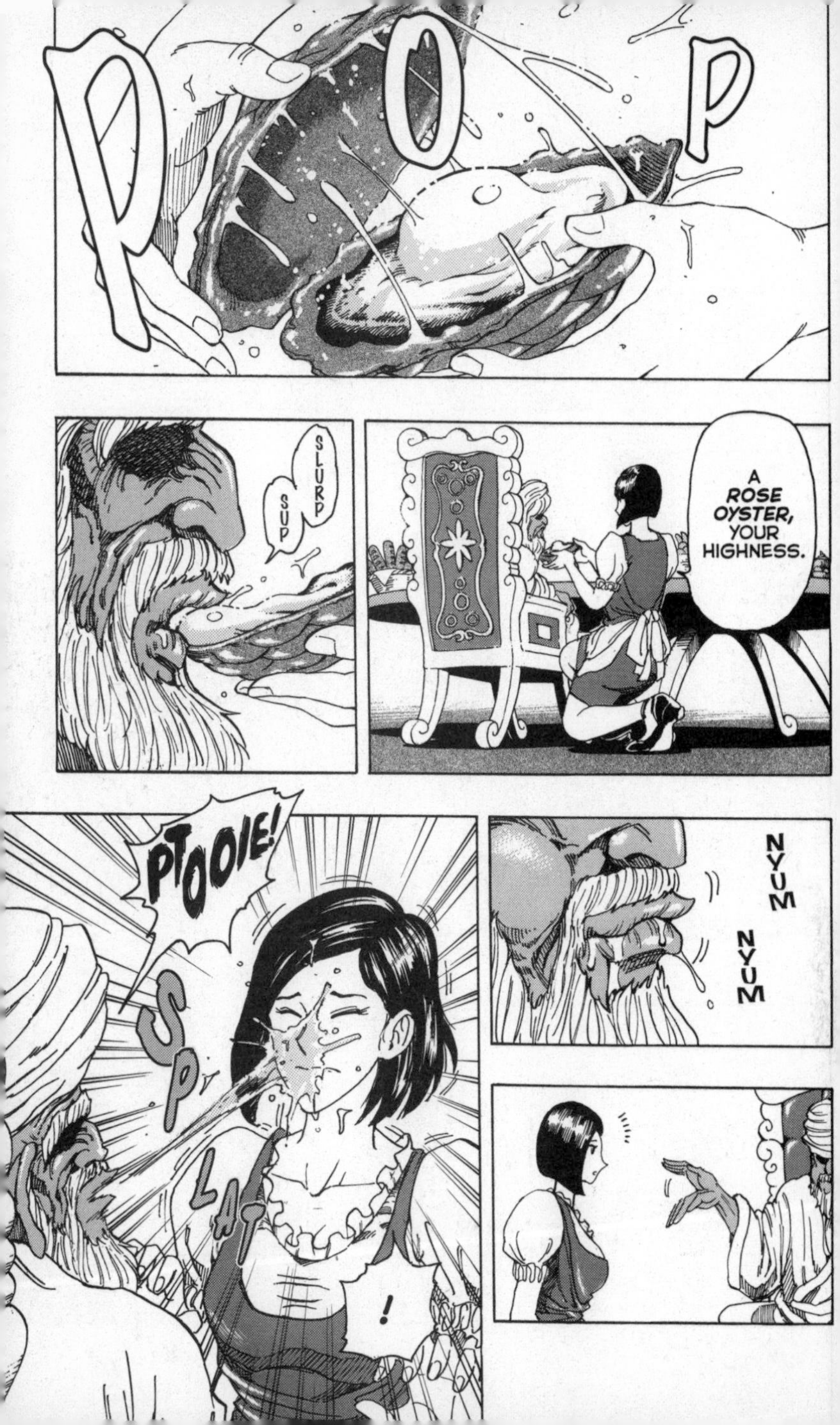
POP
A ROSE OYSTER, YOUR HIGHNESS.
SLURP
SUP
NYUM
NYUM
PTOOIE!
SPLAT
!

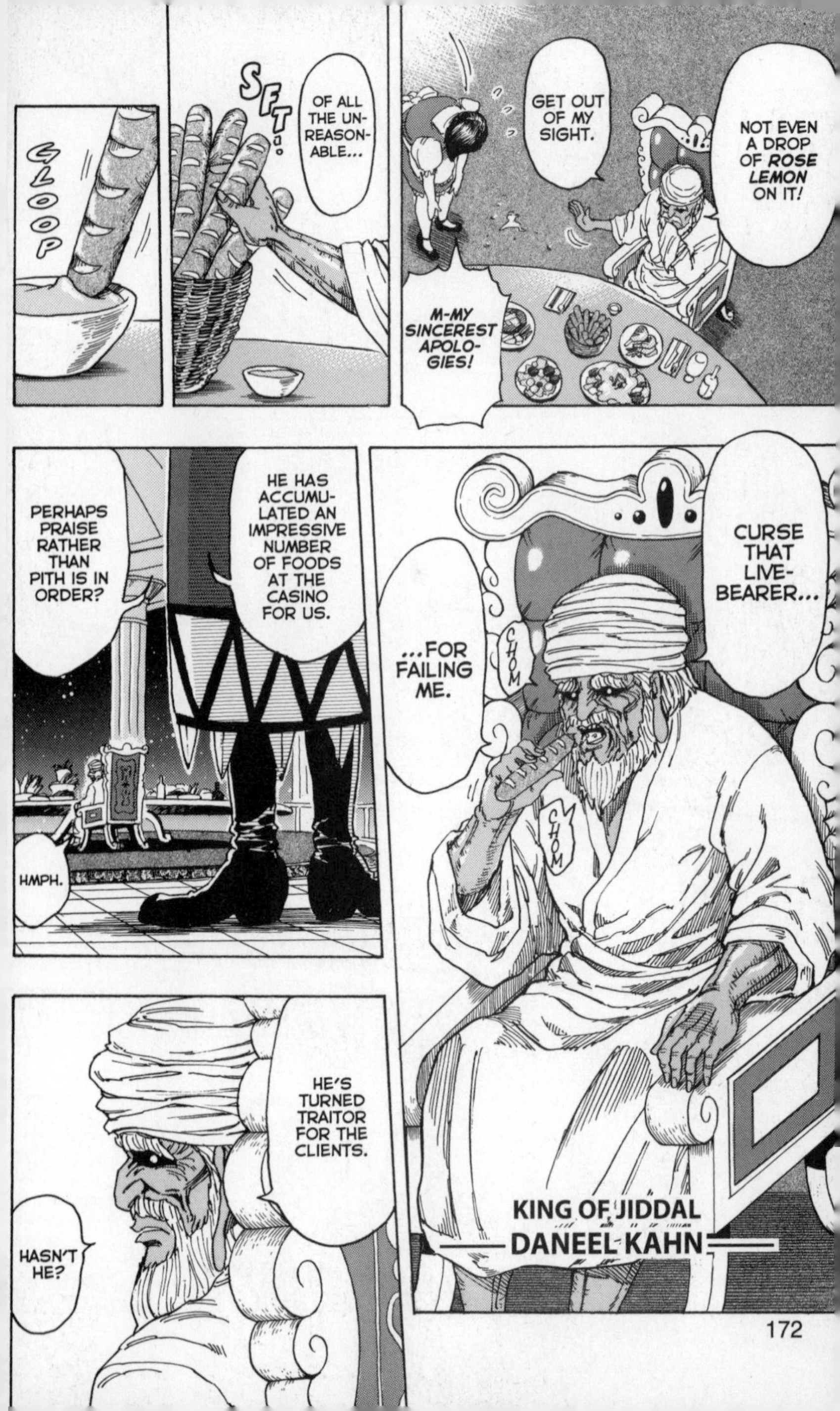
NOT EVEN A DROP OF ROSE LEMON ON IT!
GET OUT OF MY SIGHT.
M-MY SINCEREST APOLO-GIES!
SFT
OF ALL THE UN-REASON-ABLE...
GLOOP
CURSE THAT LIVE-BEARER...
CHOM
...FOR FAILING ME.
CHOM
KING OF JIDDAL
DANEEL KAHN
HE HAS ACCUMU-LATED AN IMPRESSIVE NUMBER OF FOODS AT THE CASINO FOR US.
PERHAPS PRAISE RATHER THAN PITH IS IN ORDER?
HMPH.
HE'S TURNED TRAITOR FOR THE CLIENTS.
HASN'T HE?

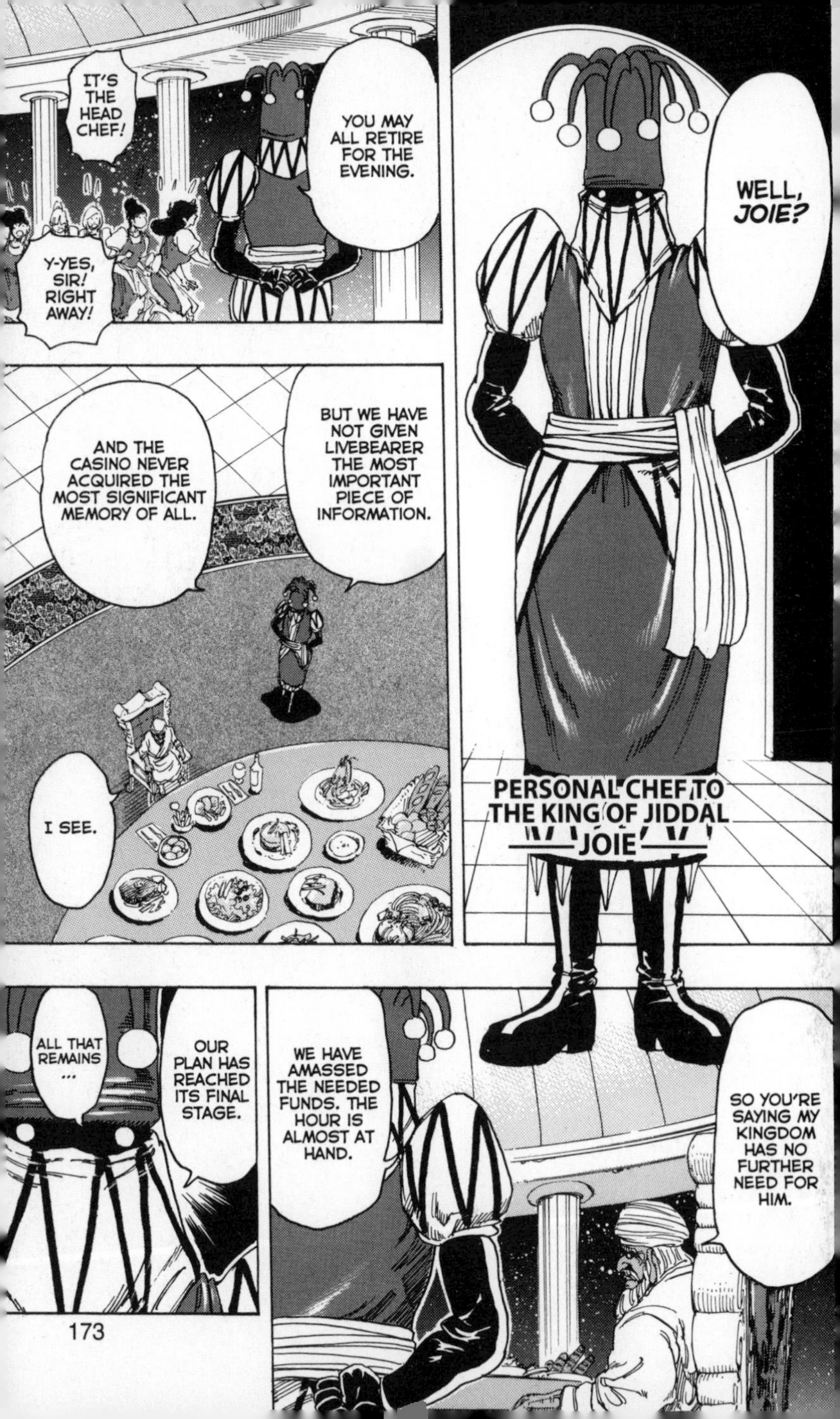
WELL, JOIE?
PERSONAL CHEF TO THE KING OF JIDDAL
JOIE
YOU MAY ALL RETIRE FOR THE EVENING.
IT'S THE HEAD CHEF!
Y-YES, SIR! RIGHT AWAY!
BUT WE HAVE NOT GIVEN LIVEBEARER THE MOST IMPORTANT PIECE OF INFORMATION.
AND THE CASINO NEVER ACQUIRED THE MOST SIGNIFICANT MEMORY OF ALL.
I SEE.
SO YOU'RE SAYING MY KINGDOM HAS NO FURTHER NEED FOR HIM.
WE HAVE AMASSED THE NEEDED FUNDS. THE HOUR IS ALMOST AT HAND.
OUR PLAN HAS REACHED ITS FINAL STAGE.
ALL THAT REMAINS ...

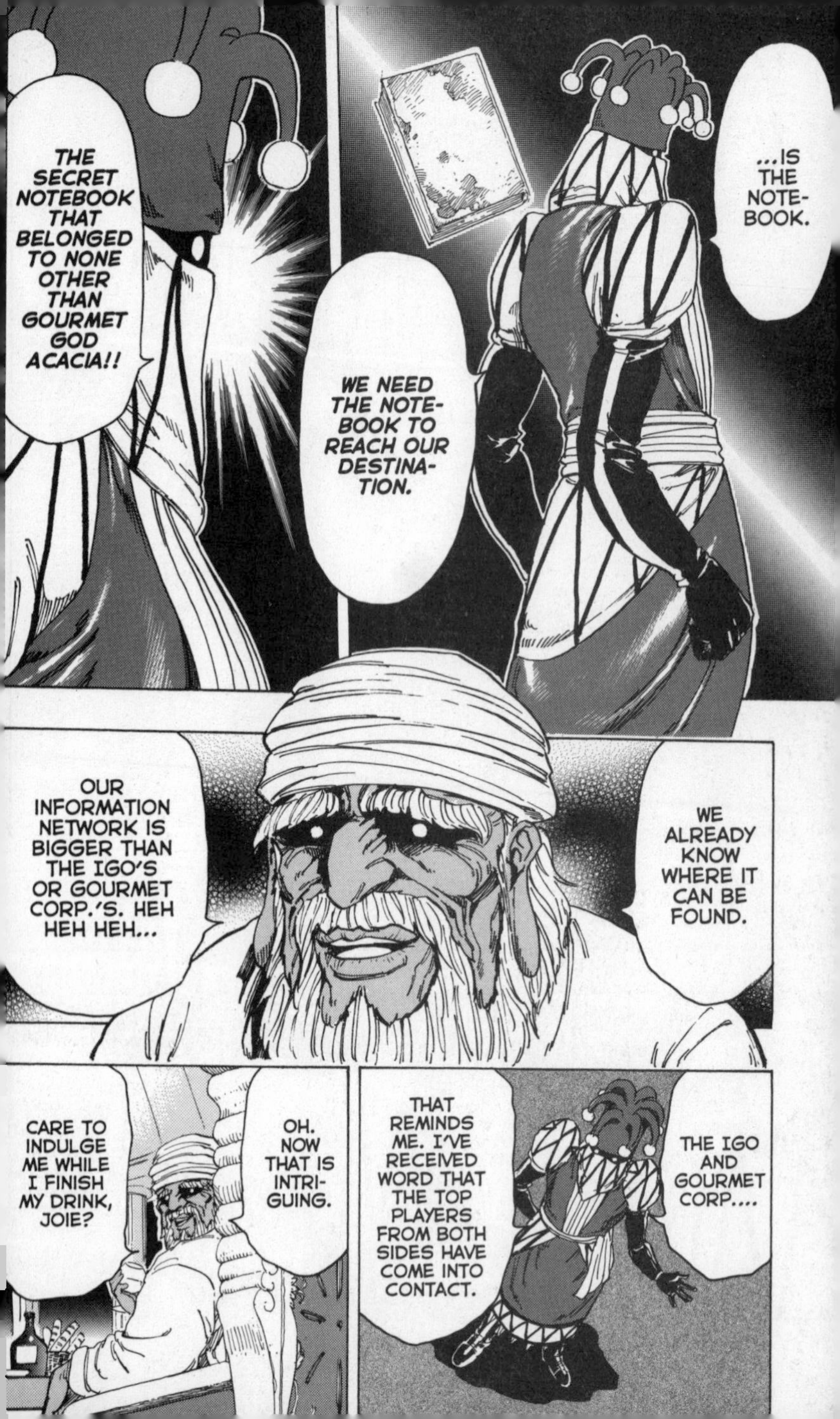
...IS THE NOTE-BOOK.
WE NEED THE NOTE-BOOK TO REACH OUR DESTINA-TION.
THE SECRET NOTEBOOK THAT BELONGED TO NONE OTHER THAN GOURMET GOD ACACIA!!
WE ALREADY KNOW WHERE IT CAN BE FOUND.
OUR INFORMATION NETWORK IS BIGGER THAN THE IGO'S OR GOURMET CORP.'S. HEH HEH HEH...
THE IGO AND GOURMET CORP....
THAT REMINDS ME. I'VE RECEIVED WORD THAT THE TOP PLAYERS FROM BOTH SIDES HAVE COME INTO CONTACT.
OH. NOW THAT IS INTRI-GUING.
CARE TO INDULGE ME WHILE I FINISH MY DRINK, JOIE?

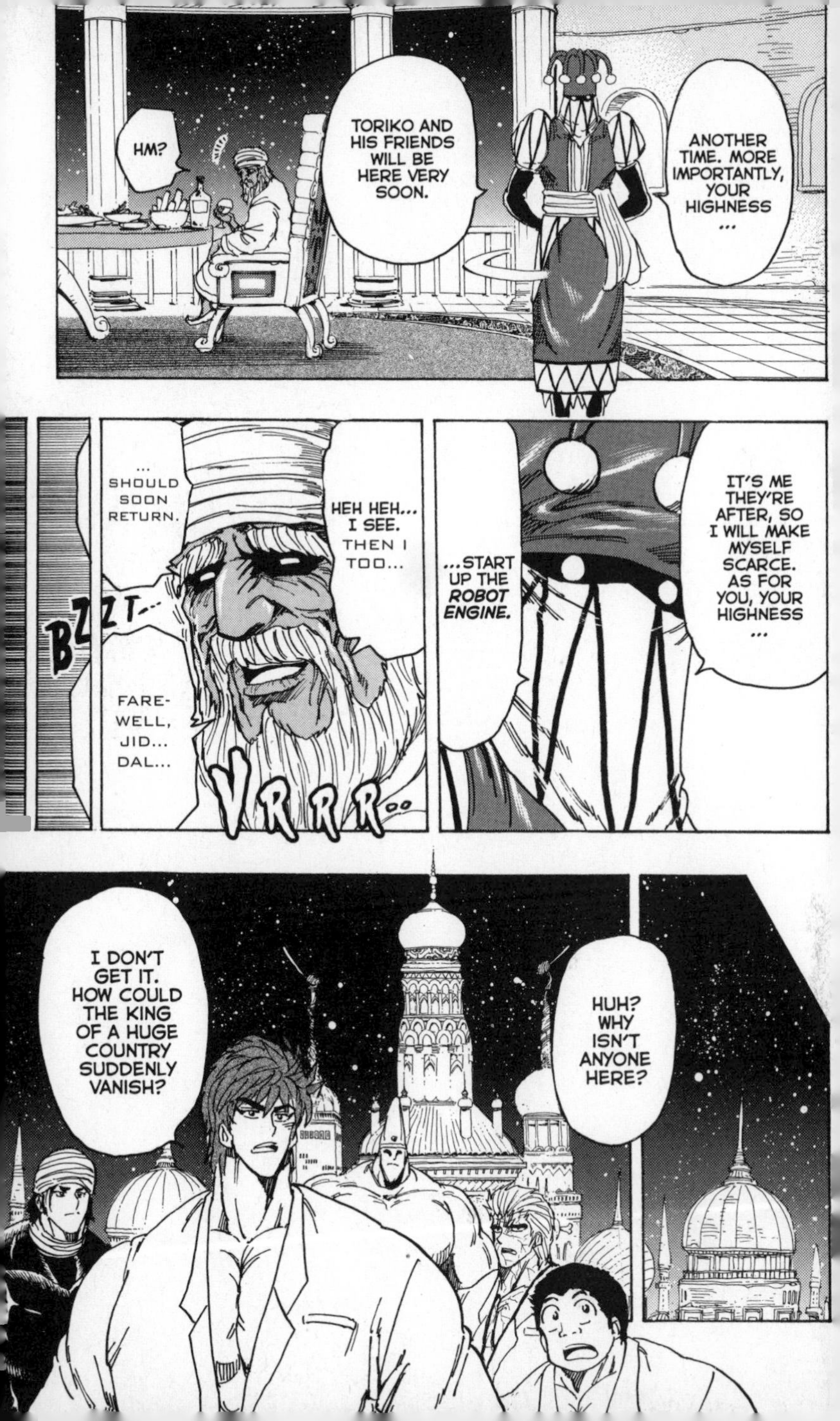
ANOTHER TIME. MORE IMPORTANTLY, YOUR HIGHNESS ...
TORIKO AND HIS FRIENDS WILL BE HERE VERY SOON.
HM?
IT'S ME THEY'RE AFTER, SO I WILL MAKE MYSELF SCARCE. AS FOR YOU, YOUR HIGHNESS ...
...START UP THE *ROBOT ENGINE.*
HEH HEH... I SEE. THEN I TOO...
... SHOULD SOON RETURN.
BZZT...
FARE-WELL, JID... DAL...
VRRR
HUH? WHY ISN'T ANYONE HERE?
I DON'T GET IT. HOW COULD THE KING OF A HUGE COUNTRY SUDDENLY VANISH?

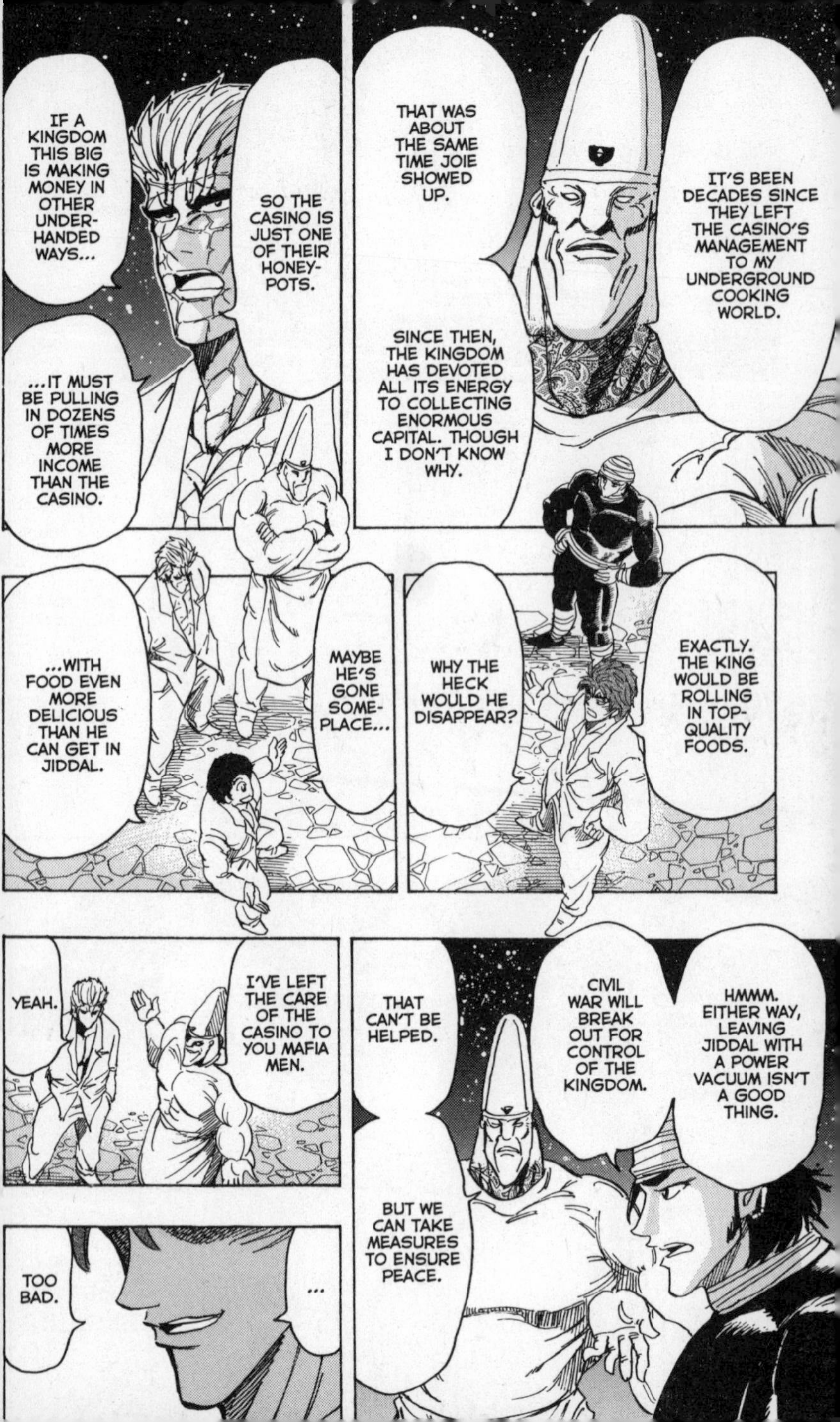
IT'S BEEN DECADES SINCE THEY LEFT THE CASINO'S MANAGEMENT TO MY UNDERGROUND COOKING WORLD.
THAT WAS ABOUT THE SAME TIME JOIE SHOWED UP.
SINCE THEN, THE KINGDOM HAS DEVOTED ALL ITS ENERGY TO COLLECTING ENORMOUS CAPITAL. THOUGH I DON'T KNOW WHY.
SO THE CASINO IS JUST ONE OF THEIR HONEY-POTS.
IF A KINGDOM THIS BIG IS MAKING MONEY IN OTHER UNDER-HANDED WAYS...
...IT MUST BE PULLING IN DOZENS OF TIMES MORE INCOME THAN THE CASINO.
EXACTLY. THE KING WOULD BE ROLLING IN TOP-QUALITY FOODS.
WHY THE HECK WOULD HE DISAPPEAR?
MAYBE HE'S GONE SOME-PLACE...
...WITH FOOD EVEN MORE DELICIOUS THAN HE CAN GET IN JIDDAL.
HMMM. EITHER WAY, LEAVING JIDDAL WITH A POWER VACUUM ISN'T A GOOD THING.
CIVIL WAR WILL BREAK OUT FOR CONTROL OF THE KINGDOM.
THAT CAN'T BE HELPED.
BUT WE CAN TAKE MEASURES TO ENSURE PEACE.
I'VE LEFT THE CARE OF THE CASINO TO YOU MAFIA MEN.
YEAH.
...
TOO BAD.

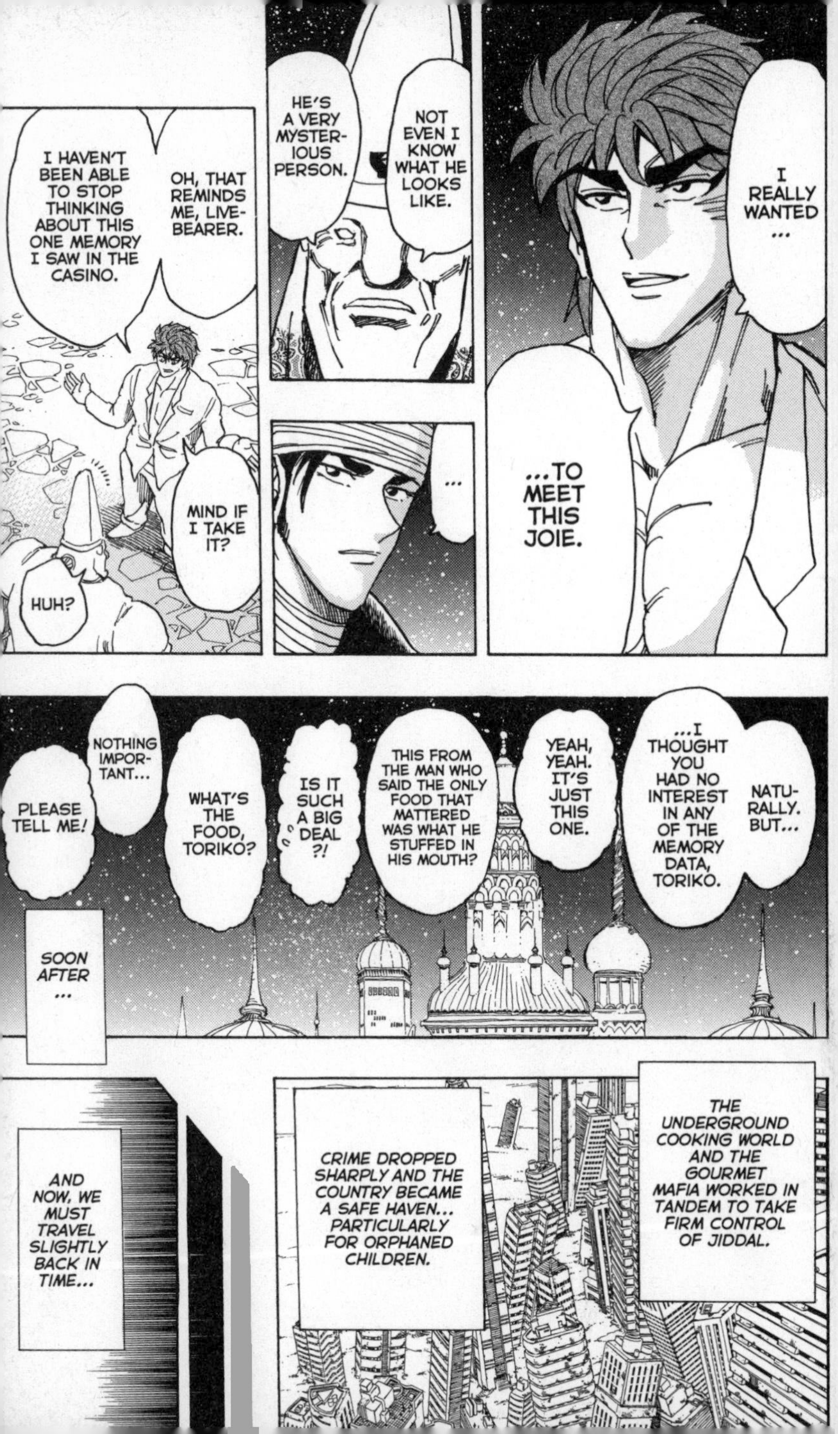
I REALLY WANTED...
...TO MEET THIS JOIE.
NOT EVEN I KNOW WHAT HE LOOKS LIKE.
HE'S A VERY MYSTERIOUS PERSON.
...
OH, THAT REMINDS ME, LIVEBEARER.
I HAVEN'T BEEN ABLE TO STOP THINKING ABOUT THIS ONE MEMORY I SAW IN THE CASINO.
MIND IF I TAKE IT?
HUH?
NATURALLY. BUT...
...I THOUGHT YOU HAD NO INTEREST IN ANY OF THE MEMORY DATA, TORIKO.
YEAH, YEAH. IT'S JUST THIS ONE.
THIS FROM THE MAN WHO SAID THE ONLY FOOD THAT MATTERED WAS WHAT HE STUFFED IN HIS MOUTH?
IS IT SUCH A BIG DEAL?!
WHAT'S THE FOOD, TORIKO?
NOTHING IMPORTANT...
PLEASE TELL ME!
SOON AFTER...
THE UNDERGROUND COOKING WORLD AND THE GOURMET MAFIA WORKED IN TANDEM TO TAKE FIRM CONTROL OF JIDDAL.
CRIME DROPPED SHARPLY AND THE COUNTRY BECAME A SAFE HAVEN... PARTICULARLY FOR ORPHANED CHILDREN.
AND NOW, WE MUST TRAVEL SLIGHTLY BACK IN TIME...

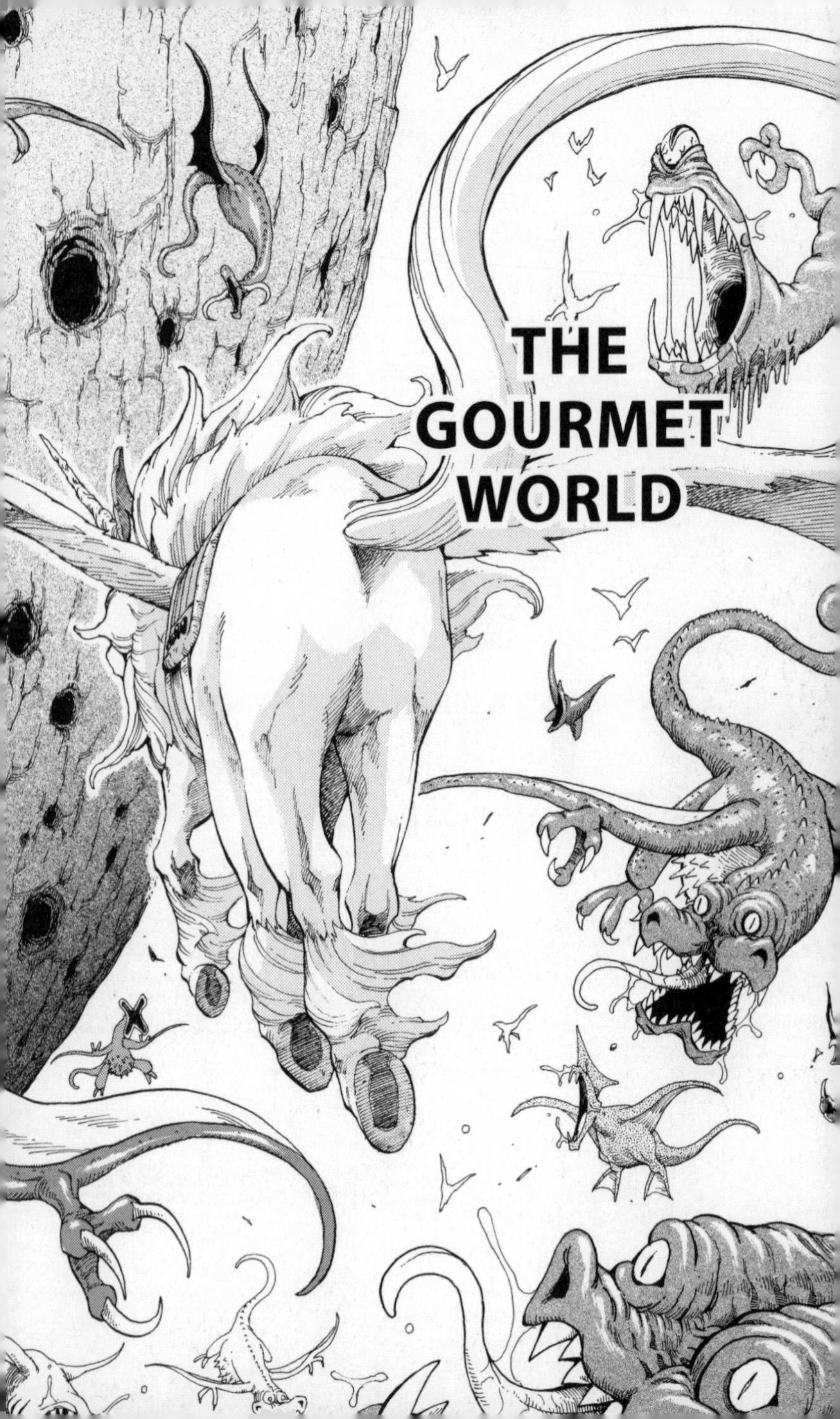
THE GOURMET WORLD

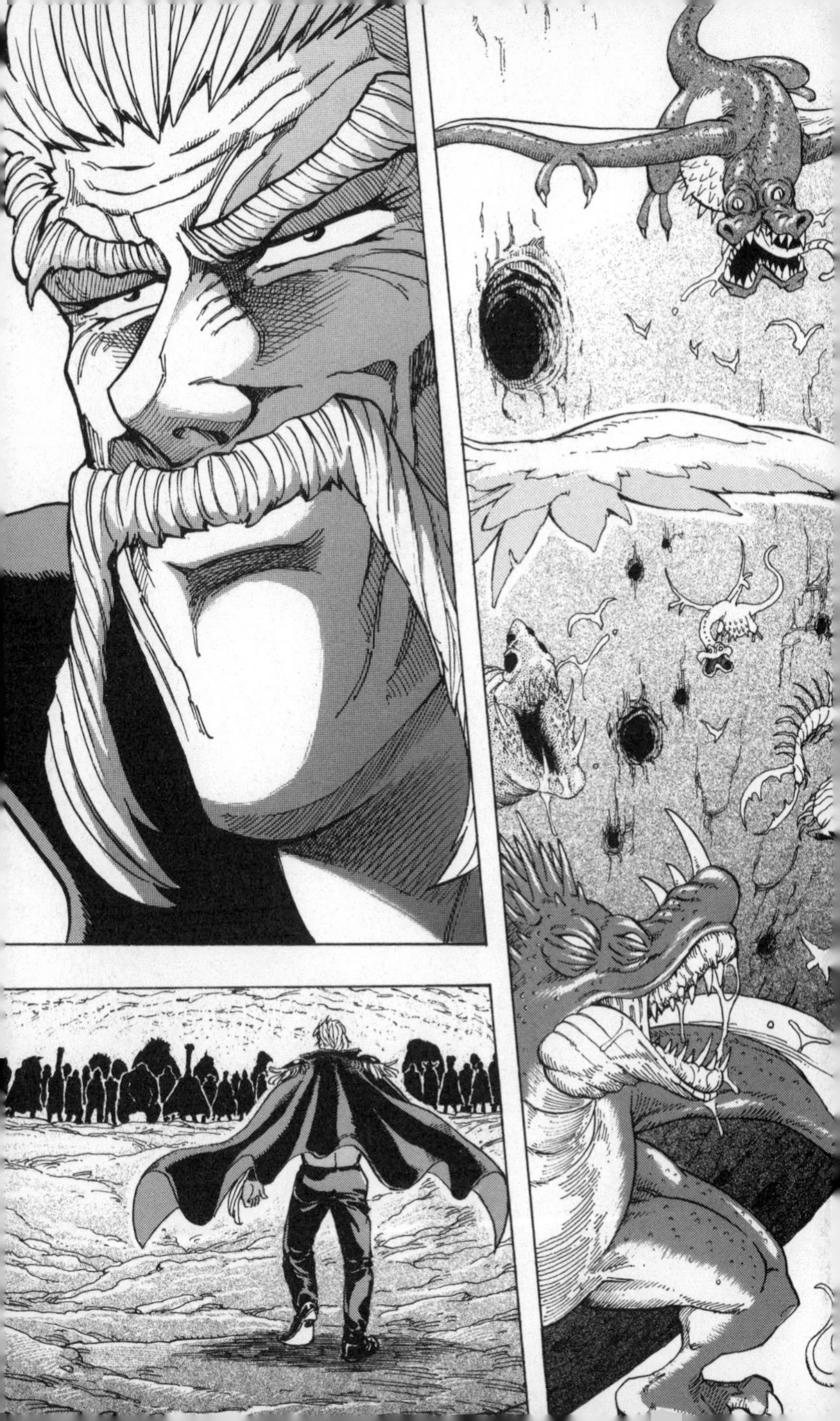

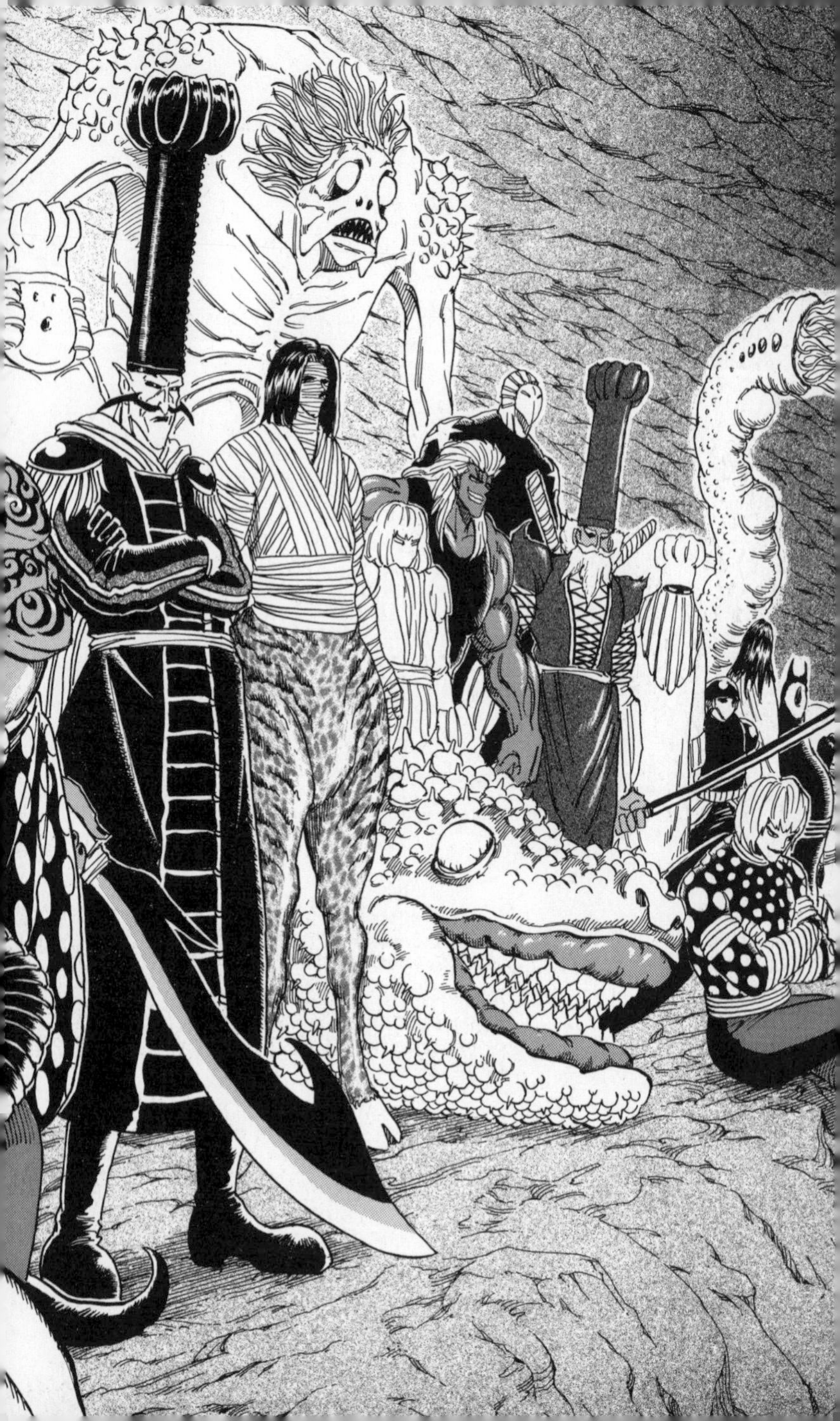

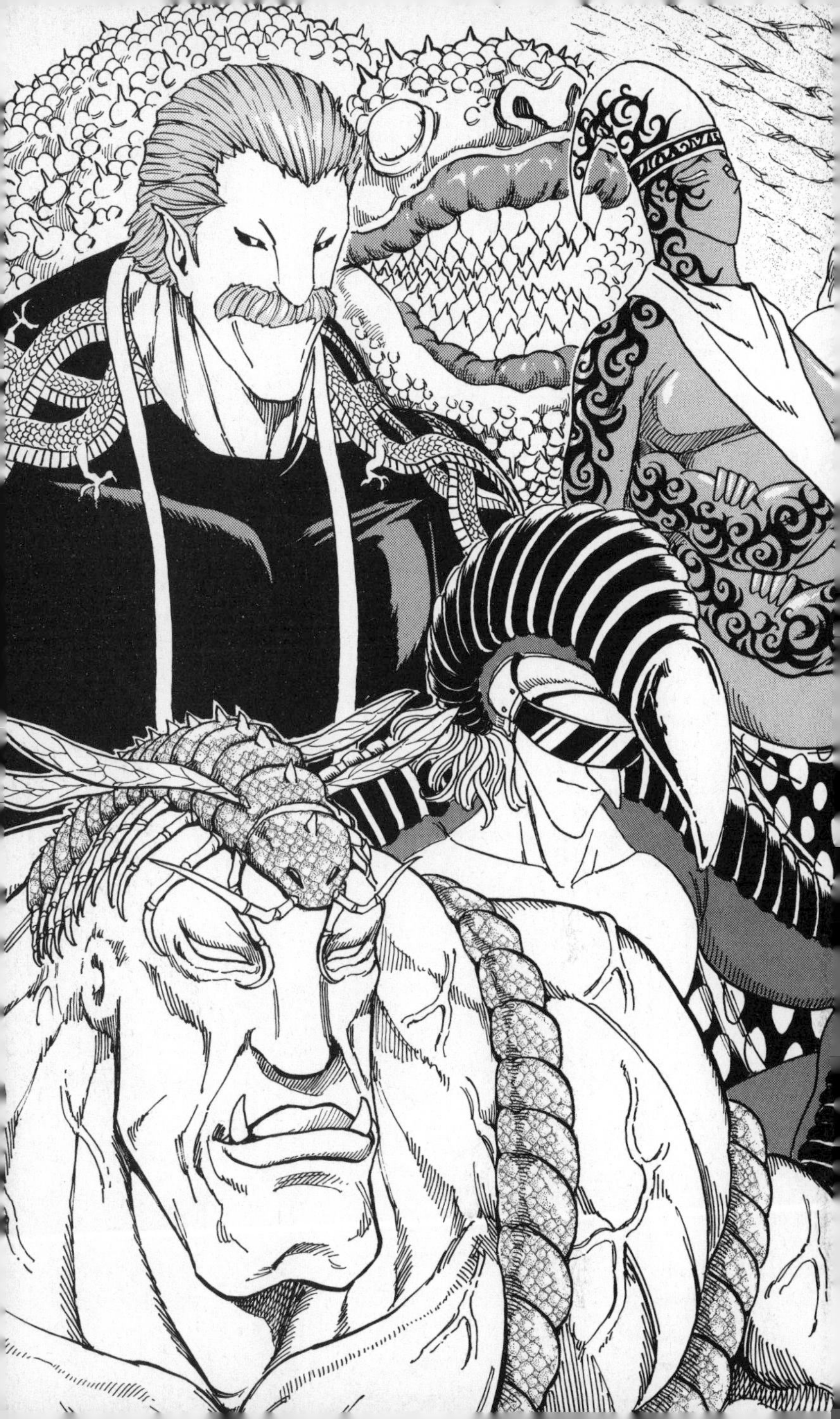

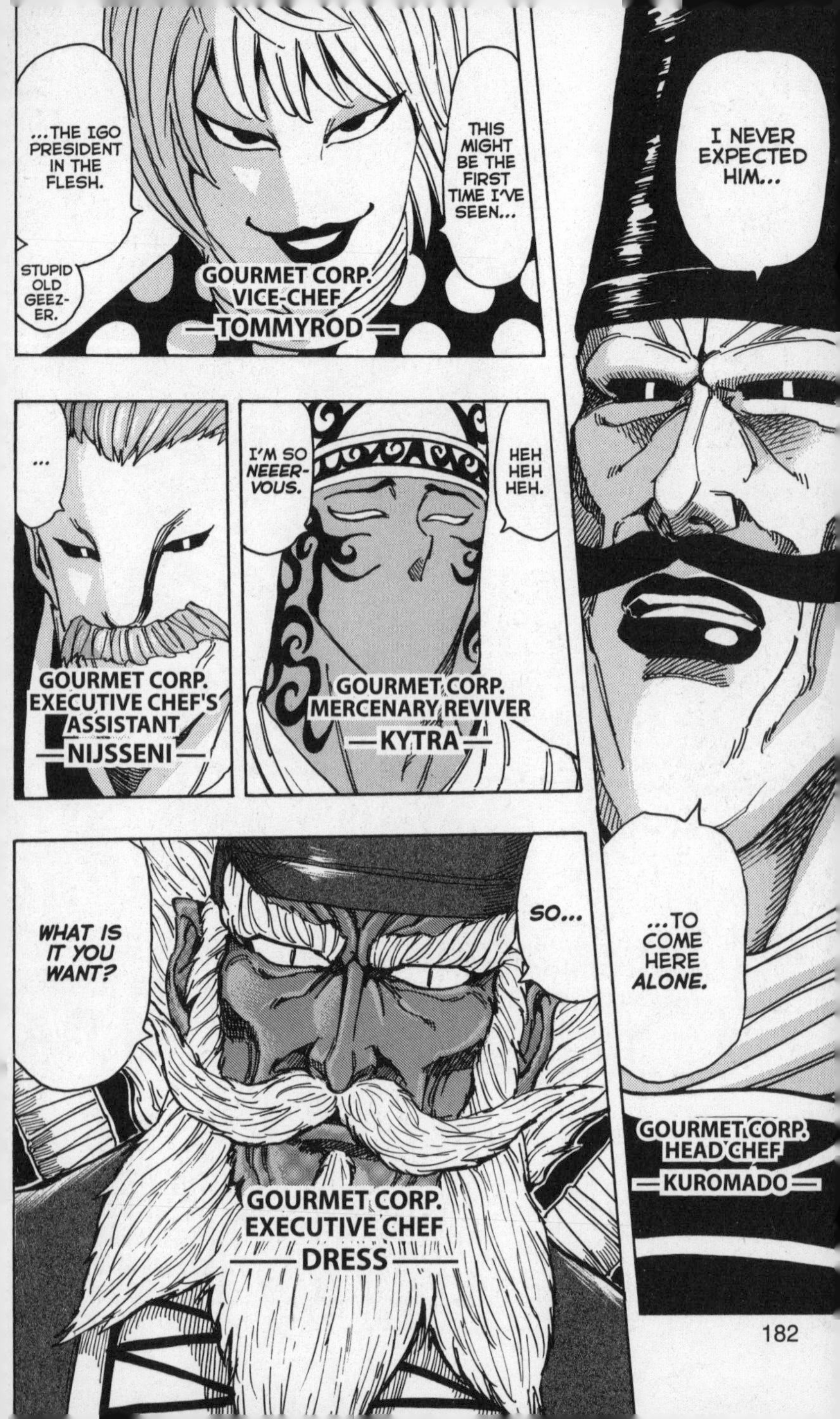
I NEVER EXPECTED HIM...
...TO COME HERE ALONE.
GOURMET CORP. HEAD CHEF —KUROMADO—
THIS MIGHT BE THE FIRST TIME I'VE SEEN...
...THE IGO PRESIDENT IN THE FLESH.
STUPID OLD GEEZER.
GOURMET CORP. VICE-CHEF —TOMMYROD—
HEH HEH HEH.
I'M SO *NEEER-VOUS.*
GOURMET CORP. MERCENARY REVIVER —KYTRA—
...
GOURMET CORP. EXECUTIVE CHEF'S ASSISTANT —NIJSSENI—
SO...
WHAT IS IT YOU WANT?
GOURMET CORP. EXECUTIVE CHEF —DRESS—

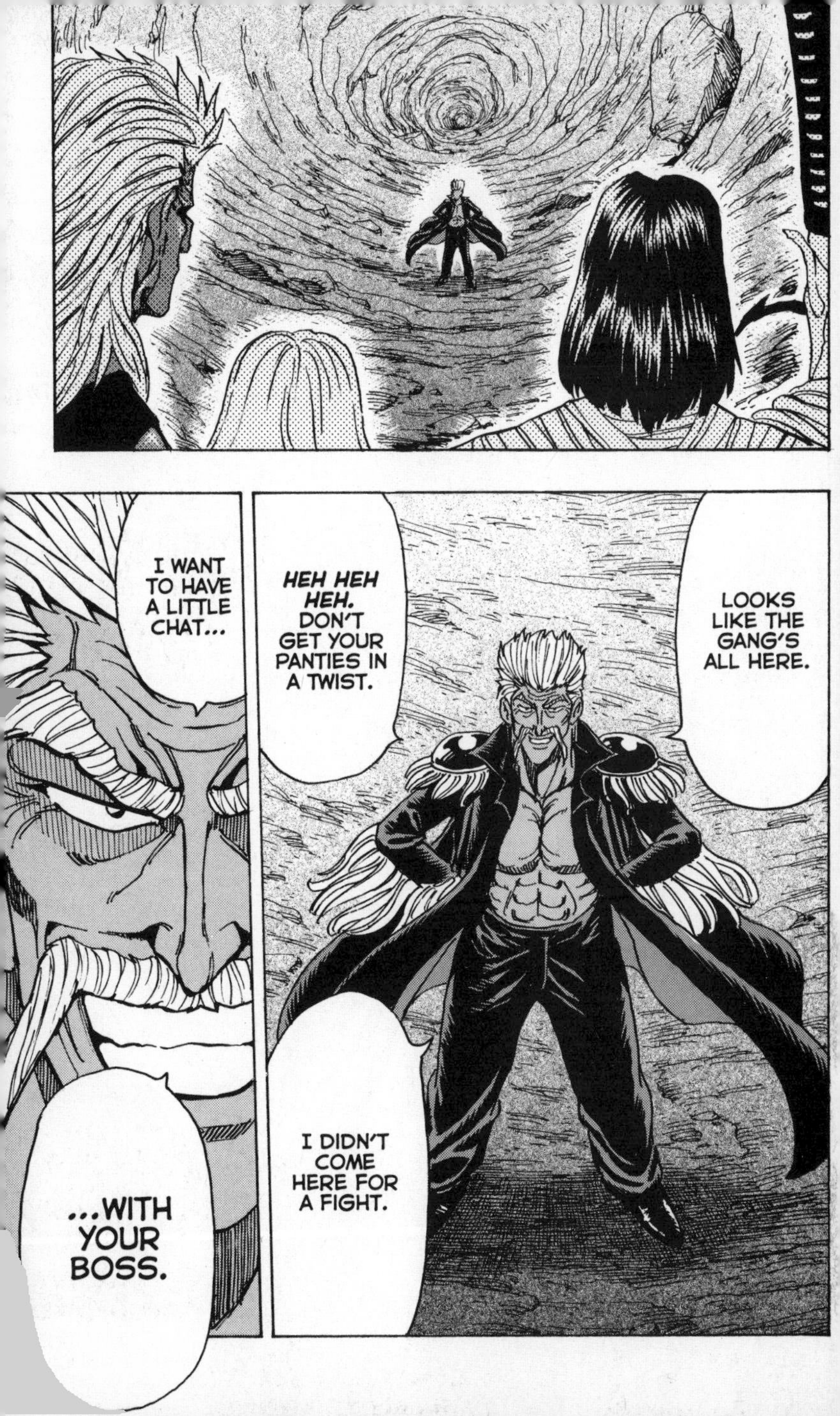
LOOKS LIKE THE GANG'S ALL HERE.
HEH HEH HEH. DON'T GET YOUR PANTIES IN A TWIST.
I DIDN'T COME HERE FOR A FIGHT.
I WANT TO HAVE A LITTLE CHAT...
...WITH YOUR BOSS.

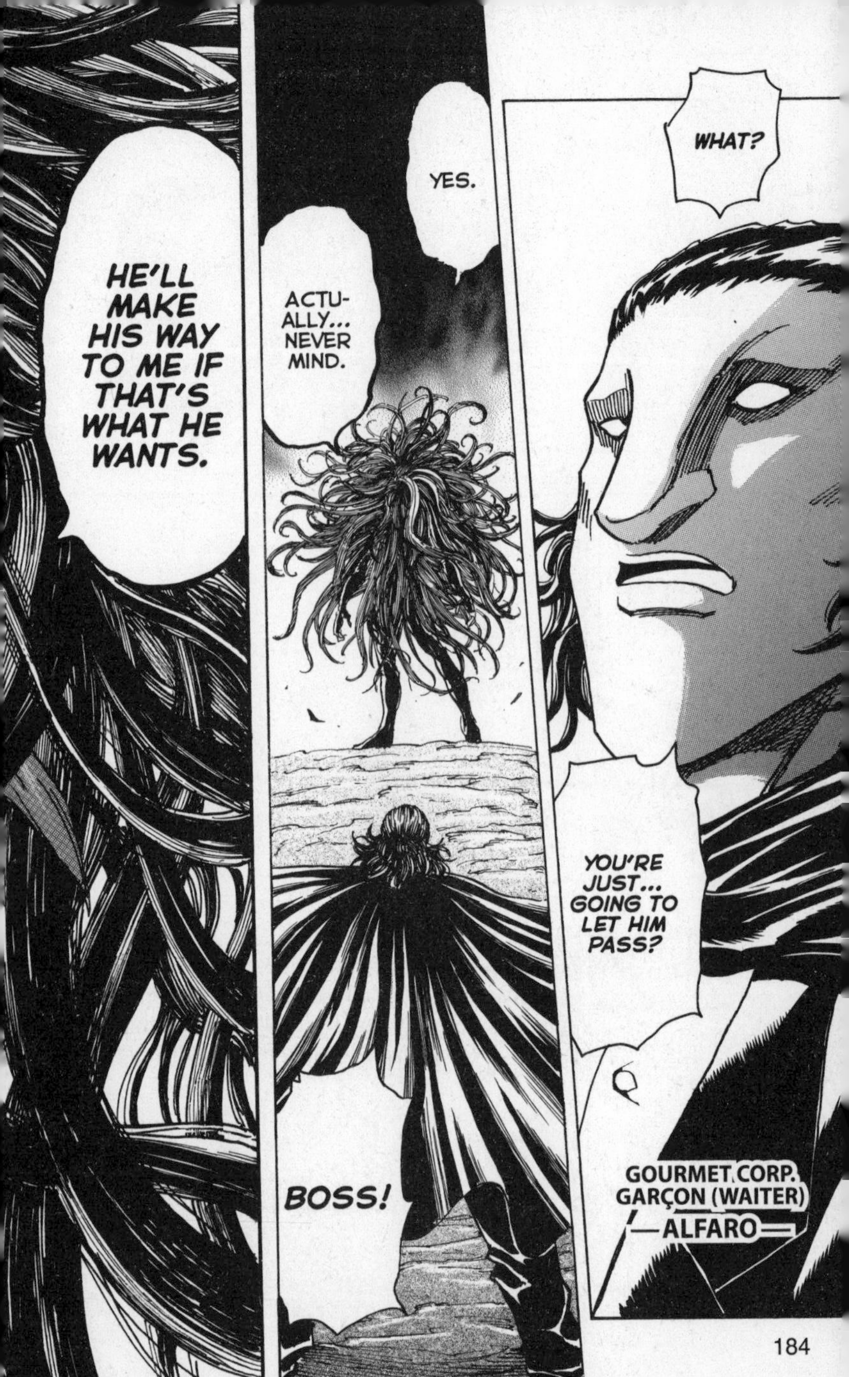
WHAT?
YOU'RE JUST... GOING TO LET HIM PASS?
GOURMET CORP. GARÇON (WAITER) —ALFARO—
YES.
ACTU-ALLY... NEVER MIND.
BOSS!
HE'LL MAKE HIS WAY TO ME IF THAT'S WHAT HE WANTS.

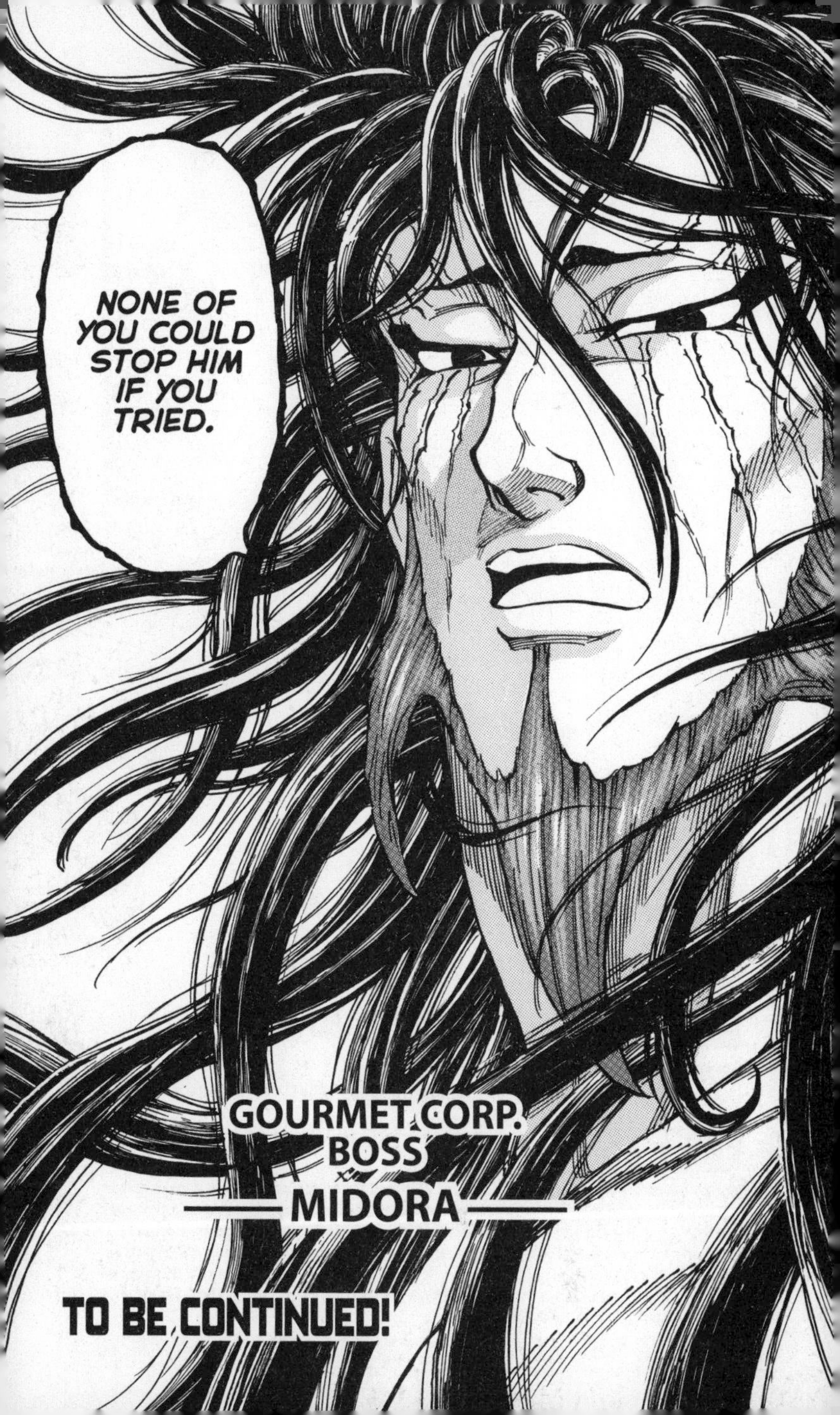
NONE OF YOU COULD STOP HIM IF YOU TRIED.
GOURMET CORP. BOSS
MIDORA
TO BE CONTINUED!

CHARACTER PROFILE

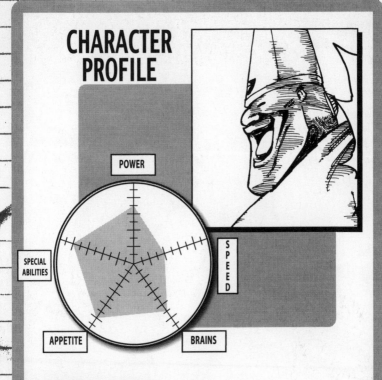

POWER

SPECIAL ABILITIES

SPEED

APPETITE

BRAINS

LIVEBEARER

AGE:	32	**BIRTHDAY:**	OCT 28
BLOOD TYPE:	B	**SIGN:**	SCORPIO
HEIGHT:	260 CM	**WEIGHT:**	SCORPIO
EYESIGHT:	20/17	**SHOE SIZE:**	WEIGHT: 330 KG

SPECIAL MOVES/ABILITIES:
- Preparation of illegal and narcotic foods

Owner of Gourmet Casino and boss of the Underground Cooking World. This shady chef deals with cuisine that doesn't make it to regular establishments and distributes illegal and drug foodstuffs. He extracts food memories from the hippocampus of the brains of patrons who lose wagers at his casino. He has an abnormal diet, as he finds supreme bliss in devouring memories. However, because he has so many food memories and methods of preparation in his possession, he is a top-notch chef. He tricks Toriko and the gang into a fixed gambling game, but ends up being done in. He has a change of heart when he witnesses Komatsu's sincerity toward food and decides to become an honest chef again.

COMING NEXT VOLUME

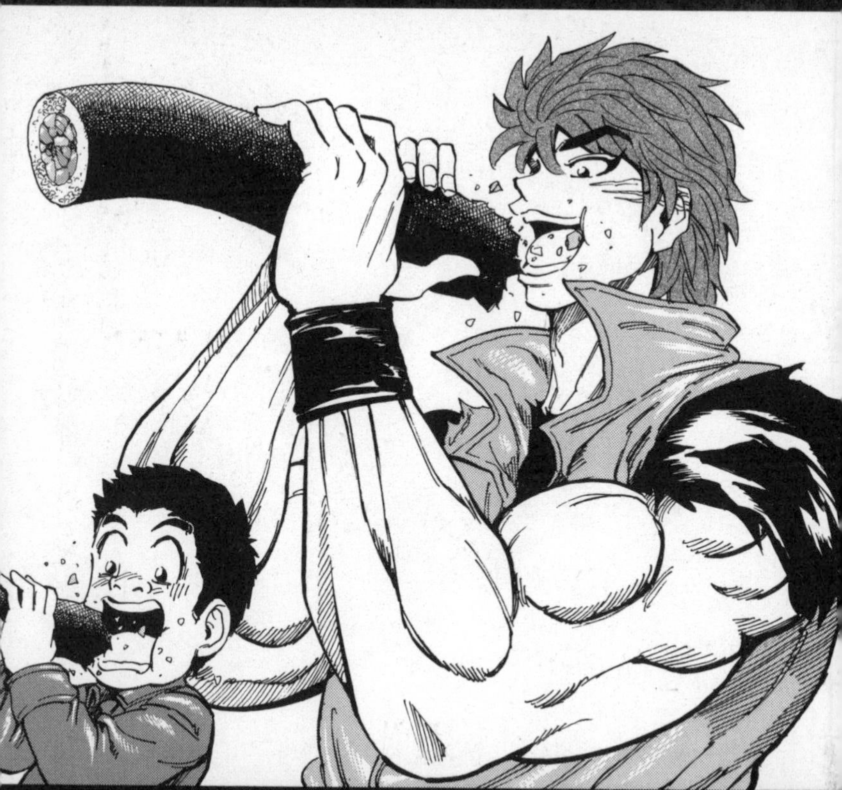

ICHIRYU AND MIDORA

The rivalry between the two superpowers of the Age of Gourmet, the International Gourmet Organization (IGO) and the nefarious Gourmet Corp., heats up when IGO President Ichiryu pays a visit to Gourmet Corp.'s headquarters in the Gourmet World. Meanwhile, Toriko and Komatsu set off on a world-spanning journey in search of some bizarre—and smelly—ingredients needed for a massive sushi roll that will guide them to the next item on their training list.

AVAILABLE FEBRUARY 2014!

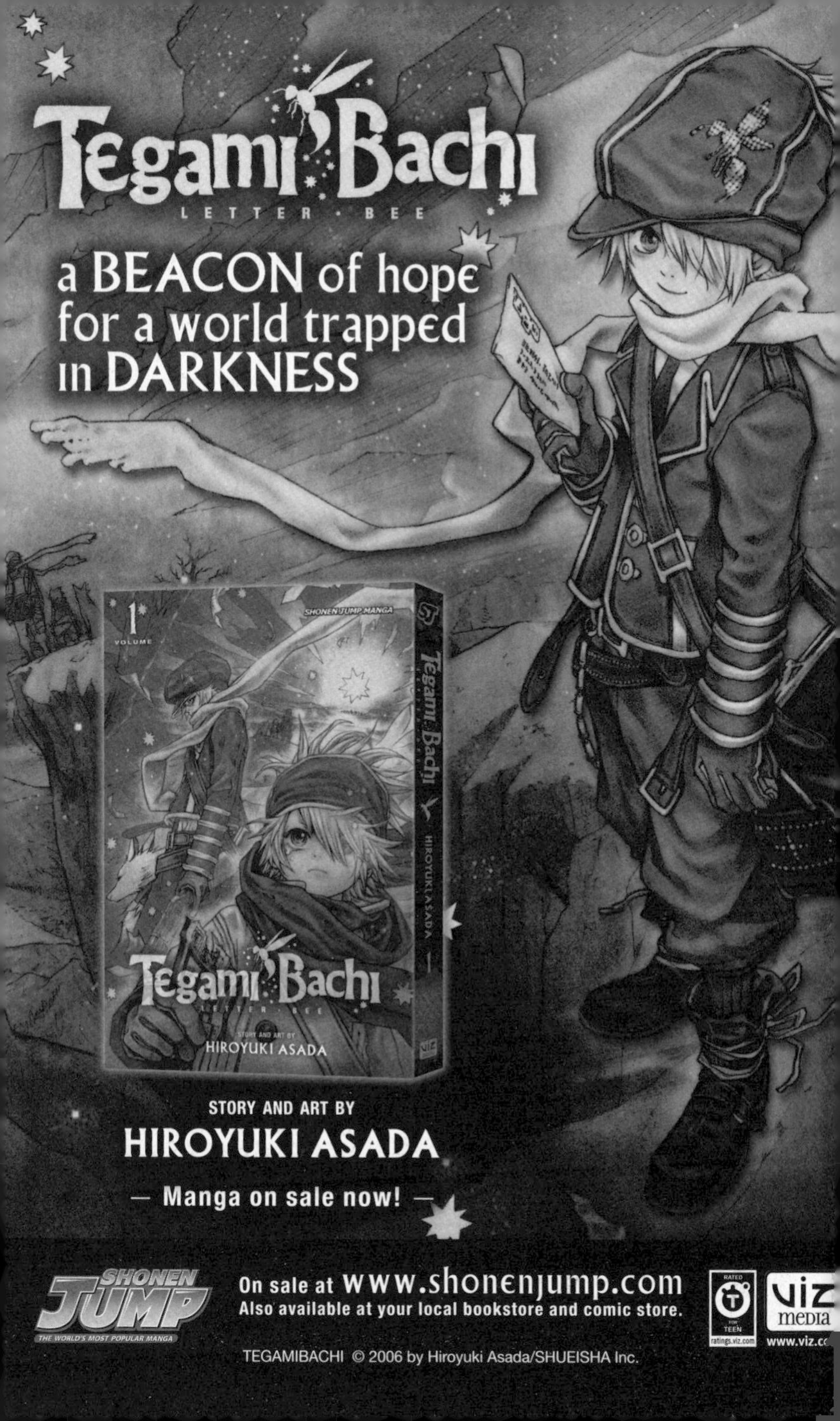
Tegami Bachi
LETTER • BEE
a BEACON of hope
for a world trapped
in DARKNESS
1
VOLUME
SHONEN JUMP MANGA
Tegami Bachi
LETTER • BEE
STORY AND ART BY
HIROYUKI ASADA
STORY AND ART BY
HIROYUKI ASADA
— Manga on sale now! —
SHONEN JUMP
THE WORLD'S MOST POPULAR MANGA
On sale at www.shonenjump.com
Also available at your local bookstore and comic store.
RATED T FOR TEEN
ratings.viz.com
viz media
www.viz.co
TEGAMIBACHI © 2006 by Hiroyuki Asada/SHUEISHA Inc.

⊔IZMANGA

Read manga anytime, anywhere!

From our newest hit series to the classics you know and love, the best manga in the world is now available digitally. Buy a volume* of digital manga for your:

iOS device (**iPad®**, **iPhone®**, **iPod® touch**) through the **VIZ Manga app**

Android-powered device (**phone or tablet**) with a browser by visiting **VIZManga.com**

Mac or PC computer by visiting VIZManga.com

VIZ Digital has loads to offer:

- 500+ ready-to-read volumes
- New volumes each week
- FREE previews
- Access on multiple devices! Create a log-in through the app so you buy a book once, and read it on your device of choice!*

To learn more, visit www.viz.com/apps

* Some series may not be available for multiple devices.
  Check the app on your device to find out what's available.

viz.com/apps

You're Reading in the Wrong Direction!!

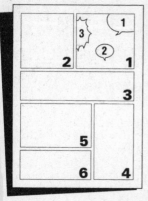

Whoops! Guess what? You're starting at the wrong end of the comic!

...It's true! In keeping with the original Japanese format, **Toriko** is meant to be read from right to left, starting in the upper-right corner.

Unlike English, which is read from left to right, Japanese is read from right to left, meaning that action, sound effects and word-balloon order are completely reversed... something which can make readers unfamiliar with Japanese feel pretty backwards themselves. For this reason, manga or Japanese comics published in the U.S. in English have sometimes been published "flopped"— that is, printed in exact reverse order, as though seen from the other side of a mirror.

By flopping pages, U.S. publishers can avoid confusing readers, but the compromise is not without its downside. For one thing, a character in a flopped manga series who once wore in the original Japanese version a T-shirt emblazoned with "M A Y" (as in "the merry month of") now wears one which reads "Y A M"! Additionally, many manga creators in Japan are themselves unhappy with the process, as some feel the mirror-imaging of their art skews their original intentions.

We are proud to bring you Mitsutoshi Shimabukuro's **Toriko** in the original unflopped format. For now, though, turn to the other side of the book and let the adventure begin...!

—Editor